Law School

Studies in Legal History

Published by the University of North Carolina Press
in association with the American Society for Legal History

Editor G. Edward White

Editorial Advisory Board

Law School

Legal Education in America

from the 1850s to the 1980s

by Robert Stevens

The University of North Carolina Press

Chapel Hill and London

© 1983 The University of North Carolina Press

Manufactured in the United States of America

Library of Congress Cataloging in Publication Data

Stevens, Robert Bocking, 1933–
  Law school.

  (Studies in legal history)
  Bibliography: p.
  Includes Index.
   1. Law—Study and teaching—United States—History.
2. Law schools—United States—History. I. Title.
II. Series.
KF272.S8   1983   340'.07'1173   82-11148
ISBN 0-8078-1537-3

For my colleagues and in memory of
Grant Gilmore and Arthur Leff

Contents

Acknowledgments

ONE of the pleasures of writing this book has been the excuse it has given me to talk with large numbers of persons, both lawyers and nonlawyers. Although it is not possible to thank all those who helped, I am grateful to each and every one. In particular, I should like to thank those who read the final or penultimate drafts of this book. This list includes Bruce Ackerman, Ralph Brown, John Heinz, William Hohenstein, Roger Lane, David Papke, John Henry Schlegel, Rosemary Stevens, Preble Stolz, Peter Teachout, William Twining, G. Edward White, and Adolphus Williams. The book has been significantly influenced by their insights and to them I am especially grateful. Of course, all would disagree with at least some of the interpretations and analyses. Mistakes, I should add, are entirely my own.

I have also been particularly fortunate with research assistance. Patricia Geoghegan of the Class of 1974 at the Yale Law School helped significantly in researching the last three decades of the nineteenth century, thereby making it possible to rethink some of the traditional interpretations of that period. Mary Benjamin of the Class of 1980 at Bryn Mawr College and the Class of 1983 at the Yale Law School worked with me during the summers of 1979 and 1980, and she not only undertook many specific research tasks but was vital in insuring that a final draft of the book was ultimately completed. I am especially indebted to her. I should also like to thank the following for source checking: Louisa Ashmead (Haverford, 1979), Robert Elwood (Haverford, 1982), Seth Fagen (Haverford, 1982), Paul Savage (Haverford, 1983) and Peter Freed (Pennsylvania Law School, 1979).

Twice the Ford Foundation has supported research efforts that finally reached culmination in this book. I also received a Research Fellowship from the National Endowment for the Humanities, which was supplemented by a grant from the Yale Institution for Social and Policy Studies. The Stanford Law School and the Institute for Advanced Legal Studies in London were gracious hosts while part of this book was being researched. The final draft of the book was written when I was a Visitor at the Socio-Legal Center and a Fellow of Wolfson College, Oxford, during Trinity Term 1981. I am most grateful to both the College and the

Center. I should also like to thank John Whitehead for his encouragement and support of my efforts to finish this book.

Since, for nearly thirty years, I was a direct participant in legal education, I should admit to my assumptions being shaped by my legal education at Oxford and Yale, practice as a member of the commercial bar in
London and with an admiralty firm in New York, and some seventeen
years as a law professor at Yale. I also had the experience of teaching at
the London School of Economics and Oxford in England and at Northwestern, Texas, and Stanford law schools in this country. My contact
with legal education over the last six years has been more peripheral and
from a rather different vantage point. I have served as a trustee of the
Vermont Law School, as provost and professor of law and history at
Tulane, and currently as president of Haverford College. If the life of the
president of a liberal arts college seems rather a far cry from the center of
legal education, I would point out that Haverford has produced, *inter
alia*, Anthony Amsterdam, John Bradway, Robert Braucher, Howard
Marshall, and Fred Rodell among a host of other law professors. I should
also add that my colleagues here, both academic and administrative,
have been uncommonly generous in their assumption that presidents
need not necessarily be illiterates.

This book inevitably builds on earlier published studies.[1] In particular,
various parts of the book build on research that originally appeared in
"Two Cheers for 1870: The American Law School," published in *Perspectives in American History*, volume 5 (1970), and republished in *Law
in American History*, edited by Bernard Bailyn and Donald Fleming
(1973). Other material, particularly parts of Chapter 6, appeared in
"Law Schools and Legal Education, 1879–1979: Lectures in Honor of
100 Years of Valparaiso Law School," 15 *Valparaiso University Law
Review* 179 (1980). At some points I have also relied on a series of empirical studies originally published under the title of "Law Schools and
Law Students" in 59 *Virginia Law Review* 551 (1973). I am grateful for
permission to reuse these various materials here.

The final version of this book has also benefited from lectures and
seminars I have given at various institutions. I particularly appreciated
the invitation to lecture at the State University of New York at Buffalo,
Temple University, and York University, Toronto. Papers to the American

1. See, for instance, "Aging Mistress: The Law School in America," 32; "Crisis in Legal
Education," in Bok, ed., "Issues in Legal Education"; "American Legal Education," 242;
"Democracy and the Legal Profession," 695. With respect to England, I have inevitably
relied on Abel-Smith and Stevens, *Lawyers and the Courts*, chaps. 1, 7, and 13; Abel-Smith
and Stevens, *In Search of Justice*, chap. 10. See also Stevens, "Unexplored Avenues in
Comparative Anglo-American Legal History," 1086.

Society for Legal History and the Yale Institute for Social and Policy Studies were also fruitful. A public lecture at the London School of Economics and seminars at Warwick and Kent universities clarified thoughts by forcing me to think comparatively. The centennial lectures delivered at Valparaiso University in 1979 helped shape the final structure of the book.

I have also been fortunate in the assistance I have received from library and archive staffs. I have made use of the archives of the national YMCA in New York, Princeton University, and the San Antonio Public Library. The Washingtoniana Collection at the Martin Luther King Library in Washington, D.C., and the Western Collection at the Denver Public Library made available their extensive holdings. I have also had access to the archives of the law schools at George Washington, John Marshall, Miami, New England (Portia), Northeastern, Pennsylvania, St. Mary's (San Antonio), San Francisco, Stanford, Suffolk, Temple, Tulane, University of California at Los Angeles, Valparaiso, Western New England (Springfield YMCA), and Yale. At the Yale Law School I should like particularly to thank Arthur Charpentier and his staff; at the Stanford Law School I should like to thank Myron Jacobstein and his staff; at Haverford I should like to thank Edwin Bronner and his staff. All were essential to the successful completion of this volume. Finally, I should like to thank Annette D'Andrea and my assistant, Ann MacKay, who typed and retyped this manuscript, and Sandra Eisdorfer, who, for the second time, took a manuscript of mine and edited it—vigorously and efficiently—for publication.

Haverford College
1 January 1982

Prologue

WRITING a general history of the American law school is relatively easy to justify. Our law schools are both powerful and mystifying. To foreign lawyers, especially the professorate, the American law school is frequently a subject of admiration as well as envy.[1] The leading American law schools appear to have an entrenched position of power in the profession, in academic life, and, indeed, in the country at large, a position that is frequently denied to the academic branches of the profession in other industrialized societies. Students from American law schools go out into a profession that appears to wield far greater power in politics, business, labor, and even in social reform than in other common-law countries. Law professors within the university appear to live something of a charmed life and, within the profession, to have a profound impact on thinking about law, procedure, and institutions. The law school is assumed to be not only at the center of professional power but a significant force in the American establishment.

To a historian or sociologist, however, perhaps the most challenging aspect of the role of the law schools has been their function in the social evolution of law, lawyers, and higher education. The centrality of law in American life, coupled with the historical functions of legal education, has insured that the schools have been at the very core of the debates about the profession and its role, as well as the nature of law itself. The history of the United States has, in many ways, been the history of the tension between equality and excellence. The history of the legal profession—and inevitably of the law schools—has similarly reflected the clash between elitism and democracy. The very concept of law, reflecting the nuances of American politics and society, has shaped and been shaped by legal education. Such phenomena alone justify a full-length study of these schools.

Until the late 1960s, there was surprisingly little serious analysis of legal education. With the exception of Reed's work for the Carnegie

---

1. For instance, Bryce said that he did "not know if there is anything in which America has advanced more beyond the mother country than in the provisions she makes for legal education." Bryce, *The American Commonwealth*, 2:623. There has been little deviation from this line by foreign observers over the last one hundred years.

Foundation,[2] little was known of the history of legal education; indeed legal history as a whole was at best a stepchild in the prestigious law schools. Although the rhetoric relating law to the social sciences had been shrill for fifty years, little data had been collected about legal education or, indeed, about the legal profession. In particular, law professors seemed almost anxious to remain ignorant of the history of legal education.

To suggest that all this has changed in the last fifteen years would be misleading, yet there have been important developments. Legal history has undergone a major renaissance; theoretical and empirical studies of law, legal services, and lawyers have become appreciably more important, and the study of professions at large has been given a prominence denied it by earlier generations.[3] A history of legal education as a whole, linking it to intellectual, political, and social trends has, however, been lacking. This book is a tentative step in that direction.

In a strange kind of way this history of legal education turns out to be parochial. If we limit our intellectual boundaries to legal education as it exists today, we need to look back little more than one hundred years to trace the founding of the institutions and concepts that have dominated the present. Not only is the time frame short, but the leading players have been relatively few. Perhaps most significant of all, legal education made but one significant breakthrough in pedagogy—the case method. The idea of learning law through studying the cases, a system that soon became associated with the Socratic system of question and answer, has dominated American legal education for the last 110 years.

This domination has not always been unquestioned. Those critical of the law schools have, understandably, attacked the case method. Yet the method has proved remarkably resilient. Introduced because of its practicality and its effectiveness in teaching black-letter rules scientifically, few would now claim it as practical; almost all would see its virtue in terms of teaching analytic skills rather than substance. Yet for all the criticism that has been leveled against the method, there has been no serious competitor. Lectures have not returned, law's philander with the social sciences has not undermined the centrality of the method, and even

2. Reed, *Training for the Public Profession of the Law*; Reed, *Present-Day Law Schools in the United States and Canada.*

3. One should perhaps add that after a century of studies of the profession—such as they were—being uniformly sycophantic, studies over the last fifteen years have generally started from the premise articulated by George Bernard Shaw in *The Doctor's Dilemma*: "All professions are conspiracies against the laity." It is possible the truth lies somewhere between the two approaches.

the advent of clinical legal education has had only a superficial impact on its centrality. The case method was, and remains, an apparently brilliant educational tool.

A teaching style that has survived, at least in appearance, without great change, has had inevitable implications. It should come as no surprise that one school—Harvard, the founder of the case method—has dominated the development of legal education for a century. Indeed, even today, Harvardization is frequently the touchstone either of academic quality or the focus for academic crises. The other most notable implication of the dominance of one teaching technique has been the cyclical nature of so-called educational innovations. All educational change has about it something of the pendulum phenomenon. Legal education has been particularly prone to appear cyclical because it has, in general, chosen as its intellectual perimeters the limits of the case method.

The predominance of Harvard as the focus of legal education also insured that the implications of the gradual acceptance of the law school as the sole method of providing legal education would be fraught with social and intellectual clashes. Harvard was the model of the nineteenth-century liberal university with a commitment to scholarship, excellence, and equality of opportunity. The last was, however, not the same as equality, and the rising immigrant groups were normally unconcerned with excellence or scholarship. Thus the bulk of legal education went on not in elite institutions concerned with such matters but in marginal proprietary or state institutions. The idea that law was a trade to be learned like any other, although it spoke to much in American history, was antithetical to the ideology of legal professionalism. The goal of leading academic institutions and of leading members of the profession was to use the law schools to raise the quality and "tone" of the legal profession in America. In this cause American pluralism was to give way to conformity and standardization. Yet the efforts by the schools that set out to cater to the bulk of aspiring lawyers may hold the key to today's structure and style. They tell us much of the decline of apprenticeship, the diversity within the profession, the search for skills, the multiplicity of meanings of policy, and the appeal of clinical studies.

In the cause of institutionalization and interchangeability, not only were law schools made to look alike but the assumption that the profession itself was homogeneous was made a canon of the new professionalism. The leaders of the bar remained remarkably impervious to the widespread evidence that the role of the American lawyer was a pluralistic one and indeed may even have become more diverse over the last century. This triumph of myth over reality fed back into the confusion about what was academic and what was practical. It also prevented intelligent discussions of the lines that might exist between the vocational, the academic, and the professional. History and political goals became the rationale for much that passed under the rubric of legal education.

Law School

1 / Once Upon a Time

A
T the time of the American Revolution, the preponderant influence on the organized part of the American legal profession was the English attorney and solicitor rather than the barrister. It was therefore natural that a system of apprenticeship coupled with a formal examination was the standard toward which leading lawyers in North America were striving at the time of independence.[1] Although only in urban areas could apprenticeship be described as compulsory in late colonial times, by 1783 few would have considered offering themselves as full-time attorneys without some period of apprenticeship.

Some colonies, however, had had a more stratified profession, and although in Virginia the separation of the upper and lower branches on a barrister-solicitor model collapsed after 1783, in the more prosperous northern states a graded bar was apparently still developing.[2] In these states, only after some years as a regular attorney could the lawyer be admitted as a barrister and practice before the supreme court of the state: still further experience was required for admission as "counselor." Evidence of how the graded system worked is tenuous,[3] but the requirements for basic practice were clear: for example, in Massachusetts it was five years of apprenticeship with a one-year reduction for college graduates.[4] No doubt what was meant by apprenticeship varied considerably from an important educational experience to gross exploitation[5] but, of the thirteen original states, only one had no prescribed period of training at all.[6] Indeed, at the time of independence the American bar may have had an even firmer structure, at least in its requirements for preparation, than either branch of the legal profession in England.

Formalized apprenticeship, together with the severing of ties with England, also led to the establishment of private law schools. They were generally outgrowths of the law offices of practitioners who had shown themselves to be particularly skilled, or popular, as teachers.[7] The most famous of these schools was the Litchfield Law School in Connecticut, formally established in 1784, which grew out of the teaching activities of Tapping Reeve during the revolutionary war. There, under the guidance of Reeve and James Gould, a course of studies based on Blackstone,[8] but adapted to the American scene, attracted students from every state in the new nation—students who were to confirm the suspicion of many that lawyers had an inside track in running for public office in America.[9] Litchfield claimed that it taught the law "as a science, and not merely nor principally as a mechanical business, nor as a collection of loose independent fragments."[10] The school, in this sense, was singularly important in developing a culture of American legal education. Other private schools —at the height of their popularity at the beginning of the nineteenth century there were a score such[11]—also played a role, although none rivaled Litchfield.

The war with England had emphasized another indigenous development. For both social and geographical reasons, the American college had already developed in the eighteenth century not only on a somewhat wider social basis than Oxford and Cambridge, but also along rather broader intellectual lines. From an early stage, moreover, bar organizations gave preferential treatment to college graduates,[12] and, apparently in response, the American college was more receptive than English universities had been to the study of the common law. There had been lectures involving politics, civil government, and international law even in the colonial period, and the need to provide some formal training for the legal profession after the Revolution accelerated that trend, an acceleration made possible by the rapid growth in the number of colleges after the Revolution.[13]

The title of first "law professor" properly belongs to Jefferson's law preceptor, George Wythe, who was appointed professor of law and police at William and Mary in 1779.[14] After that, chairs in law at the colleges expanded rapidly.[15] Exactly what these professors achieved is far from certain. Some were appointed for political rather than intellectual reasons. Some appear to have done little teaching and to have had little impact. Some followed the academic model that President Ezra Stiles of Yale had set out in 1777 in justification of teaching law in the colleges: "It is scarcely possible to enslave a Republic where the Body of the People are Civilians, well instructed in their Laws, Rights and Liberties."[16] James Kent's approach at Columbia, however, was more professional in content and, indeed, his lectures were the basis for his influential *Commentaries*. Somewhere between the two were the ill-fated efforts by David Hoffman to develop a seven-year program at the University of Maryland after 1812[17] and of Benjamin Butler, Jackson's attorney general, who developed an extensive plan for a law faculty at New York University in 1835.[18] More successful were the vocational efforts of Isaac Parker, chief justice of Massachusetts, the first appointee (1815) under the Royall bequest at Harvard,[19] although success really came only with the establishment of a law school in 1817. It is arguable that the most successful effort at liberal law teaching in colleges was Jefferson's University of Virginia, founded in 1825. Law teaching there was seen as an integral part of the undergraduate curriculum, designed to form the statesman, legislator, and judge no doubt of the appropriate Whig outlook. Although there were cutbacks almost immediately at Virginia, the "Southern tradition" of law teaching was, in general, broader than the north's.[20]

The truth, however, is that the overall efforts by the colleges to develop law as a scholarly study were not a success. Professorships frequently lapsed or remained sinecures, and serious professional training took place at the private law schools like Litchfield.[21] In a very real sense the dichotomy between the teaching of law as a liberal and liberating study and the teaching of law as a technical and professional study was already established.

In the early 1820s, a significant development occurred as far as institutional law teaching was concerned. The colleges began to provide an umbrella under which the private law schools might find shelter. The private law schools were interested in the affiliation largely because it gave prestige and because, in most states, only universities were empowered to give degrees. Why the universities were interested in the arrangement is less clear.[22] Perhaps it gave them greater influence among that powerful local elite—the lawyers. Perhaps the lawyers thought the connection would protect them from attack, or perhaps the profession and the colleges had a mutual interest in thwarting Jacksonian Democracy. The arrangements certainly cost the universities nothing. There was no hint in any of the links at this time that the law schools should be anything but self-financing.[23] Yale absorbed a local private law school in 1824 by listing the students in its catalog and appointing the "owner" of the school, Judge David Daggett, to the vacant professorship of law.[24] Harvard reorganized its law offerings in 1829, bringing in Joseph Story for prestige[25] and John Ashmun—from the Northampton Law School— to provide students.[26] When Tulane wanted to establish a law school in 1847, it absorbed the Louisiana Law School, run by the Swedish scholar, Gustavus Smith.[27] The University of North Carolina had already made a similar move.[28]

These mergers, which might be thought to have brought together the best in "academic" and "practical" law, seemed to bode well for established institutions. From 1820 onward, however, the fledgling law schools, like the fledgling medical schools, and, to a lesser extent, the colleges and universities themselves were under pressures, conveniently known as Jacksonian Democracy, which were to prevent what many were later to call "progress."

During the first two decades of the Republic the status of the profession had in fact been enhanced. The demise of the royal governors and colonial (sometimes expatriate) judges, together with the collapse of other elite groups, and the inevitable rise in importance of the supreme courts in each of the states, coupled with the coming into being of the Supreme Court in Washington, emphasized the importance of the legal profession in the country's government. Lawyers were catapulted into a political and social prominence that the profession had never enjoyed in England, with the possible exception of isolated periods in the battle between the Stuarts and the Parliamentarians in the seventeenth century. It is true that, even in these early postrevolutionary years, there was evidence of hostility toward lawyers as there was to members of other professions.[29] Nevertheless, in his observations of American society made in 1831 and 1832, Alexis de Tocqueville could express the views that have now become truisms—that the "aristocracy of America occupies the judicial bench and bar"[30] and that "scarcely any political question arises in the United States that is not resolved, sooner or later, into a judicial question."[31]

Yet generalizations about the legal profession and the role of law in the first half of the nineteenth century are hard to make. The generalizations are not made any easier by the recent trend toward distorting the role of law and lawyers in England during the eighteenth and early nineteenth centuries.[32] The tradition of judicial lawmaking that Mansfield emphasized in England was kept vigorous and active during the latter part of the eighteenth century and the early part of the nineteenth as English judges wrestled with the impact of the Industrial Revolution and developed bold new doctrines in commercial matters.[33] Indeed it was only after the Reform Act of 1832 and the rapid acceptance of utilitarian concepts and assumptions that legal formalism began to take a vise-like hold on English legal thought.[34] The style of many American state courts after the Revolution was surprisingly similar to the behavior of judges in Westminster Hall, and differences may be attributed at least as much to the varying pace of social and economic change as to the departure of the British. London was still seen by American lawyers, at least in the former colonies in the East, as the natural hub of legal thought and model for judicial behavior.

Such considerations should be borne in mind as one approaches the traditional interpretation of the rise and fall of the first American legal profession. The tone of the early studies of the legal profession was set by Charles Warren at the beginning of this century as he traced the demise of the educated American bar at the hands of the barbarian hordes of Jacksonian Democracy,[35] and this traumatic vision still characterized

Chroust's standard history of the American bar written in the 1960s.[36] The assumptions underlying this approach coincide with the conventional view of the impact of Jacksonian Democracy; there is no doubt that there were vigorous assaults on the legal profession and its status during the twenties, thirties, and forties of the nineteenth century.

Although the main thrust of Jacksonian Democracy is still accepted,[37] historians have increasingly come to question some of the early broad generalizations, and this questioning has recently been extended to the legal profession. Indeed, the questioning is perhaps especially relevant to law, since studies of those fulfilling "lawyer-jobs" in other societies suggest that lawyers or their substitutes flourish in nonstatus societies.[38] Without a monarch or a clearly defined aristocracy, with a practical utilitarian outlook, with little by way of competing professions, the new nation was almost inevitably bound to rely on lawyers to perform a wide range of functions. Lawyers became the technicians of change as the country expanded economically and geographically, a development that partly explains why even today lawyers play a more significant role in the United States than in any other developed society. It may also explain why, in connection with such roles, the evidence of the decline in professionalism during the period of Jacksonian Democracy and its immediate aftermath is particularly inconclusive.[39]

From the earliest time, as well as both before and after the Revolution, lawyers had been under various forms of attack.[40] During the 1830s the attack on "the class of lawyers" reached a remarkable pitch, for many perceived the lawyer in Tocqueville's terms—as the natural aristocrat in America—but drew different conclusions about the desirability of such elitism. The most obvious manifestation of the change was that the judiciary, in an increasing number of states, was made subject to election, but the practicing profession also fell increasingly under criticism.[41]

Some states had abolished[42] or reduced[43] the requirements for apprenticeship even before 1830. As formal education fell into disrespect, however, the outward manifestations of professionalism appeared to collapse. The guild feeling within the legal profession and the somewhat mystical view with which the common law was regarded by learned lawyers were put under pressures they had never had to face in England. In 1832, for instance, the apprenticeship requirements were greatly weakened in Maryland. They were abolished in Massachusetts in 1836, in Maine in 1837, and in New Hampshire in 1838.[44] In 1800, fourteen out of nineteen jurisdictions had required a definitive period of apprenticeship. By 1840, it was required by not more than eleven out of thirty jurisdictions. By 1860, it was required in only nine of thirty-nine jurisdictions.[45] The effect of the movement on institutionalized legal education was in many ways predictable.[46] By 1840, there were apparently only nine university-affiliated law schools with a total of 345 students.

College-connected law schools came and went with great rapidity.[47] After unsuccessful efforts in 1825 and 1835 Princeton established a law school in 1846, run by local practitioners and judges, only to abandon it in 1852 after producing six graduates. Columbian (George Washington) had a law school from 1826 to 1827 and the law school for New York University, projected by Benjamin Butler, also lasted for only one year (1838–39). In 1845, the Board of Trustees of the University of Alabama authorized the formation of a law school separate from the university, but no students came to the school and it closed in 1846.[48]

To attribute all this inhibiting atmosphere to the "excesses" of Jacksonian Democracy, however, would encourage grave dangers of misinterpretation. The colonial climate had by no means always been favorable to an organized bar, and the talk of abolishing the legal profession, which was heard again in states such as Pennsylvania early in the nineteenth century, had a long history.[49] The legal climate or culture varied considerably from state to state, and thus the role of lawyers often differed radically from one place to another. Thus some of the developments between 1820 and 1850 were undoubtedly geographic rather than intellectual. Compared with the centralized class-conscious English society, even New England was a devolved and egalitarian society, but there could be no comparison at all with the situation west of the Appalachians. Although we know too little of the role of lawyers on the frontier, it could only be expected to be different from the role of lawyers in the East, and the frontier itself provided remarkable contradictions and a surprisingly pluralistic picture.[50]

In a purely professional sense, it is of course true that many local bar associations collapsed after 1800, but recent studies have suggested that it was lawyers who lost interest in these organizations rather than that their demise reflected the triumph of antilawyer sentiment. Lawyers instead looked to legal magazines as well as to other activities to maintain professional cohesion and power.[51] It was during the early decades of the nineteenth century that the great judges were able to set out on their voyages of discovery, partly because of the power of the profession. Story had Americanized the common law with his series of treatises[52] (and incidentally beaten back any possibility that the new nation might import civil law),[53] while the Supreme Court was not only cementing judicial review but had federalized the common law with the decision in *Swift* v. *Tyson* (1842).[54] The codification movement, which reached its crescendo in the 1840s, was designed to demystify the law and was understandably opposed by lawyers;[55] yet by the fifties the reforms ridding the legal system of its feudal procedural heritage went largely unopposed. With the forms of action dead, lawyers were in a position the better to conceptualize and to rationalize the law.[56]

Thus, for all the talk of Jacksonian Democracy and for all the changes in formal rules, there seems little doubt that in major cities like Boston the leading members of the bar played a role, led a life, and enjoyed a status in 1830 little different from that of their counterparts in 1800 or 1900.[57] In Washington the Supreme Court bar moved toward its golden period.[58] On the bench it was the period of Doe[59] and Shaw.[60] By 1830, judges in Massachusetts effectively controlled juries in a way they had not even considered in colonial times.[61] The first half of the nineteenth century was a period of great judicial creativity; on this even those of differing historical perspectives agree. To Willard Hurst, this creativity signaled the courts liberating the economy;[62] to Morton Horwitz, it was a period when the judges, manifesting their class biases, operated instrumentally, in effect using formalism to oppress the masses.[63] To Karl Llewellyn, this was the period of the Grand Style;[64] to Grant Gilmore, it was the "Age of Discovery."[65] It was a period that saw the birth of law firms like Cravath, Swaine and Moore, and Cadwalader, Wickersham and Taft.[66] Lawyers were proving to be vital in the Industrial Revolution. The owners of slaves, steamboat monopolies, and banks found that they needed lawyers. Attorneys were increasingly in evidence in politics. Despite the activities of legislatures, American lawyers clung to traditional terminologies.[67]

When, in 1842, New Hampshire provided that any citizen over twenty-one was entitled to be admitted to practice, the profession in that state continued to ostracize untrained interlopers. Eventually, in 1859, this professional "inner bar" was formally recognized by the rules of the state supreme court, although the right to deny or permit admission to the bar was not restored to the court until 1872.[68] The attempts to democratize the profession in Indiana and other states were not seriously opposed by lawyers.[69] Some members of the profession even welcomed such moves as evidence of the competitive American spirit rather than as an attack on the bar per se.[70] These facts suggest that the legal profession was virtually indestructible, or at least that Karl Llewellyn was right in postulating that every society has certain "lawyer-jobs" that must be performed by someone.[71] In American society, there was virtually no profession competing for such "jobs."

These phenomena should not surprise us. Over the past decades anthropologists have taught us that the formalized aspect of social control that we call law is likely to be effective (or to penetrate, as they would say) only if it reflects generally accepted norms. Apparently there was a demand in this country—either from above or below, or perhaps from both directions—for a trained legal profession to operate an increasingly legalistic society. During the period after 1800, the graded, priest-like replicas of the English legal profession largely evaporated from the United States, and a rapid decline in formal standards for legal education and the dissolution of bar associations undoubtedly characterized the heady days of Jacksonian Democracy. The change, however, was not as precipitous as once suggested. As early as the 1850s, the pendulum began to swing back, with the refounding of law schools and increased interest in the more organized side of bar life. Law was beginning once more to be seen as a learned profession.[72]

NOTES

1. Like English solicitors, American attorneys are officers of the courts. Control of the profession therefore remains in the hands of the supreme courts, although it may be delegated to bar associations. Part of the twentieth-century movement to have an integrated bar (i.e., compulsory membership in the bar association) was an effort by the bars to have self-government as of right, along the lines of the English barristers.
2. "While, therefore, in the South, the Revolution, by closing the Inns of Court to Americans, virtually destroyed the upper bar, in the North it produced no such effect. The indigenous institution of a graded profession, which had already arisen in Massachusetts, developed and spread throughout New England, in the congenial atmosphere of the county bar system of admissions, and was extended from here to New York, and temporarily to the Northwest Territory." Reed, *Training for the Law*, 81–82. See also Nolan, "The Effect of the Revolution on the Bar," 969.
3. It is essentially Reed's, and he may have overstated the historical basis to support his proposal for a return to a graded profession. Reed, *Training for the Law*, 79 ff.
4. Ibid., 82–84.
5. John Quincy Adams recorded it at its best. Of his master, Theophilus Parsons, he wrote in 1787: "It is of great advantage of us to have Mr. Parsons in the office. He is in himself a law library, and proficient in every useful branch of service; but his chief excellency is, that no student can be more fond of proposing questions than he is of solving them. He is never at a loss, and always gives a full and ample account, not only of the subject proposed, but of all matters which have any intimate connection with it. I am persuaded that the advantage of having such an instructor is very great—." Quoted in Warren, *History of the American Bar*, 1:135.

   John Quincy Adams' father, John Adams, recorded the extensive reading in natural, common, civil, and international law that was required of him during his clerkship in Worcester, Massachusetts. Ibid., 1:136–37. There is evidence that Adams did not read all the assignments, and he was later highly critical of his preceptor. Gawalt, *The Promise of Power*, 132, 135. Thomas Jefferson thrived on what was perhaps a more practical training in Wythe's office. Jefferson, "Autobiography," in *Writings of Thomas Jefferson*, 1:4. James Kent, at Poughkeepsie, also seemed to receive a balanced education. See James Kent, "An American Law Student of a Hundred Years Ago," in AALS,

Select Essays in American Legal History, 1:837. From the careful scholarship of Paul Hamlin we now know what was available and what was recommended to law students in New York. Hamlin, *Legal Education in Colonial New York,* passim.

In Virginia, where the clerkship was not compulsory, the attrition rate was high. Smith, "Virginia Lawyers, 1680–1776," 183–84. Much of the work was that of a drudge—copying documents. The only way that most articled clerks differed from copying clerks was that the former were expected to comprehend Coke on Littleton with normally only the most marginal of assistance from their masters. Thus Jefferson, whose own experiences with Wythe had been pleasant, wrote, "I was always of the opinion that the placing of a youth to study with an attorney was rather a prejudice than a help." Ibid., 186.

The normal fee in New York for this form of servitude was £200, and there was no escaping the requirement in that province. The aristocratic William Livingstone published his feelings in *The New York Weekly Post-Boy* under a nom de plume. The rhetoric was moving, but the gist of the argument was that "not that I would be understood to mean, that the book ought entirely to supplant the Pen;—but I averr, that 'tis a monstrous absurdity to suppose, that the law is to be learnt by a perpetual copying of Precedents." Hamlin, *Legal Education in Colonial New York,* 41. Livingstone and others argued that the colleges should take up responsibility for legal education.

6. Virginia, which had the most elaborate professional structure, relied, after the Revolution, on the bar examination rather than periods of apprenticeship. Reed, *Training for the Law,* 85, 97–98. Overall, however, the examination system was as inadequate as it was in England. Ibid., 94 ff.

7. Ibid., 128 ff.

8. The first American edition of Blackstone appeared in 1771–72.

9. By the time the school finally closed in 1833, it had produced over 1,000 students, and among the 805 students whose names were recorded were 2 vice-presidents of the United States, 3 U.S. Supreme Court justices, 34 judges of state supreme courts, 6 cabinet members, 2 ministers to foreign countries, 101 members of the House of Representatives, 28 senators, 14 governors, and 10 lieutenant governors. Fisher, *Litchfield Law School: Biographical Catalogue of Students, 1774–1833,* 3, 4. Litchfield Law School, as the country's first successful law school, acquired mythical status during the nineteenth century, intermittently appearing with conflicting data in eulogies in legal periodicals. See "Law Schools and Their Course of Study," 4 *Western Jurist* 1–12 (1870); "The Litchfield Law School," 20 *Albany Law Journal* 72–73 (1879); "Methods of Legal Education," 34 *Albany Law Journal* 84–85 (1886) (which mistakenly claims that the school eventually became Harvard's Law School); and "The Litchfield Law School," 4 *Law Notes* 207–9 (1901).

10. Dwight, *Travels in New England and New York,* 4:295.

11. Reed, *Training for the Law,* 132; Hamlin, *Legal Education in Colonial New York,* 24.

12. As early as 1756, some New York counties had required only three years of work under a counselor for college graduates as opposed to seven for nongraduates. In 1771, Suffolk County in Massachusetts required all applicants to have a college education or its equivalent before entering an office. Reed, *Training for the Law,* 112–13.

13. By 1820, there were over a hundred colleges.

14. For Wythe's influence on his profession through his professorship, see Hurst, *The Growth of American Law,* 257. John Marshall studied, albeit briefly, under Wythe. Beveridge gives considerable detail about the law training at William and Mary during this period. See, especially, Beveridge, *The Life of John Marshall,* 1:157–59, 174–76.

15. In 1790, James Wilson was appointed professor of law at the College of Philadelphia

(later the University of Pennsylvania), and David Howell became professor of jurisprudence at Brown. In 1793, James Kent was appointed professor of law at Columbia College, and in 1799 George Nicholas had become professor of law and politics at Transylvania; by 1801, Elizur Goodrich was professor of law in Yale College, and in 1806 Daniel Chapman became professor of law at Middlebury. Reed, *Training for the Law*, 116–27, 134–37. See also Warren, *History of the American Bar*, 1:314 ff.

16. Chroust, *The Rise of the Legal Profession in America*, 2:189.

17. Hoffman's original *Course* was a bibliographical outline of readings arranged into thirteen "titles" plus four (later nine) "auxiliary" subjects. The plan offered training in diverse fields (including moral and political philosophy, political economy, history, and geography), although it concentrated on the divisions of law derived from Blackstone. Hoffman adhered to Blackstone's idea that the law was all-embracing, since it "applies the greatest powers of understanding to the greatest number of facts" and "embraces nearly the entire extent of human action and concerns." Although Hoffman shared the then current view of law as a moral science, he anticipated Langdell in analogizing the law to a physical science as well. The law was intrinsically moral both as to its original divine source and its consequences in human affairs, but the legal scholar, like the scientist, could comprehend the "principles" of his subject only by methodically arranging and examining its "relicks": ". . . to taste the pleasures which spring from legal research, we must [have] entered into the principles, discovered the harmonies, and arranged with method and curiosity the innumerable topics of the science, as in the caverns of the earth the accomplished and inquisitive mineralogist and geologist reap a satisfaction, and an interest unknown to the uninformed spectators." Proem.

Several of Hoffman's educational ideas flowed naturally from such a conception of law and law study. The most important was the emphasis on method. Since law was a rational science, only systematic methods could be appropriate to law study. Hoffman shared the belief of his contemporaries that the human mind was divided into a number of "faculties" such as judgment, imagination, memory, and reason, but he deplored over-reliance upon memory in learning legal rules by rote. Hence his stress on legal research and historical study. Although Hoffman recognized the uses of Blackstone's *Commentaries*, he felt that the student would best learn the reason and nature of law by retracing its development. No single treatise could substitute for this experience.

Hoffman envisioned a seven-year program staffed by six professors. The plan was never implemented, although Hoffman delivered law lectures himself for the next nine years, and for the following twenty-five continued to revise what became an 876-page treatise. Hoffman, *A Course of Legal Study Addressed to Students of Law in the United States*.

18. See Butler, *Plan for the Organization of a Law Faculty in the University of the City of New York*. It called for three years of formal education in addition to apprenticeship since law students needed "a Specific Institution for Legal Education." Ibid., 7. Classes would continue during a clerkship. Ibid., 13. They would not interfere with that office work. Ibid., 29. The school would help replace the Kinderhook Law School. NYU was to be the law school for seaboard New York, just as Hamilton was for western New York, Yale for Connecticut, and Harvard for Massachusetts. Ibid., 6.

19. The bequest was originally made in the will of Isaac Royall, who died in 1781. He may have been influenced by Viner's gift to Oxford. Sutherland, *The Law at Harvard*, xiii–xiv. Parker differentiated between the sequence at the School, which would provide study under a "capable instructor . . . as preparatory to that acquisition of practical knowledge of business which may always be better learned in the office of a distinguished counsellor." Warren, *History of the American Bar*, 1:299.

20. Bruce, *History of the University of Virginia*, 2:102–3. In 1825, the University of Virginia had 26 law students; in 1835, 67; in 1839, 71; in 1849, 66; and in 1869, 71. Reed, *Training for the Law*, 450–51.
21. Richard Pearson, for instance, ran a proprietary school at Montsville and later at Richmond Hill in North Carolina. He was said to have had over 1,000 students—many of them from out of state. He was reported to have used a type of Socratic method. Coates, "The Story of the Law School at the University of North Carolina," 8.

    Between 1786 and 1832 a blind lawyer, Peter Van Schaak, ran a law school at Kinderhook in Columbia County, New York. Over 100 students attended that school. Van Schaak, *Life of Peter Van Schaak*.

    Virginia also claimed some excellent proprietary schools. In 1810, Chancellor Creed Taylor established a law school at Richmond, which was later moved to Needham and survived until about 1830. Henry St. George Tucker, Jr., ran a school in Winchester from 1824 to 1831; John Lomax had a "strictly socratic" school in Fredericksburg from 1831 to 1844; between 1831 and 1839 Briscoe Gerard Baldwin had a proprietary school in Staunton and his place was taken by Judge Lucas Powell Thompson until 1849. It was then that John White Brockenbrough opened his Lexington Law School, with its "catechetical method of instruction," which educated 200 students before the Civil War caused its closing in 1861. Bryson, "The History of Legal Education in Virginia," 155, 176–83.
22. At the opening of the Dane Law Building in 1832, President Josiah Quincy of Harvard declared that the "community" should be "made to understand the real advantages to be anticipated from this engrafting of the study of law upon seminaries destined for public education." Although Quincy talked of the illiberalism of apprenticeship, he seemed more interested in raising the standards of the bar than in making legal education more scholarly. Miller, *Legal Mind in America*, 201, 207.
23. Reed, *Training for the Law*, 137–40; Sutherland, *Law at Harvard*, 49–59.
24. Reed, *Training for the Law*, 140–42. For reasons that can only be surmised, Yale until recently implied that it was the lineal descendant of the Litchfield Law School. See *Bulletin of Yale University: Law School (1960–1961)*, 12. "The only basis for the assertion . . . seems to be that a runaway slave 'Old Grimes,' . . . having acted as a general factotum to Litchfield students, subsequently occupied a similar position at Yale." Reed, *Training for the Law*, 131.
25. Although Story urged the student "to addict himself to the study of philosophy, of rhetoric, of history and of human nature" (Story, *Miscellaneous Writings*, 527), his actual plans for the school could scarcely have been of a more practical bent. In general, the law students at Harvard were not free to attend Harvard College courses, and Story enforced the de facto separation of law from government and politics. Ibid., 515, 535–36.
26. Reed, *Training for the Law*, 142–43. At that time there were also proprietary schools at Amherst and Needham in Massachusetts.
27. Tulane Archives, Special Collections, Howard-Tilden Library, Tulane University. See also Luis J. Banos, "The Early Years of Tulane Law School" (paper presented at the Tulane Law School, New Orleans, La., Spring 1978); Jonathan Craft, "The Law Department of the University of Louisiana" (paper presented at the Tulane Law School, New Orleans, La., Spring 1978).
28. In 1845, the University of North Carolina had taken over the proprietary law school run by Judge William Horn Battle in Chapel Hill. Coates, "The Story of the Law School at the University of North Carolina," 7.
29. For examples of the hostility toward and low status of the profession in Connecticut

and New York in the 1780s, see Horton, *James Kent*, 38. See also Gawalt, "Sources of Anti-Lawyer Sentiment in Massachusetts, 1740–1840," 283.

30. Tocqueville, *Democracy in America*, ed. Bradley, 1:282.

31. Ibid., 290.

32. See Horwitz, *The Transformation of American Law, 1780–1860*; Nelson, *Americanization of the Common Law*.

33. Stevens, "Unexplored Avenues in Comparative Anglo-American Legal History," passim.

34. Stevens, *Law and Politics*, 28–34, 77–83. The importance of all these factors is pointed up by divergent developments in England. In the years after 1832 the Parliament at Westminster met increasingly in full-time session, enacting legislation affecting many aspects of everyday life. The English civil service was expanding rapidly and, by the 1870s at the latest, was a meritocracy. In the United States, by contrast, the legislatures met rarely and were supported by the most rudimentary of civil services. Although the governors were men of power, they had little support from executive branches. The supreme courts were the only ongoing political institutions in the state capitals. The importance of lawyers was growing at the very moment when the profession appeared to be least secure. In real terms, the English models were increasingly irrelevant. The American bar was fragmenting and specializing and American judges, like American lawyers, were having roles thrust upon them that had been unknown in England.

35. Warren, *History of the American Bar*, passim.

36. Chroust, *Rise of the Legal Profession*. See, especially, vol. 2. To be treated with equal caution is the work of Perry Miller. See Miller, *The Life of the Mind in America*, 99 ff.

37. See Schlesinger, Jr., *The Age of Jackson*, chap. 25.

38. The innate contradictions are implicit in Perry Miller's work, *The Legal Mind in America*, and *The Life of the Mind in America*.

39. See, for example, Meyers, *The Jacksonian Persuasion*; and for New York, Benson, *The Concept of Jacksonian Democracy*.

40. Tocqueville had no illusions about the American scene: "In America there are no nobles or literary men, the people are apt to mistrust the wealthy, lawyers consequently form the highest political class and the most cultivated portion of society. They have therefore nothing to gain by innovation, which adds a conservative interest to their natural taste for public order. If I were asked where I place the American aristocracy, I should reply without hesitation that it is not among the rich, who are united by no common tie, but that it occupies the judicial bench and the bar."

"The more we reflect upon all that occurs in the United States, the more we shall be persuaded that the lawyers, as a body, form the most powerful, if not the only, counterpoise to the democratic element. In that country we easily perceive how the legal profession is qualified by its attributes, and even by its faults, to neutralize the vices inherent in popular government. When the American people are intoxicated by passion or carried away by the impetuosity of their ideas, they are checked and stopped by the almost invisible influence of their legal counselors. These secretly oppose their aristocratic propensities to the nation's democratic instincts, their superstitious attachment to what is old to its love of novelty, their narrow views to its immense designs, and their habitual procrastination to its ardent impatience." Tocqueville, *Democracy*, 1:288–89.

41. "I venture to predict that these innovations will sooner or later be attended with fatal consequences." Ibid., 279.

42. Northwest Territory (Indiana Territory and Ohio) in 1801–2; Georgia in 1807; Tennessee in 1809; and South Carolina in 1812.

43. New Jersey in 1817.

44. After having been established, they were also abolished almost at once in Louisiana, Mississippi, Arkansas, Wisconsin, and Iowa. For details, see Chroust, *Rise of Legal Profession*, vol. 2, chap. 3.

45. By 1860, it was required in only one southern state (South Carolina) and only one state west of the Appalachians (Ohio). Moreover, the states that retained some requirement frequently shortened the duration and reduced the formal requirement of "apprenticeship" to that of a "clerkship." Reed, *Training for the Law*, 86–87.

46. For instance, Joseph Story's appointment as law professor at Harvard in 1829 set that law school on its course toward becoming the preeminent law school in the United States. By 1844, the school had 163 students—a remarkable number for the period. But its success in these early years must not be overrated. Despite Story's unique scholarly contributions, the tone of the school was increasingly that of a trade school. As standards for admission to the bars in the different states collapsed, so did the quality of the Harvard student body. The demand, made in 1823, that students be graduates of a college or its equivalent had been so far eroded that, by 1829, students not qualified for admission to Harvard College were allowed into the law school. Students were free to come or go in mid-term and to stay for as long or as short a period as they wished. The formal plan of studies, which Isaac Parker had devised, after being scaled down from three years to one and a half, almost disappeared, and examinations were abolished. Those courses not directly related to the practice of law were dropped.

   "The reasons for these departures from the Chief Justice's plan are manifest. Harvard inconsiderately embarked upon legal education without counting the costs. This was its period of over-expansion, leading to the financial embarrassments and complete reorganization in a few years—the path travelled so often by our American universities. No support could be provided for the law school except that derived from students' fees; therefore as many students as possible must be secured and—for as long as they would pay their bills—must be retained. It was a question merely of dollars and cents. . . . If Harvard more recently has taken the lead in replacing legal education upon a graduate basis, it is only fair to recall that it was Harvard that gave the signal for encouraging a merely nominal connection between the college and the bar. She lent the prestige of her name to the doctrine that calling a practitioner a university professor is equivalent to making his proprietary law class a university school; and that an academic law degree may properly be conferred upon students entirely destitute of academic training." Reed, *Training for the Law*, 140.

47. Some sense of the state of flux in formal legal education may be gained by examining Pennsylvania. "Provincial Pennsylvanians had looked askance upon the profession of law as necessarily barratrous in its tendencies and as diametrically opposed to the Quaker tenets of good fellowship and peaceful arbitration in the solution of legal problems."

   By 1790, however, the trustees of the University of Pennsylvania determined to establish a chair of law, and James Wilson, a justice of the Supreme Court then sitting in Philadelphia, was appointed to it. The course of lectures petered out in 1791. The chair was revived in 1817, but at the end of the year the new incumbent was found to be suffering from "loss of reason." In 1850, the trustees tried again, appointing George Sharswood to the chair. This time the law department became permanent. Meanwhile, the Law Academy of Philadelphia, founded in 1821, primarily as a learned society, had begun to take on some teaching functions for law clerks, although it always sought to defer to the university.

   Outside Philadelphia, Dickinson considered establishing a law school in 1821, and in 1833 it established a nominal relationship with Judge John Reed's law school, which he founded that year in Carlisle. Reed was elected professor of law at the college; college students were allowed to attend lectures at the law school, but it was understood that "there should be no expense to the College." The law school lapsed on the death of Reed in 1850; it reappeared for a while in the 1870s and was reestablished as a separate corporation—the Dickinson School of Law—in 1890.

Many other efforts were limited to discussion. In 1834, Jefferson College talked of a law professorship; in 1839, Pennsylvania (Gettysburg) College actually made an offer to a possible incumbent as professor of law; Franklin College actually elected a professor in 1846. Hartford University (1850) and the University of Kittering (1854) were incorporated with the understanding that they would establish law schools. Lock Haven Law School was incorporated by the legislature in 1854, and in both 1859 and 1901 Bucknell University seriously considered the establishment of a law school. In 1871, Allegheny College was urged by the Methodist Board of Control to establish a law department "as soon as practicable."

Between 1838 and 1848 Marshall College ran a law school paying its professor (Judge Alexander Thompson) out of student fees. Judge James Porter became professor of jurisprudence at Lafayette in 1837; there was apparently a law school in existence at Lafayette between 1876 and 1878, and in 1896 there was some talk of reviving it yet again. Lehigh University had a law school from 1878 to 1879. Lincoln University—a black institution—had a law school from 1870 to 1873. Western University had had a law school from 1843 to 1849, and efforts were made to revive it in both 1861 and 1871. It did reappear briefly in 1872, only to collapse in 1873. After an abortive attempt to revive it in 1883, it was revived in 1895. Temple Law School was established in Philadelphia the same year. Sack, *History of Higher Education in Pennsylvania*, chap. 19.

48. It reopened in 1872. Mackenzie, "Farrah's Future," 121.
49. Friedman, *A History of American Law*, passim.
50. This is partly explained by the facts that the frontier itself was a relative concept and that there were considerable differences between the justice meted out at first instance and during the appeal process in the territorial capital. The frontier was infinitely various. On the one hand, there were lawyers and judges in the Hollywood image— men like Caesar Kasm, who practiced at the Missouri bar in the mid-1830s (Baldwin, *The Flush Times of Alabama and Mississippi*, 24–26), and John Reynolds, one of the first three elected judges under the 1818 Illinois constitution (King, "A Pioneer Court of Last Resort," 573, 576). Lawyers were often shysters, and the courtroom was often a circus. See Brackenridge, *Recollections of Persons and Places in the West*, 93, and King, "Riding the Circuit with Lincoln," 48.

At the same time, contrast the fact that the supreme court of Ohio, from its earliest years, had a highly distinguished bench (Reed, ed., *Bench and Bar of Ohio*), and the same was at least partially true in Missouri (English, *The Pioneer Lawyer and Jurist in Missouri*) as well as in other states and territories. Studies of local bars through the "frontier" period have often shown a high degree of professional organization and apparent competence. See Calhoun, *Professional Lives in America*, chap. 2, a study of lawyers in Cumberland River County, Tennessee, between 1790 and 1870. A similar conclusion was reached in a study of Wayne County (Michigan) lawyers and their education from 1796 to 1836: "There is no evidence that either the frontier lawyer of folklore or the frontier law of a hundred Western movies was a factor in the administration of justice in Wayne County during these years. Rather, the evidence is all to the contrary." Brown, "The Bar on a Frontier," 126.

See also Bloomfield, "The Texas Bar in the Nineteenth Century," 261, and Harris,

"The Frontier Lawyer's Library," 239. The same conflicting data face anyone seeking to look at legal education on the frontier. Lincoln's absence of formal training is proverbial. The Brown article, on the other hand, shows how different situations could be. So, too, one can marshal much evidence to show that "frontier" states cared at least as much about legal training and scholarship as the more "developed" eastern states. For example, Transylvania University in Kentucky began law teaching in 1799; the *Western Law Journal* coming out of Cincinnati in the 1840s was at least as sophisticated as most of its erratically published competitors in the East; and after the Civil War most of the states in the West were at least as willing as those in the East to establish rigorous standards for admission to the bar.

51. In the state as a whole, 1,408 out of 2,018 Massachusetts lawyers had been college trained between 1760 and 1840. Bloomfield, *American Lawyers in a Changing Society, 1776–1870*, chap. 5; Gawalt, *The Promise of Power*, passim. For further evidence of the stability of the profession during this period (at least in Cumberland County, Tennessee) see Calhoun, *Professional Lives in America*, chap. 3.

Partly, the change of attitude on the part of lawyers may be explained as the "critical mass" theory. The bar that had numbered 71 in Massachusetts in 1770 had grown to 493 in 1810. Nor was there an obvious decline in "quality." Between 1770 and 1840, 100 out of 184 law students in Essex County had college degrees. Gawalt, *The Promise of Power*, passim.

52. One should add that this work had begun with Kent and was soon supplemented by Parsons and later by Walker.

53. Stein, "Attraction of the Civil Law in Post-Revolutionary America," 403, 416.

54. Gilmore, *Ages of American Law*, chap. 2.

55. Reppy, ed., *David Dudley Field*, passim. See also Miller, *Life of the Mind*, 239–65, and Honnold, *The Life of the Law*, chap. 3.

56. White, *Tort Law in America*, 8–12.

57. Some flavor of this life in Boston may be gathered from reading the *American Jurist* (1828–43) and the *Law Reporter* (1838–66). See also the revealing passage in the dedication and preface of the third edition of Parsons on *Contract*, linking the Boston bar back to Bunker Hill and forward to Christopher Columbus Langdell (at the time librarian at the Harvard Law School). Parsons, *Law of Contracts*, iii–xii. See also Parsons, *Memoir of Theophilus Parsons*, passim. In one sense, too, although it oversimplifies the distinction between the common lawyers and the codifiers, Perry Miller's *The Legal Mind in America* captures this elitist tone for the period up to the Civil War.

58. Warren, *History of the American Bar*, chap. 15. The 35 or so lawyers who appeared regularly before the Supreme Court in the 1840s were from elite schools and colleges; 8 were in the Senate, 4 in the House, and 6 were attorneys general.

59. Reed, *Chief Justice*.

60. Levy, *The Law of the Commonwealth and Chief Justice Shaw*. See also Chan, *Lemuel Shaw*.

61. Nelson, *Americanization of the Common Law*, 8.

62. Hurst, *Law and Conditions of Freedom in the Nineteenth Century United States*; Hurst, *Law and Economic Growth*.

63. Horwitz, *The Transformation of American Law*, 188, 201, and passim.

64. Llewellyn, *The Common Law Tradition*, 62–72. Llewellyn's models were New York in 1842 and Ohio in 1844.

65. Gilmore, *Ages of American Law*, chap. 2.

66. Swaine, *The Cravath Firm and Its Predecessors, 1819–1947*, vol. 1; Taft, *A Century and a Half at the New York Bar*, passim.

67. This was a phenomenon noted by Bryce in the 1880s: "Prejudices survive on the shores
of the Mississippi which Bentham assailed seventy years ago when those shores were
inhabited by Indians and beavers; and in Chicago, a place which living men remember
as a lonely swamp, special demurrers, replications *de injuria*, and various elaborate
formalities of pleading which were swept away by the English Common Law Procedure
Acts of 1850 and 1852 flourish and abound to this day." Bryce, *The American
Commonwealth*, 2:625. Bryce may have been wrong on this. Medieval names continued
to be used even after the forms of action were gone. More interestingly, he added:
"Thus one finds the same dislike of theory, the same attachment to old forms, the same
unwillingness to be committed to any broad principle, which distinguished the orthodox type of English lawyer sixty years ago." Insofar as this was accurate, it represented a real difference from the high formalism of later Victorian England.
68. Reed, *Training for the Law*, 90.
69. The constitution of the State of Indiana declared: "Every person of good moral
character, being a voter, shall be entitled to admission to practice law in all courts of
justice." Article 7, Section 21 (1951). For a history of the passage of this provision at the
1850–51 constitutional convention, see Robinson, "Admission to the Bar as Provided
for in the Indiana Constitutional Convention of 1850–1851," 209. In a convention
where farmers (62) outnumbered lawyers (39) out of a total of 150, this provision was
part of a general effort to demystify the law. The convention, however, rejected the
attempt to abolish the common law of England. Ibid., 210.

The general tenor was best expressed by the delegate from Monroe County. "Mr.
Foster remarked, that when he came into this state many years ago, no one was
permitted to practice medicine, unless a graduate of the university, or who had obtained
a license from the medical institution of the state. This law had been repealed, so that
now everyone could practice in the medical profession, no matter of what grade,
regulars, Homopathists, Thompsonians, or Allopathists. In divinity, it was formerly the
custom for students not only to receive an education in divinity, but to reside for some
years at a theological Seminary or university. It is different nowadays. Why should there
be an exception made in favor of the law. These were the three liberal professions. In
other states, the practice of the law had been thrown open to all persons of good moral
character. The members of the bar would not fear competition with those who did not
understand their business. Throw the profession open to all, like medicine and divinity;
these were his sentiments." Ibid., 212. This section was adopted by a vote of 84 to 27.
70. John B. Niles opined:

> I am tired of the clamor against lawyers, and of being told that we have exclusive
> privileges, without being able to reply—you are a lawyer, too, sir. The lawyer and
> advocate under the Roman commonwealth needed no special license to practice his
> profession. Open the door wide to free competition; and integrity, learning and
> ability, will be a sufficient certificate, and without such certificate, a man will have
> but a poor practice. The law must be a vast and learned science, so long as it
> affords protection to the varied interests of civilized society. The idea of making
> every man his own lawyer by simplifying the rules of practice amounts to about as
> much as the scheme of some one who wrote a book, entitled "Every man his own
> washer-woman." [Ibid., 211–12]

Even before repeal, the courts required educational qualifications. See Gavit, "Legal
Education and Admission to the Bar," 67; Gavit, "Indiana's Constitution and the
Problem of Admission to the Bar," 595, 734.

Two apparently successful efforts to repeal the section at the turn of the century were struck down on technicalities. The provision was finally repealed in 1932 by popular vote and the repeal was upheld in *In re Todd*, 208 Ind. 168, 193 N.E. 865 (1935).

Yet, despite all the rhetoric, in 1894 there was little difference between the statistics for Indiana and its neighboring states as to the ratio of lawyers to the state population or as a percentage of state legislators. In Indiana, Illinois, Iowa, and Ohio, one in every 4 legislators was a lawyer. In Indiana, one in every 348 persons was a lawyer; in Illinois, one in every 394; in Iowa, one in every 325; and in Ohio, the figure was one in 360. See Benton, "Annual Address," 227, 244–45.

71. Llewellyn and Hoebel, *The Cheyenne Way*, chap 2.
72. According to Nathaniel W. Stephenson, Abraham Lincoln was to discover this to his chagrin in 1855. Working as associate counsel in a patent suit in Cincinnati in that year, he encountered the condescension of the college-trained senior counsel in the suit. During his return home, a conversation with Ralph Emerson elicited the following dialogue:

> Lincoln: I am going home to study law.
> Emerson: You stand at the head of the bar in Illinois now.
> Lincoln: Oh, yes, I do occupy a good position there, and I think I can get along with the way things are done there now. But these college-trained men, who have devoted their whole lives to study, are coming West, don't you see? And they study their cases as we never do. They have got as far as Cincinnati now. They will soon be in Illinois. I am going home to study law. I am as good as any of them, and when they get out to Illinois I will be ready for them. [Stephenson, *An Autobiography of Abraham Lincoln*, 118]

2 / Law, Lawyers, and Law Schools

THE resurgence of interest in the upgraded bar—even if coupled with a more instrumental "can-do" Americanized view of law—was part of a much wider trend in American life: the movement toward institutionalization.[1] There was a thirst for eighteenth-century "rationalism" often dressed up in "scientific" forms. Occupational groups felt an urge to professionalize and to stratify. The number of schools of pharmacy, for instance, rose from two in the period 1801–25 to eight between 1851 and 1875 and then to thirty-eight in the last quarter of the century. In 1801, there were twelve schools of medicine; by 1880, one hundred.[2] The college movement was accelerating at approximately the same time.[3] The founders of the University of Colorado expressed a common ideal in 1861 when they said their schools were "designated to promote and encourage the diffusion of knowledge, in all branches of learning, including the scientific, literary, theological, legal, and medical departments of instruction."[4]

The changes in the attitudes of the various occupational groups were the result, among other pressures, of the most laissez-faire of societies responding to the desires of a growing middle class for a more structured environment.[5] Less clear is the reason for the middle-class thrust. In part it was the effect of the scientism that pervaded the period; in part it was the felt need to impart order to a society dislocated by an industrial revolution and the thrust westward; in part it was a natural urge to stratify coupled with a natural (and acceptable) mechanism for differentiation. Law was to provide another such opportunity in American society.

The closing of the "safety valve" of the frontier, as proclaimed by Frederick Jackson Turner, has normally been treated in geographical terms. The frontier, however, was closing in many senses. The impact on the intellectual aspects of the American ideal was also important: "Mid-Victorians were competitive, and the serious contests of the future would be verbal. Americans would probe, joust, and examine each other in a war of words that occurred in the classroom, the courtroom, the sales-room, and the living room."[6] The last quarter of the nineteenth century was to see, on the one hand, the rapid rise of spectator sports and collegiate football and, on the other, the development of universities and the legal profession.

Sixty years after Tocqueville, Bryce noted that, "in a country where there is no titled class, no landed class, no military class, the chief distinction which popular sentiment can lay hold of as raising one set of persons above another is the character of their occupation, the degree of culture it implies, the extent to which it gives them an honorable prominence."[7] Of all the professions, the law was to become the most obvious vehicle both for claimed respectability and for upward mobility[8]—at least for white males.

Institutionalized legal education was again showing signs of life by the 1850s. There was a revival of law schools in the East (including Columbia, New York University, and the University of Pennsylvania) with the result that, by 1860, there were twenty-one law schools in existence.[9] The early catalogs of these schools provide useful pointers about their alleged purposes. In both north and south there was a feeling, which had been the rationale of Blackstone's lectures at Oxford a hundred years earlier, that law was the ideal training for a gentleman. When the faculty announced the opening of the University of Georgia Law School in 1858, it made clear that "it is not those only who intend to devote themselves to the law, that we invite to attend our school. There is in our State a large number of young men who intend to devote themselves to the honorable employment of cultivating the estates they inherit from their fathers. To them a knowledge of the general principles of law is of inestimable value."[10] New York University looked to other groups as well: "There are thousands of young men in the United States who are in possession, or will come into possession, of large estates. Many of these young men do not design to practice any profession, but nearly all are anxious to avail themselves of the advantages conferred by admission to some one of the learned professions. Many of these young men are ambitious of the honor of a seat in the Legislative Halls of the State or Nation." New York University was also anxious to appeal to "another class of young men, who are hereafter to control the mercantile and commercial interests of our country, to whom a thorough knowledge of mercantile and commercial law is indispensable. We invite ambitious, enterprising young men from all parts of the Union, who wish to acquire a thorough knowledge of our Government and Laws, to the Halls of our University."[11]

To achieve such broad purposes, the breadth of the programs was described glowingly. New York University claimed to have established its law department "in response to the imperious demand of the Public for greater facilities for acquiring a knowledge of the *science* of legislation, and the *theory* and *practice* of the law."[12] The Georgia lawyer was to be taught law "not as a collection of arbitrary rules, but as a connected logical system, founded on principles which appeal for their sanction to eternal truth." The University of Albany claimed to teach law "both as a SCIENCE and an ART."[13] Less prominently, however, the new schools admitted their real purpose. Albany castigated the "very imperfect means" of studying law in an office. "Who would think of committing a ship in the ocean to the guidance of a youth who had only studied navigation in his closets?" In Georgia it was alleged "the student is admitted to the Bar with such knowledge as he can gather, unaided, from Blackstone and Chitty." New York University deplored the office training where the students "generally pursue their studies unaided by any real instruction, or examination, or explanation. They imbibe error and truth, principles which are still in force with principles which have become obsolete; and when admitted to practice, they find, often at the cost of their unfortunate clients, that their course of study has not made them sound lawyers or correct practitioners." The middle-class urge to get ahead through structured education was receiving powerful support from the increasing dissatisfaction arising from training professionals through apprenticeship in offices.

Law was becoming a boom industry. In 1850, it was estimated that there were 23,939 lawyers; in 1870, 40,376; and by 1880, 64,137.[14] Although the basic practitioner resembled the circuit rider–office lawyer in the mold of Abraham Lincoln or perhaps even a modern cowboy movie,[15] the unleashing of the industrial might of the country and the resulting growth of large corporations, together with the "urge to professionalize," combined to promote the growth of a new type of law firm, with several partners and assistants, catering to the needs of the developing corporations.

Some of these firms had originated before the Civil War. The predecessor of the Cravath firm first emerged in upstate New York around 1820, where it pioneered the application of the trust concept to the financing of the emerging corporation. Its preeminence, however, did not come until after the Civil War, when it began handling the work of banks and railroads in New York City.[16] The career of David Dudley Field provides another example of the old giving way to the new. Until 1860, Field had a conventional law practice, based on advocacy, in New York. In that year, he hired Thomas G. Shearman to help him draft a book; by 1864, Shearman was his managing clerk, and, by 1867, a partner who hired his own clerk, John W. Sterling, fresh out of Columbia Law School. Field left for Europe in 1873 to devote himself to international arbitration, and the firm of Shearman and Sterling was born.[17] Six years later, Sullivan and Cromwell was formed.[18]

It was in this ambience that Hamilton College, as early as 1847, had appointed Theodore W. Dwight as professor of law, history, civil policy, and political economy. By 1852, the college had formally established a law department.[19] Dwight rapidly became the foremost legal educator of the revival period. He not only believed in the survival and renewal of the legal profession, but he also believed in formal training for the profession. He knew that "most of the leading lawyers had obtained their training in offices or by private reading, and were highly skeptical as to the possibilities of securing competent legal knowledge by means of professional schools."[20] Dwight, however, took the line that "principles before practice is the true watchword"[21] and sought to prove these lawyers wrong. He stood squarely in the tradition of Blackstone and Kent.

Dwight's theories[22] attracted attention from those seeking to support institutionalized training, and his position at Hamilton proved to be only a stepping-stone. At Columbia, there had been no law teaching between 1826 and 1847, and it had proceeded rather erratically thereafter. In 1857, however, as part of the emergence of the embryonic university, the School of Jurisprudence was established. In 1858, Dwight was brought in from Hamilton to run the school. His impact on the bar of New York could not have been greater. He was one of the founders of the Association of the Bar of the City of New York,[23] as well as of almost all other professional organizations established during those years. By the time he resigned in 1891, his lectures, recitations, and moots had been influential in shaping the professional lives of a remarkable proportion of leading members of the New York bar.[24]

The expansion of the law schools and the extension of the power of lawyers, both of which Dwight was promoting in the post–Civil War period, were directly related to the economic expansion and social restructuring of the country. As American industry and business firms developed rapidly, some observers expressed alarm at the prospect of the new American bar growing up under the shadow of the corporation and the trust.[25] They were, however, the few. In his commencement address at Columbia in 1867, Benjamin Silliman, a Yale man, quoted approvingly Tocqueville's praise of lawyers as "natural aristocrats"[26] and explained that the role of Columbia's graduates would not be to litigate but to work with businessmen, especially in Wall Street: "I believe that no place on earth is daily trodden by more [men] of honor, enterprise, generosity, faith and integrity—than that on which the setting sun casts the shadow of the spire of Trinity." Columbia's position as the leading law school was so prominent that Silliman referred to Columbia as "the very *West Point* of the Profession."[27]

Columbia was to maintain this prominence as the most important of the law schools, or more accurately, law programs, through the seventies. The refounding of the school by Dwight had, in effect, thrown down the gauntlet to practitioners. At its best, apprenticeship at that time was all that clinical legal education is claimed to be today: close supervision of a student by his principal in real-life encounters. Yet few apprenticeships worked out that way. Indeed, even when principals were diligent, the chances of any one office offering a good all-around training were small.[28] Dwight was not attempting to remove law training entirely from the office—most of the students spent part of each day in such offices[29]—but to make each case occur in an academic setting. This was accomplished by a series of expository lectures, supplemented by examinations, recitations, quizzes, and moots. The system called for exposition in the grand manner.

Despite fears to the contrary, few in the profession—especially its leaders—were prepared to fight the move away from apprenticeship and toward law school. By 1870, professional journals were vying with one another in appeals for improving the legal profession.[30] An article published both in the *Albany Law Journal* and the *Western Jurist* (Cincinnati) wondered why the legal profession "should be so utterly regardless of its own fair name, and careless of the honors which ought to be connected with the practice of so noble a profession as to admit so readily horde upon horde . . . within its precincts, with scarcely a voucher for the ability or worth, morally or intellectually, of such applicants as choose to present themselves."[31] In no time at all the concept of providing part of legal training through an institution known as the law school had become associated with the parallel aspect of institutionalization—the urge to raise standards and so make the bar more competent and more exclusive.[32]

The desire to raise standards did not, however, mean that the profession would necessarily accept law school training without reservations. The vast majority of the legal profession until the turn of the century still experienced only on-the-job legal education.[33] The law schools were offering instead a systematic, academic experience designed to upgrade the intellectual quality of law and lawyers and thus enhance their professional status. There had been, so it was claimed by the 1870s, a "downward tendency," and law had gone from "a liberal science to a mechanical trade."[34] Yet "the science of law was the science of mankind," and lawyers were being urged to "help solve the moral problems upon which the progress of the law depends."[35] Despite this appeal to ideology, a few practitioners saw the dangers of using too academic a training. In a different article, for instance, the *Albany Law Journal* argued that moots were of no more value to law students than counterfeit sickness would be to a medical student.[36]

The dispute was, however, relatively muted. No one at that time was suggesting that all three years of training should be spent in law school.[37] The leadership of the bar was fighting for something much more fundamental: a generalized requirement of apprenticeship, part of which might be "served" in law school, and an effective bar examination.[38] As a substitute for part of the apprenticeship, law school made good sense to most sections of the legal community. Thus calls for a structured legal education were reiterated throughout this period, both by eastern lawyers who saw themselves as setting the country's standards and by members of the profession from the South and West who feared to fall behind the times.

The leaders of the bar were conscious that, by calling for a more rigorous training and more systematic bar examinations,[39] entry to the profession would become narrower and, in one respect at least, less democratic. Perhaps Abe Lincoln had *not* been to law school; his casual passing of the bar examination (and his casual view as a bar examiner) had become part of the profession's lore.[40] Yet the profession's desire to raise standards would soon overcome the "outmoded" democratic tendencies of the Jacksonian era.

Professional standards in 1860 had been largely nonexistent. In that year, a specific period of law study, as a necessary qualification for admission to the bar, was required in only nine out of thirty-nine jurisdictions, and even law study had come to be thought of as less an apprenticeship and more a clerkship.[41] The bar examination, although required in all states but Indiana and New Hampshire, was everywhere oral and normally casual. In only nine states was there anything approaching a bar examining committee.[42] The leaders of the legal profession, surveying the situation, came to the conclusion that the status quo could not and should not be maintained. As the Civil War came to a close, the legal establishment turned its attention to raising standards for entry into the profession.

In the period between 1870 to 1890, admission to the bar tightened noticeably. By 1890, twenty-three of the thirty-nine jurisdictions required a formal period of study or apprenticeship. Meanwhile, states gradually adopted the committee system for examining for the bar and when, in 1878, New Hampshire established a permanent examining committee to be financed from the fees paid by students, the future pattern was set.[43] During this period, the written bar examination, which in 1870 had existed only in New York, was increasingly accepted as the norm.[44]

A belief in the technocratic and egalitarian aspects of examinations in general—a conviction that was encouraging reform of university and civil service in England—allowed the more ready acceptance of bar examinations in this country. Yet the apparent logic of such a neat utilitarian solution blunted political and social concerns about those who, because they were poor, were ill prepared. The theme that pushed reform forward was that one owed the obligation to society to raise standards. As an Illinois lawyer put it in 1879, "in a matter as important as that of raising the standards of professional honesty and ability, the convenience of the applicant for admission to the bar ought not to be consulted or estimated."[45]

The new process did not happen without controversy. One manifestation of the "better mousetrap" was the dispute over the diploma privilege. The origins of the issue were found in New York. In the 1850s, the state had no required period of law study[46] and only an erratic oral examination for applicants to the bar.[47] Without such requirements, it was difficult for law schools to attract students, but Theodore Dwight seemed to have come up with a solution to the problem in 1855, when he arranged for law students at Hamilton to be admitted to practice automatically after being examined by three counselors (i.e., lawyers), all of whom were teaching at the school.[48] In an era when law schools were seen as an expanded form of office practice, this was not irrational. In 1859, the diploma privilege was extended to Albany Law School and, in the following year, to Columbia and New York universities.[49] With this privilege, it was possible for the law schools to attract increasing numbers of students and, in the case of Columbia, to keep them for two years. The bar examination might not be particularly effective, but either the desire to avoid it through the diploma privilege or to learn law systematically was enough to keep the law schools economically viable.[50]

The bar leadership was not pleased with the diploma privilege, which it felt took control of entry into the profession away from practitioners and gave it to legal educators. Lewis Delafield stated unequivocally that "lawyers are public officers and upon principle no private body should appoint to public office," but he noted that 2,400 law students in New York took advantage of the privilege between 1860 and 1875.[51] Other opponents of the diploma privilege included those schools who could not get it and resented, for financial and prestige reasons, those schools that could. Harvard was not granted the privilege, and others found in that situation a way of attacking Columbia and other schools that had the right. "We should suppose that if even Cambridge may not claim for the possessors of its diploma an unquestioned admittance to the honors and profits of the Massachusetts bar, the lesser law schools throughout the country might submit to the same rule."[52]

Dwight fought to keep the privilege for Columbia, pointing out the weakness of the state bar exam and the strengths of a law school education,[53] but to little avail. In 1875, the Association of the Bar of the City of New York appointed a special investigative committee with Lewis Delafield as chairman to examine the problem. The committee not surprisingly called for the abolition of the privilege and the substitution of a permanent examining board, with a written, uniform bar examination.[54] In the same year, the judges of the Supreme Court, meeting in Albany, formally called on the legislature to repeal the diploma privilege.[55] The collapse of the system had begun, but its death was a slow one, and it was not abolished completely in New York until new rules were made in 1882. As the schools had surmised, the number of students fell, but not as dramatically as the schools had feared.[56] Once New York had abandoned the system, the diploma privilege came under attack in other states. It did not, however, disappear.[57]

Yet the diploma-privilege dispute was but an internal struggle within the general movement to raise the qualifications for entry to the profession. The instigator of a national organization to raise standards proved to be the American Social Science Association and its president, Lewis Delafield—the leading opponent of the diploma privilege. Delafield boldly attacked the "prevalent notion among laymen, which is shared by many professional men and has found expression from certain judges, that the gates to the bar should be wide open, and easy admission allowed to all applicants." Such a laissez-faire approach, Delafield observed, suggested that law was a trade, whereas, he argued, it was a public calling. In return for the grant of a monopoly, the state was entitled to demand character and learning of its lawyers. Delafield attacked any "leveling tendency" and maintained that the "unworthy" had to be "excluded" and "rejected."[58]

That was the message of Delafield's speech delivered to the American Social Science Association at its meeting in Saratoga in 1876. His call clearly met a need, and the 1877 meeting of the association urged the formation of a national lawyer's group.[59] The creation of the American Bar Association (ABA) in 1878 was largely the result of these meetings.[60] The ABA was, however, a tiny organization, having only 750 members in 1888. Nevertheless, the raising of the standards of the profession was high on its agenda from the beginning,[61] and its members listened carefully to what Delafield said. His call had been tripartite: "The best system would be . . . to require that all applicants should learn the principles of the law in a school, then apply them for at least a year in an office, and finally pass a public examination by impartial examiners appointed by the courts."[62] Because law schools were being founded, or refounded, across the country, office practice was being reemphasized by periods of apprenticeship, and the "impartial examiners" were appearing, this solution had some practical merit. It was in response to this utilitarian call that the modern law school movement accelerated.

NOTES

1. See, generally, Boorstin, *The Americans*, vol. 3; Bledstein, *The Culture of Professionalism*; and Larson, *The Rise of Professionalism*.
2. Bledstein, *The Culture of Professionalism*, 84. Similarly, veterinary schools went from zero in 1800 and 1850 to 15 in 1900, and medical schools, numbering 12 in 1800, numbered 186 a century later.
3. "By 1870 there were more institutions in America awarding bachelor's degrees, more medical schools and more law schools than in all Europe." Ibid., 33.
4. Davis, *Glory Colorado!*, 6. Other universities started in this period include Johns Hopkins University in 1876 (French, *A History of the University Founded by Johns Hopkins*), and Syracuse University in 1871 (Galpin, *Syracuse University*).
5. A recent study of professionalism categorized such developments as "a collective assertion of special social status and . . . a collective process of upward social mobility." Larson, *The Rise of Professionalism*, xvi.
6. Bledstein, *The Culture of Professionalism*, 73.
7. Bryce, *The American Commonwealth*, 2:626.
8. Earlier in his book, Bryce had said, "The lawyers best deserve to be called the leading class, less powerful in proportion to their numbers than the capitalist, but more powerful as a whole, since more numerous and more locally active." Ibid., 303. Lawyers themselves were all too well aware of their influence. *The Albany Law Journal* told its readers in 1870 that "in every age of civilized man, the lawyers have been an important instrument in the work of refining and elevating the race." "An Address to Law Students," 1:165. Even before this, in 1853, *Livingston's Monthly Law Magazine* had nothing but praise for the leaders of the bar, "those Americans now living whose talents, energy and enterprise, while affording an instructive lesson to mankind, seem worthy of being held up as examples for emulation. A knowledge of those whose substantial fame rests upon their attainments, character and success must exert a wholesome influence on the rising generation of the American people." 1 *Livingston Monthly Law Magazine* 71 (Jan. 1853).
9. Reed, *Training for the Law*, 152–54. On the general similarity of early schools, see ibid., 154–59. Although the University of Pennsylvania had had a professorship of law since 1790, its law school was not reestablished until 1852. See Patterson, "The Law School of the University of Pennsylvania," 99, 106. Columbia Law School, which Dwight incorrectly claims to have been the first in New York, was established in 1858. See Dwight, "Columbia College Law School, New York," 141. New York University Law School was originally established in 1838, only eight years after the incorporation of the university itself. For an outsider's view of it at this early stage, see "Law School of the New York University," 1 *The Law Reporter* 121 (1838). After an early collapse it was refounded in the 1850s.
10. The announcement continued: "They expect to be the Legislators of the land; they expect to make themselves useful to their counties as Judges of the Superior Courts;

they will confer blessings on their poorer neighbors, by settling disputes among them. To do these things well, and to maintain that position of honor and respect that the Georgia planters ought to occupy, some familiarity with the law is indispensable." University of Georgia, Law Department, *Announcement*, Athens, 1 June 1859.

11. New York University, Law Department, *Annual Announcement of Lectures, 1858–59*, 9–10.

12. Ibid., 10–11.

13. *Circular and Catalogues of the Law School of the University of Albany for the Year 1856–57*, 9.

14. Reed, *Training for the Law*, 442.

15. See, for instance, the career of William W. Dixon. His father had come from England, became a successful practitioner in New York, and ended his practicing career in Illinois. William was admitted to the Iowa bar in 1858, specialized in mining law, and later practiced in Tennessee, Arkansas, California, and Nevada, finishing his career in Montana. See *University of Montana, Dedication and History: School of Law* 24–25 (1961).

16. See Swaine, *The Cravath Firm and Its Predecessors, 1819–1948*; Hurst, *The Growth of American Law*, 303–7. The ascendancy of the Wall Street firm might have been threatened by defections to direct corporate employment. In the 1890s, a partner left the Cravath firm to become counsel to the Santa Fe Railroad and another was lost as counsel to the J. P. Morgan Co. Despite these losses, however, by 1900, the firm had five partners and five associates.

17. See Earle, *Mr. Shearman and Mr. Sterling and How They Grew*. Although Field had continued his largely courtroom practice, Shearman became increasingly involved with such captains of industry as Gould and Vanderbilt. When Field left, the corporate side of the firm increased in importance. The Rockefellers brought oil work, and the firm also handled steel, cotton, coal, and a concern that eventually became the First National City Bank. By 1880, Shearman and Sterling even had the latest status symbols: the telephone and the typewriter. Ibid., 14, 125, 137.

In other parts of the country, too, the forerunners of the large law firms of the mid-twentieth century were beginning. In 1885, there were only some 11,000 persons in Los Angeles, but the city's development was active enough to encourage Jackson Graves to go into partnership with Henry O'Melveny, the beginning of the law firm that went on to become O'Melveny and Myers. Clary, *History of the Law Firm of O'Melveny and Myers*, vol. 1, chap. 5. Ten years earlier Wayne MacVeogh, a Yale College man who had clerked with James Lewis in West Chester, Pa., and then mixed law and politics, moved his office from Harrisburg to Philadelphia. He joined forces with the scholarly George Tucker Bispham who had been at the University of Pennsylvania both as an undergraduate and as a law student and had then published a book on equity. The partnership was soon representing the Pennsylvania Railroad and the Girard Bank. It became Dechert, Price & Rhoads. Massey, Jr., *Dechert, Price and Rhoads*, chap. 1.

18. See Sullivan and Cromwell, *A Century at Law, 1879–1979*; Dean, *William Nelson Cromwell*.

19. Goebel, ed., *A History of the School of Law, Columbia University*, 34.

20. Ibid., 42.

21. Ibid., 35.

22. Dwight described his method of instruction in the first issue of the *Green Bag*. The students received daily reading assignments that they were expected to complete before an oral "quiz" on the subject. "To make the assignment effective, he is questioned on the topic, mainly to make it certain that he has studied the subject and has in a measure

comprehended it, and is thus in a position to listen with advantage to expositions."
Attendance at lectures, at least at first, was mandatory, so that the student would learn
to "relish" the subject. Dwight noted that no method could work for the student of
"average powers" as well as for the gifted one, and the college graduates would have
already experienced, and therefore have been comfortable with, his way of teaching.
Dwight declared in 1889 that "during a period of thirty years not a single instance has
transpired of any former student's expressing dissatisfaction with it." See Dwight,
"Columbia College Law School, New York," 141, 146.

23. Martin, *Causes and Conflicts*, 135–36, 195–96.

24. Goebel, *School of Law, Columbia*, 40–41.

25. See, for example, Bryce, *The American Commonwealth*, 2:628. "The growth of
enormously rich and powerful corporations, willing to pay vast sums for questionable
services, has seduced the virtue of some counsel whose eminence makes their example
important."

26. *Address by Benjamin D. Silliman before the Graduating Class of the Law School of
Columbia College* (12 May 1867).

27. Ibid.

28. In 1896, Charles Libby noted that "study in an office resolves itself into the reading of
text-books, with occasional furtive glimpses of the details of cases passing through the
office. How unsatisfactory such a method of studying law is, and how little likely to
develop a comprehension of the law as a science." Libby, "Legal Education," 27. The
1870s and 1880s saw discussion and debate on the merits and demerits of apprenticeship, but the proceedings of bar association meetings and bar association reports by the
1890s show general agreement that apprenticeship alone was inadequate preparation
for the legal profession. Close supervision of apprentices and clerks was rare, and the
areas of law studied were often limited in scope and applicable only to local jurisdictions. Another difficulty was that so many law offices were hiring professional clerks
(often former law students unable to find employment in the profession) that there was
little or no work left for an apprentice in such an office. See "Lawyer's Clerks: Their
Duties, Their Pay, and Their Many Discouragements," 56 *Albany Law Journal* 12
(1897). Some articles stressed the difficulties experienced by the practicing lawyers. "In
truth there is nothing that a busy lawyer would sooner run from than a young
gentleman who would exact an hour of his time every day instructing him in the
elementary principles of the law." Jones, "Report of the Committee on Legal Education
and Admission to the Bar," 97, 100. J. A. Hutchinson (of West Virginia) explained the
system to the ABA in this way: "The applicant for admission spends a year or two
thumbing Blackstone or Kent, or both, with now and then a dip into Chitty or Starkie,
in the lonesome, dusty, dreary round of a country attorney's office, where he was left to
work his way as best he could with little to guide him except his common sense (which
often was no guidance at all). He may have asked a few vague questions and received a
few vague answers." "Appendix to the Report of the Committee on Legal Education," 4
ABA Reports 278 (1881).

One of the difficulties of analyzing the controversy about apprenticeship (or clerkship) is that there are relatively few descriptions about how the system worked in the
nineteenth century that can be regarded as typical. Generally, atypical eulogies or bla-
tant attacks have survived. Those who wrote about their experience from the time of
Adams and Kent were scarcely typical practitioners. What is clear from biographies and
from histories is that in the late nineteenth century there was still a strong feeling, even
on the part of those who did go to law school, that a clerkship, although not mandatory,
was essential for the practitioner who intended to get to the top. For example, Joseph

Choate, after graduating from Harvard College and attending the Harvard Law School
in the 1850s, was an "apprentice" to Leverett Saltonstall and then clerked for four years
for Butler, Evarts and Southmayd. Strong, *Joseph H. Choate*, 23–25. After graduating
from Hamilton and NYU in the 1860s, Elihu Root worked for Mann and Parsons,
staying "one year, serving, as was the custom, his apprenticeship without pay." Jessup,
Elihu Root, 1:66. Henry O'Melveny's "apprenticeship" in Los Angeles in the 1880s
took place after O'Melveny had been admitted to the bar. Clary, *O'Melveny and
Meyers*, 38–40.

In Philadelphia, John Marshall Gest attended both the University of Pennsylvania
Law School and clerked in a law office concurrently. "I shall never forget my first day in
a law office. I was given Sharswood's Blackstone to read, and sundry writs and prae-
cipes to prepare from forms, the very nature of which I had never heard before. This
was our daily routine. We filed papers in the Prothonotary's office, drew deeds and
mortgages, mechanics liens and many other things *ejusdem generis*, we attended
sheriff's sales; we went to the offices of the Recorder of Deeds and the Register of Wills
for conveyances and mortgage searches, for the title insurance companies were then
almost unknown and little used. . . . In this way we learned practice." Gest, *Legal Education in Philadelphia Fifty Years Ago*, 16.

29. See Dwight, "Admission to the Bar," 142.
30. See, for example, "An Address to Law Students," 1 *Albany Law Journal* 165 (1870):
"In every age of civilized man, the lawyers have been an important instrument in the
work of elevating and refining the race."

The following selected bibliography gives some indication of the extent and general
applicability of these appeals which extend through the 1870s to the 1880s: "Admissions to the Bar," 1 *Central Law Journal* 353 (1874); Miller, "The Ideals of the Legal
Profession," *1874–1881 Iowa State Bar Association Proceedings* 194 (1912); "Law
Schools," 12 *Chicago Legal News* 273 (1880); Osborn, "Annual Address," 2 *Ohio
State Bar Association Reports* 71 (1881); "Report of the Committee on Legal Education and Admission to the Bar," *Tennessee Bar Association Reports* 50 (1882): "We
think we can trace a decline in the general practitioner at the bar, even in our time";
"Legal Education," 3 *Kentucky Bar Association Reports* 16 (1884).

Of course, not all were enthusiastic about the idea of change. See, for example,
"Admission to the Bar," 15 *American Law Review* 295 (1881): "Changes have
followed each other in rapid succession, so that it might almost seem that the present
generation of students exists only for the purpose of being subjected to experiments, on
the result of which will depend the course to be adopted in the training of their more
fortunate successors."

31. Concerning examinations for admission to the bar, see 1 *Albany Law Journal* 350
(1870), reprinted in 4 *Western Jurist* 306 (1870). William Hammond agreed that the
"bar is probably more easily accessible than any other profession or trade by which
men can make a livelihood." Hammond, "The Legal Profession—Its Past—Its Present
—Its Duty," 1, 13.
32. See, for example, Hammond, "Legal Education and the Study of Jurisprudence in the
West and North West," 165; Hammond, "Legal Education and the Present State of the
Literature of the Law," 292.
33. For the typical experience of a prosperous son of a family in Carrollton, Missouri, see
Barber, *Missouri Lawyer*, chap. 1. His apprenticeship, begun in 1896, was divided
between reading Blackstone, Kent, and Chitty and copying and filing. The process
ended with a four-hour oral exam ("never before or since have I had such exacting
demands made upon my mental powers and knowledge"). Ibid., 15.

34. Washburn, "Legal Education: Why?," 213, 215.
35. Ibid., 216.
36. See "Law Apprenticeships," 5 *Albany Law Journal* 97 (1872). In fairness, the article admitted that "the time spent by a young man in a law office is, to a great extent, wasted." Ibid., 98. The article advocated formal apprenticeship rather than clerkship, contending that something like code pleading had to be learned in a law office. See also "Law School," 12 *Albany Law Journal* 212 (1875).
37. E.g., the remarks of J. J. Alexander of Baltimore, saying of law students who attend only law school "that perhaps the course of most of them resembles too much the scheme of education of priests and monks." 4 *ABA Reports* 287 (1881).
38. "Not until the bar shall awaken to the necessity of imposing the most stringent requirements for admission to practice, and thus preclude therefrom all such as have not the most undoubted qualifications, will the profession of law be an honor unto itself, or anything but a target for idle and sarcastic remark and ridicule." "Admission to the Bar," 4 *Western Jurist* 308, reprinted from 1 *Albany Law Journal*, 350.
39. See letter from "Juvenis" noting that "so indifferent are the committees to these requirements, however, that a casual *private* examination of five or ten minutes suffices to get the requisite certificate," 1 *Central Law Journal* 353 (1874); a reprint of an article from the *New York Daily Register* ("Examinations for Admission to the Bar") in 7 *Chicago Legal News* 38 (1874), asserting the article was equally applicable to Chicago; Hammond, "The Legal Profession," 13, noting, "I have never heard an examination, East or West, for which a young man of fair talents and education could not have been prepared by an experienced trainer in three months." The list could be endless, ranging from New York and New Jersey to Georgia, but it includes: Delafield, "The Conditions of Admission to the Bar," 7 *Pennsylvania Monthly* 968 (1876); "Examinations for Admission to the Bar," 3 *New Jersey Law Journal* 95 (1880); "Admission to the Bar," ibid., vol. 5, 95 (1882); 6 *Alabama State Bar Association Reports* (1884), citing the conditions of the South after the Civil War as one obstacle to raising standards; "Legal Education," 3 *Kentucky Bar Association Reports* 16 (1884); "The Learned Fifth," 1 *Columbia Jurist* 89 (1885), printing fifteen questions from a New York bar exam, and reproaching them for their irrelevancy; and "Report of the Committee on Legal Education and Admission to the Bar," 4 *Georgia Bar Association Reports* 178, 184–85 (1887), fearing that "members [of the examining committee] are friendly to the candidate and anxious to secure his admission."
40. See Hurst, *Growth of American Law*, 281–83.
41. Reed, *Training for the Law*, 87. In the jurisdictions where a period of law study had survived, it had been reduced to two years in Maryland, North Carolina, and Ohio. Other states, including Connecticut, Rhode Island, Vermont, New Jersey, Pennsylvania, and Delaware, required three years of study. Clerkship was a sign of degeneration from apprenticeship, a change from the idealized student studying law texts with his master to a "hurrying to chambers and answering to his principal's causes, or driving as a copyist through a mass of manuscript, or keeping a register of daily business." In this type of clerkship, law could only be learned in "a hap-hazard way." Dwight, "Education in Law Schools in the City of New York Compared With That Obtained in Law Offices," 157, 159.
42. A successful attempt to pass the bar examination by a black lawyer is described in Bloomfield, *American Lawyers in a Changing Society*, 314–16.
43. Reed, *Training for the Law*, 102–3. Change, however, came slowly. Huey Long's oral bar examination in 1915 is part of Louisiana lore. When asked by George Terriberry, an admiralty practitioner, what he knew about admiralty, Long replied, "Nothing." When

pressed about how he would handle an admiralty matter, Long announced, "I'd associate Mr. Terriberry with me and divide the fee with him." Long passed. Williams, *Huey Long*, 81.

44. See, for example, "Examination for Admission to the Bar in Virginia—the Past—the Future," 2 *Virginia Law Register* 310 (1896); "Examinations in Law for Admission to the Bar in the State of New York," 20 *Proceedings New York State Bar Association*; "Legal Education," 44 *American Law Register* 361 (1896); "Report of the Committee on Legal Education," 2 *Pennsylvania Bar Association Reports* 128 (1896). Many of these reports and articles suggested that the written examination be supplemented by an oral examination in cases of questionable results. An oral examination as the sole criterion for admission to the bar was, however, condemned by all. "The examinations are oral in almost every instance, by a picked-up committee whose members have no special preparation for their work and who have not given it any thought or attention." "Report of the Committee on Legal Education and Admission to the Bar," 17 *Texas Bar Association Proceedings* (1898). In "How Shall Our Bar Examinations be Conducted?," 3 *Western Reserve Law Journal* 129 (1897), questions from the bar examination in Suffolk County, Massachusetts, were published as an example of the proper form of a written examination. The following question was typical:

> A was the owner of a stable situated on a public highway, in which he kept several horses. A had placed a sign extending from this stable over the highway, in violation of a city ordinance. With negligence on A's part, a horse escaped from the stable and damaged B's garden. In a severe tempest the sign blew down and fell on C, then lawfully traveling on the highway. Can B recover against A for the injury to his garden? Can C against A for his personal injury? [Ibid., 133]

For other reports recommending or approving the use of written examinations, see Libby, "Legal Education"; Rogers, "Legal Education."

45. Armstrong, "The Terms of Study of the Law Student," 354. Correspondents pointed out that Armstrong's solution would exclude the poor, but not necessarily those of low morals or intellect. Ibid., 367.

46. The 1846 constitution provided that "any male citizen of the age of twenty-one years, of good moral character, and who possesses the requisite qualifications of learning and ability shall be entitled to admission to practice in all the courts of this state."

47. The many rulings are neatly cataloged in "Examination for Admission to the Bar" printed originally in the *New York Daily Register*, 16 October 1874, and reprinted in 7 *Chicago Legal News* 38 (1874).

48. Reed suggested that the original establishment of a separate bar committee for examining Hamilton graduates was "a reasonable attempt to reduce geographical inconvenience . . . but the practical operation even of this act . . . could not have been very different from complete exemption from court control." Reed, *Training for the Law*, 251. In 1866, Pomeroy asked the state supreme court to nominate three prominent lawyers to conduct the final examinations at New York University. Jessup, *Elihu Root*, 1:62.

49. The history is usefully reviewed in Association of the Bar of the City of New York, *Report of a Committee on Admission to the Bar* 3–6 (1876). Actually, the diploma privilege had existed before its appearance in New York but had not attracted as much attention. It was available in Virginia from 1842 to 1849 and later in Louisiana when the University of Louisiana was given the privilege in 1855. The University of Louisiana later became Tulane.

50. The *Albany Law Journal* gave extensive coverage to the problem of whether or not

Columbia should keep this privilege. "Current Topics," 9 *Albany Law Journal* 336 (1874); "Correspondence," ibid., vol. 9, 361; "Law Schools—Admission to the Bar," ibid., vol. 9, 406; "Admission to the Bar," ibid., vol. 2, 360 (1865); "Admission to the Bar," ibid., vol. 13, 142 (1876). *The Nation* also addressed the topic. "The Work," 22 *The Nation* 90 (1876); "The Bar and the Law Schools," ibid., vol. 22, 109. Other, more distant journals, also discussed it. See "Law Schools," 8 *Western Jurist* 584 (1874); "Law Schools—Admissions to the Bar," 1 *Central Law Journal* 320–21 (1874); "Law Schools—Reform Needed," ibid., vol. 1, 335; "Law Schools—Admission to the Bar," ibid., vol. 1, 360; "Law Schools," ibid., vol. 1, 419. "The Conditions of Admissions to the Bar," 7 *Pennsylvania Monthly* 968 (1876); "Legal Education," 12 *Canada Law Journal* 187 (1876).

51. Delafield, "The Conditions of Admission to the Bar," 964–67.
52. "Admission to the Bar," 1 *Central Law Journal* 321.
53. Dwight, "Education in Law Schools," 157–66.
54. Report of the Committee on Admission to the Bar, 29–31. The report stated:

> None of the professors whom we had the pleasure of hearing gave any reason why the law schools should have the privileges now enjoyed except that schools ought to be encouraged; and they all expressed the apprehension that were the privileges repealed the numbers of students would largely diminish.
> We cannot concur with the first reason, and as to the second, we are of the opinion that those who are deterred from the study of law on this account will be no loss. [Ibid., 13]

55. Goebel, *School of Law, Columbia*, 105.
56. In 1881–82, there were 471 students at Columbia; in 1882–83, 400; 1883–84, 365; 1884–85, 365; 1885–86, 345. Ibid., 106–7, 433. Dwight could even say "It is creditable to the young men studying the law, that they still crowd the law schools, notwithstanding that they have no exclusive privileges." Ibid., 107–8.
57. In 1890, the privilege was enjoyed by 26 schools in sixteen states. The ABA declared itself against the privilege in 1892, 1908, 1918, and 1921. The AALS condemned it in 1901. It was still in force (at least partially) in thirteen states in 1928. Reed, *Present-Day Law Schools*, 53–54.
58. Delafield, "The Conditions of Admissions to the Bar," 960.
59. The Bar Association of the City of New York had been founded in 1870. See Martin, *Causes and Conflicts*. For an account of the growth of state and local bars during this period, see Reed, *Training for the Law*, 206.
60. For a useful account of how the ASSA gave birth to the ABA, as well as the perspective of one who could legitimately claim it was "really my child," see Goetsch, *Essays on Simeon E. Baldwin*, 24–30. Baldwin had not only helped save the Yale Law School from extinction in 1869, but he was a mainstay of the school for fifty years. He also served as governor of Connecticut.
61. Rogers, "The American Bar Association in Retrospect," 172. See also Smith, "History of the Activity of the American Bar Association in Relation to Legal Education and Admission to the Bar," 1.
62. Delafield, "Conditions of Admission to the Bar," 969.

3 / Harvard Decrees the Structure and Content

UNTIL the 1870s, there were no modern universities in America, only colleges where Greek, Latin, moral philosophy, and mathematics were taught through lectures and recitations. Although there had been some lessening of rigidity earlier in the century[1] and even during the colonial period, the modernizing breezes blew strongly only in the years after 1865. Yale and Princeton set themselves against the trend, but Harvard, under the presidency of Charles Eliot, a scientist appointed in 1869, set out to conquer new (if not all) worlds. Eliot believed in an aristocracy of talent and declared open season on all subjects, claiming virtually everything as suitable for university study. These decades saw not only the endowing of great private universities[2] and the founding of land grant colleges under the Morrill Act[3] but also the emergence of smaller, private colleges around the nation[4] and, by the 1880s, of a new species of proprietary professional school.

Such success as American legal education had had before the Civil War had been achieved through proprietary schools[5] such as the Litchfield Law School. Several universities had acquired proprietary law schools before the war, but the resulting law departments, whether at Harvard or Tulane, were marginal to the main purpose of these institutions, which was the providing of a four-year, highly structured, liberal arts education. The four-year liberal arts syllabus, which included all those areas thought appropriate for the education of the young, did allow the president (or in some cases a so-called professor of law who was what we would now call an adjunct faculty member) to deliver some thoughts during the fourth year on political economy, or international or constitutional law. Such developments had little to do with the Story School at Harvard or the Daggett School at Yale, which also taught undergraduates. These latter schools were not designed for the elegant training of the mind. Strategically, they were in competition for students with the four-year liberal arts curriculum; tactically, they were profit-making professional institutions; educationally, they were primarily trade schools.

The law school that Christopher Columbus Langdell inherited, as dean, in 1870 was an adjunct of what was to become Harvard University,

but it had no relation to Harvard College.[6] Students in general chose
either law school or college, not both. At best they might take a few
courses in the college. Some students might transfer to the "school" after
one or two years of college, or after a college degree, but most came
directly from high school and a minority after a degree at Harvard or
elsewhere. A similar situation prevailed at Yale, Columbia, and Pennsylvania and even more vividly at less prestigious schools.[7] Thus, during the
last thirty years of the nineteenth century and the first two decades of the
twentieth, although the norm for formal American legal education moved
from one to two to three years, it did so essentially as an undergraduate
curriculum.[8]

Columbia's growth after 1850 and its position as leader of the law
school "improvement" movement was ultimately overshadowed by the
rise of the Harvard Law School in the decades after 1870. The attack on
the old order at the Harvard Law School began effectively with an un-
signed article (written by Oliver Wendell Holmes, Jr., and Arthur Sedg-
wick),[9] but the school's rise is attributable primarily to two appointments:
those of Eliot as president[10] and of Langdell[11] to the newly created post
of dean of the law school in 1870.[12] During Langdell's deanship, which
lasted until 1895,[13] Harvard not only became the preeminent law school
in the country, but institutionalized legal training was established as de
rigeur for leaders of the profession. Moreover, law was accepted, finally
and irrevocably, as an appropriate study for university education.[14]
Much of the credit (or responsibility) for this ought to belong not to
Langdell (who frequently seemed unaware of the revolution he was en-
gendering) but to Eliot, whose innovations on both the undergraduate
and graduate level of the university had a powerful influence over Langdell.[15] It was largely through Eliot's efforts and his "social relations"
that the Harvard Law School method was accepted by other schools and
scholars; Langdell, taciturn and studious, surrounded his work with a
"deep silence."[16]

It is, however, with Langdell's name that the various reforms that took
place while he was at Harvard[17] and rapidly spread through American
legal education have been associated. Langdell and Eliot found the Harvard Law School a two-year operation, at best, with students free to start
at any point. Langdell, as dean, at once established first- and second-year
courses—what became known as the graded curriculum. The long-term
goals, however, were far grander. In addition to the development of a
system of teaching that emphasized the analysis of appellate cases, it was
Langdell's goal to turn the legal profession into a university-educated
one—and not at the undergraduate level but at a level that required a
three-year post-baccalaureate degree.[18] The proposed three-year degree

became a reality before law was recognized as a graduate study. In 1871 the LL.B. was extended from eighteen months to two years, in 1876 the Board of Overseers agreed to a regulation designed to encourage candidates for the LL.B. to study for three years, and in 1899 the mandatory three-year goal was reached,[19] although there was still flexibility even at Harvard.[20]

Other schools slowly picked up the three-year requirement after an initial flirtation with the idea of a two-year LL.B. with optional higher degrees.[21] The move to make law a graduate program, however, moved appreciably more slowly. By the beginning of World War I, only Harvard and Pennsylvania had established any serious claim to have the law curriculum treated as a graduate one,[22] and at least at the University of Pennsylvania the assumption was that law school and clerking in an office would be done concurrently.[23] When universities like Stanford brought law into the curriculum, they adopted the traditional pattern whereby law became an undergraduate division of the university like arts and sciences and which, in the case of Stanford, awarded an A.B. degree.[24] By 1921, however, when Alfred Z. Reed produced his first report on legal education for the Carnegie Foundation, Stanford, together with Columbia, Western Reserve, and Yale law schools required a college degree, except from those enrolled as undergraduates in the same university.

Changes during this period were not primarily of this order. Nationwide, the chief change in the early part of the twentieth century was to bring admissions' standards at the law schools up to the level of other undergraduate programs. This was not always easy to achieve even at schools with well-known names. For instance, in 1899 when Cornell moved to apply to the law school the admissions standards by then applied elsewhere in the university, namely, four years of high school, the entering class fell from 125 to 62.[25] The same "fall off" often resulted when schools moved beyond the high school diploma requirement. When the University of Minnesota Law School began to require one year of college work in 1909, the first-year class fell from 203 to 69.[26]

For the last decades of the nineteenth century and the first of the twentieth, the role of the typical law school was much closer to the Lawrence Scientific School of Harvard[27] or the Sheffield Scientific School of Yale,[28] that is, to a technical school serving undergraduates and usually with a second-class status. When Hugo Black appeared at the University of Alabama in 1904, he was unable to gain admission to the Academic Department (the College of Arts and Sciences). He was, however, accepted without difficulty at the law school.[29] Three years earlier, there had been some unpleasantness at Georgetown. Although the College at Georgetown had serious standards, the law school did not even require graduation from high school for admission. Opponents of Georgetown's athletic programs were irritated to discover a disproportionate number of Georgetown's athletes enrolled in the law school.[30]

Harvard, however, continued to be both the market leader and professional exemplar, and Harvard's innovations concerned not only its student body but also its faculty. The appointment of James Barr Ames in 1873 as an assistant professor of law was considered a milestone. He was the first of a new breed of academic lawyer, a law graduate with limited experience of practice who was appointed for his scholarly and teaching potential. Ames, a recent Harvard Law graduate who had scarcely practiced law, was exactly the type of professor Langdell demanded: "A teacher of law should be a person who accompanies his pupils on a road which is new to them, but with which he is well acquainted from having often traveled it before. What qualifies a person, therefore, to teach law, is not experience in the work of a lawyer's office, not experience in dealing with men, not experience in the trial or argument of cases, not experience, in short, in using law, but experience in learning law."[31] Thus the case system was seen as so self-contained that the hand of a practitioner was not to sully its purity. Despite a Harvard Board of Overseers that was "reluctant" and "dubious" about his appointment, Ames succeeded at Harvard in turning the case method into a faith.[32] He was popular with the students and apparently had a greater facility for teaching than the originator of the method, Langdell.[33] Of Ames' appointment,[34] Eliot said: "In due course . . . there will be produced in this country a body of men learned in the law, who have never been on the bench or at the bar, but who nevertheless hold positions of great weight and influence as teachers of the law, as expounders, systematizers and historians. This, I venture to predict, is one of the most far-reaching changes in the organization of the profession that has ever been made in our country."[35]

Until Ames' appointment (and the practice, in general, continued after it) law professors had been either practitioners taking a few hours away from the office each week to conduct classes, or full-time teachers who had had extensive experience as practitioners before appointment. Ames' appointment set a trend that helped to bring the law school further into the mainstream of the burgeoning American higher education industry and began to lead it away from the profession. Although Ames, even more than Langdell, emphasized doctrine, his appointment created, for the first time, a division in the legal profession between the "academics" and the "practitioners," a separation that would not only logically lead to the creation of the Association of American Law Schools (AALS) in 1900 as an entity separate from the ABA, but would also cause increased confusion and controversy in the disputes over standards in the early twentieth century.

Harvard had taken the lead in the creation of the new method of teaching, the new structural standards, and the new type of educator thought to be needed by American legal education. What was covered in the curriculum, however, changed little; not surprisingly, here, too, Harvard was dominant. In the early years of the nineteenth century the formal subjects of instruction had varied considerably,[36] but by 1900 Langdell and Ames had overseen the emergence of a remarkable uniformity in curricula. Moreover, these essentially professionally oriented curricula[37] were based on the Harvard curriculum of 1852[38] as revised— in the light of professional needs—during Langdell's time.[39]

The size and influence of Harvard was such that almost all university-affiliated schools were only too anxious to emulate its developments.[40] A few of the national schools tried to be less professional than Harvard by offering courses in such areas as international law,[41] comparative law, and jurisprudence,[42] and other schools early brought in the embryonic social science of economics and government.[43] It was not, however, easy. Columbia under Dwight had been as hostile to any nonlaw subjects as had Langdell's Harvard. Francis Lieber, the political scientist who sought a foothold at Columbia, learned this to his cost.[44] On the other hand, in 1887 Yale had even introduced an alternative degree, the Bachelor of Civil Laws (B.C.L.), designed "for those not intending to enter any active business or professional career but who wish to acquire an enlarged acquaintance with our political and legal systems, and the rules by which they are governed."[45] Although this attempt to establish a nonprofessional law school degree must be counted a failure,[46] it pointed up some fundamental questions hinted at by the creation of "academic" lawyers.

The issues were posed more starkly in the story of Harvard's involvement with the founding of the University of Chicago Law School. In 1900, when William Rainey Harper, the president of the new University of Chicago, was ready to open a law school, he turned to President Eliot and Dean Ames for advice and support. (Indeed, he lunched with the Harvard Law School faculty and pleaded with them to "come over into Macedonia and help us.") In the meantime, sentiments on the Midway were rather different. Gulusha Anderson of the divinity faculty, a member of the Steering Committee, wrote to Harper, warning that "Harvard is theoretical, doctrinaire, and should not have the privilege of just putting down its counter-part here; we are more practical and direct and all the better for that."

In face of such opposition, preparations for a law school nevertheless proceeded, and plans were made for Joseph Beale to be seconded from Harvard to Chicago as dean. Meanwhile, Ernst Freund, a political scientist on the Chicago Steering Committee, drafted a circular about the new law school, paying the usual homage to the school's obligation "to cultivate and encourage the scientific study of systematic and comparative jurisprudence, legal history and the principles of legislation." The unexpected aspect was that the document also foresaw, in addition to the courses taught at Harvard, the teaching of international law. What was more, the document suggested electives in the second year in such novel subjects as taxation, constitutional law, jurisprudence, and Roman law. When he heard of these suggestions, Beale was horrified. "We have no such subjects in our curriculum," he announced, with an air of finality. Said Dean Ames, "We are unanimously opposed to the teaching of anything but pure law in our department. . . . We think that no one but a lawyer, teaching law, should be a member of a Law Faculty." Beale petulantly announced, "I can be of no use in such a law school," but he went to Chicago nonetheless. The experiment worked satisfactorily, and the result turned out to be much closer to Harvard than Beale had feared or some of the Chicago faculty had hoped.[47]

Indeed, at many schools there appeared to be a gulf between rhetoric and reality, springing from the reception that the law schools, designed for professional or even vocational training, were given by the universities, which were increasingly seeing themselves as centers of scholarship. In the 1890s, for instance, President Welling of Columbian (George Washington) University liked to talk of the Columbian Law School as a School of Comparative Jurisprudence.[48] The truth was that it was a successful night school helping government clerks get through the bar examination.[49] Georgetown, which was packing in nearly one thousand part-time students in its only program—the night school—in the 1890s, still went through the pretense of insisting that it was especially interested in "nonlegal" subjects like legal ethics, legal philosophy, and legal history.[50] Of the three leading schools in Washington, however, the most pretentious was Catholic University. Not only was the law school enthroned in the School of Social Sciences, but, as part of its academic pretensions, it offered no less than three doctoral degrees in common and civil law. Yet the school had to scratch and scrape to find faculty and, when two resigned before term began in 1899, the dean informed the president that "it is a very difficult matter to obtain candidates such as you desire for the law school of the University. We are at our wit's end every year to find material sufficient for the work at the meager salary we are able to pay."[51]

The conflict between academic pretensions and the reality of the marketplace was increasingly obvious. Nor was it clear that the homogenized and stylized Harvard curriculum made sense for every law school. A problem with having a standard national curriculum soon manifested itself in the less prestigious local law schools.[52] Albert Kales of Illinois suggested in 1909 that, since between 65 to 95 percent of law students at the University of Illinois intended to practice locally after graduating, a standard curriculum based on the development of legal reasoning was less pertinent to the career goals of such students than learning the law of their particular jurisdiction.[53] This point raised another question that would concern those who aspired to be legal scholars: Was American law really (or should it be) a unitary system, as Langdell had claimed? In adapting the case system to teach the methodology that became known as "thinking like a lawyer," Ames and Keener had decided it should, and the goals of the National Conference of Commissioners on Uniform State Laws clearly supported them. Yet the issue was to remain a persistent and nagging one.

Such questioning caused scarcely a ripple at the national law schools. When the United States Commissioner of Education published a list of curricula at the law schools in 1891,[54] Harvard offered only twenty-two subjects while Yale offered fifty-five, of which eighteen were listed as "nontechnical." The next largest number of courses was offered by Northwestern, of which only five fell into the nontechnical category.[55] These differences were partially ironed out in the ensuing years when the elective system, finally introduced at Harvard by Langdell and ultimately accepted in 1896,[56] spread rapidly to other leading schools.[57] Although broader and elective approaches became the norm at national schools, at the less prestigious schools the story was very different.[58] Albert Kales' observations about the needs of local practitioners and James Hall's hesitations about the use of electives for local law schools seemed to be proving themselves accurate. With respect to the core curriculum, however, virtually all these schools had accepted the Harvard model by 1920.[59]

In the fifty years from 1870 to 1920, one school was intellectually, structurally, professionally, financially, socially, and numerically to overwhelm all the others. Some worried that an "educational octopus" had achieved far too firm and pervasive a grip on the system.[60] Perhaps, though, among others, there was some relief that at least there was a basis for professional unification; someone had finally defined "the law" by creating an orthodox educational system and a structure and curriculum for it. Legal education had failed, in an earlier period, to produce the aristocracy that Tocqueville had purported to see. Now, at least, the law school could be recognized as the cradle of "technique" and produce the technocrats needed to man the new system.

NOTES

1. Ticknor at Harvard had introduced modern languages, and Silliman at Yale had taught chemistry and geology. Amherst experimented with electives and a modern curriculum, and Jefferson's Virginia sought a more "egalitarian" university. See, generally, Veysey, *Emergence of the American University*.

2. During these years, Trinity College in North Carolina gradually expanded under its president, Crowell, and tried to "modernize." Lack of money prevented fulfillment of this ambition while the school was run and supported by the Methodist church. After almost failing, it was saved in the 1890s by donations from the Methodist tobacco manufacturer, Benjamin Duke, and other members of his family. In 1904, a law school was started. Porter, *Trinity and Duke*, passim. Elsewhere, the Baptists, who had started Chicago University in 1857, were forced to close the school in 1886. With donations from John D. Rockefeller, a Baptist, the school was reopened in 1890, with William Rainey Harper, a Yale graduate, as president. Plans for law and medical schools were well advanced by the turn of the century. Storr, *Harper's University*, passim.

3. The 1862 act established a land grant for state colleges that were to teach courses primarily in agriculture and the mechanical arts. In 1890, the Morrill Act was amended to provide monetary grants in addition to grants of land. Some states opened up new schools (Ohio, West Virginia, Arkansas, California); others used the funds to allow private schools to open up the new departments (Yale, Brown, Dartmouth, Cornell). Of these latter four only Cornell remains a land-grant institution today. Rudolph, *The American College and University*, 252–53.

4. Valparaiso, in Indiana, is one example of such a college. Originally founded by the Methodists as the Valparaiso Male and Female College in 1859, financial difficulties forced it to suspend classes in 1869. But by 1878 the school had been reorganized by Henry Baker Brown as the Northern Indiana Normal School and Business Institute. In 1879, an associated law school was opened and by 1900 the Normal School became Valparaiso College. In 1905, the law school was merged with the college and 1907 saw the incorporation of Valparaiso University. The university became a Lutheran institution in the 1920s. *Indiana: A Guide to the Hoosier State*, 310 (1947), and Valparaiso University Law School, *Announcement for the Sessions of 1978–1979*, 8 (1978).

5. There were some proprietary schools along the lines of the Litchfield School even after the Civil War. For instance, in 1878 John H. Dillard and Robert B. Dick established the Greensboro Law School, which had 87 students in its second year of operation. Coates, "The Story of the Law School at the University of North Carolina," 7. For one view of the impact of the war on the South, see Foster, writing in 1884, who argued that it would take years "to readjust and harmonize the disordered conditions of our political and social organization" resulting from the Civil War. "Public opinion and the statute laws are working hand in hand for the protection of the people from the ignorance, arrogance, dishonesty, extortion, and want of skill in those who undertake to serve the people as teachers, physicians, lawyers." Rising standards were also to aid in the reconstruction of Southern society and government. Foster, "Report of the Committee on Legal Education and Admission to the Bar," 124, 132.

6. Noah Porter's statement in his inaugural address as president of Yale in 1871 that he felt the law school was important to the university was considered quite unusual at the time. See Hicks, *Yale Law School, 1869–1894*, 8.

7. When the Northern Indiana Normal School began its college law course in 1879, this was an undergraduate program, as were the other offerings of the school. The 1879 catalog of the Northern Indiana Normal School and Business Institute (now Valparaiso) listed no entrance requirements for admission to its newly founded law school. By 1900, the catalog simply stated: "All persons of good moral character are entitled to enrollment in any class, at any time, on payment of tuition." After two years of three terms each, students were awarded an LL.B.

The University of Indiana law department, which closed in 1877, was also an undergraduate enterprise. Classes were often held on a temporary basis, and the years between 1842 and 1877 saw a rapid succession of short-term faculty appointments and resignations. Despite an enrollment of forty-one students in 1877, the law school was forced to close. In the absence of tuition, the university found itself unable to pay salaries sufficient to attract competent professors. In 1889, the school reopened under the leadership of Judge David B. Banta. See Wylie, *Indiana University, 1820–1890*, 56–90.

Columbian (George Washington) stipulated in its catalog only that "the applicant for admission is required to furnish evidence of having received an education fitting him for the study of law." In the catalog for 1899–1900, this was raised to high school graduation or its equivalent.

8. In 1898, Simeon Baldwin estimated that less than 20 percent of law students were college graduates. Baldwin, "The Readjustment of the Collegiate to the Professional Course," 1.

This lassitude on the part of the law schools, which probably feared a drop in admissions if they raised their standards too quickly, was not reflected in a similar attitude on the part of the bar. Many legal practitioners seemed eager to promote this additional requirement. In 1905, the majority of the members of the Illinois bar indicated their approval ("Inquiry into the Present Condition of Legal Education," 39 *American Law Review* 581 [1905]), but Lawrence Maxwell in 1915 argued that none should be allowed into the profession except those with a proper liberal education. Maxwell, "The Importance of a Pre-Legal Education as a Preparation for the Practice of Law," 29. H. A. Bronsen of North Dakota stressed the extra time and effort needed for the noncollege graduate to succeed in law school. "The Advisability of a Longer Law School Course and of a Higher Standard of Admission," 85. That did not mean, however, that the entire bar favored such additional standards, and the controversy over such considerations was to be a major one in the early years of the century.

There was lobbying to require not only a prelaw liberal education but also a strongly classical one. See, for instance, the remarks of both practitioners and academics at the symposium, "The Value of Humanistic, Particularly Classical, Studies as a Preparation for the Study of Law, from the Point of View of the Profession," at the Classical Conference at Ann Arbor, March 1907. Starr (Chicago bar), "The Value to the Lawyer of Training in the Classics," 409. Harlow Davock (Detroit bar) added the thought that "above all else in importance is the peculiar quality of the training offered by Latin and Greek, which develops the mind for the analysis of the intricate questions presented in the practice of law. . . . The man who succeeds in life is he who has gained the command of his own mental processes through close, hard work, such as is instilled from the study of Latin, Greek and mathematics." Ibid., 430–31.

In 1909, the AALS Committee on prelegal studies reported that the primary prerequisites for law school were English, Greek or Latin, German or French, math or science, history, and experimental psychology. 2 *American Law School Review* 333 (1909).

9. "Harvard University Law School," 5 *American Law Review* 177 (1870).

10. Charles William Eliot was born in Boston in 1834 and graduated from Harvard in 1853. He was a mathematics tutor and an assistant professor of mathematics and chemistry at Harvard from 1854 to 1863, traveled in Europe for about a year, and then returned to Massachusetts in 1865 to become a professor of chemistry at MIT, a position he held until he became president of Harvard.

11. Langdell was born in New Boston, New Hampshire, in 1826. After working his way through Exeter, he attended Harvard College from 1848 to 1849, but he did not earn a degree. He returned to Harvard in 1851, this time entering the law school and working as a law school librarian while studying law. He received his LL.B. in 1853 and practiced law in New York City until Eliot offered him the Dane Professorship of Law in January 1870. See Sutherland, *The Law at Harvard*, 165–66.

Eliot explained how he had come to know Langdell: "I remembered that when I was a junior in college in the year 1851–1852, and used to go often in the early evening to the room of a friend who was in the Divinity School, I there heard a young man who was making notes to Parsons on Contract talk about law. He was generally eating his supper at the time, standing up in front of the fire and eating with good appetite a bowl of brown bread and milk. I was a mere boy; only eighteen years old; but it was given to me to understand that I was listening to a man of genius. In the year 1870, I recalled the remarkable character of that young man's expertise, sought him in New York and induced him to become Dane Professor." Cited in Hurst, *The Law Makers*, 261–62.

12. Dean was a new title; the position Langdell accepted was basically secretary of the faculty. Langdell made the deanship the significant post it is today. Sutherland, *The Law at Harvard*, 166–67; Harvard Law School Association, *Centennial History of the Harvard Law School, 1817–1917*, 27 (1917). For a description of the meeting at which Langdell was elected dean, see Henry James, *Charles W. Eliot*, 1:268, and Charles W. Eliot, *A Late Harvest*, 47–48.

13. For a perceptive systematic analysis of Langdell's achievements, see Stolz, "Clinical Experience in American Legal Education," 55.

14. Woodard, "The Limits of Legal Realism," 709–18.

15. Chase cites Touraine's estimate of Eliot's role in the development of Harvard University. According to Touraine, "Harvard's success [could not] be adequately understood without taking into account Eliot's personal role. A Tory democrat, an eminent member of the mercantile aristocracy, a conservative, a Unitarian, a foe of trade unions and of compulsory elementary education, he was also a rationalist and a Darwinian, concerned with the formation of a social elite with a high sense of social responsibilities. . . . Under the influence of Spencer, and his interpreter, Thomas Huxley, Eliot applied the evolutionary outlook to the whole field of knowledge. Knowledge must proceed from the simple to the complex, according to the experimental method that starts from facts to arrive at theory." Eliot's work in particular affected the law school, undergraduate science work, and the school of medicine. Chase, "The Birth of the Modern Law School," 329, 333.

16. Ibid., 339.

17. "If intractable opposition rose, individuals could be sacrificed in behalf of the larger vision in which Eliot believed and which he, at the same time, embodied. So it is not difficult to understand why Eliot might be willing to confuse at times exactly who was responsible for what." Ibid., 345.

18. In the mid-1890s, more than three-quarters of the students had degrees; at Columbia, fewer than half had degrees; at Northwestern, it was 39 percent; at Yale, it was 31 percent; at Michigan, it was 17 percent. In New York State, as many as 35 percent of bar applicants held degrees, but nationwide the figure was 8 percent in the last decade of the nineteenth century. Auerbach, *Unequal Justice*, 94–95.

19. Columbia, eventually succumbing to the case method, was to move to a three-year curriculum eight days after Dwight and his followers resigned to protest against the new method in 1891. Goebel, *School of Law, Columbia*, 45. The students already enrolled were irate about the unilateral extension of the program, and a large part of the second-year class—including many who became well-known lawyers—refused to stay for a third year. Ibid., 151–52.

20. Samuel Williston's autobiography relates a story that gives some idea both of Harvard's eagerness to establish a three-year degree and of the problems encountered in doing it. Having received his undergraduate diploma from Harvard in 1882, he spent a short time working and then entered Harvard Law School. He noted, "Two years was the most that ever had been required and probably a majority of the students who attended law schools were satisfied with one year or one and a half years of scholastic training. In consequence of this custom and of the somewhat limited curriculum of the Harvard Law School, many of its students left at the end of two years, and I planned to do this." Williston changed his mind about leaving and decided to stay for the third year only when the faculty offered him a scholarship of $150, the entire tuition for the year. See Williston, *Life and Law*, 83. John Henry Wigmore, in the Class of 1887 at the Harvard Law School, followed the normal procedure and did not attend classes during the third year but merely took the examinations. Roalfe, *John Henry Wigmore* 10.

21. Reed, *Training in the Law*, 176. The only long-term result of this movement was the somewhat equivocal degrees of LL.M., S.J.D., and the like. Ibid., 172. Columbia had the first graduate program, a one-year LL.M. course, between 1863 and 1865. Harvard and Boston University each tried a similar program a few years later. Ibid., 176. Of such programs, Yale's one- or two-year graduate course, begun in 1876, seems to have been the first successful one. *Report of Acting Dean, Yale Law School, 1902–03*, 103; Reed, *Training for the Law*, 176. By 1890, there were eight schools offering graduate work, although a few others had tried and abandoned the project. Ibid. Some of these "graduate" degrees were still offered to supplement a two-year LL.B.

   One early use for the graduate course was for nonlegal subject areas. Ibid., 304. Yale's early political history and sociology courses were offered in the Doctor of Civil Law program. Hicks, *Yale Law School, 1869–1894*, 27. Roman law was a frequent area of emphasis, as in a doctoral program begun at Harvard in 1910–11. Sutherland, *Law at Harvard*, 233.

   Aside from this use of the extra year as a place for separate, "glued-on" subject matter (Reed's phrase), the graduate programs were apparently of minor importance to the law schools. Harvard seems to have been the exception. The S.J.D. course covered (besides the expected Roman law and jurisprudence) modern problems in international law, administrative law, and reform of criminal procedure. *Centennial History of the Harvard Law School*, 59; Redlich, *Common Law and the Case Method*, 46n. Although Columbia and Yale both maintained active programs (Yale, for instance, usually had ten to twenty resident graduate students), it was not until the 1920s that they announced graduate work geared toward a firm objective—research and preparation for teaching. Goebel, *School of Law, Columbia*, 333; *Report of the President of Yale University, 1922–23*, 198; *Report of the President of Yale University, 1926–27*, 118.

22. The Harvard Law School first called for a degree (or equivalent exam) for admission in

1875. Although President Eliot approved, the Board of Overseers rejected the plan. The first announced admissions requirement of a college degree was in 1895–96, but there were exceptions made and the ruling was not fully effective until 1909. Warren, *History of the Harvard Law School and of Early Legal Conditions in America*, 394–98. It has been calculated, however, that between 1896 and 1910 only 49 of the 3,488 admitted to the Harvard Law School did not have a college degree. Seligman, *The High Citadel*, 41–42.

The University of Pennsylvania announced the requirement of a college degree in 1916. Some schools, rather than requiring a degree before college, had compulsory entrance examinations for those applicants who had not attended college. See, for example, Rogers, "Law School of the University of Michigan," 189–208. The law school of the State University of Iowa did not require a college degree in 1889 but said it was advisable. See McClaim, "Law Department of the State University of Iowa," 374. When John W. Davis went to Washington and Lee Law School in 1894, only two of the roughly sixty students had undergraduate degrees. Davis incidentally took advantage of the arrangement that allowed any student to complete law school in one year. Because of the financial panic in 1893, Davis had already spent fourteen months "reading law" in his father's office. Harbaugh, *Lawyer's Lawyer*, 19–24. Washington and Lee University Law School had come into being in 1870 when the proprietary Lexington Law School had become affiliated with Washington University. Bryson, "The History of Legal Education in Virginia," 155.

It should be remembered, however, that even the schools with the highest requirements remained relatively unselective until the 1930s. Arthur Sutherland noted, "In 1910 achievement of an undergraduate degree from a respectable American college, passport to the Harvard Law School, was still no very extraordinary feat of record. This was the era of the 'gentleman's C.'" Sutherland, *The Law at Harvard*, 221. Law school records of these years regularly included statistics on the number failed after exams. Between 1904 and 1908, for instance, Yale dropped 174 students because of failing work; only 5 of these were college graduates. *Report of the Dean, Yale Law School, 1908–1909*, 219. Harvard's exams were notoriously difficult, with sometimes over one-third of a class failing. Sutherland, *Law at Harvard*, 221. Columbia also required course exams during these years, but not until 1914 were they designed with the intent of failing the poorer students. Goebel, *School of Law, Columbia*, 233, 473n.

The Harvard Law School also continued to fight to have the B.A. reduced from four years to three. When the term of law school study was lengthened to three years in 1877, the Academic Council considered shortening the B.A. curriculum to three years for prelaw students. In 1890, the faculty voted to accept this proposal, but it was rejected by the Board of Overseers. In 1901, however, President Eliot was still urging the shortened degree period for prelaw students. Abbott, *The Undergraduate Study of Law*, 1.

Indeed, during these years of attempts to lengthen the law course, there was a great deal of interest among some of the law schools in cutting the total time required for college and law school work. Dean Rogers of Yale noted in his 1904 report, "There has been a growing conviction among thoughtful educators that it ought to be possible to obtain the degree in Arts and that in Law in six years" (155). The popular "combined program" that resulted from such convictions involved the admission of qualified seniors from the local college to all or part of the first-year curriculum; by the usual plan, the student could count this law work toward both degrees. At both Yale and Harvard such arrangements were made in the 1890s. Pierson, *Yale: College and University, 1871–1937*, 1:213; Warren, *History of the Harvard Law School*, 2:469.

Eventually the combined arts and law programs lost favor, as the records of college seniors generally compared unfavorably with those of other law students.

23. "By 1887 the process of legal education had become a somewhat haphazard combination of office work and law school education. I was registered with the firm of Biddle and Ward and was also entered as a first-year student in the law school at the University of Pennsylvania. There was increasing co-operation between the offices of the bar and the law school. The rise of full-time professors was in its infancy. In almost all cases the lecturers in the schools were practitioners who had a flair for teaching. There really were only two branches of the profession, the practicing bar and the judges." Pepper, *Philadelphia Lawyer*, 48.

24. Mitchell, *Stanford University, 1916–1941*, 86. By 1921, another 4 schools required three years of college work; another 23, two years; and a further 20, one year of college work, although this still left more than half the schools requiring only high school graduation or less. Reed, *Training for the Law*, 392–93.

25. Woodruff, "History of the Cornell Law School," 91. After that, "progress" was rapid. In 1911, one year of college was required; in 1919, two. Ibid., 99–100.

26. Stein, "In Pursuit of Excellence—A History of the University of Minnesota Law School," 511.

27. The Lawrence Scientific School was established in 1847, using a contribution from Abbott Lawrence, a railroad man. By 1890, however, its faculty, doing poorly largely because of competition from MIT, had merged with that of the college to form the Faculty of Arts and Sciences. See Morison, *Three Centuries of Harvard, 1636–1936*, 279–80, 306, 371.

28. The Yale Corporation created the first two chairs in science in 1846, but it was not until 1858 that Joseph E. Sheffield's endowments insured the survival of the "Yale Scientific School." In 1871, the school was "incorporate[d] . . . as a separate legal identity under its own Board of Trustees," accepting both graduate and undergraduate students. Eventually, as science programs were accepted as part of the regular undergraduate program, the school became "nothing more than a legal fiction." See Furness, *The Graduate School of Yale*, 28–37, 82–89.

29. Black, "Reminiscences," 1, 7. Whereas Mr. Justice Black bounced between different parts of the university, Senator Albert Beveridge, arriving in Indianapolis in 1886 with a B.A. degree from DePauw, determined to become an apprentice of the future president, Benjamin Harrison. Harrison rejected the overtures. Beveridge, instead, was taken as an apprentice by the future senator, Joseph McDonald. Within six months he was given a salary, after twelve he was chief clerk, after fourteen, de facto, the junior partner. Bowen, *Beveridge and the Progressive Era*, 32–33.

30. Durkin, *Georgetown University: The Middle Years, 1840–1900*, 252.

31. Cited in Seligman, *The High Citadel*, 37.

32. As a kind of counterweight, the Board of Overseers also appointed James B. Thayer to the faculty and for his first two years he used the lecture method. At the same time, Harvard also hired John Chipman Gray, one of the founders of the leading Boston law firm of Ropes and Gray. Seligman, *The High Citadel*, 37–38. Eliot's efforts were apparently crucial in the appointment of Ames; indeed, it may have been mainly his idea. Fessenden, "The Rebirth of the Harvard Law School," 493, 511.

33. Seligman, *The High Citadel*, 37.

34. Ames arrived in 1873. The enrollment in 1873–74 was 141, increasing only slightly to 144 in 1874–75, but by 1875–76, enrollment had jumped to 173. Ibid., 37.

35. Cited in Sutherland, *The Law at Harvard*, 184.

36. At the Litchfield Law School the areas of the law as defined by Blackstone were the

topics of instruction. Roger Baldwin's manuscript notes from the Litchfield Law School in 1813 devote the following pages to these topics: Introductory (50), Domestic Relations (194), Executors and Administrators (69), Sheriffs and Gaolers (41), Contracts with Its Actions (378), Torts (74), Evidence (72), Pleading (281), Practice (68), The Law Merchant (266), Equity (51), Criminal Law (64), Real Property with Its Actions (364). Reed, *Training for the Law*, 453.

Some of the early college professors offered a broader curriculum and more academic fare oriented toward politics and government, and some of this wider approach, which Currie has called the "Southern Tradition," survived as late as the 1890s. Currie, "The Materials of Law Study," pt. 1, p. 375.

37. The ever-industrious Reed made the following calculation of relative percentages (*Training for the Law*, 454):

	Blackstone 1765–1769	Litchfield 1794	Litchfield 1813	Harvard 1835–1838
The Law Merchant, Contracts, etc.	2	31	33	40
Equity	2	4	3	14
Pleading Practice and Evidence	13	13	21	14
Criminal Law	21	0	3	0
Real Property	25	18	18	7
Other Branches and Introductory	37	34	22	25
	100	100	100	100

38. By that year, the curriculum had stabilized: Blackstone and Kent, Property, Equity, Contracts, Bailments and Corporations, Partnership and Agency, Shipping and Constitutional Law, Pleading and Evidence, Insurance and Sales, Conflicts, Bills and Notes, Criminal Law, Wills, Arbitration, Domestic Relations, and Bankruptcy. Ibid., 458.

39. Additions after 1870 were Torts (1870), Jurisprudence (1872), Federal Procedure (1872), Trusts (1874), Mortgages (1876), Suretyship (1882), Quasi-Contracts (1886), Damages (1890), Municipal Corporations (1908), Restraint of Trade (1916); by that date Bailments had become Carriers, and the course in Blackstone and Kent had been dropped. For full details, see Reed, *Training for the Law*, 458.

40. Columbia attempted a large-scale curriculum revision in 1903–4, but divided opinion about what should be changed resulted in no action being taken. Goebel, *School of Law, Columbia*, 189–90.

41. International law was, however, offered sporadically at Harvard after 1899. *Centennial History of the Harvard Law School*, 76.

Charles Shepard suggested in 1915 that schools not requiring a college degree for entry might adapt their curricula to the differing qualifications of their students. Thus such nonprofessional courses as international law, history, economics, government, sociology, and political philosophy could be required work for noncollege graduates, and they could be electives for those with a college degree. Shepard, "The Education of the Lawyer in Relation to Public Service," 220.

For a revealing analysis of the continued role of law in the undergraduate college, see Colby, "The Collegiate Study of Law." Colby was Parker Professor of Law at Dartmouth.

42. Reed, *Training for the Law*, 299–301. Simeon E. Baldwin of Yale suggested an elementary course in law to give the student a better understanding of law and its impact on American society, noting that "it is better to explain the foundation of a building by examining one of its rooms than by looking at a few of its shingles." See Baldwin, "The Study of Elementary Law, the Proper Beginning of a Legal Education," 1.

43. Reed, *Training for the Law*, 302–3. For instance, Yale, from 1874 onward, advertised "a broad course of studies," which not only included courses on "political science and history" but also, as Reed noted rather quaintly, "invaded even the economists' field." This probably referred to an early effort to teach taxation, or possibly it was a reference to courses on public finance and the economics of transportation. Reed, *Training for the Law*, 302. The catalog for 1874–75 records among the first-year courses International Law, History of American Law, General Jurisprudence and the Common Law, English Constitutional Law, Medical Jurisprudence, and Methods of Study and Mental Discipline (given by President Porter). In the second, and final, year there were lectures on International Law, Comparative Jurisprudence, Roman Law, American Constitutional Law, Ecclesiastical Law, and Political Economy. Hicks, *Yale Law School, 1869–1894*, 30.

44. Lieber, a political refugee from Prussia, taught at the College (University) of South Carolina from 1835 to 1856 and then resigned, primarily because of his antislavery views. (In the 1840s, Story had attempted to have a chair established for him at the Harvard Law School.) In 1857, Lieber was appointed professor of history and political science at Columbia College and, when the Law School was established the following year, the trustees appointed him as a professor in that school, too (together with the professor of moral philosophy, Charles Nairne). In 1860, however, Dwight refused to allow mandatory exams in Lieber's subjects, unlike Dwight's own, and the trustees supported Dwight. Lieber limped along, dominated by Dwight, until his resignation in 1872. Goebel, *School of Law, Columbia*, chap. 3.

45. Hicks, *Yale Law School, 1869–1894*, 36.

46. The course was two years long, covering elementary and American law, international law, public and private, general jurisprudence, political science, the Institutes of Justinian and the Pandects. By the time it was abolished, in 1916, the degree had been conferred on only nine persons. Ibid., 36–37. Yale was to toy with similar experiments from that day to this.

47. Ellsworth, *Law on the Midway*, passim.
    Eugene Wambaugh made demands similar to those of Beale when, in 1892, he was offered and accepted (but did not take up) the deanship of Western Reserve Law School. He insisted on three things for a three-year LL.B.: the case method, a full-time student body, and "rigorous admissions standards." Cramer, *The Law School at Case Western Reserve University*, 25.

48. Kayser, *Bricks Without Straw*, 150. The method of teaching had probably changed little since 1870 when the lecture method was used by the two professors on the faculty who taught from four books: Blackstone's *Commentaries*, Williams' *Real Property*, Williams' *Personal Property*, and Chitty's *Contract*. King, "The Law School 45 Years Ago."

49. In fairness, in 1902, after George Washington had joined the AALS, the night school plan was abandoned. Classes were taught in the early morning and late afternoon, and in 1903 two full-time professors were added. Jones, "The George Washington University Law School." By 1906, President Welling reported to the board that George

Washington was "no longer a night school or a University whose prime purpose was to educate government clerks." *Columbian-George Washington Law School Association Bulletin,* 1921.

50. Durkin, *Georgetown University,* 95.

51. Hogan, *The Catholic University of America, 1896–1903,* 51.

52. It was not entirely irrelevant at the prestigious schools. Despite all the commitment to a few "basic principles," Harvard began teaching a course in Massachusetts practice in 1890 and New York practice in 1892. *Centennial History,* 84.

53. See Kales, "A Further Word on the Next Step in the Evolution of the Case Book," 11. Henry Ballantine, a supporter of Kales' point of view, suggested that special emphasis should be put on finding cases referring to local jurisdictions. Ballantine, "Adapting the Case Book to the Needs of Professional Training," 135.

54. *1890–91 Report of the Commissioner of Education,* 376–416 (1894).

55. Reed, *Training for the Law,* 352.

56. Langdell's justification for using electives was that they provided an opportunity to develop new courses and thereby to maintain a "balanced" curriculum. Full acceptance of the elective system carried the implication of necessary reliance on the competence of the students to plan their own programs. Ibid., 308–9.

57. Ibid., 306–11. Some had already adopted the idea, and in 1897, the Committee on Legal Education and Admission to the Bar of the ABA was recommending the use of electives. See 20 *Reports of the American Bar Association* 366–67 (1897). By 1905, the president of the AALS was reporting that electives held a "considerable" place in many law schools and a "commanding" place in some. See Huffcut, 248. James Parker Hall, dean of the University of Chicago, felt that electives could be useful but would not be valuable for local law schools, which required primarily practical courses.

58. "[T]he course of study in . . . [fifty-six university-affiliated schools] . . . is, with a very few exceptions, confined to the branches of practical private law which a student finds of use in the first years of his practice. It is the technical rather than the scientific or philosophic view of law which is taught." U.S. Department of Education, *Report of the Commissioner 1890–91,* 378.

59. Reed listed the standard subjects offered in the 1920s: Agency, Bailment and Carriers, Bankruptcy, Bills and Notes, Conflicts, Constitutional Law, Contracts, Corporations (private), Corporations (public), Damages, Domestic Relations, Equity, Evidence, Insurance, Mortgages, Partnership, Pleadings, Property, Quasi-Contracts, Sales, Suretyship, Torts, Trusts, Wills and Administration. Reed, *Present-Day Law Schools,* 254. It was beyond doubt a Harvard curriculum. As an article in the AALS journal put it in 1922, legal education was "cast in a common mold" and had "slavishly imitated the program of instruction and methods" at "one or two of (our) older and more influential schools." Spencer and Harno, "The Correlation of Law and College Subjects," 85.

60. For example, Archer, *The Educational Octopus.*

4 / Harvard Sets the Style

CHARLES Eliot argued in his 1869 inaugural address that "universities should embrace all knowledge."[1] German scientism had taken on a North American hue. Although Thorstein Veblen was later to complain that "a school of law no more belongs in a university than a school of . . . dancing,"[2] Eliot saw nothing wrong in teaching dancing—indeed, making it compulsory—at Harvard.[3] By the end of the century, universities and colleges across the country were attempting to achieve the goal of practicality[4] by broadening course offerings and creating new departments to include disciplines well beyond the traditional curricula of the English and American universities of 1850.[5]

By the beginning of the twentieth century, these efforts had succeeded so well that the intellectuals of the Progressive period became concerned that American higher education was too relevant and too practical.[6] Even the most prestigious of the private universities were thought to have absorbed too enthusiastically the arguments of Spencer and Huxley that education should serve the needs of an increasingly specialized industrial society.[7] Just as Abraham Flexner by the 1920s was to express horror at the commercialization of Nicholas Murray Butler's Columbia, so even earlier the elite law schools were seen as increasingly bent on serving corporate law firms,[8] while other academic schools and departments similarly specialized in preparing for specific careers.[9] The classic concept of the liberal education was giving way to a modernized pluralistic undergraduate education. The elective had destroyed the classical concept of a liberal education, but the major had yet to produce its pale imitation of a serious education. Although something called a liberal education survived, professional training, both at the undergraduate and graduate level, achieved, at least with the general public, a new respectability. Leaders in the universities, meanwhile, regarded the organization of professional training as an exciting challenge. As Eliot said, "to impart information and cultivate the taste are indeed sought in education, but the great desideratum is the development of power in action."[10] The elite law schools grew alongside the burgeoning corporate law firms.

The "real life" emphasis at the leading universities fitted in well with the scientific spirit that spread through academia, producing the new disciplines that were to go a long way toward eradicating the trivium and quadrivium of liberal education. Just as there was to be a "scientific" base for history, the classics, and politics,[11] the spirit of science was to invade the law. The spirit at Harvard during these years is perhaps best exemplified in the words of John Fiske, professor of philosophy in Harvard College: "The truth of any proposition, for scientific purposes, is determined by its agreement with observed phenomena, and not by its incongruity with some assumed metaphysical basis."[12] Moving from lectures and quizzes about rules to the examination of cases was the law schools' apparent passport to academic respectability.[13] The case method proved to be a brilliant and effective vehicle for the "imaginative activity" of the law. Generations of law students were to be weaned on determining relevant facts, making arguments to a law professor masquerading as a court, and justifying or destroying judicial opinions in terms of legal "rightness" and, later, in terms of the nonlegal desirability of some principle or another.

Harvard's most obvious area of dominance was its teaching approach. The case method, although not an original creation of Langdell's,[14] became known as his by virtue of his determined and systematic application of the approach.[15] Intellectually, Langdell shared with Dwight the assumption that law was a science: "If law be not a science, a university will best consult its own dignity in declining to teach it. If it be not a science, it is a species of handicraft, and may best be learned by serving an apprenticeship to one who practices." Langdell, however, had already concluded that "law, considered as a science, consists of certain principles or doctrines. To have such a mastery of these as to be able to apply them with constant facility and certainty to the ever-tangled skein of human affairs, is what constitutes a true lawyer . . . and the shortest and the best, if not the only way of mastering the doctrine effectually is by studying the cases in which it is embodied. . . . Moreover, the number of legal doctrines is much less than is commonly supposed."[16] Although Langdell talked of science in a nineteenth-century way, his vision of legal science would have been acceptable to Bacon.

The Langdell approach not only limited itself strictly to legal rules but also involved the assumption that principles were best discovered in appellate court opinions. Langdell argued that the general principles of law derived from this process cut across state lines and perhaps across national boundaries (or extended at least as far as the Royal Courts of Justice in London), a denial of those differences in local law that had been evident, even if offensive, to the Federalists since the colonial period. In time, this particular assumption of national applicability was to undermine the idea that each state was a viable legal system in its own right. Langdell's approach also assumed that the study of appellate cases would lead to remedying the judicial deviations from established principles that had occurred in preceding decades. In theory this sounded ideal, as did Langdell's claim for the system as a unitary, self-contained, value-free, and consistent set of principles that could then be applied to each new case as it occurred.

It was especially these last few assumptions that underlay what became known as the case method. Teaching at Harvard Law School under Langdell's influence consisted of the professor and a large number of students analyzing appellate decisions, primarily in terms of doctrinal logic. This enterprise became entangled with the question-and-answer technique, similar in purpose and form to the traditional law school "quiz," a merger that rather pretentiously came to be known as the Socratic method.[17] Although the case class (and the Socratic method) were ultimately to be justified under a different rationale,[18] their original purpose was to isolate and analyze the relatively few principles of the common law that the Harvard system postulated and to show how some (presumably non-Harvard trained) judges had deviated from them.[19]

Although Eliot's vision of science had many of the attributes of the twentieth-century's view, Langdell's did not. His most coherent exposition of his own particular scientific theory was published in the English *Law Quarterly Review* in 1887. He explained that he was attempting by his example to put American law faculties in much the same position as that of faculties in continental Europe. "To accomplish these objects, so far as they depended upon the law school, it was indispensable to establish at least two things—that law is a science, and that all the available materials of that science are contained in printed books."[20] Langdell's confusion between science as an empirical and as a rational activity was to continue. In his confusion, however, Langdell never wavered in his view that law was a science and that the center of legal education was the library: "We have also constantly inculcated the idea that the library is the proper workshop of professors and students alike; that it is to us all that the laboratories of the university are to the chemists and physicists, the museum of natural history to the zoologists, the botanical garden to the botanists."[21]

Those who believed that the law was a pure science took the appropriate parts of Langdell's statements literally. It was his colleague Eugene Wambaugh who propounded the acid test for discovering the *ratio decidendi* of a case:

> First frame carefully the supposed proposition of law. Let him (the student) then insert in the proposition a word reversing its meaning. Let him then inquire whether, if the court had conceived this new

proposition to be good and had had it in mind, the decision would have been the same. If the answer be affirmative, then, however excellent the original proposition may be, the case is not a precedent for that proposition; if the answer be negative, the case is authority for the original proposition and possibly for other propositions also. In short, when a case turns only on one point, the proposition or doctrine of the case, the reason of the decision, the *ratio decidendi* must be a general rule without which the case would have been decided otherwise.[22]

This interpretation of law, however, tended to ignore the vital feature of the case system that not only Langdell but also Eliot and Ames wished to emphasize. Adopting "practicality" as the watchword of their era in legal education as well as in the university in general, these men sought first to point out the impracticalities of earlier methods of legal education and then to stress the pragmatism of the case method. Eliot, in his inaugural address, announced that "the actual problem to be solved is not what to teach, but how to teach."[23] He may have been somewhat unfair in saying of the earlier system that "the lecturer pumps laboriously into sieves. The water may be wholesome but it runs through,"[24] yet Ames' view of the earlier recitation method was equally unrelenting. It was not "a virile system. It treats the student not as a man, but as a school boy reciting his lines."[25]

Ames' words reveal these educators' recognition that, as the "scientific" approach implied practicality, practicality in turn implied an acceptance of the Darwinian, or survival of the fittest, approach. In turn, this acceptance implied approval of the scientific. This machismo view of the case method was neatly caught in the *Centennial History of the Harvard Law School*. The student, it suggested, "is the invitee upon the case-system premise, who, like the invitee in the reported cases, soon finds himself fallen into a pit. He is given no map carefully charting and laying out all the byways and corners of the legal field, but is left, to a certain extent, to find his way by himself. His scramble out of difficulties, if successful, leaves him feeling that he has built up a knowledge of law for himself. The legal content of his mind has a personal nature; he has made it himself."[26] Ames would not have wanted anyone to forget, however, that, in addition to its "virility," the case system was fundamentally practical. "If we cannot summon at will the living clients, we can put at the service of the students . . . the adjudicated cases of the multitude of clients who have had their day in court."[27] Langdell, in his casebook on contracts, was careful to emphasize the case method as the practical way to legal competence.[28] Even the Harvard Board of Overseers made certain that the practical, or perhaps pragmatic, approach was evident at the law school by maintaining a balance between the schoolmen and the practitioners holding posts as professors.[29] Increasingly, however, as Langdell's system traveled, this link with practice was to weaken.

At Harvard, the special combination of Eliot, Langdell, and Ames produced an educational system unusually well adapted to its time and place. Eliot provided the inspiration and "power in action," Langdell was its first practitioner and therefore its symbol, and, finally, the talent and perhaps youthful enthusiasm of Ames helped to perfect and perpetuate the system.[30] The case method fulfilled the latest requirements in modern education: it was "scientific," practical, and somewhat Darwinian. It was based on the assumption of a unitary, principled system of objective doctrines that seemed or were made to seem to provide consistent responses. In theory, the case method was to produce mechanistic answers to legal questions;[31] yet it managed to create an aura of the survival of the fittest.

Beyond the basic characteristics of the case method and the types of school it tended to create, the system had a further feature that would allow its success to be perpetuated—a certain amount of adaptability. Although Langdell's approach had not originally included any detail on classroom techniques,[32] the system rapidly absorbed the Socratic aspects of the recitation and the quiz.[33] Ames and Louis Brandeis were enthusiastic about Langdell's teaching,[34] but others were more reserved. Of the course in equity practice, Roscoe Pound said: "It was a curious course. . . . Langdell was always worried about 'Why?' and 'How?' He didn't care particularly whether you knew a rule or could state the rule or not, but how did the court do this? And why did it do it? That was his approach all the time."[35] Joseph Beale commented that Langdell had been "too academic; and many of his students said, if they did not really feel, that his teaching was magnificent, but was not law."[36] Although Langdell had set out to teach law as a series of definable, objective, and interrelated rules, the genius of his system appeared to be to emphasize methodology by examining the irrational and the discretionary.

It is not without significance that the history of philosophy at Harvard makes no mention of Langdell, although he was dean of the Law School during the "Golden Age" of Harvard philosophy.[37] Later academics, like William Keener,[38] were more sophisticated and saw the law as more complex, with an infinite variety of principles.[39] This led Keener and others to place less emphasis on the genius of the case method as a means of teaching the substantive principles of law, but to stress more strongly the case method's unique ability to instill a sense of legal process in the student's mind. In other words, the main claim for the case method increasingly became its ability to teach the skill of thinking like a lawyer. Methodology rather than substance became the nub of the system. Indeed, led by Ames, a new type of casebook, embodying this rather different approach, was developed. In Ames' nine casebooks, the cases were grouped by subjects and had been chosen for their "striking facts and vivid opinions,"[40] instead of being printed chronologically as were Langdell's (so that students might trace "by slow steps the historical development of legal ideas").

By 1907 Ames had put his imprimatur on the transition:[41]

> The object arrived at by us at Cambridge is the power of legal reasoning, and we think we can best get that by putting before the students the best models to be found in the history of English and American law, because we believe that men who are trained, by examining the opinions of the greatest judges the English Common Law System has produced, are in a better position to know what legal reasoning is and are more likely to possess the power of solving legal problems than they would be by taking up the study of the law of any particular state.[42]

Although Langdell emphasized the case method as a means of studying rules scientifically, in practice he was the instrument of change in a different direction.

The lasting influence of the case method was to transfer the basis of American legal education from substance to procedure and to make the focus of American legal scholarship—or at least legal theory—increasingly one of process rather than doctrine. The early practitioners of Ames' "vocation of law professor" may not have appreciated what they were doing. Yet Langdell set the style when he moved from examination questions in essay form, calling for the systematic exposition of rules, to a primitive problem method. By this move he not only outraged many students,[43] but ensured that American law would take the atomistic rather than the unitary approach that distinguishes it from other common-law systems today. Ames and his colleagues for a while sought to coordinate their casebooks with the relevant textbooks,[44] but they soon abandoned that attempt and resorted to the catch-all phrase that the case method "trained legal minds."[45]

"Science" and "practicality" remained the watchwords of the case method. Keener certainly believed that "under this system the student must look upon the law as a science consisting of a body of principles to be found in adjudged cases,"[46] and he continued to argue that "in other words, the student is practically doing, under the guidance of an instructor, what he will be required to do without guidance as a lawyer. While the student's reasoning powers are thus being constantly developed, and while he is gaining the power of analysis and synthesis, he is gaining knowledge of what the law actually is."[47] The case method showed itself not only to be a brilliant teaching device but jurisprudentially to allow a wide spectrum of opinions within its doors.

If the leading universities had "received the faith" by 1891, the American Bar Association had not. That failure was not entirely surprising. The fashionability of the case method was in so many ways ironic, for that was the period when the leadership of the profession was passing from courtroom lawyers to the office lawyers who sought to avoid litigation. Meanwhile, the law schools were favoring a system that appeared designed to produce litigators. The leaders of the bar were men who thought that "jurisprudence," even if they did not quite understand what it meant, was a "good." Similarly, studying civil law systems based on Roman law, with which Langdell would not have been comfortable, was also attractive to them,[48] and at ABA meetings there was a good deal of talk about the need for more social science in the legal curriculum.[49] In short, the ABA, although a strong supporter of structured legal education, was not the natural ally of the case method nor of legal education limited solely to the study of legal rules.

Practitioners had always had some doubts about the case method, both intellectually and politically. As early as 1876 the *Central Law Journal* had condemned the system "which we understand to involve a wide and somewhat indiscriminate reading of cases—some of them overruled."[50] There was some doubt about the ability of faculty to handle the system,[51] and "the rumor spread abroad that young men were fitted not for the bar, but for the Antiquarian Society."[52] Even John Chipman Gray was forced to admit that "given a dunce for a teacher, and a dunce for a student, the study of cases would not be the surest mode to get into the Bar. . . . it does need a fairly moderate amount of intelligence."[53] This was the point the opponents of the case method pressed. Henry Wade Rogers of Michigan insisted that "it was quite unsuited to the average student,"[54] and Theodore Dwight refused to concede that the case method was better "for any student," but he was clear it was "inferior to true teaching in its effects upon those of average powers."[55] The leaders of the bar were trying to upgrade the profession intellectually, but they were not attempting to impose a system that might exclude their children from becoming lawyers.

The leaders of the bar might be confused about what was "scientific," but "they knew what they liked." They were especially attracted to the high formalism of the English judiciary, a formalism that had grown higher with each succeeding expansion of the parliamentary franchise.

Although Langdell might talk the language of "scientism," many in the bar rightly feared that what Langdell was up to would undermine the elegant symmetry that they sought as they gave their support to organizations like the National Conference of Commissioners on Uniform State Laws, which operated under the umbrella of the ABA after 1892. They were also concerned that the case method might encourage litigation, something the new breed of corporate lawyers viewed with increasing disdain and dislike. Dominating the ABA, these lawyers were attracted to English procedure, which, with its system of costs, discouraged litigation. Although the case law schools were training lawyers for the emerging corporate law firms, those very law firms believed the case method to be a Trojan Horse in their midst.

It was in this context that the 1891 report of the ABA Committee on Legal Education attacked the heart of the Harvard system. Having announced "it would be beneath the dignity of the Association or even of its humblest committee to take part however incidentally in controversies which necessarily must become more or less personal,"[56] the committee proceeded to oppose the attempt to make law a graduate study[57] and attacked the case method as "unscientific." The report argued that the ideal work of the lawyer was to be done by knowing the rules and keeping clients out of court. Teaching decisions without systematically instilling rules led to the "great evil" manifested by young lawyers who were all too willing to litigate, did not restrain their clients, cited cases on both sides in their briefs, and left all responsibility to the court. "This is plain language, but we believe that it only expresses the inevitable result of much teaching which is now given to beginners, and that the Association has no higher duty than plainly to point it out."[58]

Students, the committee felt, should be taught basic rules:

> Is it not equally clear that the special applications to particular facts, and especially such parts of them as depend merely upon the decision of the courts, should be kept back until the principles of law are thoroughly fixed in the mind of the student? The law is not made by cases in any other sense than as every science is created by the thought and experiments of the men who pursued it. . . . In this respect the law differs from no other science, since all sciences deal with general notions and general truths only. The specific difference of law lies in the fact that these general conceptions or ultimate facts are determined by the common consent of the people, or by the express act of the legislature. There can be no appeal, as in natural science, to observation to correct them. Authority is conclusive, and

that authority is to be found only in the recorded decisions of the Courts upon their application to a great variety of cases.[59]

Whatever might be happening at Columbia, the Dwights were in control of the ABA's Committee on Legal Education.

The 1892 annual meeting of the ABA was as vigorous in its assaults. It formally announced that Keener was "wrong" if he believed that cases were a source of law.[60] The report, however, concluded that "the law schools of the country are in good hands," because many instructors were practicing lawyers. Yet the attacks on the case method continued. "A limitation of the case method, and probably an unavoidable one, is its confinement to the doubtful part of the law and disregard of the great but settled principles upon which so much of the lawyer's reasoning depends. . . . The result of this elaborate study of actual disputes, and ignoring of the settled doctrines that have grown out of past ones, is a class of graduates admirably calculated to argue any side of any controversy, or to make briefs for those who do so, but quite unable to advise a client when he is safe from litigation. . . . The student should not be so trained as to think he is to be a mere hired gladiator."[61] This was praise for the English model, and there was no doubt at whom the slingshots were aimed: "It is absurd to expect that a class of beginners will strike out a scientific method for themselves in a mass of such 'practical' rubbish, merely because we deafen them with praises of the logical consistency and scientific character of the law."[62] The assault on the case method continued during the debates: "The study of cases *only* (if such method anywhere prevails) seems to me to be in danger of presenting the law in too disconnected, isolated and detached fragments, rather than in one continuous and steady flow, and would fail to indicate the bearing and relation of one case upon another, and their mutual interdependence upon each other, and would lack the vivifying and unifying quality which a properly prepared lecture may have."[63]

As it turned out, the ABA meetings of 1891 and 1892 were the last serious doubts the legal establishment expressed about the case method. By the 1893 annual meeting, the Harvard and Keener forces were much more in control and, although there was criticism of the case method, it was relatively muted.[64] Nothing seemed capable of stopping the growth of the case method, or of tarnishing the prestige of its creator, Harvard. As Eliot mused, contemplating the Harvard Law School: "If there be a more successful school in our country or in the world for any profession, I can only say that I do not know where it is. The school seems to have reached the climax of success in professional education."[65] The school, however, did not feel entirely secure. Ames reported that Moorfield Storey, president elect of the ABA in 1895 and an opponent of the case method, "ought not to give loose rein to his censorious spirit." It was not clear in Cambridge that they had finally won.[66]

On the other hand, with the appointment of Harvard's William Keener to Columbia's faculty in 1890, the Langdell method had begun to drive out the Dwight method at that school. Although Keener had announced that "the method of teaching by cases has grown steadily in favor since its introduction in the Harvard Law School, and has almost universally commended itself to those who examined it, or have seen its fruits," most of the Columbia faculty did not share his view. Dwight himself resigned in 1891 followed by other faculty members. Despite these protests, Keener, with the encouragement of President Low, continued to combine the benefits of the case method with those of the lecture method.[67] Although the Columbia Law School faculty had not necessarily accepted the lead of Langdell at Harvard, Low had clearly decided to follow in Eliot's footsteps. Another milestone occurred when Eliot, on the retirement of Langdell in 1895, chose Ames as the next dean of the Harvard Law School.

The American legal profession had undoubtedly been "ripe for development" when Dwight and Langdell appeared on the scene. Among the national schools, it was becoming increasingly clear as the century drew to a close that it was Langdell's Harvard rather than Dwight's Columbia that was at the pinnacle of the hierarchy of schools. By 1895, Harvard had grown to ten professors and over 400 students. By 1907, the number of students had risen to more than 700, with fourteen professors.[68] Although Columbia had more than 400 students in 1890, by 1907, it had dropped, although only temporarily, to less than 250 students.[69]

Even taking into account these considerations, the fashionability of the Langdell system grew with remarkable rapidity. For a short time, it was a phenomenon largely confined to certain elite schools, but once such schools as Columbia had fallen to the trend, others followed in quick succession. Wigmore's and Abbott's appointments at Northwestern in 1893 and Beale's at Chicago in 1900 were further signals of the change. President Eliot opined to Wigmore, "I congratulate you on having got into a missionary diocese. On the whole, missionary work is the most interesting part of the teachers' function, and there is great need for it in the teaching of law."[70] Beale advised Wigmore, "I wish you the greatest success in your good work in the West. I don't believe you will find it at all unprofitable to have at least one man with you working in the old way. We can convince only by comparison of results; that was the course of things here and at Columbia, and I have no doubt it will be equally true at Northwestern."[71] Yale could not be included for consideration in this elite group, since at the time its sponsoring institution chose to remain predominantly a college rather than joining Harvard, Columbia, and Chicago in transforming itself into a university. Indeed, at the turn of the century, Yale reflected the general tenor of the typical law school. Of his battles with the ABA, Ames replied: "From the Yale man I did not expect any sympathy. It was with much interest that I am waiting for the first sign of conversion at the Yale Law School."[72] It was not to be long in coming.[73]

When William Howard Taft, then district judge in Ohio and dean of the law school of the University of Cincinnati on the side, reorganized the school in 1895, he did it on the basis of the case method.[74] By 1900, the newly created five full-time faculty members at Stanford all used the Harvard system, citing William Keener as their role model.[75] The leading state universities were just as anxious to import the Harvard technique. The 1890s saw the case method arrive in Madison, Wisconsin, when President Charles Adams brought in Charles Gregory as associate dean. Edwin E. Bryant, the dean, who had been running the Wisconsin Law School as an "ideal law office," attacked the case method as "narrow, slow and unprofessional."[76] When Harry Richards became dean in 1903, however, the case method had finally won, and Richards was able to address himself to what he perceived as more important issues such as how to Harvardize other schools and prevent the "less worthy" from creeping into the legal profession.[77] The pattern was similar at most university-affiliated law schools, including the less prestigious,[78] which saw the innovation as a way of gaining academic recognition.[79] Hastings Law School adopted the Harvard case method with the arrival of Warren Olney and dropped the Pomeroy case method.[80] Moreover, the appearance of the case method was almost invariably linked with rising admissions standards as well as longer law programs.[81] Tulane succumbed to the case method in 1906 when Monte Lemann and Ralph Schwarz, just returned from Harvard, joined the law faculty as lecturers. Only a year after they introduced the case method, a high school diploma was required for admission to the school, and the law course was extended to three years.

Even at Yale, it was possible to trace the increasing influence of the case method, a development that, so it was alleged, transformed Yale and thus allowed it to enter the ranks of the "elite."[82] The school had always been proud of the "Yale Method" of instruction, which consisted of lectures and daily recitations.[83] Although the printing and selling of separate cases to Yale students in order to supplement textbooks had begun as early as 1891, the case method of instruction itself was not used until 1903–4 and then only for third-year students. The pressure of the new religion made itself fully felt that year when Arthur Corbin joined the faculty—as the first full-time faculty member in addition to the dean. Corbin was soon using a combination of text and casebook even for first-year students. John W. Edgeton and William Reynolds Vance joined him in these heresies. By 1912, the Rubicon had been crossed. The Yale Law faculty resolved "that in case the instructor in charge of any course shall prefer to make use of the case system of instruction in such course, he shall be permitted to do so, with the consent of the Dean." The following year, almost all the courses, in all three years, were taught by the case method.[84] The wheel had come at least half circle; it only remained to appoint a Harvard man as dean of Yale. The "blow" fell in 1916 when Thomas Swan accepted the post. Despite the gradual transition to the case method that had appeared to be taking place, not all members of the faculty were pleased. One member wrote, "It soon became increasingly apparent that the ideal of the new administration was actually to convert and transform the Yale Law School into a sort of replica of the Harvard Law School—and that replica subsequently turned out to be a poor and feeble one. So before the close of the first year of Dean Swan's administration in July, 1917, many of our faculty, including myself, resigned."[85]

Other schools, although succumbing to the encroachment of the case method, also displayed some resistance in the process. The case method came to Valparaiso University in the academic year 1908–9. The faculty obviously was not entirely convinced. The catalog for that year discussed the marvels of the case method, but one can visualize a stormy faculty meeting out of which there emerged the proviso in the catalog that added the following: "Yet the study of the entire body of law from cases alone is laborious, wasteful of time, necessarily fragmentary and unsystematic. The average student who is required to gain all his knowledge from case studies becomes after a time so saturated with cases that his powers of discrimination are dulled." So there was still an incentive, the faculty thought, to read treatises. Not everyone was enthused about Langdell and his system.[86]

Some legal practitioners still viewed the new method of education with skepticism, but already, as early as the 1880s, the prestige of the case method was apparent. The editors of the *American Law Review* reported that in their opinion "any student of English and American law, who will subject himself to that system for a time sufficient to acquire the habits belonging to it, will be for that reason a more thorough lawyer, a more formidable adversary, and a sounder counsellor than he otherwise would have become."[87] Justice Holmes, at one time a skeptic, after experimenting with Langdell's method, reported that "after a week or two, when the first confusing novelty was over, I found that my class examined the question proposed with an accuracy of view which they never could have learned from textbooks and which often exceeded that to be found in the textbooks. I, at least, if no one else, gained a good deal from our daily encounter."[88]

By the beginning of the twentieth century, then, the case method, although far from unanimously approved, was recognized as *the* innovation in legal education. Its success, though largely the result of the confluence between its drama and its ability to engage students in imaginative activity, was related to other factors. No doubt part of the method's popularity was snobbism; once elite law schools had decided to approve of the system, those aspiring to be considered elite rapidly followed. Such elitism, however, may have been not only on the part of the institutions but also on the part of the individuals within them. Law professors undoubtedly relished their increasing power and influence in the classroom and happily made the change from treatise-reading clerk to flamboyant actor in a drama. Moreover, the law student felt the appeal, too. By the 1890s, going to law school was no longer a rarity; a law student who wanted product differentiation sought out a case-method school. A certain amount of practicality also went along with this student attitude, and the new breed of academic lawyers taking over legal education was interested in teaching in case-method schools.

Even with all these features in its favor, the case-method system also held a trump card—finance. The vast success of Langdell's method enabled the establishment of the large-size class. Although numbers fluctuated, Langdell in general managed Harvard with one professor for every seventy-five students;[89] the case method combined with the Socratic method enabled classes to expand to the size of the largest lecture hall. Its Socratic aspect justified the abandonment of the recitation and the quiz, the "exercises" used at good schools relying on the lecture method. Indeed, the lecture had been merged with the quiz in a teaching method that expanded the personalized aspects of earlier methods to classes that could compete with the largest lectures. The case method was thus both cheaper as well as more exciting for both teacher and student. Such was the prestige of Harvard that law schools emulating its teaching method could scarcely ask for a "better" faculty-student ratio. Any educational program or innovation that allowed one man to teach even more students was not unwelcome to university administrators. The "Harvard method of instruction" meant that law schools could be self-supporting.[90] President Eliot smiled on Langdell's Celtic wisdom in having invented the financially attractive case-method system and Langdell, in return, purred.[91]

The combination of adaptability and consistency insured the success of the case method. By 1906, Professor James Scott of George Washington Law School declared: "The method which best trains the student in legal thinking and in legal reasoning, [i.e., the case method] is necessarily the best method for the student of law."[92] By 1902, twelve of the ninety-two law schools listed in the country "had equivocally accepted the case system," and, by 1907, that number had risen to over thirty.[93] A group of men had accurately sensed the mood of their era and—perhaps inadvertently—had produced the stimuli that would most animate it. Science, apparent practicality, elitism, financial success, and "thinking like a lawyer" produced an "unbeatable combination."

NOTES

1. Eliot, Inaugural Address at Harvard College (1869); reprinted in Hofstadter and Smith, eds., *American Higher Education*, 2:601.
2. Veblen, *Higher Learning in America*.
3. "I have often said that if I were compelled to have a required subject in Harvard College, I would make it dancing if I could." Charles Eliot, "Inaugural Address," in Hofstadter and Smith, *American Higher Education*, 601.
4. See, for example, the address of Justice Samuel F. Miller in 1879, stating, "I am a strong believer in the rapidly growing opinion, that in the accelerated pace at which modern human beings are propelled, under the influence of railroads, telegraphs, and the press, it is, in nine cases out of ten, absurd to spend the usual period of four collegiate years in the study of dead languages and theoretical mathematics." Miller, "The Ideals of the Legal Profession," 202.
5. For general discussions of this broadening of curricula, see Veysey, *The Emergence of the American University*; Buck, *Social Sciences at Harvard, 1860–1920*; Haskell, *The Emergence of Professional Social Science*.

   Charles Homer Haskins, president of Columbia University, was to claim for the social sciences, in 1915, what had previously been claimed for the classics: "They are practical, not in the narrow sense as leading to a livelihood, but in the larger sense of preparing for life." Rudolph, *The American College and University*, 365. The late nineteenth century saw the breakdown of the dominance of the traditional classical curriculum. As with law, the importance of such subjects as history or economics was not readily accepted until they too obeyed the late nineteenth-century idealization of science and empiricism. By adopting "inductive" methods into their courses, professors of the "humanities" also gained recognition of their fields as legitimate courses of study in the same way law professors had. Veysey argues that the urge to broaden the curriculum of American universities was not successful until the end of the nineteenth century because of financial constraints that were only lessened by growth in the national wealth following the Civil War. Further motivation was provided by a wish to outdo European universities.
6. Veysey, *Emergence of the American University*, 90. Similarly, Veblen wrote: "These schools devote themselves with great singleness to the training of practitioners, as distinct from jurists; and their teachers stand in relation to their students analogous to

that which the 'coaches' stand to the athletes. What is had in view is the exigencies, expedients, and strategy of successful practice; and not so much a grasp of even those quasi-scientific articles of metaphysics that lie at the root of the legal system. What is required and inculcated in the way of a knowledge of these elements of law is a familiarity with their strategic use." Veblen, *Higher Learning in America*, 155.

7. Considering the attitude of the profession, this could perhaps be seen as making a virtue of necessity on the part of the law schools. See, for example, the attitude of Thomas N. Raynor, of the South Carolina bar, who noted that "our State has, to put it mildly, been exceedingly merciful in its requirements for admission to the bar" and then cited the theory of the survival of the fittest as justification for blocking the unqualified from entering the profession. Raynor, "Necessity of Preparation for the Bar," 61.

8. Once again, the bar seemed to see this as the appropriate if not always the most desirable method. R. T. W. Duke felt compelled to admit that students would have to learn something about corporate law. "The law-merchant, the laws relating to money and negotiable instruments, the laws governing private property rights, as important as they are and ever will be, are gradually being overshadowed by that vast cloud, in which, without perfect form, are seen the laws relating to the rights, duties and liabilities of those huge monsters—corporations." Duke, "Some Thoughts on the Study and Practice of Law," 133.

9. Veysey, *The Emergence of the American University*, 67–68.

10. Ibid., 91. "Power in action" was no glib phrase for Eliot. Not only did it describe Eliot well; his use of it also indicated his realization that such power was vital to success in the changing society of his period. John Jay Chapman spoke of him in this way concerning one example of his activities—fund raising:

> Eliot in his financial rhapsodies drew golden tears down Pluto's cheek, and he built his college. The music was crude; it was not Apollo's lute: it was the hurdy-gurdy of pig-iron and the stockyards. To this music rose the wails of Harvard, and of all our colleges,—our solemn temples, theaters, clinics, dormitories, museums. . . . They are the symbols of contemporary America,—inevitable, necessary, the portals of the future. As for Eliot's share in all of them, all one can say, is, What wonderful manipulation of an era, what masterly politics. [Quoted in Chase, "Birth of the Modern Law School," 339]

11. For the rise of economics, see O'Connor, *Origins of Academic Economics in the United States*; of psychology, see Roback, *History of American Psychology*; of history, see John Higham, with Leonard Kreger and Felix Gilbert, *History*; and of the more skeptically greeted sociology, see Mills, *Sociology and Pragmatism* and Odum, *American Sociology*. For the emergence of political science, see Bernard Crick, *The American Science of Politics*. See also, generally, Buck, *Social Sciences at Harvard, 1860–1920*.

12. John Fiske, *Outline of Cosmic Philosophy*, 1:272.

13. Nor should one merely sneer at these changes. With respect to the reforms in the law and medical schools, Eliot wrote:

> So long as lectures were the only means of teaching in the law and medical schools of this University, the heterogeneous character of the class did not much affect the efficiency of the instruction, except so far as the lecturers felt obliged to adapt their teaching to the ignorant and untrained portion of their audience. But with the adoption of catechetical methods in both schools, the presence in the recitation room of a considerable proportion of persons whose minds were rude and unformed became at once a serious impediment. The large use of examinations in

writing also brought into plain sight the shocking illiteracy of a part of the students. [Quoted in Warren, *History of the American Bar*, 2:396]

14. See Chase, "The Birth of the Modern Law School," 332–43. See also Hastings College of Law, *Golden Jubilee Book, 1878–1928* (1928), where it describes how John Pomeroy taught equity from the cases at New York University. This pre-Langdellian use of the case method is confirmed by Philip Jessup in his biography of Root, who took a law degree at NYU in 1867. Jessup, *Elihu Root*, 1:61. When Pomeroy went to Hastings in 1878, the trustees forced him to use the lecture method, but he soon returned to a modified form of the case method.

15. Langdell's determination almost lost him his job. During his first year of teaching, he was extremely unpopular, regarded as an "old crank." The number of students in his class dropped to seven or eight. As law school enrollment also decreased, apparently as a result of the adoption of the case method, by 1874 there were rumors that Langdell might be fired. Just in time the tide turned, and the Langdell method gained popularity and approval. Seligman, *The High Citadel*, 35. See also Gilmore, *The Ages of American Law*, 41–48.

16. Langdell, *A Selection of Cases on the Law of Contracts*, vii. At p. iv, Langdell noted: "It seemed to me, therefore, to be possible to take such a branch of the law as Contracts, for example, and, without exceeding comparatively moderate limits, to select, classify, and arrange all the cases which had contributed in any important degree to the growth, development or establishment of any of its essential doctrines."

President Eliot later noted: "Professor Langdell's method resembled the laboratory method of teaching physical science, although he believed that the only laboratory the Law School needed was a library of printed books." Eliot, *A Late Harvest*, 54.

17. For a picturesque, if brief, description of Langdell's initial attempts to use his new system, see Chase, "The Birth of the Modern Law School," 329–30.

18. As with the case method, the Socratic method was not solely an inspired revival at Harvard. Dwight had described his own method as "Socratic, illustrative and expository." Cited in Goebel, *School of Law, Columbia*, 55, n. 14.

19. Reed, *Training for the Law*, 376, 378. Langdell's casebook style was a chronological collection of (mostly old) cases on a few major points. The development of principles was the criterion for the selection of cases. *Cases in Equity Pleading* (1878) and *A Selection of Cases on Contracts* (1879) included summaries of the law covered in the cases, "concise but profound, which have been useful to the student."

Langdell included a disclaimer in the later work: "As the summary was written for the sake of the cases, and the two were designed to be companions, the cases constitute the . . . authority cited in the Summary. When other authorities are cited, it is for some special purpose, it being no part of the writer's object to make a collection of authorities upon the subject discussed. . . . [I]t is always assumed that the reader has [the cases] before him, and that, if he is already not familiar with them, he will make himself so." Langdell, *Summary of the Law of Contracts*. The volume nevertheless included 108 pages of summary.

Later casebooks discontinued the practice, except for James Barr Ames' *Selection of Cases on the Law of Bills and Notes* and Joseph H. Beale's *Selection of Cases on the Conflict of Laws*. *Centennial History of the Harvard Law School*, 80–81.

20. Langdell, "Harvard Celebration Speeches," 124.

21. Ibid. As mentioned earlier, Eliot's theories on legal education often provided a basis for or paralleled those of Langdell. See, for example, Eliot's 1874 comparison of the study of medicine and the study of law:

Medicine and surgery must be learned, partly, it is true, from books, but largely from the bodies of the sick and wounded; whereas law is to be learned almost exclusively from the books in which its principles and precedents are recorded, digested, and explained. The medical student must spend a large part of his time in hospitals; but a law student who should habitually attend courts, except during the short period when he is acquainting himself with office work and practice, would waste his time. The law library, and not the court or law office, is the real analogue of the hospital. [Quoted in Chase, "Birth of the Modern Law School," 341–42]

22. Wambaugh, *The Study of Cases*, 17–18.

23. Hofstadter and Smith, *American Higher Education*, 617.

24. Ibid., 610. Although perhaps exaggerating the weakness of the lecture system, Eliot was not completely inaccurate in gauging the increasingly negative view of this system on the part of legal educators, many of whom waged a strong attack on lecturing. The inherently "dry and unillustrated style" of lectures was felt to be one of the major problems with the method. Dennis, "Object-Teaching in Law Schools," 228. Another difficulty was the probability that students would miss, or fail to retain, the material. "Only an imperfect and erroneous knowledge of law can result from such a system." Case, "Methods of Legal Study," 69. Professor Tiedeman noted that if all students were well-trained before coming to law school, the lecture system would be superior to other systems, but "the variety and lack of training of incoming students made lecturing undesirable as the sole method of instruction." Tiedeman, "Methods of Legal Education," 150, 151. Simeon E. Baldwin summed up the worst features of the lecture system, which although the easiest recourse of the law teacher, "is a nasty review of some large subject by one familiar with it, before many who are unfamiliar with it. To make it of lasting value, there must be either a taking or transcribing of notes, or resort to published works on the same topic." Baldwin, "The Recitation System," 1, 2. By and large it was not the use of lecturing in itself that was condemned but the use of lecturing as the only method of teaching. Not everyone agreed with Eliot's outright condemnation.

25. Ames, *Lectures on Legal History and Miscellaneous Essays*, 362.

26. *Centennial History*, 130.

27. Not all contemporary observers, however, agreed with Harvard's view. Dwight and his followers were, not surprisingly, some of the most outspoken opponents. See Dwight, "What Shall We Do When We Leave Law School?," 63. Dwight stated: "Reading law cases in a haphazard way leads to mental dissipation. . . . Law decisions are but a labyrinth. Woe to the man who busies himself with them without a clue . . . to guide him." Ibid., 64. John Dillon, a supporter of Dwight's position, noted: "It will not do to turn a beginner in the study of law over to the 1,000 cases which have been decided. . . . It is best to first outline principles, then have students read textbooks and one or more leading cases." Dillon, "Method and Purposes of Legal Education," 10, 12. See also Smith, "The True Method of Legal Education," 211.

28. Langdell, *Cases on Contracts*, viii.

29. See, generally, Edward Warren, *Spartan Education*. The hiring of Thayer to offset Ames was only one example of this approach. Warren, a member of the Class of 1900, described how the trend was continued. In his day, the "big four" were Thayer, Gray, Smith, and Ames. His role model was Gray, who spent only two days a week at the school and practiced the remainder of the week. After returning to Harvard as an assistant professor in 1904, Warren himself opened a law office in Boston. He did this, he claimed, with the encouragement of President Eliot, who wanted some of the faculty

to remain practitioners. The arrangement permitted Warren to cancel 5 percent of his classes. Ibid., 13.

30. The romantic may wish to assimilate these three to the then contemporaneous builders of modern Italy—Mazzini, Cavour, and Garibaldi, described by G. M. Trevelyan as "the heart, the mind, the sword" of a unified Italy.

See also Sutherland, *The Law at Harvard*, 162–204: "Eliot's energy, his unflagging and understanding interest in the progress of the Law School through four decades, his insight into the qualities its teachers required, his willingness to risk innovation, his continuous support of Langdell and Ames, all were essential to the transformation effected in their deanships." Ibid., 164.

31. G. Edward White has noted "that educated postwar Americans were attracted to an ideology that imposed upon their universe a sense of order derived not from religious, metaphysical or transcendental dogmas but from an organized control of the new features of the American industrial environment." Having "lost faith in the ideal of liberated transcendental man," these people looked for control and organization in such devices as the case method. White, *Tort Law in America*, 22–26.

32. For a discussion of the extent of questions and answers in noncase schools, see, for example, Baldwin, "The Recitation System."

33. Fessenden, "The Rebirth of the Harvard Law School," 398–508; Beale, "Professor Langdell—His Later Teaching Days," 10; Bachelder, "Christopher C. Langdell," 440–41.

34. Ames, *Lectures on Legal History*, 362–63; Mason, *The Brandeis Way*, 34–38.

35. Sutherland, "One Man in His Time," 7, 10.

36. Beale, "Professor Langdell," 10.

37. Kucklich, *The Rise of American Philosophy*.

38. Keener, *Cases on the Law of Quasi-Contracts*, iii–iv.

39. The preponderant jurisprudential view today would be to side with Langdell but to admit that the application of the principles varies considerably with the multitude of fact situations.

40. Ames' first casebook, *Cases on Torts*, was published in 1875. *The Centennial History* describes his approach. "It was Ames who really fixed the type of case book in American law schools. His decisions were chosen, not with a purpose of tracing by slow steps the historical development of legal ideas, but with the design, through the selection of striking facts and vivid opinions, of stimulating the thoughts of the student, and leading his mind on by one step after another until he had become familiar with the fundamental principles of the subject and the reasons for them. . . . His method became, at least for his pupils, the typical method of teaching by cases: Keener followed it, and later Wambaugh, Williston, Beale, and their younger colleagues." *Centennial History*, p. 81. On Ames' book see also White, *Tort Law in America*, 18 ff.

41. The change was most clearly perceived by Josef Redlich, professor of law in the University of Vienna, who was brought to this country in 1913 by the Carnegie Foundation to study the case method of instruction. Redlich, *The Common Law and the Case Method*. See, especially, "Shift of Emphasis under Langdell's Successors: Training the Legal Mind," in ibid., 23–25.

42. Ames made these remarks during a discussion of a paper by Albert Kales. 31 *Report of the American Bar Association* 1025 (1907).

43. Bachelder, "Christopher C. Langdell," 441.

44. Phelps, "Methods of Legal Education," 148–49.

45. Keener, *Cases on Quasi-Contracts*; Keener, "The Inductive Method in Legal Education," 28 *American Law Review* 709 (1894).

46. Keener, *Cases on Quasi-Contracts*, iv.
47. Keener, "The Inductive Method in Legal Education," 17 *Reports of the American Bar Association* 482 (1894).
48. "Dean Langdell thought that English and American law should be studied by itself without admixture of other subjects, such as government, economics, international law, or Roman law." Eliot, *A Late Harvest*, 53.
49. "Report of Committee on Legal Education," 4 *ABA Proceedings* 327–29 (1881). The 1881 committee also agreed that ideally there should be more social science in the law school curriculum, to prepare the lawyer for his roles as lawyer, party leader, diplomat, director of finance or education, judge, legislator, and statesman. That, however, was far in the future; the immediate need was to prepare the working lawyer. Ibid., 330–32.
50. "The Higher Legal Education," 3 *Central Law Journal* 540 (1876).
51. The president of the Maine State Bar Association feared that many legal educators did not understand the system. Kibby, "Legal Education," 33.
52. Schouler, "Cases Without Treatises," 1. In general, however, Schouler approved of what Harvard had done, because he believed the pure case system had been considerably relaxed.
53. Grey, "Cases and Treatises," 756, 758.
54. Rogers, "Law School of the University of Michigan," 194. Rogers obviously changed his mind. As president of Northwestern he recruited Wigmore who imported the case method, and he went on to be dean of the Yale Law School as it was succumbing to the case method.
55. Dwight, "Columbia College Law School of New York," 146.
56. "Report of Committee on Legal Education," 14 *ABA Proceedings* 332 (1891).
57. "Admission to the school should not be restricted to the graduates of colleges, as has sometimes been proposed, but should be open to all who have a good English education." Ibid., 331.
58. Ibid., 334.
59. Ibid., 335–40.
60. "Report of Committee on Legal Education," 15 *ABA Proceedings* 317, 323 (1892).
61. Ibid., 340–41.
62. Ibid., 350.
63. Ibid., 368. See also Appendix, "Memorandum from Boston University Law School."
64. See McClain, "The Best of Using Cases in Teaching Law," 16 *ABA Reports* 401 (1893).
65. Cited in Sutherland, *The Law at Harvard*, vii.
66. Roalfe, *John Henry Wigmore*, 36.
67. Goebel, *School of Law, Columbia*, 140.
68. Sutherland, *Law at Harvard*, 215.
69. Reed, *Training for the Law*, 195–96.
70. Roalfe, *John Henry Wigmore*, 33.
71. Ibid., 35–36.
72. Ibid., 36.
73. By the mid-1890s, the U.S. Commissioner of Education estimated that three law schools used the case method exclusively, seven made some use of the case method, thirty-three used primarily lectures, and twenty-four mainly relied on textbooks. U.S., *Report of the Commissioner of Education, 1893–94*, vol. 1. The Pennsylvania Bar Association reported that the "new method" was in almost exclusive use at Harvard, Northwestern, the University of Pennsylvania, Stanford, the University of Iowa, and Columbia. 1 *Pennsylvania Bar Association Reports* 118 (1895).

74. Address by William Howard Taft at the dedication of the College of Law, University of
    Cincinnati, *Dedication* 8–9 (1925). Taft, however, may have been somewhat abashed
    when in 1897 he felt compelled to write to Harvard faculty members to obtain an
    explanation of just how to use the method. In that year the law school was finally
    merged with the university. McGrave, *The University of Cincinnati*, 130–31.
75. Kirkwood and Owens, *A Brief History of the Stanford Law School*, 14.
76. "Case lawyers . . . elevated reason above moral sense and pridefully asserted that
    reason alone could guide judicial decisions. Viewed in this way, the mechanical
    application of precedents threatened the image of the lawyer as a free moral agent and
    in so doing threatened to undermine what to many nineteenth century lawyers was the
    essence of 'professional conduct.'" Johnson, *Schooled Lawyers*, 118.
77. Ibid., 102–6, 117–18.
78. In 1896, Cornell reported that "case books have been used for substantially all the
    work of the curriculum except practice work." Woodruff, "History of Cornell Law
    School," 104. At Notre Dame, the case method was first used in 1889 and by 1905
    dominated the school. Moore, *A Century of Law at Notre Dame*, 24, 27. Dean Tucker
    at Washington and Lee fought hard against the case method, but in 1916, E. Merril
    Dodd, a Harvard graduate, introduced it and by 1923 it was triumphant. Bryson,
    "History of Legal Education in Virginia," 197. The Richmond College of Law, an
    evening school, purported to be "the first to use it [the case method] in the South,"
    when Walter Scott McNeill arrived from Harvard in 1905. Mays, *The Pursuit of
    Excellence*, 19.
79. Dean Saunders of the Tulane Law School is reported as saying: "In an endeavor to
    make the law school equal to the best in the country, the method used at Harvard in
    teaching will be adopted here. That is known as the case method, and the pupils are
    taught the principles of law by being given cases to study, instead of being told a lot of
    principles, with no opportunity of seeing the application of these principles." *New
    Orleans Daily Picayune*, 16 August 1906, 2.
80. Barnes, *Hastings College of Law*, 128. The case method was irretrievably established
    with the arrival of Robert W. Harrison, LL.B. Harvard, Class of 1898, as an assistant
    professor in 1901.
        When the law school was opened at the University of Oklahoma in 1909, the first
    dean—Julian Charles Monnet—had recently received an LL.B. from Harvard. He was
    a believer. Gittinger, *The University of Oklahoma, 1892–1942*, 61; McKown, *The
    Dean*, passim.
81. Wisconsin first moved to a three-year program in 1894. It had already added the
    requirement of a high school diploma in 1889 and by 1892 began to "recommend"
    some college study for its applicants. Johnson, *Schooled Lawyers*, 87. Thus, by the time
    of Richards' victory in 1903, the school had already brought other standards up to the
    profession's goals.
        At Northwestern, the three-year law course first arrived in 1895. Rahl and Schwerin,
    Northwestern University School of Law. When Valparaiso introduced the case method
    in 1907, the admissions requirement of a high school education or the equivalent was
    added. In 1917, under Dean Bowman, the school lengthened the program from two to
    three years and began an Arts-Law curriculum. University Archives, Valparaiso
    University, Valparaiso, Ind.
82. See Schlegel, "American Legal Realism and Empirical Social Science," 464.
83. Hicks, *Yale Law School, 1869–1894*, 28–35. The announcement for 1887–88
    reported that "the Method of instruction . . . is mainly that of recitations. It is the
    conviction of the Faculty of this Department, as well as the tradition of the University,

that definite and permanent impressions concerning the principles and rules of any abstract science are best acquired by the study of standard textbooks in private, followed by the examinations and explanations of the recitation room." Ibid., 33.

84. Ibid., 43–44.

85. Sherman, *Academic Adventures*, 193.

86. One example of a true die-hard institution was the University of Virginia. The school, after the exhortations by Thomas Jefferson to treat law in the most liberal manner, fell under the spell of John Barbee Minor, who taught law there from 1845 to 1895. This time span led the historian of the Virginia Law School, with perhaps more southern courtesy than historical accuracy, to suggest that "Minor and Langdell were the most influential American legal educators in the last half of the nineteenth century." Minor's educational philosophy was that "the 'foundation' of legal study 'should be broad and deeply laid'; that law students should be instructed in practical know-how as well as in legal theory and reasoning; that the materials to be studied should be treatises, statutes, and selected legal opinions; that instruction should be conducted by the lecture method and the questioning of students in class; that there should be daily written tests and periodic examinations." The educational philosophy lived on. As late as 1921, Dean Lile was still arguing against the case method. Ritchie, *The First Hundred Years*, 54.

87. "General Notes: Law Students," 15 *American Law Review* 348 (1881).

88. Oliver Wendell Holmes, Jr., "The Use and Meaning of Law Schools, and Their Method of Instruction," 923. Gilmore has analyzed the relationship between Langdell and Holmes:

> Langdell's thought was crude and simplistic. Holmes's thought was subtle, sophisticated, and, in the last analysis, highly ambiguous. Holmes's accomplishment was to make Langdellianism intellectually respectable. He provided an apparently convincing demonstration that it was possible, on a high level of intellectual discourse, to reduce all principles of liability to a single, philosophically continuous series and to construct a unitary theory which would explain all conceivable single instances and thus make it unnecessary to look with any particularity at what was actually going on in the real world. Langdellian jurisprudence and Holmesian jurisprudence were like the parallel lines which have arrived at infinity and have met. [Gilmore, *Ages of American Law*, 56.]

89. For details of Langdell's financing see *Centennial History*, passim.

One of the compensations of this poor faculty-student ratio was that Harvard paid its law professors well. Bryce was shocked by the low salaries paid to American university professors generally "compared with the general wealth of the country and the cost of living." Exceptions to this were at the "new" University of Chicago, where a few professors earned $7,000, and at the Harvard Law School, which paid its professors $5,000. Bryce, *The American Commonwealth*, 2:672.

90. In order to understand the spread of the case method one must look at the structure and funding of the university-connected law schools. The "best" type of law school at the time of the Civil War had only three full-time faculty members. Michigan added a fourth in 1866, a number attained by Columbia and Harvard in 1874. As numbers rose, and as the connections with universities became closer, doubt came to be thrown on the financial basis of the law schools. Until then, the vast majority of institutions, even those attached to universities, were enterprises controlled by the faculty, which divided both profits and losses. In this sense, the only "nonproprietary" schools at the time of the Civil War were Virginia, Harvard, and Michigan. However, the situation changed slowly. Columbia put Dwight on a salary in 1878, and, from its inception in 1887,

Cornell Law School was financially an integral part of the university. After that, the other leading universities followed suit: Pennsylvania in 1888, New York University in 1899, Northwestern in 1891, North Carolina in 1899, and Yale in 1904. The independent law schools and some of those only marginally attached to "institutions of higher learning" never gave up their financial independence or, as some would have it, proprietary purpose, and many would argue that even the most prestigious schools never quite shook off the proprietary image. See Reed, *Training for the Law*, 183–92; Reed, *Present-Day Law Schools*, 102.

The law school was in general the poor relation in the university. At Yale, for instance, the 1906–7 figures showed that the average cost of instruction per law student of $115 was the lowest per capita figure for cost of instruction in the university, and the Law School's endowment at the turn of the century ($82,814 in 1899) was among the lowest of the departmental endowments. *Reports of President, Yale University, 1907–08*, 15, and *1920–21*, 21. In terms of the demands on the budget, however, the beginning years of the twentieth century were quite unpressured for Yale and a few fortunate others. For the decade beginning in 1900–1901, Yale's income exceeded expenditures by nearly $58,000. *Report of the Dean, Yale Law School, 1910–11*, 218. Harvard was also well out of debt—for 1902, income totaled $23,000 more than expenses. *Centennial History*, chart following p. 376. The years of financial pressure came earlier, during the establishment and early growth of the school, and later, when expanded funds for buildings, scholarships, and library endowments began to be required. Yet the relative prosperity of the early 1900s was probably limited to a handful of schools. Reed's 1925 figures show Yale and Harvard at the top of the income scale. Carnegie Foundation, *Annual Review of Legal Education* 5 (1928). It is safe to assume that few other schools were as well off financially in the earlier years. Indeed, there is considerable evidence that some schools could not afford the $10 annual subscription to join the AALS.

91. "President Eliot was delighted. . . . 'The University in taking this action is only doing its duty to the learned professions of Law and Medicine, which have been for fifty years in process of degradation through the barbarous practice of admitting to them persons wholly destitute of academic culture . . . to their own lasting injury and that of the community.' . . . Eliot then advanced the unexpected—though, as it turned out, wholly accurate—argument that raising standards was also good business for the university: 'An institution which has any legal prestige and power, will make a money profit by raising its standard, and that either at once or in a very short time. Its demand for greater attainments on the part of its students will be quickly responded to, and this improved class of students will in a marvelously short time so increase the reputation and influence of the institution as to make its privilege and its rewards more valued and more valuable." Seligman, *The High Citadel*, 38–39. The *Centennial History* reported that when Langdell came the school had an endowment of less than $37,000 but a surplus of $25,000 (46–47). A later report on finance noted that "from the beginning of the Langdell period the school has been uniformly prosperous; and except nominally for a year while Langdell Hall was being paid for there has been no deficit in the accounts of the school." *Centennial History*, 378.

92. Scott, "The Study of the Law," 4.

93. Seligman, *The High Citadel*, 43.

5 / The Market Explodes

THE ABA's urge to upgrade the legal profession, a revived intellectual interest in law and related disciplines, and the emergence of the modern university closely paralleled one another. It was during this period that the new law school industry became more clearly integrated with the burgeoning universities. For the leading law schools this move was probably made for reasons of social prestige and, in economic terms, for reasons of market differentiation. It is also arguable, however, that the move was made as a way of avoiding consumer (student) control.[1] From a sociological point of view, the professional and academic developments have been described as the "epitome of social stratification."[2] Although in Iowa William Hammond might wonder how the profession could demand a college degree before law school because there were in fact more lawyers than college graduates in America,[3] everyone could agree that there was need for better law schools to improve the wholly inadequate clerkship.

Princeton, which had had a law school (not surprisingly, through the franchising of a proprietary school) from 1848 to 1852, toyed with the idea of returning to (and thus inevitably improving) the burgeoning field of legal education. The first steps came in 1890, when President Francis Patton wrote, "We have Princeton philosophy, Princeton theology, but we have to go to Harvard and Columbia for our law—that is a shame. Just as soon as I find a man with half a million, I am going to found a law school."[4] In 1891 Princeton considered starting a law school in New York City when Dwight defected from Columbia,[5] but again nothing happened.

Schools that did come to fruition did not all move at the same pace. When Mrs. Stanford and President David Starr Jordan were building the Leland Stanford, Jr., University, they began by bringing Nathan Abbott from Northwestern in 1893, but there was no full legal program until 1899.[6] Iowa Law School, on the other hand, had begun in 1865, and it became a part of the state university in 1868.[7] By the 1880s, the school was producing the majority of lawyers in the state and was cautiously arguing in favor of higher standards.[8] Michigan rapidly established itself as the premier school in the Midwest, averaging two hundred students a year by the late 1860s.[9]

Some schools, like Cornell, set out to be "scholarly," calling for "a resident faculty of competent men whose duty is to give their predominant energies to the labor of imparting education," while encouraging students to take courses in the School of History and Political Science.[10] Boston University, on the other hand, founded in 1872 by those who disagreed with the appearance of the case method at Harvard, claimed to teach "the science of law with a view to its application" and, unlike Harvard, to keep students in touch with practicing attorneys.[11] The University of Pennsylvania tried, as it was to do so often in later generations, to cover all bases. It was close to the profession, yet it was one of the earliest schools to offer degrees beyond the LL.B.[12] In some ways, if there were a typical law school, it was the Buffalo Law School begun in 1887. It was started by the local bar, as a substitute for an exclusively clerking experience. It was practical, part-time, inexpensive, and open to women and immigrant groups.[13]

Part-time law schools opened up a whole new sector of the legal education market. The first of these was established in the 1860s for students who had full-time jobs—and not by any means always jobs in law offices. They began in Washington, D.C., where the size of the civil service had grown rapidly during the Civil War. Columbian College (George Washington) led the way in 1865 with a program designed to serve federal employees whose workday then ended at three in the afternoon.[14] In 1870, new rivals—Georgetown and National—grew up in the District of Columbia.[15] The movement spread rapidly. Whereas Washington had a predominantly white, Anglo-Saxon population,[16] in the late 1880s part-time schools began to spring up in the cities with heavy immigrant populations. Moreover, immigrant groups early saw the importance of both education and of law in America[17] as well as the need and advantage of being a lawyer. Northwestern College of Law was opened in Portland, Oregon, in 1884. The year 1888 saw the establishment of evening law divisions at Metropolis Law School in New York City (later absorbed by New York University) and Chicago College of Law (later Chicago-Kent). Then the University of Minnesota opened a night school in 1892 in an effort to increase the size of its student body.[18] Baltimore University (later absorbed by the University of Maryland) began its part-time program in 1889.[19] The nineties were to see an even more dramatic expansion.

The rationales for part-time education were legion. Georgetown had allegedly set out to provide an elite, theoretical law school education but ended with a thriving evening program of one thousand students. The rationalization used was that in Rome the general of the Society of Jesus was worried about anti-Jesuit sentiment in the United States. When, in 1897, the general said that Georgetown's professional schools should be conducted without ostentation ("sine strepitu") and should not be of the highest kind ("altiora minime quaerendo"),[20] Georgetown obliged by running one of the largest and most lucrative part-time programs in the nation.

The invention of the typewriter no doubt released more part-time students for day schools (the female secretary having replaced the male clerk), and the addition of gas and electric lighting probably encouraged the growth of evening institutions. In 1891, when the New York Law School, led by disciples of Dwight, demonstrated that university affiliation was not a prerequisite to the right to grant degrees, the night and part-time law school movement was firmly launched.[21] By the time it was discovered that law schools could even be run at a profit, the proprietary school had returned in full force.

During the period 1889–90, there were six full-time schools with three- or four-year courses, with some 1,192 students, one mixed day and night school with 134 students, and nine night schools with 403 students, as contrasted with fifty-one "pure" day schools with 3,949 students. The fifty-five part-time and short-course schools had 3,294 students. By 1899–1900, the twenty-four full-time full-course schools could claim 3,992 students. The seventy-four other schools, however, had some 7,631 students.[22] Although the massive expansion of part-time legal education, especially in schools unrelated to universities, was to come in the period immediately after 1900, the primacy and confidence of the national schools were being shaken as early as 1895.[23] A new group of students had arrived. They saw, even more clearly than those with better qualifications, that law school was essentially the gateway to a professional career with the attendant prospects of social advancement and economic improvement, rather than primarily an educational experience.[24]

With an existing demand for effectively educated workers, the need was for appropriate opportunities and facilities. Schools like Columbian and Chicago-Kent could not have succeeded without, from the beginning, the existence of a powerful interest on the part of consumers in the marketplace. As the second generation of immigrants began to savor the benefits of rising living standards and free public education, the luxury of going on for higher education, once a preserve of the wealthier classes, became a feasible goal for some of the less well-to-do. Many eagerly grasped the chance; a society mouthing the teachings of Darwin and Spencer, while demanding increasingly specialized workers, was no place for the uneducated.

The success of the part-time schools alarmed the leaders of the profession. They realized that powerful forces, societal demands, appropriate facilities, and simple practicality had not only prompted the second proprietary school movement but also apparently insured its success. In 1870 there had been 1,200 law students in twenty-one law schools (or 4 law students per 100,000 of population). This figure had risen to 4,500 students in sixty-one law schools (or 7 per 100,000 of population) by 1890.[25] The explosion, however, produced the antithesis of uniformity. As states once again began to require apprenticeship, and law schools were offered as an alternative to apprenticeship, "law schools, which previously had been very similar one to another, began now to be strung out in a serial line, as it were: at one end, those that were taking advantage of restrictive state regulations to make themselves as good as they knew how; at the other extreme, schools that profited by this freedom in another way and endeavored to do little more than to provide the training needed to pass superficial bar examinations. All these schools conferred the same degree. No authority made their relative merits clear."[26]

By 1916, there were twenty-four "high entrance full-time schools" with 4,778 students, forty-three "low entrance schools offering full-time courses of standard length" with 7,918 students, fifty "part-time schools offering courses of standard length" with 7,464 students, and twenty-three "short-course schools" with 2,043 students. The law school movement had remarkable success; by 1917, only seven states did not have a law school. Perhaps equally important, legal education had become urbanized. By 1917, 59 percent of cities over 100,000 had law schools: Chicago had nine, Washington eight, New York five, and St. Louis and San Francisco four each.[27]

Battle lines between the establishment law schools and the proprietary schools[28] were not always clearly drawn. When William Rainey Harper's new University of Chicago, financed by Rockefeller money, was beginning its law school, there was at first a suggestion that it should absorb Columbian (George Washington) in D.C.[29] (They were both Baptist in origin, and Columbian had vied for Rockefeller's money.) The District of Columbia "market" produced at least one delightful vignette that underlined the status situation. Archbishop Satolli, the apostolic delegate, decided in 1894 that the way to build up a law (and medical) faculty quickly at Catholic University would be to transfer the ones currently existing at Jesuit-run Georgetown. Satolli cleared the plan with both Pope Leo XIII and the general of the Society of Jesus, but he omitted to clear it with either Catholic or Georgetown universities. The first intimation either institution had that such a change was contemplated was a letter that the apostolic delegate addressed to the deans of the law and medical faculties at Georgetown, instructing them that the "wish of the Holy Father is that our faculty aggregate to the Catholic University."[30] The Jesuit institution was to receive $175,000 in cash for this transfer, and the initial reaction of President Joseph Richards of Georgetown was positive, if somewhat Machiavellian: "Our consent would show a disinterested desire on our part to do whatever the Holy Father may think best for Catholic education in the country, and at the same time would open the way for the [Catholic] University to be transferred to us at some time."[31]

Although the president's initial reaction was calm, the same could not be said about either of the Georgetown deans. Papal infallibility was then, after all, only two decades old, at least in its modern, rather extreme, form. Upon receipt of the letter the dean of the law school announced unequivocally that the transfer "cannot be carried into effect by a direct mandate from Pope Leo XIII."[32] The dean of the medical school—another layman—was no more amused. The deans pressured the president, and he reported to Rome that the deans were "dumbfounded at the very suggestion." He explained to the father-general's assistant that the transfer should not go through because it would be perceived by Protestant students as evidence of "Catholic Chicanery."[33]

Catholic University, the would-be recipient of the boon, reacted in an intriguing way to receipt of the news of the proposed move. It shared Georgetown's displeasure, but for a far different reason. As the school's rector, Bishop John Joseph Keane, later wrote, "The schools in question were not the kind of schools of Law and Medicine that we hoped to organize; as they were night schools, frequented mostly by young men who were government employees during the day and had only the evening hours to fit themselves for professions, whereas our institution was to have true university-schools, working their students all day long."[34] In short, the Georgetown Law School was not good enough for Catholic University. The Satolli incident showed just how stratified institutionalized legal education had become by 1894, and the disputes had only just begun.

As the lesser law schools emerged, however, commercial or neocommercial arrangements were frequent. The Blackstone Law School, organized in Denver in 1888, entered into a contract with the University of Denver in 1892 to become the law faculty of the university. Not only was the faculty paid through fees, but until the 1920s, the books in the library were owned by the professors.[35] There were equally complex arrangements regarding other law schools. Union College of Law originally opened in 1859 as the law department of the (old) Chicago University, beating out Northwestern, which had hoped to have the school affiliated with it. In 1873, Chicago University and Northwestern became joint managers of Union. When the Chicago University closed in 1886, Northwestern took over sole management, and, in 1891, Union College of Law became the official law school of Northwestern University.[36] In rather the same way St. Louis Law School, founded in 1867, after a series of vicissitudes ultimately became the law school of Washington University.[37]

This was the age of deals—mergers, reorganizations, market opportunities, and the rest—which affected legal education as much as any other industry.[38] The new schools that were starting at the turn of the century were particularly aware of this and sometimes were better able to take advantage of such opportunities than the more established ones. In 1872, the Albany Law School rechartered itself as a constituent part of Union University, based on Union College. The Cincinnati Law School, originally begun in 1879, again became a part of the University of Cincinnati by contract in 1897, broke free again in 1910, but had its stock bought up by the university in 1917. North Carolina, which had had a series of well-known old-style proprietary law schools, had a law professor at its state university from the 1840s on, but it was not until the 1870s that law students were even regarded as on par with "real" undergraduates and not until the 1890s that the law professor was paid by salary rather than through student fees.[39] This established university was soon challenged by an enterprising newcomer. Wake Forest began to offer classes in 1894, and ten years later it could claim that 40 percent of the practitioners in the state had attended the school.[40]

North Carolina was not the only state university that faced problems with funding from its state government. In California, the reluctance of the state to become involved in legal education had led to the gift by former Chief Justice Serranus Clinton Hastings[41] to establish what became known as the Hastings School of Law.[42] The grant, made in 1878, was to be for a graduate school of law and Hastings himself modestly assumed the deanship. Ten years later, though, the school was experiencing difficulty in enforcing even the requirement of a high school diploma from potential students.[43] In the southern part of the state, a group of law clerks, who had been meeting to discuss the law, agreed in 1896 to hire a preceptor; three years later they incorporated themselves as the Los Angeles Law School. This school in turn was absorbed by the University of Southern California after it established its law school in 1903.[44]

St. Lawrence University, a liberal arts college in northern New York State, provided a particularly intriguing example of the "can-do" period of legal education. Its own law school lasted only two years (1869–71), and for the next thirty years the right to grant law degrees remained dormant. In 1903, Norman Hefley, running a highly successful proprietary business school in Brooklyn, decided to branch out into law. His school possessed no power to grant degrees, something he appreciated only after he had been running the law school for a year. The dean of the Brooklyn

Law School, however, discovered in the catalog of St. Lawrence that it had the unexercised power to grant law degrees. St. Lawrence, a liberal arts college catering mainly to WASP families in upstate New York, then got together with Brooklyn Law School, catering to immigrant families from the ghettoes, and the law school became a "branch" of the college 360 miles to the north.[45] By 1929, with 3,312 students, Brooklyn was the second largest school in the nation, serving a predominantly immigrant student body.[46] The historian of St. Lawrence coyly noted: "The School also prospered financially; a sizeable surplus was accumulated and the community [i.e., St. Lawrence] was compensated for its sponsorship and educational guidance."[47] An established, "respectable" university had thus recognized and benefited from the economic viability of a downstate proprietary school.

Sometimes the intellectual "success" of a university law school was the inspiration for the establishment of a proprietary or at least a nonelite school. In Wisconsin, the state university, founded in 1848, followed the usual pattern of four basic undergraduate divisions: academic, education, medicine, and law.[48] It took some twenty years to get the law school started, and until this century its costs were expected to be borne by student fees.[49] At first, the law school saw itself as supplementing office training, although it did obtain the diploma privilege.[50] Later, in the 1890s and the following decade Wisconsin became Harvardized and grew in national reputation. This elitist development created a need for a different type of law school for a different clientele. In response, Marquette Law School, which traded in "practicality" and served mainly immigrants and the poor, opened in 1908. So, too, when, in 1911, the University of Minnesota Law School appointed a dean from Yale (William Reynolds Vance) with a mission to "raise standards," he responded by phasing out the night program at the university. The result was predictable: the St. Paul College of Law, founded in 1900 as a night school, flourished, and two more proprietary schools—Minneapolis College of Law (1912) and Minnesota College of Law (1913)—appeared.[51]

Although cooperative adventures between universities and proprietary schools sometimes worked, as with St. Lawrence and Brooklyn, the interaction between Marquette and Wisconsin was probably more typical of the period. The proprietary school was generally seen as the competitor, and not the potential complement, of the university school. Perhaps the attitude toward each proprietary school in the final analysis amounted to a partially hidden but pervasive distinction—redolent of the battles about welfare—between the worthy poor and the unworthy poor. This distinction was often clearly evident on the local level. Boston, for instance, was the locus of fierce competition. With Harvard next door in Cambridge, and Boston University firmly planted in the middle of the city, probably only the most intrepid would open a proprietary school. Early in this century, however, two schools took up the challenge: the Boston YMCA Law School and Gleason Archer's Suffolk Law School.

Those who attended the YMCA school apparently were considered to be the worthy poor. The YMCA's origin—it was begun by Sir George Williams' evangelical organization—as well as its continued success throughout this country, undoubtedly contributed to its acceptance. The organization had first seriously entered the field of education in the 1890s, and by the early 1920s it was running 365 schools, covering a multitude of subjects, with over 120,000 students. At least 10 of these were law schools, of which the most important of all was the Boston venture.[52]

From its beginnings, the Boston YMCA Law School received favorable treatment from the establishment. In 1897, the Lowell Institute began to offer its classes through the YMCA, including such subjects as elementary electricity, advanced electricity, and law. The following year the YMCA founded its own Department of Law, with James Barr Ames, the dean of Harvard Law School, on the podium as the first lecture was delivered. The YMCA's educational work prospered, and it was later segregated into Northeastern College. The faculty included many leading practitioners—Brandeis, for example, taught there in the evenings. By 1917 the YMCA Law School had a branch in Worcester and, by 1921, branches in Springfield and Providence.[53]

Although YMCA schools prospered in Boston and around the country, other proprietary schools did not achieve success as easily. Gleason Archer's Suffolk Law School in Boston had to compete with Northeastern's more elite faculty[54] without any help from the profession, which saw his school as an encouragement to the "unworthy" poor. Archer, who wrote his first autobiography at age thirty-five in 1915, saw two main dangers in society: the "reds" (Communists) and the "crimsons" (Harvard). Opening law schools to the poor was his attempt to establish bulwarks against the encroachment of both these sinister forces.[55] Beginning in 1906, Suffolk taught a highly practical course, mainly by the pedagogical technique of the lecturer dictating notes.[56] Archer had no hesitation in battling President A. Lawrence Lowell of Harvard, and in 1914 succeeded in obtaining a state charter despite Harvard's opposition.[57] After that, expansion was rapid—to 460 students in 1915, 1,512 in 1922, and 2,018 in 1924. By 1928 Archer could still claim that Suffolk was the largest school of law in the world, boasting nearly 4,000 students.

Other areas beside Boston were to have YMCA successes. The Toledo YMCA Law School migrated from the "Y" to the University of Toledo one year after its founding in 1908, a fact perhaps not unrelated to the sudden departure of the YMCA education secretary after he had bounced several checks.[58] In 1908, the Youngstown YMCA also went into the law school business and, by 1911, was reported to provide an effective bar-cramming course. It prospered despite its having to compete with the other courses offered by the YMCA—mechanical drawing, metallurgy, business, stenography, English for New Americans, the employed boys' school, sign writing, shop, mathematics, and automobile repair.[59] In Cincinnati, the "Night Law School," established as a branch of the Cincinnati and Hamilton County YMCA as early as 1893, moved to the main YMCA building in 1917.[60] The great growth of YMCA law schools was a challenge to its Catholic arch-rival, the Knights of Columbus. The Knights had over $10 million for support of servicemen when the Armistice was declared in 1918, and they channeled those funds into a kind of a Catholic forerunner of the G.I. Bill. Included in this plan were law schools for the worthy Catholic poor.[61]

It thus became increasingly possible for white males, even poor immigrants, to qualify for the legal profession. The portals were far narrower for blacks and women. Although blacks seem to have entered the legal profession in this country sooner than women, their success was more limited.[62] Already facing social ostracism, they fought white middle-class prejudice against blacks practicing law. There are few recorded stories of black lawyers in the nineteenth century; the law journals of the time were clearly not comfortable with the subject. The career of John Mercer Langston was exceptional. The son of a Virginia planter and a half-black, half-Indian slave, he entered Oberlin, one of four colleges in the country then admitting blacks, in 1849. After studying theology and then clerking under Philemon Bliss, he received a license to practice from an Ohio court in 1854. (Some have attributed his success in this endeavor to his appearance, which allowed him to pass as white.) He eventually went on to be the first dean of Howard Law School, which opened in 1868, and later acted as president of Howard University.[63] Howard's Law School ought to have increased the number of black lawyers quickly, and for a while it did flourish because of the absence of admission requirements, a two-year program, and a reasonable supply of government clerks to fill its evening program.[64] Then it fell on harder times. In 1877, the District moved to require three years of training for lawyers. In 1879, Congress announced that none of its appropriation might be used for Howard's professional schools.[65] In 1887, Howard had 12 law students (8 blacks),[66] and it almost went out of business in the financial panic of 1893.[67] Census figures show that although black lawyers nationwide, at one point, outnumbered women lawyers, reaching 431 in 1890,[68] the

Jim Crow system took its toll. By 1900, their number was only 728, below that for women.[69]

This era of institutionalization and competition in the law school market had also been the period of the emergence of women in both the professions and the universities. "Early feminism was a conscious revolt against both the Victorian ethos and the far older belief in female inferiority. It appeared first among the educated, middle-class women who became involved in the abolitionist movement and then found their participation threatened by current ideas about the appropriate female role."[70] In the legal profession the progress of women toward recognition and equality was particularly slow. Women found it more difficult to become lawyers than doctors, for example, because the legal profession was institutionalized and had, in general, been granted licensing powers earlier than the medical profession.

Arabella Mansfield was probably the first woman in modern times to be allowed to join the bar when she was admitted in Iowa in 1869, and Lemma Bankaloo, admitted to the Missouri bar the following year, was probably the first woman to try a case, in St. Louis in March 1870.[71] In that same year the first woman on record to have received a law degree was Ada Kepley from Union College of Law in Illinois (Northwestern).[72] The federal courts, however, were less willing to admit women, denying admission in 1869 to Myra Bradwell, the successful editor of the *Chicago Legal News*, who wished to join the Illinois bar. The U.S. Supreme Court upheld the exclusion with Mr. Justice Joseph Bradley giving his notorious opinion that "the natural and proper timidity and delicacy which belongs to the female sex evidently unfits it for many of the occupations of civil life. . . . The paramount destiny and mission of women are to fulfill the noble and benign offices of wife and mother. This is the law of the creator. And the rules of civil society must be adapted to the general contribution of things, and cannot be based on exceptional cases."[73] In 1878, Belva Lockwood, however, completed her successful campaign to have the federal courts opened to women attorneys.[74]

Despite the intimidation from the Supreme Court women fought for their right to be lawyers. As early as 1869 the University of Iowa admitted women law students. The chief justice of the state, Austin Adams, declared that their presence so enhanced "the cause of liberal education that women of society in Dubuque entered the Law School, to encourage by their presence the young women students, and give them countenance."[75] Michigan soon followed Iowa's lead and in 1872 Boston University Law School admitted women. In 1878 two women successfully sued to be admitted to the first class at Hastings Law School.[76] The elite law schools, however, remained hostile. A Yale Law School alumnus opined in 1872, "In theory I am in favor of their studying law and practicing law, provided they are ugly." In 1886 Alice Ruth Jordon actually registered at the Yale Law School, arguing accurately that "there isn't a thing in your catalogue that bars women." That very year the Yale Corporation hastened to include the words, "It is to be understood that the courses of instruction are open to the male sex only."[77] In 1883, the Trustees of Columbian (George Washington) University in the District had been prepared to admit women, but the law faculty, which included two Supreme Court Justices, held that "the admission of women into the Law School was not required by any public want. In the whole history of the institution only one woman has applied for admission and her wants were adequately supplied by the Law School of Howard University in this city."[78] By the turn of the century, this intransigence had led Ellen Spencer Mussey and Emma Gillett to found the Washington Law School for women and men.[79] Overall, the census reported 5 women lawyers in the United States in 1870. As of 1880, it listed 75 and, by 1900, there were 1,010.[80]

The rise of the suffragist movement increased the pressure on the law schools.[81] In 1899 the Women Lawyers' Club of New York was founded, and in the same year a major effort was made to have the Harvard Law School thrown open to women. There was a bitter faculty debate, with Langdell opposing the admission of women and Thayer expressing the prevailing view that "he should regret the presence of a woman in his classes, because he feared it might affect the excellence of the work of men; but he could not deny the inherent justice of the claim." The faculty thereupon agreed to admit women if Radcliffe would admit them as graduate students. Radcliffe was willing, but the Harvard Corporation vetoed the idea.[82] Partly, but only partly, in response to this, in 1908, Portia Law School was founded in Boston. The genesis of the only law school with an all women student body was more complex. It was the brainchild of Arthur W. MacLean, Gleason Archer's law partner. The evidence suggests that it was begun as a commercial enterprise—MacLean gaining the women's market and Archer the men's. Certainly their friendship withered when MacLean finally admitted men to the LL.B.[83] In the meantime, however, a significant number of high school graduates in the Boston area gained a law school education at Portia.[84]

When the *Women Lawyers' Journal* began in 1911, nationally the situation was little changed. In that year women law graduates were refused admission to practice in Arkansas and Georgia,[85] and the Washington School of Law was still advertising that it was "the only law school south of Philadelphia admitting women."[86] In 1915, Harvard once again refused to admit women, and in response, Joseph Beale established the Cambridge Law School for Women, announcing that "the Cambridge Law School for Women will be as nearly as possible a replica of the Harvard Law School as is possible to make it." Even such high aspirations coupled with applicants from Radcliffe, Smith, and Bryn Mawr were not enough to make the school prosper.[87] World War I, however, encouraged the movement. By 1918, there were 177 women studying law in D.C.,[88] and in that year not only were women admitted to membership in the ABA but they were also admitted to Fordham and Yale law schools.[89] Although Harvard was not to admit women until 1950, women had made progress in entering many of those institutions that were effectively controlling the emerging legal profession, at the very moment that the Flexner reforms were driving them out of the medical profession.[90]

NOTES

1. First, "Competition in the Legal Education Industry," 311, 341.
2. Larson, *The Rise of Professionalism*, 166–67.
3. Hammond, "Legal Education and the Study of Jurisprudence," 170, 176.
4. Thomas Jefferson Wertenbaker, *Princeton, 1746–1896*, 377.
5. In 1835, Princeton had tried to persuade another Columbia defector, Chancellor Kent, to help start a school of law. Kent replied that "I am far too advanced in life to start new enterprises." Ibid., 229–30.
6. By 1900, the Stanford Law School had 145 students and a faculty of five full-time professors. See Mitchell, *Stanford University, 1916–1941*, 86; Kirkwood and Owens, "A Brief History of the Stanford Law School"; and Reed, *Present-Day Law Schools*, 412.
7. Hansen, "The Early History of the College of Law, State University of Iowa, 1865–1884," 31, 41. The school claimed to have been the first law school west of the Mississippi.
8. From 1884 to 1889, over half of the lawyers admitted by the state supreme court were from this law school. In 1889, Iowa was calling for higher standards, but it realized that "it is not in the power of the Law Schools to force advancement in this direction beyond the slow process of public sentiment." McClain, "Law Department of the State University of Iowa," 376.
9. Rogers, "The Law Department of Michigan University," 129, 133. By 1889, the school was second in size of student body only to Harvard. Dean Rogers (later to be president of Northwestern and dean at Yale), particularly vocal in legal periodicals, claimed the Michigan Law School had a longer alumni roll than any other in the country. Rogers, "Law School of the University of Michigan," 198. By 1900, the number of students had risen to 883. Reed, *Present-Day Law Schools*, 454.
10. Founded in 1887, the school had 55 students in its first entering class and 104 by 1889. Hutchins, "The Cornell University School of Law," 473, 486, 487.
11. Swasey, "Boston University Law School," 54–65; and Curtis, "The Boston University Law School," 218–25.

12. In 1889, the law school of the University of Pennsylvania had six faculty members, 144 students, and met on the sixth floor of the Girard Trust Company in the heart of Philadelphia. The school offered postgraduate work leading to the LL.M. Patterson, "The Law School of the University of Pennsylvania," 106, 107.

13. "The Law School was in fact the enterprise of the Buffalo Bar, in the interest of the more thorough and effective training of its future members. The school placed a strong emphasis on its direct connections with law offices in Buffalo. Its first class graduated in 1889, and all of the graduates who attempted to pass the bar succeeded." Norton, "The Buffalo Law School," 421, 426. At this point the law school was part of Niagara University. Pederson, *The Buffalo Law School*, 23–24. The school soon moved to the business district to establish closer connections with the law offices. "It is a practical school, . . . it points out to its students the things they will most need to know in successfully practicing their profession and making a living." From an entering class of 12 in 1887, the number of students rose to over 100 by 1889. "Buffalo Law School and the Bar of Erie County," 59 *Albany Law Journal* 25, 27 (1899). The school became the third school of the University of Buffalo in 1891. Pederson, *Buffalo Law School*, 42.

14. Even that hour was "loosely enforced." Kayser, *Bricks Without Straw*, 128. By 1884–85, the Columbian catalog reported that "the exercises of the School are all held after the usual office hours, which close at 4 o'clock . . . enabling young men engaged in office duties to avail themselves of the facilities of the school." Ibid., 5. By 1891–92, there were no classes before 6:00 p.m. Columbian University, *Law School Catalog, 1891–1892*. The trustees were conscious of what they were doing when the school was refounded in 1865. A trustee commiteee reported "the presence here of many young men with college degrees or literary backgrounds, working in the government, but with much time on their hands and looking forward to law." Kayser, *Bricks Without Straw*, 124. The school was prosperous. By 1867, the (part-time) faculty hoped to make $2,000 to $3,000 each per annum. Ibid., 131.

15. National was incorporated in 1869 and began operations in 1870. Although it had medical and dental schools (1884–1903) at different points and a college was attached in the 1920s, National University was basically a law school. It merged with George Washington in 1954.

16. Of the eighty-two men appearing in the *Columbian University Law School Year Book for 1895*, only one was clearly not born in the United States—virtually all appeared to be ethnically British. Some fifty-one worked in federal offices, many of them saying they had come to Washington in the federal service in order to go to law school. Several were patent examiners or clerks to congressmen or congressional committees. Others were merely clerks or stenographers in government offices. Ten were clerking in law offices—and of these, two or three had already been called to the bar. Three worked for patent firms, two for banks, three were in business. Two were realtors, three were teachers, two were clerks or stenographers outside government. The eight who appeared to have no job included the only four who had undergraduate degrees.

17. The New York Legal Aid Society began as the result of activities of German immigrants. Smith, *Justice and the Poor*, 134. Irish lawyers advertised for Irish clients in Boston. Handlin, *Boston's Immigrants*, 74. Nor did all the Irish lawyers train in offices or at marginal law schools. Patrick Collins, a Fenian, and the first Irish state senator in Massachusetts, attended the Harvard Law School in 1871 and was later admitted to the bar. Ibid., 224.

18. The night school added 45 students to the Law School total. Stein, "In Pursuit of Excellence," 494.

19. Reed, *Training for the Law*, 396–97.

20. Durkin, *Georgetown University*, 222.
21. Reed, *Training for the Law*, 192. By 1891, Dwight had had enough. His fight against the Harvard method had been unavailing, and the case method was encroaching on the foundations of the "Columbia System." His resignation in that year was followed shortly by those of professors George Chase and Robert Petty, also protesting against the abandonment of the Dwight method. These "disciples" of Dwight started the New York Law School to continue the work of "the greatest living teacher of that peculiar system of law, which may comprehensively be styled the English and American jurisprudence." 2 *The Counsellor* [*of New York Law School*] 10 (1892–93). See also Goebel, *School of Law, Columbia*, 145. The new school came to offer Columbia serious competition in the 1890s. Columbia's numbers fell from a high of 623 in 1890–91 to a low of 265 in 1892–93. Ibid., 447. In its first session, the New York Law School had 345 students. 1 *The Counsellor* 19–20 (1891–92).
22. Reed, *Present-Day Law Schools*, 531. In 1899–1900, the first figure omits two schools, the latter five. Much of the writing on the 1890s has been misleading because of the unreliable 1893 report of the U.S. Commissioner of Education. Reed, *Training for the Law*, 465.
23. Some flavor of the competition between the national schools and the others may be gained from the rapid rise and fall in the size of schools. Ignoring the fluctuations during the Civil War (on this see Carnegie Foundation for the Advancement of Teaching, *Review of Legal Education 1918*, 1–12 [1918]), in 1870 the largest law school was the University of Michigan, with some 400 students, having burst into prominence under Cooley. Columbian (George Washington) was second largest followed by Columbia, Harvard, Albany, and Virginia. Ten years later Columbia led with 573, followed by Michigan and Hastings. In 1890, Columbia and Michigan were still the largest, but each was about to face serious local competition from rival part-time schools. From 1911 to 1922, Georgetown was the largest law school, with over 1,000 students. See, generally, Reed, *Training for the Law*, 195–97.
24. On this see the comment of the principal of the Law Society's School of Law in London: "With Mr. Reed a 'part-time' school is one which caters largely for students who are not, at the time of attendance at any rate, in any sense lawyers, or even law students as most Englishmen understand the term. They may be students who hope at some future date to make a serious effort to qualify as members of the legal profession, or they may be merely business men and women who find a smattering of certain legal topics useful in their various callings. In any case, these students are mainly engaged, for the time being, in other pursuits." Jenks, "Legal Training in America," 152, 154–55.
25. Reed, *Training for the Law*, 442.
26. Reed, *Present-Day Law Schools*, 13, discussing the "Creative Period, 1865–1890."
27. Reed, *Training for the Law*, 193–95, 448–49. Moreover, Pennsylvania, along with Delaware, had been the only two states to maintain prelegal education, even during the Jacksonian period. Ibid., 314. Philadelphia had only two schools presumably because the Pennsylvania preceptor system effectively prevented those without a legal sponsor from attending law school.
28. In terms of numbers, Georgetown, which opened in 1870, led the list with 1,052 students. Fordham, which had started operations in New York City only fifteen years earlier, came in fifth, and Suffolk, not incorporated until 1911, was sixth on the list. Reed, *Training for the Law*, 425, 429, 430, 452.
29. See Ellsworth, *Law on the Midway*, 31. Harper made the suggestion in 1890 and the president of Columbian, James C. Welling, also proposed the takeover in 1893. Harper, however, seemed to have lost interest as his plans became more developed.

30. Ahern, *The Catholic University of America, 1887–1896*, 98–108.
31. Durkin, *Georgetown University*, 219.
32. Ahern, *The Catholic University*, passim. Dean Hamilton went on to say: "The Law Department of the University of Georgetown was organized by graduates of the Academic Department, through love for the old and honored institution. The faculty serves not only because of monied considerations or salaries, but because of their love for, and interest in, the University of Georgetown; and the proposition of transfer is not only impracticable but borders close upon an offense." Ibid., 102.
33. Durkin, *Georgetown University*, 217.
34. Ibid. Dean William C. Robinson had lofty plans for his school and had been impressed with the progress of the recent past. "Hitherto in the United States, the legal profession has been regarded so much as a trade and the lawyer as . . . the mere agent and servant of his client." The recognition of "law as a science" was changing that, and Robinson wanted no part of a system of legal education which seemed to return to the concept of law as a trade. See Robinson, "A Study of Legal Education."
35. Indeed, the faculty was paid two ways: a salary based on the number of hours the professor had taught, paid out of the profits of the institution, and shares of stock in the library association. Reed, *Present-Day Law Schools*, 87.
36. Rahl and Schwertin, *Northwestern University School of Law*; Babb, "Union College of Law, Chicago," 330. By 1900, the school had 211 students. Reed, *Present-Day Law Schools*, 479.
37. Its first graduating class in 1869 had twelve students; by 1889, it had over eighty students, and an endowment of $77,000. Allen, "The St. Louis Law School," 283, 288, 291.
38. Market influence inevitably led to an emphasis on price, particularly among smaller or new schools that might have a greater hope of attracting students through low fees. One example of this technique was the catalog of Valparaiso University, which included the Law School for the first time in 1879. The cover bore the legend, "Expenses are less here than any similar institution in the West." Inside, it was claimed that the student could attend the law course "for less than half the expense they would necessarily incur at any other similar institution." By 1900, Valparaiso was able to claim that "expenses are less here than any other school in the land." Under "Expenses" the *Catalog* noted that one reason its boarding charges were so low was that "one of the principals of the school, who has given the subject of dietary many years of careful study, gives this department his personal attention." University Archives, Valparaiso University, Valparaiso, Ind.
39. Coates, "Law School of University of North Carolina," 17–23.
40. *Dedication of the New Building of the School of Law: Wake Forest College* (1957).
41. Hastings had a fascinating career. Born in New York in 1814, he migrated to Indiana and then to Iowa. At the age of twenty-four, he was a member of the Iowa legislature. In 1846, Hastings became a member of the United States Congress representing an Iowa district. By 1848, he was chief justice of the Iowa Supreme Court, and, following the Gold Rush in 1849, he became chief justice of California. He had attended neither college nor law school but had read law while he was the principal of an academy in New York, a post he had attained at the age of twenty. In 1851, Hastings became attorney general of California but resigned two years later to engage full time in making money. Hastings College of Law, *Golden Jubilee Book, 1878–1928* (1928).
42. By 1889, the school had 77 students and was encountering hostility since many felt it was producing too many lawyers. Slack, "Hastings College of Law," 524; Hastings College of Law, *Golden Jubilee Book, 1878–1928*. For a discussion of the ambiguous legal position of Hastings, see Reed, *Present-Day Law Schools*, 85–86. Although Judge

Hastings apparently agreed to the articles of affiliation, his board did not. Then a constitutional amendment in 1918 appeared to give the Law School the benefits, but not the burdens, of being a part of the University of California. One of the most remarkable aspects of this relationship was the late retiring age, which, even with recent changes, has allowed Hastings to have distinguished teachers who have retired from other schools.

43. Hastings College of Law, *Golden Jubilee Book, 1878–1928.*

44. In these early years the faculty was paid $1.12 per hour for teaching, and, appropriately enough, the football coach was one of the early teachers at the law school. University of Southern California, *Dedication Ceremonies: School of Law Building*, 35 (1926).

45. Richardson, *Dedication of the Brooklyn Law School (St. Lawrence University).*

46. Until St. John's Law School was founded in 1925, there was no competition on Long Island. "Brooklyn was a fertile field for a professional school not only because of its large and growing population, but also because it was the home of a plain people, the largest center of foreign-born and the children of foreigners in the United States. Perhaps . . . (St. Lawrence) . . . did not fully realize how much it meant to Jewish, Italian, and other peoples struggling for a living to have their sons enter the professional class and secure a university degree. No sacrifice was too great for this. . . . The great service of the school was that it offered a professional education for those who would have found it very difficult and often impossible to get it elsewhere." Pink and Delmage, *Candle in the Wilderness*, 241.

47. Ibid., 240.

48. Curtis and Carstensen, *The University of Wisconsin*, vol. 1, passim.

49. Such delays were not atypical in state universities. The 1868 charter of the University of California called for the establishment of a College of Law. After various false starts, the university "adopted" Hastings College of Law in 1878; but in 1906 the university decided to have its "own" law school, based on the department of jurisprudence at Berkeley, which had begun teaching in 1881 and had moved to a three-year professional LL.B. program in 1902. A 1908 circular was directed to the California bar, calling for "not merely a law department of good standing, but a center of legal education of the highest rank—a Harvard and Columbia of the West." Ferrier, *Origin and Development of the University of California*, 432–34, 459, 593, 596.

50. Johnson, *Schooled Lawyers*, 78.

51. Stein, "In Pursuit of Excellence," 864, 867. Vance was practicing what he preached. He had argued that 40 percent of the "leaders of men in New York City who hold themselves out to practice law are without sufficient legitimate business to afford a living income; . . . [some] starve, others steal and a few go to Sing Sing." Vance, "The Function of the State Supported Law School," 410.

52. See, generally, Bouseman, "The Pulled Away College," 10. In this and following sections I have made use of the archives of the National Council of YMCAs, New York. See also Hopkins, *The History of the Y.M.C.A. in North America.*

　　In 1919 there were seven YMCA law schools. By 1936, there were ten such schools. Bouseman, *The Pulled Away College*, 84. See also Hutchins, "Birth and Development of the Salmon P. Chase College School of Law within the Structural Organization of the Y.M.C.A."

53. See Mary O'Byrne, "A Y.M.C.A. Law School: Northeastern University School of Law, 1898–1945" (paper presented to the History Department, Yale College, 1976); Jackson, "NU Law School," 10.

54. O'Byrne, "A Y.M.C.A. Law School," 22.

55. See Archer, *The Educational Octopus*, passim.

56. But see Archer, *Suffolk Law School Systems and the Case Method of Teaching Law* (1924).
57. See Archer, *The Impossible Task*; Archer, "Fifty Years of Suffolk University," Alumni Banquet Booklet (1956), Law School Archives, Suffolk Law School, Boston, Mass.
58. First, "Legal Education and the Law School of the Past," 135, examines the Toledo Law School as a study in economic history.
59. Zimmerman, "A History of the Youngstown Law School."
60. Dieffenbach, "The Origin and Development of the Salmon P. Chase College of Law," 1.
61. *Report of the Supreme Board of Directors, Knights of Columbus: Educational and Welfare Activities for the Fiscal Year Ended June 30, 1925.* See also Columbus University, School of Law and School of Accountancy, *Announcement, 1932–1933*, 10:

> Columbus University . . . owes its creation to the expenditures by the national body of the Knights of Columbus of surplus war funds . . . utilized to establish free scholarships to all World War veterans. . . . When this fund became depleted the local councils of the Knights of Columbus took over the institution and pledged to carry it on. It became necessary to abandon the free scholarships to veterans but the new sponsors, motivated only by a desire to make education financially accessible to many who might otherwise be precluded, adopted the policy that tuition rates should be established and maintained at an absolute minimum.

62. There is some evidence of black lawyers in New Orleans even before the Civil War. Robert Morris, a black, practiced in Boston before the Civil War. Handlin, *Boston's Immigrants*, 70.
63. Howard graduated 10 blacks in the first Law School class. See also "John Mercer Langston and the Training of Black Lawyers," in Bloomfield, *American Lawyers in a Changing Society*, 302.
64. Logan, *Howard University*, 48.
65. Ibid., 87, 120.
66. Ibid., 86.
67. Statistics fluctuated wildly. In 1892, 29 LL.B.s were awarded; in 1900, 1; in 1903, 23. Ibid., 133.
68. The 1850 census, for instance, reported four black lawyers in New York City.
69. U.S. Department of Commerce, Bureau of the Census, *Negro Population: 1790–1915*, 526 (1918).
70. Petters, "The Legal Education of Women," 234.
71. Martin, "Admissions of Women to the Bar," 76, 78.
72. Harris, *Beyond Her Sphere*, 112.
73. *Bradwell* v. *The State*, 83 U.S. 130, 131 (1873).
74. "Shall Women be Admitted to the Bar?," 1 *The Legal News* (Montreal) 184 (1878). Myra Bradwell's *Chicago Legal News* noted the new law and inquired as to why women should not be allowed to vote. "Those vine-clinging creatures who profess to be so much shocked at the idea of voting, will not be compelled to use the privilege if they do not desire it." "Admission of Women to the Bar," 11 *Chicago Legal News* 179 (1897).
75. Petters, "The Legal Education of Women," 234.
76. The two women, having won on the grounds that Hastings was part of the university and that the university accepted women, in the end did not attend the law school. Slack, "Hastings College of Law," 518, 520.
77. Hicks, *Yale Law School, 1869–1894*, 72–76.
78. Keyser, *Bricks Without Straw*, 166.

79. Mrs. Mussey had become a lawyer by clerking for her husband; Miss Gillett, although white, had attended Howard in 1880. White middle-class women had previously, to the discomfort of their families, attended "the negro college." When Gillett and Mussey began teaching their courses—Mussey teaching constitutional law and Gillett the common law according to Blackstone—the idea had been that it would prepare women for Columbian. But once again, in 1899, Columbian turned the women down. "Mrs. Mussey was told that conservative members still insisted that women had not the mentality for law." Mussey ultimately was driven to found her own school—and in 1898 the Washington College of Law was incorporated. Hathaway, *Fate Rides a Tortoise*, chap. 12.

   By the 1890s, New York University had a "Women's Law Class." These were lectures given by the faculty to acquaint women with their rights. They were not courses for credit. Petters, "The Legal Education of Women," 239.

80. U.S. Department of the Interior, Bureau of the Census, *Women in Gainful Occupations, 1870–1970*, 42 (1979).

81. For a survey of the situation of women in the law, state by state, in 1900, see Petters, "The Legal Education of Women." Thirty-four states admitted women, the largest number being in Illinois (87). Ibid., 234.

82. *Centennial History*, 55.

83. When the LL.M. was started in 1925, it was open to both men and women. This was part of MacLean's strategy to open the school to both sexes. Portia had finally been chartered and given the right to award degrees in 1918. In 1929, the Massachusetts Department of Education refused to allow the school to award degrees to men because the standards of the women's school were too low. *Evening Globe* (Boston), 5 March 1929. Men were finally admitted to the LL.B. in 1938. Law School Archives, New England (Portia) Law School, Boston, Mass.

84. According to the *Portia Law School Catalog, 1925–1926*, 12, the size of the student body was as follows:

1908–9	2	1917–18	91
1909–10	10	1918–19	106
1910–11	24	1919–20	131
1911–12	32	1920–21	177
1912–13	32	1921–22	226
1913–14	30	1922–23	303
1914–15	40	1923–24	338
1915–16	46	1924–25	384
1916–17	76		

The catalog argued that "there is a far greater proportion of women than men who attain high standards in almost any kind of classroom work." Ibid., 19. It also claimed that "the majority of our women are successfully practicing law in Massachusetts today, and have proved their ability particularly in cases relating to real estate, wills, administration of estates, and in laws affecting the home, especially when acting in an advisory capacity for clients of their own sex."

85. 1 *Women Lawyers' Journal* 11 (1911).

86. Ibid., 7.

87. Ibid., vol. 5, p. 15 (1915). See also *New York Times Magazine*, 3 October 1915. It is said that Beale abandoned the school when his daughter, one of the first students, decided to drop out to marry.

88. 98 at the Washington School of Law, 58 at George Washington, 18 at National, and 3 at Howard. 9 *Women Lawyers' Journal* 6 (1919).
89. Ibid., vol. 8, pp. 5, 13 (1918).
90. In 1870, there had been 544 women physicians (0.8 percent of the total); by 1890, 4,557 (4.4 percent); and by 1910, 9,015 (6 percent). As the Flexner reforms drove out of existence most of the women's medical colleges and the "mixed" medical schools retrenched on the number of women, numbers fell. By 1930, there were only 6,825 women physicians in the U.S., representing 4.4 percent of the total. The percentage of women physicians in Boston fell from 18.2 percent in 1900 to 5.8 percent in 1960. Walsh, *Doctors Wanted*, chap. 6.

6 / The Establishment Attempts to Control the Market

THE institutionalized legal profession, spearheaded by the American Bar Association, which grew up in the last two decades of the nineteenth century and the first two of the twentieth, had absorbed the spirit of utilitarianism of the period. The profession was seen as part of the movement for industrialization, and it was not therefore surprising that its leaders were concerned with interchangeability and obsessed with standardization—two aspects of the industrial spirit. Since the new approach was the work of a narrow elite who could look back to the nativism of the 1840s, there was broad acceptance among those leaders of the superiority of northern European stock. As the Congress held hearings on immigration, which ultimately led to the National Origins Act of 1924, restricting immigration especially from eastern and southern Europe, the profession again made its ethnic assumptions part of "progress."

The American legal profession had always been a pluralistic one, with its members playing widely contrasting roles. Although Shearman and Sterling and the other large firms on Wall Street were increasingly involved in policy issues for corporations, the vast majority of lawyers in New York City were solo practitioners, many of them eking out a living, if not as "ambulance chasers," at least on the economic margins of the lower middle class. With the development of part-time and evening schools, for the first time the stratification of the profession was linked to an unacknowledged but obvious hierarchy developing among the law schools. It was impossible for the ABA to ignore the situation; indeed, it had been formed in 1878 primarily to "improve" the profession.[1] The association might have opted for institutionalizing diversity, although that would have run counter to the egalitarian ethos of the nation. It would have seemed even more un-American in the last part of the nineteenth century, a period when standardization was a national watchword, not only in the profession but throughout industry and commerce.[2] Whatever doubts members had about the case method, almost all were adamant that a uniform type of law school should control entry to the profession.

At its first meeting in 1879, the ABA Committee on Legal Education and Admissions to the Bar not only urged national comity for lawyers of three years standing—its original chore—but it began the crusade for an expansive program for standardization.[3] The committee accepted as axiomatic that bar standards had declined between 1840 and 1870, and it was equally adamant that "membership in a great and learned profession like the law, ought to carry with it presumption of merit; and experience and distinction are of right entitled to distinctions."[4] The committee had no doubt, since "education is the parent of public and private virtue," that the improvement should take place in law schools where law would be studied "scientifically."[5] Not that the committee was satisfied with the majority of law schools that did exist; their courses of study were too short, they were too concerned with enrollments, examinations were shallow, and degrees were "thrown away on the undeserving and the ignorant."[6] Law schools needed to be brought closer to the profession and to "submit to restraints which the necessity of the case make indispensable."[7] The model was to be the scientific training of France and Germany. There was a need for "a full scientific course upon the Roman civil law," and allegations were made that constitutional history and political science were neglected.[8] At all costs the "proneness" of law students "to be practical" had to be "combatted."[9] The outcome of all of this was that, in addition to the comity practices, the committee resolved that there should be "public maintenance" of law schools with at least four well-paid and efficient teachers, written examinations for graduation, the requirement of a law degree before practice, the recommendation by state and local bars of graded (i.e., sequential) law school programs for three years, and a curriculum based on David Hoffman's plan for legal education.[10]

The report was signed by only three persons and, although it foreshadowed with remarkable clarity the direction of institutionalized legal education, it was not to find immediate support in the ABA at large. Thus in 1880 a rather milder version was introduced,[11] and it was not until 1881 that the association as a whole became involved in what was to be a century-long crusade. In that year, the ABA House of Delegates passed a resolution recommending (not attempting to require) attendance at law school for three years, although it also urged law schools to let students complete the work in less than three years. It further recommended that all states give credit toward apprenticeship for time spent in law school.[12] The importance of law school was explained by a delegate from Maryland on the ground that it "would materially tend to diminish the number of those who, without the necessary provision and equipment, crept into the profession by the personal influence of their preceptors, who are anxious to relieve themselves of the encumbrance of a dull student by turning him into an incompetent lawyer."[13]

Not everyone was, however, uncritical about the transferring of responsibilities to law schools. Another Maryland delegate complained that "the course of most of them resembles too much the scheme of education of priests and monks. . . . I have found that students of law schools are not generally as proficient as others in drawing pleadings, deeds, and the like, and in the knowledge of actual practice."[14] Overall, however, as a delegate from Alabama put it: "If the members of the bar were organized into a guild or corporation, and were authorized and required by law to prescribe the terms and conditions upon which new members would be admitted, there can be little doubt that a high standard of qualifications for admission to the bar would result."[15]

Having made a fairly vigorous start,[16] the ABA settled down during the eighties to being little more than the social organization of the nation's leading lawyers. This lethargy led, in 1888, to the establishment of a rival organization, the National Bar Association (NBA), based, as was the American Medical Association, on delegates from local bar associations.[17] The ABA responded to the competition by courting local delegates and in 1889 the NBA began to collapse.[18] The competitive escapade, however, helped revive the ABA's Committee on Legal Education, under the chairmanship of William Hammond, by then chancellor of St. Louis Law School (Washington University). The committee set its sights lower than some of its predecessors, calling, in 1890, for admission by the highest court in each state and two years of required law study, during which students would spend as much time as possible in law school.[19] Although the resolution was not passed, the direction for consensus was becoming clear.

The annual meeting of the ABA in 1891 was spent discussing data on admissions to the bar and bar examinations. The need to return to serious bar examinations had been encouraged partly by the temper of the times and partly as a response to the diploma privilege of which the ABA disapproved. As the diploma privilege declined, the bar examination necessarily became a more serious activity, if only to justify removing such authority from the schools. Written bar examinations appeared in some counties of Massachusetts in 1870[20] and in New York in 1877.[21] Local bar associations, both for prestige and for competitive reasons, generally fought hard to have the states impose strong bar admission requirements. After 1878 the ABA added its voice. Slowly, boards of examiners, normally controlled by local bar associations, replaced the supreme courts as the examining authorities. Beginning with New Hampshire in 1876, statewide boards were established that financed themselves out of applicants' fees. A pattern of delegation also appeared. The legislature normally delegated control of the examination to the supreme court, which, in turn, delegated its responsibilities to a board of bar examiners. In practice the board was almost invariably controlled by the state bar associations.[22] Professional self-regulation had taken another important step forward.[23]

The 1891 ABA annual meeting was, however, an opportunity once again to emphasize the importance of attending law school. It was of considerable concern to the Committee on Legal Education that only one-fifth of the lawyers admitted each year had been to law school, that no state required attendance at law school, and that there was little chance of the latter being achieved "within the present generation."[24] The resolution on the 1891 report came on for discussion at the slimly attended 1892 annual meeting of the ABA. It was to prove to be the most important such discussion thus far. The association passed a resolution calling for two years of legal education, with the assumption that those years would be in law school. Although there was agreement that only two years could be required, there was also agreement that postgraduate courses should be provided for those who could stay longer. Commercial schools and the diploma privilege were officially deprecated, and the resolution that bar exams should be run by the highest court in the state was finally passed. It was again recommended that law schools be maintained by the states and have at least one full-time faculty member.[25] The strength of interest in the 1891 committee report led to the founding of the first ABA section in 1893, the Section of Legal Education and Admissions to the Bar.[26] The section immediately took up the issue of the length of law school,[27] and, as part of this general trend, in 1895 the section approved a resolution, which it sent on to the House of Delegates, calling for a mandatory three years of law school.[28] Although the resolution was sent back to the Committee on Legal Education, positions were hardening.

Despite all the rhetoric and resolutions, the ABA had at best the power of persuasion, and by 1895 it had had virtually no impact in raising the educational standards of lawyers. As a result of these efforts by the organized bar, it is true that time spent in law school came to be counted as time spent in a law office, as states gradually increased (or restored) the requirement for some kind of apprenticeship or clerkship. Yet no state required attendance at law school, and the majority of lawyers in the 1890s had seen the inside neither of a college nor of a law school. Several states did not even require graduation from high school for admission to the bar. It was galling to the leaders of the bar that there had been a dramatic revival in formal training for divinity and medicine but, at best, a desultory revival in law.[29]

The elite lawyer in the 1890s headed for the newly emerging law firms in Wall Street might well graduate from Yale College and the Harvard Law School and then spend his first few years working for the firm learning practical skills. The typical lawyer, however, in almost any state, might begin practice on his own without any institutional training, perhaps without even a high school diploma, and often with no or only minimal office training. Indeed, it was the "voluntariness" of the American system that had so impressed James Bryce.[30] He praised the outstanding work of the leading law schools and declared that "here at least the principle of demand and supply works to perfection. No one is obliged to attend these courses in order to obtain admission to practice, and the [bar] examinations are generally too lax to require elaborate preparation. But the instruction is found so valuable, so helpful for professional success, that young men throng the lecture halls, willingly spending two or three years in the scientific study of the law which they might have spent in the chambers of a practicing lawyer as pupils or as junior partners."[31] This was not the ABA ideal.

Although the future looked bleak, the bar was not willing to give up its program of "professionalization." In 1896, the ABA approved the requirement of a high school diploma and two years of law study for bar admission. By 1897, the period of study required was lengthened to three years, with the hope that state legislatures would not only approve but also restrict the method of study to that of attending law school.[32] In 1908, the association was discussing a requirement of two years of college before law school,[33] although its official requirement was still a high school diploma (and would remain so until 1921). In 1909, 1911, and 1912, the ABA Section of Legal Education again recommended as standard rules for admission to the bar either four years in a law office or three years in law school followed by either a graduate year or a law-office year.[34]

In the meantime, a new lobbying force was at work. The new profession of "academic lawyers" created by Ames' appointment at Harvard had had no unifying organization of its own. Practicing lawyers had the ABA, but that association did not devote as much time to legal education as most law professors felt it should, and, in addition, it had dared to criticize the case method. In 1899, the ABA, under pressure from the new breed of academic lawyer, called for the establishment of an organization of "reputable" law schools, which came into being in 1900, with twenty-five members, as the Association of American Law Schools.[35] Membership was open to schools rather than individuals,[36] and the schools were required to meet certain minimum standards; students were to have a high school diploma, courses had to be two years long (thirty weeks a year), and students were required to have access to a library with U.S. reports and local state reports.[37] The association raised the minimum requirement for membership to a three-year law school program in 1905, and after 1907 two-year schools were denied membership. By 1912, the AALS would no longer accept members with day and night sessions of equal length.[38] At the annual meeting that year it was argued that "the maintenance of regular courses of instruction in law at night, parallel to courses in the day, tends inevitably to lower educational standards." The association therefore solemnly resolved that "the policy of the Association shall be not to admit to membership hereafter any law school pursuing this course."[39] The gauntlet had been thrown down.

By 1916, the AALS was prepared to go further still and debate a resolution not to recognize any night work after 1920. Although the resolution was ultimately referred to the Executive Committee, positions were hardening. It was in that debate that Eugene Gilmore, a law professor at Wisconsin, later to be president of the University of Iowa announced: "The universities can turn out all the lawyers the country needs; we don't have to sit up nights to find ways for the poor boy to come to the Bar."[40] At that same meeting, the association adopted a requirement of three "substantially" full-time faculty members, despite the threats of Marquette and Pittsburgh that "if you adopt it to take effect at once, we shall withdraw. We are not willing to be in this association by suffrance nor to agree to conditions that would suddenly disarrange our present organization."[41]

The ABA, unlike the American Medical Association (AMA), was only a voluntary organization of individuals, and it did not have the elaborate infrastructure developed by the physicians at the county and state level. The 1901 Committee on Legal Education report pointed out that although the AMA had prompted the creation of state boards of health that were successfully forcing students into medical schools, the ABA could not get legislation passed to force law students to go to law schools.[42] Moreover, although the ABA undoubtedly contained the leaders of the profession, it represented only a tiny proportion of the bar as a whole. In 1900, only 1.3 percent of lawyers were members; by 1920, a little over 9 percent were members.[43]

The AALS was in a similar position. In the first two decades of this century, it was representing a steadily smaller proportion of the total law school population,[44] partly through losses as member schools, which could not keep up with requirements, were dropped,[45] but mainly through the growth of nonmember proprietary and part-time schools.[46] Leaders of the AALS noted this with concern and quoted discouraging statistics to various meetings of the association,[47] but the growth of the competitor schools continued nonetheless. Since the ABA and AALS represented such a small percentage of the legal population, their members generally found it difficult to have their reforms enacted into law by state legislatures, which, although they had many lawyers in their membership, often had few with elite educational backgrounds and practices. A problem that contributed to this difficulty was that the ABA and AALS did not necessarily always work in concert; their part of the iceberg was not only merely a tip but it was also cracked.

Although "in its infancy it [the AALS] seemed to enjoy a filial relationship with the American Bar Association,"[48] the vision of unity soon faded. "Both corporate firm lawyer and the university law teacher were new men of power in a new age. Twin offspring of modernization and specialization in an urban industrial society, they displayed sibling rivalries and tendencies."[49] The two groups met together until 1914, at which time the ABA, perhaps intentionally, switched its annual meetings to a date during the school term when it would be difficult for law professors to attend.

The confusion caused by the differing standards of the AALS and the ABA probably made it easier for state legislatures to avoid the standards being promulgated and propagated by the profession. In 1870, only sixteen jurisdictions prescribed some period of office practice for the aspiring lawyer, and none allowed time spent in law school to be counted in lieu of such requirements.[50] As Bryce noted, law schools were by then competing in an open market; he did not explain that the typical AALS school was unhappy with the situation. In response to this open market, different schools looked for methods to minimize or eliminate competition. These attempts often involved efforts to control or at least utilize local legislation.

An early example of this was the diploma privilege, which gave legislative approval to individual law schools to determine the quality of student needed to pass the bar. The ABA opposed the privilege from the time of its creation and sought to institute local bar examinations, controlled by practitioners, as a better way of improving standards. Although the privilege was abolished locally by some jurisdictions, little major action took place nationally, until 1892, when the ABA began an outright attack. The system declined more rapidly after the ABA assault. In 1917, the numerous California and Minnesota schools lost the privilege, although twenty-two schools in fifteen states still enjoyed its advantages.[51] (Even in 1965 four states had some form of diploma privilege.)[52] By the 1920s, however, the end of the privilege as a major force was in sight.

As with the abolition of the diploma privilege, the initiation of state bar examinations by legislatures was predominantly the result of the activities of the ABA and local bar associations. By 1917, centralized boards of bar examiners existed in thirty-seven jurisdictions.[53] At the same time, the number of jurisdictions requiring some formal period of training—either in law school or a law office—rose rapidly. In 1860, only nine out of thirty-nine jurisdictions required it. In 1890, the requirement had risen to twenty-three out of forty-nine. By 1917, the requirement had reached thirty-six out of forty-nine, with twenty-eight demanding a three-year period.[54]

With bar associations giving the lead, various state legislatures had acted to raise the standards of the legal profession. Even in 1917, however, there was no state that required attendance at law school. To the AALS this was intolerable. Although the ABA was in theory committed to the necessity of attendance at a law school, it seemed to the AALS that not nearly enough was being done.[55] Several times the ABA had hesitated to push through its House of Delegates an increase in college or law school requirements when it had had the political opportunity.[56] Worst of all, the number of students in non-AALS schools continued to increase. The AALS knew something had to be done.

The motives behind the urge of the AALS, eventually joined by the ABA, to reform legal education in the United States are complex. In a detailed economic study, Harry First labeled the AALS as a cartel and argued that each of the "reforms" undertaken or encouraged by the AALS had less to do with educational concerns than it did with the urge to control the market.[57] By enforcing elitist controls, the leading law schools hoped to eliminate profitable non-AALS schools with whom they were at a disadvantage economically by "going outside the market," suppressing competition, and enforcing higher standards that would allow the schools, rather than the student population, to control the legal education market.[58] Jerold Auerbach argued, from the perspective of a social historian, that the ideology of the case method as a "science" led legal educators to believe that they could reform society and its evils ultimately through their skills as scientists.[59] Envisioning themselves as leaders of society, they felt they could allow into the field only those who upheld the same moral values and ideology and had the same intellectual background as they did; they had to keep out "the poorly educated, the ill-prepared, and the morally weak candidates,"[60] which inevitably included non-native-born Americans.[61] The efforts to raise standards, in Auerbach's view, were primarily concerned with keeping out Jews, blacks, and immigrants.[62]

The leaders of both the bar and the law schools were elitist by definition, and such economic and social arguments each contain a strong element of truth. As Franklin Danaher said to the ABA Section of Legal Education in 1915: "You can produce a moral and intelligent bar, by raising the standard, not only of education, but along economic lines so that every Tom, Dick and Harry cannot come to the Bar."[63] Yet it would be wrong to view the issue solely from such limited points of view; the motives behind raising standards were numerous. The overall thrust of the movement to raise standards was part of the far larger movement toward institutionalization, and, whatever else motivated the leaders of the bar, they were committed to an ethical, educated bar. The elite schools could not simply impose their whims but had to adjust to the fundamental realities of a heterogeneous grouping of law schools;[64] the elitism was often more vocal than active.[65] Yet the objections of second- and third-level law schools, in combination with the competition between the ABA and the AALS, may well have slowed the process of raising standards, but it certainly did not stop it. Although economic considerations seem to have prevented the professional groups from condemning some less elite schools outright, when it came to blocking the entry of immigrants into the schools and the bar, there were fewer objections to the crusade.

It is true that the leaders of the bar shared the then current assumptions about the ethnic superiority of native white Americans. The schools that catered to immigrants apparently were so low in the view of the elite that, despite their possible economic power, the associations were quick to attempt to crush them. In 1909, ignoring a plea from John Henry Wigmore that "we had better recognize cosmopolitan conditions and not for the sake of a theory have a rule which would prevent us in the next 20 years from doing a little more justice to our great foreign populations," the Section of Legal Education of the ABA adopted a requirement that lawyers had to be American citizens.[66] Although the poor American law student was still a commodity to be considered in the marketplace, or at least sufficiently so to slow immediate rules against him, prejudice against foreigners throughout the country seemed to guarantee the immediate need to block their path.

Although the academic lawyers often argued the need to rid society of the night schools to insure competent, public-spirited, and ethical lawyers[67] as the basis for exclusionary moves, ABA members were more blunt. World War I merely made matters worse.[68] Legal politicians found that the legal profession was a means by which Jews, immigrants, and city-dwellers might undermine the American way of life.[69] An ABA delegate from West Virginia argued forcefully in favor of prelaw college training "where proper principles are inculcated, and where the spirit of the American government is formed." The "influx of foreigners" into the cities consisted of "an uneducated mass of men who have no conception of our constitutional government."[70] A New York delegate defended the college requirement of prelaw training with even less sophistication: it was "absolutely necessary" to have lawyers "able to read, write and talk the English language—not Bohemian, not Gaelic, not Yiddish, but English."[71]

Some have suggested that Auerbach overstated the case in emphasizing the efforts of the ABA and AALS to keep out immigrants, yet wherever one looks in the literature of the period, the establishment expressed concern about the background of those who were alleged to be demeaning the bar. The academic profession could at times be just as blunt as members of the bar. In Connecticut, for example, there was little doubt about such prejudices, and the attitude of its leading university certainly fed this atmosphere. In 1922, the Yale Board of Admissions was deeply concerned about "the Jewish problem." In that same year, a Yale psychologist warned the state bar association that "this invasion of foreign stock" was undermining "the finer professional spirit and feeling which characterizes the professional training of the typical American lawyer." Dean Swan of the Yale Law School suggested to the state bar in 1923 that students with foreign parents should be required to remain longer in college than native-born Americans before being admitted to law school.[72] At a Yale faculty meeting in the same year, Swan argued against using grades as the basis of limiting enrollment to the law school, because such a development would admit students of "foreign" rather than "old American" parentage, and Yale would become a school with an "inferior student body ethically and socially."[73]

In short, the attack on night and part-time schools that opened the twentieth century seems to have been a confusing mixture of public interest, economic opportunism, and ethnic prejudice. Another factor, related to all of these, yet somewhat different, was "professional pride." It had its roots in the "culture of professionalism" of the late nineteenth century. Lawyers and law professors had recently founded their professional organizations; they jealously guarded these institutions from any who might be considered interlopers. "Science" and the orthodoxy of the case method had given them a solid base for their pride,[74] and anyone who did not follow the new religious creed was robbing them of their solidity and standing.[75] Legal periodical articles from the end of the century resound with praises of the glories of the legal profession;[76] one writer went so far as to say, "the lawyer is the first messenger between

God and man."[77] Often these articles detailed or presumed an idealistic, but attainable, vision of a lawyer, which could be achieved through high standards. It was not unimportant that the same periodicals were also filled with lamentations about overcrowding and pleas for the raising of standards.[78]

The image of the poor or immigrant law school student was far from this ideal. He (or in a very few cases, she) could probably not afford to go to a school that taught by the case method, or even taught through a full-time program, and his preparation would probably have been inadequate for the training at a case-method school. The only way to retain the ideal of the perfect lawyer was to get rid of schools that did not follow orthodox methods or that admitted students who had not followed a conventional educational pattern. The professionals hoped to accomplish this by urging state legislatures to raise prelaw and law school structural requirements so high that these law schools would be deprived of their natural markets, the lower socioeconomic groups. By the beginning of World War I, however, the campaign did not seem to be working; division in the ranks of the ABA and AALS, combined with unresponsive state legislatures, prevented the march toward the "perfect" legal profession.[79]

The final straw had been the Flexner Report, published in 1910.[80] The medical profession, facing similar "problems" with standards, had acted earlier and more decisively to "improve" the situation. In 1904, the AMA founded its Council on Medical Education, which later sparked the establishment of the Flexner investigation. Even before the report was published, Flexner's visitations had closed many marginal medical schools.[81] In 1900, there were 160 medical schools with 25,213 students, compared with 102 law schools with 12,516 students. By the time the Flexner Report was published, the number of medical schools had fallen to 131 with only 21,394 students, while there were no less than 124 law schools with 19,567 students. Flexnerism would only allow the "scientific" medical schools to survive.

In the succeeding years, the position changed even more rapidly. By 1917, there were only 94 medical schools left and by 1919–20 the number was down to 85 with 13,789 students. By then, there were no less than 146 law schools with 24,503 students.[82] At the same time, standards for admission to medical school had been revised rapidly. In 1914, a high school diploma was demanded; in 1916, one year of college; in 1918, two.[83] Moreover, states had lent their weight to the enforcement of higher standards. These changes were galling both to the leading academic and to practicing lawyers—it offended their professional pride—

although probably for different reasons. Whereas medical education had "sanitized" itself and driven out the night school, the part-time medical school, and the school with inadequate facilities and poor faculty, their equivalents in the law appeared to be thriving.[84] Indeed, the proprietary law schools, with their graduates appearing in increasing numbers in the state legislatures, were by then normally free to grant degrees.[85] For the standardizers the future seemed grim.

NOTES

1. The prime mover behind the ABA was Judge Simeon E. Baldwin of New Haven, who was also a professor at the Yale Law School. He was later to serve as governor of Connecticut. On his work with the ABA see, especially, Jackson, *Simeon Eben Baldwin,* 79–81.

The call for the founding meeting of the association went out in January 1878, signed by fourteen lawyers from twelve states. Seventy-five lawyers from twenty-one jurisdictions attended (out of sixty thousand U.S. practitioners). The improvement of legal education was not stated as one of the objects of the association, but a Committee on Legal Education and Admissions to the Bar was one of seven original standing committees. At the first meeting, in July 1878, the committee was instructed to develop at the next annual meeting some plan for uniform bar admissions throughout the nation. Rogers, "The American Bar Association in Retrospect," 172; Reed, *Training for the Law,* 207–8; Smith, "History of the Activity of the American Bar Association in Relation to Legal Education and Admission to the Bar," 1.

2. The culmination of this movement was the establishment of the U.S. Bureau of Standards in 1901. The House Committee on Coinage, Weights, and Measures declared in 1900 that "no more essential aid could be given to manufacturing, commerce, the makers of scientific instruments, the scientific work of the Government, of schools, colleges and universities than by the establishment of the institution proposed in the bill." One of the leading forces behind the bill—and the whole standardization movement—was Henry S. Pritchett, superintendent of the Coast and Geodetic Survey. Pritchett, "The Story of the Establishment of the NBS," 281. Pritchett meanwhile became president of MIT and then, after losing the confidence of the MIT faculty for suggesting a merger with Harvard, president of the Carnegie Foundation, where he commissioned the Flexner and Reed reports. Cochrane, *Measures for Progress.*

3. State and local bar associations were encouraged to press for equal rights and privileges in their own states for lawyers from other states who had practiced for three years in the highest court of the states of which they were a citizen. 2 *ABA Reports* 235 (1879).

4. Ibid., 211–12. The ABA debates of 1881 returned to this theme. Nathan Webb of Portland, Maine, complained that standards had been high until 1843 when "under the impulse of prejudice against lawyers, diligently excited by a class of demagogues, the legislature swept away all existing rules." "Appendix to Report on Legal Education," 4 *ABA Reports* 241 (1881). Webb explained that the bar evaded the rule by not recognizing those who had not studied law. Ibid., 241. John Shirley from Andover, New Hampshire, explained that state's "open door" policy on the ground that "it was said that they [lawyers] were exclusive; that they did not represent the people; that the

judges were lawyers, and that the courts and bar conspired together to shut out the most deserving people in the state." At bar meetings, "moral character" lawyers were not recognized. Ibid., 243, 244.

5. "Report of the Committee on Legal Education and Admissions to the Bar," 2 *ABA Reports* 209, 212, 216–17 (1879).

6. Ibid., 217.

7. Ibid., 219.

8. Ibid., 220. There was also a warning, however, that things would never be quite like Paris or London: "Our social system, the ardor of our youth to embark in life, the impossibility of restraining it beyond the age of legal freedom, and other considerations that might be enumerated, would render the imposition of such conditions impracticable at this time in this country." Ibid., 288. "The long preparations at the Lycées and the didactic learning of the Facultés de Droit would never be tolerated by our legislators or endured by our people." W. Preston (Kentucky), "Appendix to the Report on Legal Education," 4 *ABA Reports* 289 (1881). The situation was particularly acute on the frontier: "There is great difficulty in compelling adequate preparation for admission to the bar in the western states. The pressure of young men is excessive. The profession here is full of men without considerable general culture. They cannot, therefore, well appreciate it, nor are they naturally disposed to require it in others." James M. Woolworth (Nebraska), ibid., 300.

9. Ibid., 223. The report added: "Youth is the season for forming character, and there is no danger whatever in this time of the world, and in this country in particular, that the influences to which young men are submitted may not tend to make out of them persons sufficiently practical." Ibid., 224. At the same time the speakers looked to a pedagogical system that was not singularly imaginative. Lectures, for instance, should be repetitive to drive home points, and practicality was not dead. Professors, it was held, should be aided by "scientific practical instructors." Ibid., 229.

10. The plan, as accepted by the committee, called for thirteen heads of education during the three years of law school: moral and political philosophy, elementary and constitutional principles of the municipal law of England, laws of real rights and real remedies, law of personal rights and personal remedies, law of equity, lex mercatoria, crimes and punishments, law of nations, admiralty and maritime, civil or Roman law, U.S. Constitution, comparative jurisprudence including other U.S. States, and political economy. Ibid., 235–36.

11. It called for ABA support for the maintenance of law schools, a recommended list of courses, and a recommendation for comity in admissions. The suggestion of required attendance at law school was defeated. Smith, "History of the A.B.A.," 2.

12. Speakers talked about the gradual comeback they were witnessing in institutionalized legal education. "Report of Committee on Legal Education," 4 *ABA Reports* 237 (1881). Bowdoin was considering establishing a law school (242); New Hampshire lawyers were "increasingly" studying at Cambridge, Boston, Albany, and Ann Arbor (242); as the result of the reestablishment of bar exams in New Hampshire in 1876, "students of law are now studying law instead of loafing about offices" (249); the newly established law school at the University of Maryland "has done much to promote the study of the law, and elevate the standards of qualifications for admission to the bar" (264).

13. Ibid., 265.

14. J. J. Alexander (Baltimore), ibid., 265.

15. D. S. Troy, ibid., 281–82.

16. "The time spent in any chartered and properly conducted law school ought to be counted

in any state as equivalent to the same time in an attorney's office in such state, in computing the period of study, prescribed for applicants for admission to the Bar" (Resolution 3). 4 *ABA Proceedings* 28–30 (1881).

17. Its founder and first president, James A. Broadhead of Missouri, told the ABA that his organization represented 2,000 of the 10,000 lawyers in local bar associations. Reed, *Training for the Law*, 209–12.

18. Its name, however, survived as the national organization of black lawyers.

19. It began its 1890 report with the words, "The Standing Committee on Legal Education hesitates to break the record of masterly inactivity formed by the unremitting efforts of their predecessors for at least ten successive years. . . ." 13 *ABA Reports* 327 (1890).

20. Reed suggested that it was because Harvard students did poorly in this bar examination that Langdell introduced his rigorous annual examinations. Reed, *Training for the Law*, 357.

21. Until this point bar examinations were largely meaningless. An Alabama delegate to the ABA could "call to my recollection no instance in which a license was refused" (D. S. Troy). "Report of Committee on Legal Education," 4 *ABA Reports* 281 (1881). For other examples of the perfunctory nature of the exam, see ibid., 285 (Tennessee); 290 (Kentucky); 296 (Illinois).

22. Gilb, *Hidden Hierarchies*, 63.

23. By 1917, centralized boards of bar examiners existed in thirty-seven jurisdictions. Ibid., 102–3.

24. 14 *ABA Reports* 301, 330–31 (1891). Frustration was evident in the report. "Can any intelligent lawyer believe that in a popular government like ours the State may properly exclude ignorance and incompetence from preying on the bodies of citizens, but must allow them free scope to prey upon their estates, to introduce quarrel and disorder in their social as well as business relations, and even to make the State itself the object of their spoil?" Ibid., 319. "Every added requirement of education, every increase in the standard of trained and cultivated fitness for the task of a lifetime makes the contest more equal and the chance of success for the worthiest better, as it diminishes the start gained by native genius or inherited wealth and the other advantages of birth or fortune that imply no real fitness for the execution of high trust." Ibid., 320.

25. Reed, *Present-Day Law Schools*, 99–100, 110, 113, 261, 267.

26. Twenty-seven men enrolled in the section. It was open to any ABA member and could make recommendations directly to the association, which then could refer them back to the Committee on Legal Education. Ibid., 22–23.

27. Before the section considered the issue, it heard Austin Abbott argue the case for more jurisprudence and the teaching of procedure. "Existing Questions of Legal Education," 16 *ABA Reports* 371 (1893). There was also an interesting discussion of the type of legal subjects that still belonged in a B.A. See Williston, "Legal Education," ibid., 390. He argued in favor of the historical teaching of law in college.

28. Reed, *Present-Day Law Schools*, 23.

29. See Appendix B to the report of the ABA Committee on Legal Education in 1891. "Report of the Committee on Legal Education," 14 *ABA Reports* 353 (1891). In 1878, there were 3,012 law students in law schools of whom 703 had undergraduate degrees. The figures for theology were 4,320 (1,186) and medicine 9,942 (760). By 1889–90, the numbers were law 3,517 (793), theology 7,927 (2,876), and medicine 13,879 (1,376). It was argued that although most theological and medical students had returned to institutionalized training, only 20 percent of those who intended to practice law had done so.

30. "In most states the judges impose some sort of examination on persons seeking to be

admitted to practice, often delegating the duty of questioning the candidate to two or three counsel named for the purpose. Candidates are sometimes required to have read for a certain period in a lawyer's office, but this condition is easily evaded, and the examination, nowhere strict, is often little better than a form or a farce. Notwithstanding this laxity, the level of legal attainment is in some cities as high or higher than among either the barristers or the solicitors of London. This is due to the extraordinary excellence of many of the law schools." The passage continues with the remark, "I do not know if there is anything in which America has advanced more beyond the mother country than in the provision she makes for legal education." Bryce had been professor of civil law at Oxford. Bryce, *The American Commonwealth*, 2:623. With this should be contrasted the opening remark of Albert V. Dicey's inaugural lecture at Oxford in 1883, *Can English Law Be Taught in the Universities?*: "If the question whether English law can be taught at the Universities could be submitted in the form of a case to a body of eminent counsel, there is no doubt whatever as to what would be their answer. They would reply with unanimity and without hesitation that English law must be learned and cannot be taught, and that the only places where it can be learned are the law courts and chambers" (1). For the same mood of pessimism see also Bryce's valedictory lecture, *Legal Studies in the University of Oxford* (1893), cited and discussed in Abel-Smith and Stevens, *Lawyers and the Courts*, 166 ff.

31. Bryce, *The American Commonwealth*, 2:623.

32. Although not well chronicled, clerkship in law offices was already on the decline. See Danaher, "Courses of Study for Law Clerks," 559. After describing the various programs available for law clerks, he opined that law office preparation could at best be a substitute for law school. Some still took the view that the ideal solution was a mixture of law school and law office work. See Swindlehurst, "Legal Education and Law Practice," 214. This was not a view shared by the deans of leading law schools. In 1903, the AALS conducted a survey, asking, "Is apprenticeship in a law office advisable while pursuing a course of study in a law school?" Six deans (Yale, New York University, Cincinnati, Louisville, Boston, and Hastings) said no and four (Kansas, Iowa, Tennessee, and Wisconsin) yes. Two were undecided. 1 *American Law School Review* 83 (1903). Even among those who favored a merging of the two experiences, there was a growing feeling that law school experience should come before office experience. Richards, "Shall Law Schools Give Credit for Office Study?," 514.

33. By 1900, Harvard was already requiring a college degree for admission, and Columbia and Chicago had indicated that they would soon do likewise. *Report of the Acting Dean, Yale Law School, 1901–02*, 115. Yale was talking about such a requirement, but President Hadley wrote in 1902 that "the interests of the public, and in the long run of the universities themselves also, would be adversely affected by the requirement of a college education for admission to the professional schools." *Report of President, Yale University, 1901–02*, 14. Just four years later, however, Dean Henry Rogers of Yale was arguing in favor of an immediate increase in admission standards. *Report of the Dean, Yale Law School, 1905–06*, 149. Yale's admission requirement became in 1909–10 the equivalent of two years of college work, and this, in turn, was raised in 1911–12 to four years as the basic standard. Hicks, *Yale Law School, 1895–1915*, 42–43. The enrollment fell from 438 in 1908–9 to 133 in 1914–15. Hadley, *Arthur Twining Hadley*, 157. In 1916–17, there were still only seven schools requiring at least three years of college for admission. Carnegie Foundation, *Annual Review of Legal Education, 1918*, 3.

34. Reed, *Present-Day Law Schools*, 49, 51, 131; Sullivan, "The Professional Associations

and Legal Education," 412–15. As of 1908, four years was also approved for part-time law school study; by 1916–17, however, only about one-quarter of the night schools offered four years and a few offered only two. Carnegie Foundation, *Annual Review of Legal Education, 1918,* 3; ibid., *1921,* 6.

35. By 1901, the membership was at 32. This was less than one-third of the 108 law schools in existence. See Seavey, "The Association of American Law Schools in Retrospect," 158. This article confirms the suggestion that some schools did not join the AALS because they could not afford the $10 annual dues.

36. There is disagreement as to the true meaning of this distinction. By emphasizing that invitations to the association were sent to schools and that, upon demand, votes within the organization were taken by school, Harry First argues that legal education in this period was controlled by a cartel of law schools seeking to control the market. First, "Competition in the Legal Education Industry," 335. Reed, on the other hand, looked upon the group as a collection of individual law teachers, noting that the governing bodies of the law schools were not the delegates.

37. Seavey, "The Association of American Law Schools," 158. One school was expelled in 1903, and another 9 had withdrawn by 1910. In 1915, Hastings was terminated because of inadequate library facilities. Reed, *Present-Day Law Schools,* 28.

38. Stolz, "Training for the Public Profession of the Law," in Packer and Ehrlich, *New Directions in Legal Education,* passim; Reed, *Present-Day Law Schools,* 25, 28, 110, 314; Sullivan, "Professional Associations," 410.

39. Reed, *Present-Day Law Schools,* 314. Reed argued that "the policy itself is more defensible than the reasons addressed in its support. . . . The preamble suggests . . . that any attempt to meet the need of possible law students who have only their evenings free for school study and attendance is a compromise with evil. . . . The actual resolution could be defended on the quite different ground that an increasingly definite separation of part time from full time education would operate to the ultimate benefit of both." Ibid. The position of the elite law schools was put most graciously by Arthur Corbin: "If a part-time law school, with instructors whose chief thought and energy are devoted to active practice, using a textbook or lecture method, can know and teach the law as it is, to comparatively uneducated students, devoting comparatively little of their time to law study and can turn such students into 'broadly and thoroughly trained experts,' then my colleagues and I ought to resign and go into another business." Corbin, "Democracy and Education for the Bar," 728–29. In the same debate, Joseph Beale of Harvard took a different tack: "The night schools are here to stay; they fill a real need; they educate real lawyers" (751).

40. 4 *American Law School Review* 26 (1916).
   The remark stuck in the craw of Edward T. Lee, dean of the John Marshall Law School, who argued "don't slam the door in the face of brains." Lee, *The Study of Law and Proper Preparation,* 5–6. At the 1918 meeting of the ABA's Section of Legal Education, Lee noted, no doubt to the irritation of members, that "the ancient and modern chosen people"—by which he meant the Jews and the Irish—predominated in the evening schools in Chicago. Not surprisingly, he also argued that the best work was done in the evening. 4 *American Law School Review* 379 (1918).

41. 4 *American Law School Review* 279 (1916).

42. 24 *Reports of the American Bar Association* 400 (1901).

43. Reed, *Training for the Law,* 216. Roughly 10 percent of the members actually attended meetings. Ibid., 218.

44. In 1901, 52 percent of law school students were in AALS schools, leaving 48 percent in non-AALS schools. By 1910, the balance had changed; the figures, respectively, were 46

percent and 54 percent. By 1926, the contrast was even more noticeable, standing at 35 percent in AALS schools, and 65 percent in non-AALS schools. Reed, *Present-Day Law Schools,* 29.

45. See First, "Competition in the Legal Industry," 336–37, 344.

46. Between 1901 and 1916 the numbers of students attending AALS schools rose by 24.9 percent; those attending nonmember schools rose by more than 100 percent. Auerbach, "Enmity and Amity," 565, n. 47.

47. See First, "Competition in the Legal Education Industry," 347.

48. Auerbach, *Unequal Justice,* 89.

49. Ibid., 74.

50. Reed, *Training for the Law,* 266.

51. Ibid.

52. "Admission to the Bar by State, 1965," 35 *The Bar Examiner* 89–90 (1966). The states in question were Mississippi, Montana, West Virginia, and Wisconsin.

53. Reed, *Training for the Law,* 102–3.

54. Ibid., 90–91.

55. During the first forty-four meetings of the American Bar Association, resolutions concerning legal education or admissions were adopted on only nine occasions. Reed, *Training for the Law,* 18–19.

56. First, "Competition in the Legal Education Industry," 352.

57. "If legal education is an industry, then the AALS is a trade association, 'an organized group of producers of broadly similar commodities or services.' We might therefore expect to find that the AALS has engaged in activities similar to those engaged in by industrial trade associations (subject to the modification that the firms it represents are seeking maximization of elitist preferences rather than maximization of profit). These activities would include the gathering and dissemination of data regarding supply and demand, attempts to control output, standardization of products sold, control over 'ethics,' lobbying and facilitation of uniform pricing procedures. An examination of the AALS's activities reveals direct evidence that, with the exception of price regulation, it is engaged in all of these practices." Ibid., 332–33.

58. Ibid., 332–60.

59. "In an age of reform, teachers perceived law as an instrument of social engineering, with broad public implications that transcended client-caretaking." Auerbach, *Unequal Justice,* 76. Auerbach quotes William Draper Lewis of the University of Pennsylvania as saying in 1906, "If, as a profession, we are awake to our failure to perform our public duties, it is the small class of men who are devoting their lives to legal teaching who must point the way." Ibid., 82.

60. Ibid., 107, quoting the president of the Carnegie Foundation.

61. "Although lawyers spoke the language of professionalism, their vocabulary often masked hostility toward those who threatened the hegemony of Anglo-Saxon Protestant culture. . . . In a rehearsal for postwar efforts, teachers and practitioners began to play variations on the themes of anti-urbanism, anti-Semitism and nativism." Ibid., 99.

62. See, in general, ibid., 74–124. Auerbach does suggest, though, a motive beyond simple xenophobia: in bar exams, the graduates of elite schools did not always compare favorably with students of nonelite schools.

63. 3 *American Law School Review* 35 (1911).

64. "The recurrent problem, however, was how to reach an agreement on standards acceptable to member schools with divergent interests and strengths. Had the AALS simply tried to enunciate what a group of law schools believed were the 'best' educational standards, it would not have had this problem; but it never saw itself as

representative of only a small segment of the industry." First, "Competition in the Legal Education Industry," 343.

65. In 1918, when a proposal was made to combine the ABA's Section of Legal Education with the AALS, it met objections from delegates who feared that the "great Eastern law schools" would take control of the section, causing it "to commit hari-kari, first bequeathing or devising to the AALS all of its functions and powers." 4 *American Law School Review* 389 (1918).

In 1919, the AALS passed a resolution limiting credit for night school work, to be met by objections from various faculty members of Marquette Law School. Franz Eschweller said, "We do not feel that we ought to be asked to sacrifice the interests of those who from poor families from force of circumstances are compelled to attend the night school a year longer than those who take the day school because it may seem wiser for those who do not maintain the night school themselves to adopt such a stringent recommendation." 4 *American Law School Review* 526 (1919). The Milwaukee law school faculty, having its attention called to this resolution, passed a resolution unanimously against this resolution. "We want to go at the thing with you; but my God! don't pass a thing which will compel us to leave this when we are doing a public service." Ibid.

66. 2 *American Law School Review* 316 (1909).

67. But the underlying approach may have been similar. As early as 1915 the dean of the Wisconsin Law School had commented: "If you examine the class rolls of the night school in our great cities, you will encounter a very large proportion of foreign names. Emigrants and sons of emigrants remembering the respectable standing of the advocate in their own home, covet the title as a badge of distinction. The result is a host of shrewd young men, imperfectly educated, crammed so they can pass the bar examinations, all deeply impressed with the philosophy of getting on, but viewing the Code of Ethics with uncomprehending eyes. It is this class of lawyers that cause Grievance Committees of Bar Associations the most trouble." Richards, "Progress in Legal Education," 63.

68. A German-born lawyer was disbarred in Texas for saying "Germany is going to win the war and . . . I hope she does." Auerbach, *Unequal Justice*, 104.

69. 15 *Handbook of A.A.L.S.* 107. The standard had been set by Charles Harts Lorne at the 1913 meeting of the Section of Legal Education, when he argued the need to exclude the "class of candidate found chiefly in the larger cities, whose character at the time they apply for admission to the bar is such as to make it probable that they would be unworthy members." 3 *American Law School Review* 368 (1913). Anti-Semitism was rife. For example, at the 1915 meeting of the section, the chairman, Walter George Smith, snidely referred to "the most ancient race" who are "surprised when informed they have done anything wrong." 4 *American Law School Review* 32 (1915).

70. Richards, "Progress in Legal Education," 60.

71. Ibid., 67.

72. Haldeman and Goetsch, *A History of the First One Hundred Years of the Connecticut Bar Association, 1875–1975*, 11.

73. Schlegel, "American Legal Realism," 472, n. 89.

74. Edward Lee of the John Marshall Law School noted that because of lack of time, most night schools could not utilize the case method. Lee, "Evening Law Schools," 290. Lee also claimed that the night schools included representatives of nearly every country in Europe—Christians and Jews, white and black and yellow and even "native Americans."

75. Charles Carusi, dean of National Union Law School, in defending the night schools,

accurately noted that one objection to them was that they represented the old type of law school. He saw the "case method" schools as interested only in the "habits of thought prevalent in purely educational circles." Carusi, "Legal Education and the Bar," 91. Carusi was also willing to defend the correspondence schools such as La Salle Extension University.

76. A selection of these would include: H. B. Hutchens, "Legal Education: Its Relation to the People and the State," 1 *Publications of the Michigan Political Science Association* 1–25 (1895) (attributing the success of the American government to the participation of lawyers); George B. Dorris, "Admission to the Bar," 6 *Oregon Bar Association Proceedings* 43–47 (1896); Richard L. Hand, "Preparation for the Bar," 53 *Albany Law Journal* 119–47 (1896) (proclaiming the integrity and indifference to wealth of lawyers); Franklin J. Dickman, "The Demand for a High Standard of Legal Culture and Education," 3 *Western Reserve Law Journal* 109–18 (1897) (law is "consecrated to the cause of science" and "derived from the depths of philosophy"); Richard C. Jones, "Report of the Committee on Legal Education and Admission to the Bar," 21 *Alabama State Bar Association Proceedings* 97–104 (1898) ("It is a fact beyond question that lawyers in the United States are the leaders of public thought in times of peace and war").

77. Dorris, "Admission to the Bar," 46.

78. See Jordan, "Pettifogging Law Schools and the Untrained Bar," 19; "Examinations for Admission to the Bar in Virginia—the Future," 2 *Virginia Law Register* 310–11. "It is not pessimism to recognize on every hand, in the eager crowding of young men by hundreds—indeed thousands—into our profession and in the deficiency exhibited by so many of these of any adequate concept of what admission to the bar should mean to them that the recruiting of our ranks is the result of processes far from satisfying and giving little promise of escape from very undesirable not to say serious consequences." "Report of the Committee on Education," 2 *Maryland State Bar Association Reports* 67–77 (1897).

79. Reed, in his 1928 report, recorded a story that the leaders of the bar would have pointed to in horror as an example of what low standards could lead to:

> The following episode seems also worth rescuing from oblivion. The enterprising Mr. X, Philippine soldier, socialist propagandist, biological experimenter, after having prepared himself for the California Bar, started a class in San Francisco. He eventually moved to the town of M, married one of his first class of graduates, took her in as a junior partner, and in 1914 was found conducting in the back offices of this law firm of X and X the "M School of Law." Unhampered by scholastic tradition, he has devised a new method of legal instruction, rendered possible by his ingenious discovery that legal definitions can be printed on pieces of celluloid with an ordinary typewriter. Throwing these definitions on a screen by the aid of a magic lantern, he supplemented these exhibitions, held two evenings a week, by running comment, and so appealed to eye and ear at once. Strangers, in the town of M, making a round of the moving picture houses, took in his show along with the rest, thus establishing the value of this pedagogic innovation. At intervals, typed sheets, containing such questions as "Define the difference between a nuncupative and an oleographic (sic) will" were distributed as tests to the students. His school would have been more successful if he had not recently been obliged to serve a term in jail for violating a city ordinance against making stump speeches without a license. Not merely were his educational activities temporarily interrupted by this untoward incident, but also two young University of Chicago graduates seized the

occasion to occupy his former offices, and under the name of the "M Law School," to launch a rival institution. [Reed, *Present-Day Law Schools*, 73, n. 2]

80. Flexner, *Medical Education in the United States and Canada.*
81. For this period of medical education, see Stevens, *American Medicine and the Public Interest*, chap. 3.
82. Reed, *Training for the Law*, 443.
83. Stolz, "Training for the Law," 8.
84. Another thing that irritated the leaders of the bar was that with the "improvement" of medical education had gone an increase in power and membership of the AMA. Membership rose from a little over 8,000 in 1900 to 33,000 in 1914. The ABA membership was stable at about 8,000. ABA, *Special Communication in re the Membership Situation* (1 January 1914).
85. Reed, *Training for the Law*, 192.

7 / Standoff: Redlich, Reed, and Root

A LTHOUGH "a number of [Boston Law] firms excluded the largely Irish graduates of Suffolk Law,"[1] Gleason Archer's claims and those of the other proprietary schools across the nation were not music to the ears of the ABA and AALS. The ABA had announced in 1879 that "there is little, if any, dispute now as to the relative merits of education by means of law schools and that gotten by mere practice or training in apprenticeship as an attorney's clerk. Without disparagement of mere practical advantages, the verdict of the best informed is in favor of the schools."[2] Clearly proprietary schools were not what the declaration meant, but by the twentieth century these institutions were appearing in increasing numbers. The ABA and the newly created AALS moved against them. Their motivations were complex, involving public, professional, financial, and social considerations.

The Flexner Report may have been galling to the ABA, but, because of this indignation and the report's success, it also deeply impressed the association. Three years after the Flexner Report was published, the ABA decided enough was enough, and the members of the Committee on Legal Education and Admissions to the Bar announced that it was "most anxious to have a similar investigation made by the Carnegie Foundation into the conditions under which the work of legal education is carried on in this country."[3] The president of the Carnegie Foundation, Henry S. Pritchett, was also anxious to undertake a study of legal education along the lines of the Flexner Report; indeed, he had wanted to look at lawyers before he had looked at physicians but had been rebuffed. Thus, for the next twenty years, Alfred Z. Reed, a nonlawyer member of the staff of the Carnegie Foundation, conducted a series of studies of legal education and the legal profession.[4] His first report, *Training for the Public Profession of the Law*, was published in 1921. It was the most important document he was to produce as well as the most radical.

Reed's 1921 report was not actually the first, but the second, major report to discuss American legal education. Josef Redlich, an Austrian observer, had already published *The Common Law and the Case Method in American University Law Schools* in 1914, also under the auspices of the Carnegie Foundation. The conversion of the leading schools to the case method had already largely occurred by the time of this report.

Redlich had, however, visited only 10 schools,[5] and by 1909—four years before his visit—there had been no less than 124 law schools with 19,498 students.[6] The leading case-method schools, the type most heavily represented in the study, could hardly indicate the state of all the schools, and in this regard, Redlich's views were bound to be less important than Reed's.[7]

To understand Reed's views on the profession and the excitement they caused, one must reflect a little on the rapid growth of the law school. Redlich, although he visited mainly elite schools, dimly perceived that there were at least two markets. He noted that "the fundamentally democratic idea which pervades everything in America" prevented even the most elite schools from resembling Oxford and Cambridge. "Even in the Harvard Law School, and to a large extent in the excellent law schools of the state universities of Michigan and Wisconsin, or in the two Chicago universities, students of all classes of the population are to be found, the sons of farmers as well as those belonging to the urban middle classes." He also asserted that the proprietary schools "supply the needs primarily of those social strata whose sons are not thinking of university education in either the American or the continental sense. They consider the legal profession as a trade, like any other, and regard legal education in the same light as commercial education in a commercial school."[8]

Seven years later, Reed painted the picture with broader strokes and in more grandiose hues. In terms similar to those used by Flexner, Reed viewed the legal profession in ways that are reminiscent of the idealized portraits of the legal profession traditionally articulated by leaders of the bar, but he drew very different conclusions that some would regard as peculiarly modern. Law, like medicine, was a "public profession." In Reed's opinion, "practicing lawyers do not merely render to the community a social service, which the community is interested in having them render well. They are part of the governing mechanism of the state. Their functions are in a broad sense political. This is not due primarily to the circumstance that a large proportion of our legislative and administrative officials, and virtually all of our judges, are chosen from among this practically ruling class. . . . It springs even more fundamentally from the fact, early discovered, that private individuals cannot secure justice without the aid of a special professional order to represent and to advise them."[9]

Although the leaders of the bar had earlier used the public functions of lawyers to justify raising standards and to restrict the practice of law to only a carefully and scientifically trained elite, Reed ultimately drew just the opposite conclusion. He saw the America of the 1920s as a pluralistic society being presented with a theoretically unitary bar.[10] He saw a brighter situation in the quality of the leaders of the profession, whose intellectual grasp of the law had improved with the development of law schools, but the contrast between this sector and the other end of the profession, which he believed was progressively worsening, stood out sharply against the formal theory of a unified bar.[11]

Unlike most of the leaders of the bar, Reed was prepared to argue that a unitary bar was doomed to failure. He opposed the establishment of those universal standards—either through bar examinations or through accreditation—designed to drive out the intellectually less fashionable schools. In the long run, he saw the need for lawyers of differing skills and qualifications serving different purposes and different elements in society. Indeed, he proposed institutionalizing the inherent differences within the profession. To buttress these differences, Reed described at least four different categories of law school that he had uncovered and at least three of which he believed deserved to survive.[12] It was his support for a differentiated bar and for different types of law schools that brought Reed face to face with the forces demanding uniformity.[13]

These forces, although probably unaware of the extent of heresy to be revealed in Reed's report, were not unprepared when it did appear. Although after 1914, the ABA and the AALS no longer met at the same time, the interests of their leaderships remained close. Even while Reed was still working on his report, the ABA Section of Legal Education and Admissions to the Bar, faced with the continuing rapid growth of "inferior" schools, began to suggest stronger rules.[14] Although not brought to a vote, the draft rules proposed by the section in 1916 and 1917 called for attendance at law school as a prerequisite for taking the bar examination (three years at a full-time or four years at a part-time school).[15] In the meantime, however, the AALS, somewhat dissatisfied with the efforts of the ABA, was trying an outflanking movement. It, too, sought to "do a Flexner" and drive out the "less good" schools. The problem was that there were three competing gamekeepers: the Committee on Legal Education of the ABA, the Section of Legal Education of the ABA, and the AALS. The campaign to streamline the structure, begun in 1915, was carried to its logical conclusion in the remarks of the president of the AALS in 1916—Walter Wheeler Cook. He called for a Council on Legal Education along the lines of the Council on Medical Education. In 1917, the AALS put on the pressure by formally requesting the ABA to appoint such a council. In great haste, and virtually without debate, the ABA approved the establishment of the council at its 1917 convention (in effect turning the committee into the council) but, anxious "to prevent control of the section from passing into the hands of . . . the Law School Association,"[16] made it much less powerful than the AALS had hoped.

To placate the AALS, the ABA at once staffed the council with the pillars of the academic legal establishment—the deans of Harvard, Wisconsin, Minnesota, Columbia, and Northwestern.

The committee-council then tried to absorb the section and, effectively, the State Board of Bar Examiners. It failed, and, within two years, for internal political reasons related to centralization, the ABA decided to abolish the committee-council and substitute a council controlled by the section. The leading law schools fought against the move but lost at the 1919 convention. The AALS was displeased and responded by raising its own rules for membership, in effect finally excluding part-time schools. Moreover, the AALS members decided on a strategy to take over the ABA Section of Legal Education through the simple expedient of attending meetings in force, since the ABA, unlike the AALS, was based on individual membership.[17]

The AALS plan succeeded; professors packed the 1920 meeting of the ABA Section of Legal Education and Admissions to the Bar and were able both to insure that established law teachers had a strong say in section policy and also to pressure the association into appointing a Committee on Legal Education that was ultimately chaired by Elihu Root. Root's committee, in the midst of various strong and conflicting forces, worked out a compromise solution. It reported that "only in law school could an adequate legal education be obtained" and that two years of college should be required before admission to law school. At the same time, night schools could achieve legitimate status on the condition that they became four-year institutions. Bar examiners were placated by the formal disapproval of the diploma privilege. The ABA was called on to invest the Council on Legal Education with the power to accredit schools.

The section accepted the report, and Root and Chief Justice William Howard Taft piloted it to approval at the 1921 ABA convention. At most, however, the ABA could only hope to be persuasive.[18] The association, therefore, sponsored a conference of local and state bar associations the following year and persuaded them to give general endorsement to the work of the ABA.[19] If the ABA-endorsed Root Report had in fact been implemented in the 1920s, the unified bar that so clearly attracted the leaders of the profession would have been in sight. All this while, however, Reed had been working on his report, sulking because he felt that Reginald Heber Smith in his 1919 report on *Justice and the Poor* had stolen some of his thunder. At last, however, the report was ready, one month after the Root Report had been published.[20]

Reed's completed initial report for the Carnegie Foundation, *Training for the Public Profession of the Law*, had suggested that the de facto stratified bar be accepted de jure. Although the basic theme startled his readers, the proposal was not novel; from time to time writers had toyed with the idea of the return to a graded profession. Langdell in the 1870s had sometimes talked of his graduates as "counsellors" and "advocates" rather than as attorneys.[21] Walter Wheeler Cook and Wesley Hohfeld at Yale had been suggesting the idea of a differentiated bar during the years when Reed was collecting his material.[22] Reed's suggestion in his first report that the most democratic, egalitarian, and American solution would be a differentiated bar, with differing types of law schools, nonetheless managed to offend both his ABA and AALS audiences.[23]

The ABA represented the most successful practitioners, and it was an elite committed to raising the standards of legal education generally. The AALS consisted of the elite law schools, who dreamed of the day when all but the full-time university-affiliated law schools would have gone the way of the proprietary medical schools. The Root committee, which had seen the Reed Report in draft, opined:[24] "In spite of the diversity of human relations with respect to which the work of lawyers is done, the intellectual requisites are in all cases substantially the same. . . . All require high moral character and substantially the same intellectual preparation."[25] Meanwhile, Arthur Corbin of Yale, in his presidential address to the AALS, spent much of his speech rejecting any concept of a differentiated bar.[26]

On its surface, the ABA–AALS position looked the more democratic of the two. The idea of reinstituting the English concept of a divided bar—which some said the Reed proposals implied—seemed redolent of the class-conscious colonial period in, say, Virginia. As the medical profession was to discover, however, although driving out the worst medical schools might increase the quality of service to the middle class, it ran the danger of depriving the poor of all medical care. Some have argued that many of the ills of inadequate medical care in the 1980s can be traced to the success of the Flexner Report in transforming medical education into a scientific, university-based profession.[27] If the ABA–AALS approach had been successful, legal services might have been even more inadequately distributed in this country than they are today. There might also have been fewer incompetent lawyers.

Even in the 1980s the evidence suggests that the bar is still far from unitary, no matter what its leaders like to believe. The issue of standards, egalitarianism, and the public responsibility of the profession that were emphasized by Reed and those who objected to the Root Report would remain. In the 1920s, this hardly meant that the ABA and AALS had lost the battle. Doing their best to ignore Reed and the leaders of the proprietary schools, the two associations, united since joint meetings came back once again in 1920,[28] would press on until their "ideals" gradually bore fruit. The seed had been planted. The law schools and their requirements had become the center of professional debate, and they had already had a profound effect on American legal culture. Their efforts to standardize and raise legal education requirements, however, proceeded only slowly.

Although the ABA and the AALS shared the joint concern over standards and egalitarianism, the law schools themselves found additional sources of worry. The case method, by the second decade of this century the standard teaching system for leading AALS law schools, first came under systematic, critical analysis around the time of World War I. Since leading legal academics had to a considerable extent based their reputations and professionalization on the science of the Harvard technique, any concentrated attack on its orthodoxy was a serious threat. Despite the excellence of the case method in teaching legal analysis, it would be strange if such a novel system had no disadvantages. It did, and many of the drawbacks were isolated and publicized by Josef Redlich in his 1914 study of the case method. They were then reemphasized seven years later in Reed's first report.

The case method certainly had been criticized before. Schools that envied Harvard's success hoped that the teaching system would be its Achilles' heel and felt free to snipe. Dwight provided a particularly virulent example of this license, and he had been supported by various groups within the bar. Students never felt the same enthusiasm for the case method as did the faculty. Rarely had systematic outside criticism, however, been heard—rarely, that is, until the arrival of Redlich and Reed. Each hired as an impartial observer with a certain amount of expertise, one a foreigner and the other a nonlawyer, their attacks could not be dismissed as diatribes by jealous competitors or less than outstanding students, although the law school establishment was not above suggesting that Redlich had listened to "gossip."[29]

The very success of the case method meant that it was soon to be used in all the years of law school, and as the case method came to be regarded less as a means of transferring information about substantive rules and more as a means of teaching legal methodology, complaints began to be heard from students about its repetitive nature. Redlich had already noted that the system was essentially geared to teaching common law and that, for teaching statutory and other materials, different methods of instruction would be more appropriate.[30] As it was, he attributed part of the method's success to the fact that, in 1913, there was still widespread use of textbooks in conjunction with case classes.[31] Also, although deeply impressed by the Socratic method, he felt it would not have been nearly so successful had it not been supplemented by moots, law clubs,[32] individual advice from professors,[33] and, perhaps most important of all, the law reviews.[34]

The law reviews, however, were for the few. What of the discussion of cases in the large classes? Redlich noted that "for a considerable period only the particularly quick or talented students take part in the debates."[35] Indeed, the introduction of the case method of instruction had been opposed by Dwight at Columbia because it was not suited to the "great and important class of men of average ability" that "exists and always will exist in the profession. . . . These men must be trained as well as those of superior powers."[36] In the long run, leading law schools largely solved the "problem" of the slower student by introducing competitive admissions. For such schools, the major issue that returned to plague them was the students' growing psychological hostility toward the case method. In the less prestigious schools, however, Redlich's concern about the lack of attention to all but the most talented or outspoken students would remain pertinent, particularly so because of the unfavorable student-faculty ratios that the case method either tolerated or encouraged.

From the viewpoint of his own didactic Germanic education, Josef Redlich saw other dangers in addition to the plight of the average student. He felt that an obsessive use of the system might well—in fact already did—undermine the scientific treatment of law for which Langdell and his associates had called:

> [I]t cannot be denied that the literary powers of the new generation
> of American teachers were for many years very largely expended
> upon supplying the new aids to law school work and instruction—
> the case books, that is to say—which the new method demanded.
> This task has been accomplished in the last generation in an
> eminently comprehensive and satisfactory manner. . . . But on
> the other hand, it is equally certain that this kind of literary activity
> has prevented many forceful writers among modern American law
> teachers from cultivating the fields of legal history and dogmatic
> literature as fruitfully as they might otherwise have done.[37]

His suggestion for remedying at least some of these defects was to lengthen the law degree to four years, "for this would render possible a larger number not only of analytic exercises, but also of lecture courses." These, in turn, "would undoubtedly greatly stimulate the production of strictly scientific literature in American law."[38] Related to all these concerns was Redlich's perception of the effect of the case method on the approach to legal history and legal theory. Redlich rued the absence of scientific literature that expounded areas of the law in great depth, the nonexistence of introductory courses that explained fundamental concepts, and lectures that gave an overview of the law. He sensed that the common law in America was moving toward an "atomistic" and away from a "monistic" intellectual approach.[39]

A final theme—merely mentioned by Redlich—was the absence of a practical side to law studies. The concept of the scientific approach carried with it, almost of necessity, some notion of the practical experiment—the clinical experience. The great intellectual theme of the Flexner Report had been the need to turn the training of medical students away from abstract lectures and back to the laboratory and the ward, where they could be exposed to the "real thing"—the cadaver and its predecessor, the patient. Langdell had originally claimed that although law students, learning by his method, were removed from the files and clients found in the law office, the law classroom and library were the laboratories in which the student had his "clinical" (or, as Langdell would have been more likely to say, practical or scientific) experience.

Redlich dutifully recorded contemporary lawyers' theories about the clinical component in the case method, but he was unconvinced by them. Keener and Pound had taken over from Langdell and Ames, drawing even closer parallels to the laboratory than had Langdell's rather abstract theorizing. In 1888, Keener had claimed, "Under this system the student must look upon the law as a science consisting of a body of principles to be found in the adjudged cases, the cases being to him what the specimen is to the geologist."[40] Roscoe Pound, who had begun his career as a biologist, put it somewhat more graphically in his inaugural lecture at Nebraska in 1903: "As teachers of science were slow to put the microscope and the scalpel into the hands of students and permit them to study nature, not books, so have we been fearful of putting reports into their hands, and permitting them to study the living law."[41] That definition, assimilating clinical studies to the study of appellate decisions, was not adequate for Redlich.[42]

In fairness, even the leading members of the ABA, who normally gave the schoolmen what they wanted, were again having doubts about the new legal elite being trained in an atmosphere of total academic legal immersion. It was one thing to exclude from the profession part-time law students who were taught by part-time teachers, but the bar worried as the leading schools increasingly had students who had no contemporaneous practical experience taught by faculty members who had little or no experience of practice. At the 1909 ABA meeting, Franklin Danaher of the New York Board of Examiners said his state had made a "grievous error" in allowing students to take the bar examination without serving some time in a clerkship.[43] In 1910 the ABA recommended that, after three years of law school, students have a mandatory one-year clerkship, and the AALS was urged to support the recommendation.[44] In 1913, the ABA formally asked the AALS to accept the rule, but, led by Henry Rogers, the academics balked.[45] To them it was abundantly clear that the case method was practical; the obtuseness of practitioners seemed to know no bounds.

Nevertheless, many of Redlich's reservations about the case method were shared by Alfred Reed. After noting that "not literally all good things are first thought of in Cambridge," he strongly implied that Langdell had, to some extent, been making a virtue out of necessity in his development of the case method.[46] The number of cases had become absurdly large[47] and their craftsmanship progressively worse,[48] so that restating principles through a limited number of cases had become a convenient method of expounding the law. Like Redlich, Reed also appreciated that the case method, during its life, had been transformed. As it became clear that the number of principles of the law was greater than Langdell had predicted—or at least that the experience of the law was wider than its logic—the purpose of the method became not merely "to put its students into possession of some definite field of knowledge, however small. The case method law school no longer professes to give its students a present mastery of judge-made law. It prepares them merely to master judge-made law in the future."[49] This change was nowhere better symbolized than in the introduction of electives at Harvard in 1886. The idea that law school was solely for mastery of "the law"—a well-defined entity—was on the wane.

Reed, however, was blunter in his criticism than Redlich had been:

> The fiction that even generalized national judge-made law was to be mastered, was abandoned. Portions of it were to be mastered, but large portions of it were avowedly not. American law became for the student not a field to be surveyed broadly, but a thicket, within which a partial clearing, pointing in the right direction, is made. The young practitioner is then equipped with a "trained mind," as with a trusty axe, and commissioned to spend the rest of his life chopping his way through the tangle.[50]

In common with Redlich, Reed also regretted the absence of good scholarly treatises. He offered three explanations:

> We have not had in our law schools until recently many men— we probably have not many even to-day—who knew enough about the law to be able to produce good textbooks. . . . The number of

classroom hours assigned to the individual instructor who teaches by the exceptionally arduous case method is often too great to leave him time and energy for productive work. And in addition there is the sometimes hazy feeling that the production of texts, which facilitate dogmatic instruction in the law, is opposed to the main purpose for which these schools exist.[51]

In fact Reed was not as hostile to the case method as these quotations make him sound. He readily admitted "that lawyers who had been trained in this way outstripped in practice the product of other methods."[52] What basically concerned Reed was the homogenization of legal education through the pervasiveness of the Harvard case method. The method worked exceedingly well with a full-time college-prepared student body who might be expected to read the material before class and to be in a position to reflect on it. More important to its success, however, was the available faculty: "I believe that while in the hands of a genuine scholar, skilled in the socratic method, the case method is indubitably the best, in the hands of a mediocre man it is the very worst of all possible modes of instruction."[53] Thus Reed viewed with horror the spread of the teaching method to the fastest-growing sector of the law school market—the night schools[54]—where he felt the typical instructor was ill equipped to make use of the case method. As the rest of his report made clear, this criticism was not intended to indicate opposition to the night schools themselves. Rather, the fact that competitive pressures in a supposedly unitary system of legal education had forced the night law schools to adopt a method inappropriate to the ability and needs of their faculty and students was simply another indication that the market in reality was, and should be, pluralistic. Only by admitting the different needs of the heterogeneous population of law schools and lawyers could the most appropriate teaching methods for each be used.

What truth was there in the criticism offered in the Redlich and Reed reports? Was the increasing distance between the case method and practical problems inherent in the nature of the case method, or was it more the result of hiring as professors those who had little or no experience of practice?[55] Was it fair to say that the case method inhibited research and discouraged the best minds from publishing research on law rather than about law?[56] The questions to be left to the 1970s and 1980s included such fundamental issues as whether the law schools were any more than high-grade schools of rhetoric and, more uncharitably, whether their tendency was to produce analytic giants but moral pygmies. In recent years, the case method has been attacked for fostering the notion of the lawyer as an "objective scientist" who discovers fundamental principles rather than a system of training that would eschew technicalities and encourage an advocate to use "basic social and moral values" to make legal rules.[57] Such a juxtaposition inevitably oversimplifies; indeed, it is arguable that the reverse was the ultimate impact of the case method. There was, however, undoubtedly something lost, intellectually and morally, in the blind obedience to German scientism. In retrospect, the period of high formalism in the life of the case method has about it a touch of the ludicrous. From the very beginning there were inherent contradictions in the scholarly and the pedagogical aspects of the case method, yet its contribution was enormous.

Although admitting that there were problems with the case method, unrestricted criticism of Harvard and its system was no more warrantable than unquestioning acceptance. An important, though perhaps now unnecessary, point to reiterate is that the belief in law as a science was not limited to Harvard's disciples, but it was instead one of the most publicized examples of adherence to a common methodology of the era. It was, after all, a Yale Law School professor who became dean of social sciences at Catholic University who wrote, in the 1890s, that "law as a science is a body of fundamental principles and of deductions drawn therefrom in reference to the right ordering of social conduct. The principles are universal, admitting neither exception nor qualifications. The intellect in deriving legitimate deductions from the principles follows the legitimate process of logic, over which the will has no control, and which are always and everywhere the same, whatever may be the subject of investigation."[58]

The case method itself, despite its tendency to promote a uniform curriculum, had many facets. To Oliver Wendell Holmes, Jr., it was not a narrow experience, leading only to a scientific analysis. Discussing the advocates of the case method, he noted: "They have said that to make general principle worth anything you must give it a body. You must show in which way and how far it would be applied actually in an actual system. You must show how it gradually emerged as the felt reconciliation of concrete instances, no one of which established it in terms. Finally, you must show its historic relations to other principles, often of very different dates and origins, and thus set it in the perspective, without which its properties will never be truly judged."[59] Holmes, in short, was able to embrace Langdellian "scientism" and yet manage, at the same time and in the view of many, to lay the groundwork for Realism. Holmes knew the importance of the "dragon" of legal history, and, in the same article, he noted both how the case method was "to teach in the grand manner and to make lawyers"[60] and also that "under the influence of German Science [the case method] is gradually drawing legal history into its sphere."[61] Seen in this light, the case method had an intellectual purpose akin to the emerging social sciences. No doubt Holmes knew what he was doing, and certainly the absence of any serious theoretical underpinnings to the Langdellian innovations made it easy for him to translate the scientific search for rules into a scientific analysis of facts. There was, moreover, enough latitude in the Harvard model to justify Holmes' proto-Realist interpretation of the intellectual purposes of the case method.

However much Holmes, Redlich, Reed, and contemporary academics and professionals might argue back and forth about the various merits and demerits of the case method, and however nervous the leading academics might be made by criticism of the method, by the time of the 1921 reports there could be no question that the system was the inevitable accoutrement of the majority of American law schools. The steamroller seemed to be rolling inexorably on. The case method had succeeded in the face of the opposition of state universities, elite private universities, and the skepticism of an Austrian observer and a Carnegie Foundation investigator. It was not merely a fad of the late Victorian era but the standard of the twentieth century. By the 1920s, anybody who was anybody in the law school "industry" used the case method. It was only the Archers and the Lees[62] who would "rather fight than switch."

NOTES

1. Trout, *Boston, the Great Depression and the New Deal*, 16.
2. "Report of the Committee on Legal Education of the American Bar Association," 2 *Reports of the ABA* 209–36.
3. Letter dated 7 February 1913. Cited in Stolz, "Training for the Law," 8.
4. Reed was born in Colorado, the son of a physician in Colorado Springs. Graduating from Harvard College in 1897, he spent the next fifteen years as a private tutor in New York while working on his Ph.D. at Columbia. He completed the Ph.D. in 1911, joined the Carnegie Foundation in 1913 in charge of legal studies at the age of 38, and continued in that post until 1934. He died in 1949. *Who Was Who, 1950,* 2:441.
5. Redlich, *Common Law and the Case Method*, vi. Of these schools, six were at that time using the case method: New York University, Columbia, Harvard, Michigan, Northwestern, and Chicago. Ibid., 26.
6. The first Reed report is important for many reasons, not the least of them being its statistical exhaustiveness. Some sense of the growth of legal education may be obtained from the following: when Dwight was appointed to Columbia, there had been 18 law schools with between five hundred and six hundred students. When the Civil War broke out, there were 22 law schools. Reed recorded that the number of law schools doubled between 1870 and 1890 and doubled again between 1890 and 1910. When the report was published, there were 142 law schools. Reed, *Training for the Law*, 193.
7. President Pritchett was disappointed by the quality of the Redlich report. The original

was written in German, and it is believed that Pritchett and Reed had to struggle to translate it. The introduction, by Pritchett, has been described as "lukewarm and dry." The report, however, was not the last that the foundation heard of Redlich. In the 1920s, when he had fallen on hard financial times, he approached the foundation for support. Savage, *Fruit of an Impulse*, 111. Redlich ultimately spent the years 1926 to 1935 in Cambridge, Massachusetts.

8. Redlich, *Common Law and the Case Method*, 70. Although admitting that "these more or less commercial schools . . . have not the slightest significance from the point of view of scientific legal instruction," Redlich argued that the proprietary schools "correspond to real requirements of the American people. . . . They have their warrant in the economic life of the nation, and are firmly rooted in the old democratic view of the legal profession as a practical trade." Ibid., 70–71.

9. Reed, *Training for the Law*, 3.

10. "The evil—the very great evil—of the present situation, as a result of which all part-time legal education now rests under a justified cloud, lies in the perpetuation of the theory of a unitary bar, whose attainments are to be tested by uniform examinations. This formula, once adequate to the needs of sparsely settled communities, has been carried over into a period when it is no longer workable. Under the notion that there is such a thing as 'a' standard lawyer, radically different educational ideals are brought into conflict with one another, to their mutual injury; this in the face of the fact that they actually produce radically different types of practitioners. To begin with, the night schools are damaged by the obligation placed upon them to cover the same curriculum as the day schools. . . .

"The conventional picture of our bar examination system that is commonly drawn is as follows: The state, through its examining board, is supposed to test all applicants for admission to the bar—in most cases after they have already been subjected to tests provided by the schools. The actual situation is that neither the tests of the state nor those of the law schools serve to prevent incompetents from flooding the profession. Taking into consideration the effect of night law schools advertising in artificially stimulating a demand for legal education, there can be little question but that, in spite of all recent efforts to raise bar examination standards, more incompetents are to-day admitted to the bar than when, under laxer former requirements for admission and a far smaller development of good law schools than we now possess, the generality of actual applicants nevertheless received a sound training in the office of an old-fashioned practitioner." Ibid., 57–59. A critic might well argue that Reed was being more than a little naive about the social forces that had transformed America in the latter part of the nineteenth century.

11. "The dark side of the present situation has been shown. Its bright side is that there has been at all times an element in the profession that has carried on the old traditions of the English bar. Originally composed for the most part of college graduates who studied in the best law offices, this element—although still very hazily defined—now tends to be composed of college graduates who have studied in the best law schools. While in its lower ranges the bar . . . has been getting worse and worse, on top, at least from the point of intellectual mastery of the law . . . the development of law schools has made it better and better. Thus, beneath the formula of a technically unified bar within each state, the profession has actually become widely differentiated." Ibid., 60.

12. Eleven percent of the schools consisted of those 16 schools whose work could be completed in less than three years of either part- or full-time study. These schools were "clearly destined to disappear." Next, with 21 percent, came those 30 "high-entrance full-time schools," all attached to colleges or universities, and almost all of whom "have

acknowledged the leadership of Harvard, and teach national law by the case method." Third, 29 percent of the schools (or 40) came into a miscellaneous category of low-entrance full-time schools, requiring little or no prior education. Reed assumed these would survive for students who were not able to take the seven-year training of the national schools, yet could afford to study full time for three years. Finally, there were part-time schools—55 of them (or 39 percent). Almost all were proprietary and unattached to universities. "This group . . . is not in good repute among those who cherish the highest educational and professional ideals," who indeed were bent on destroying such schools. "In the judgement of the writer, it is neither possible, nor having due regard to the fundamental principles for which the American common-wealth has been supposed to stand, would it be desirable, to abolish this now definitely established and rapidly growing educational type. Efforts had much better be directed toward transforming it into something far better than it now is." Ibid., 414–16.

13. "The development of differing types of legal education has established in legal practice groups of lawyers of different types, each of which has been properly interested in perpetuating its kind. Under the influence of an inherited prepossession, however, each has thought it necessary, not only to do this, but also to impose upon the totality of practitioners its own special conception of legal education. . . . The scholarly law school dean properly seeks to build up a 'nursery for judges' that will make American law what American law ought to be. The practitioner bar examiner, with his satellite schools, properly seeks to prepare students for the immediate practice of the law as it is. The night school authorities, finally, see most clearly that the interests not only of the individual but of the community demand that participation in the making and adminis-tration of the law shall be kept accessible to Lincoln's plain people. All these are worthy ideals. But no single institution, pursuing its special aim, can attain both the others as well. Attempts by each type of law school to carry the entire burden of legal education produce such unsuccessful results as to bring the entire body of practitioners into disrepute." Ibid., 417–18.

14. Donna Fossum, "Law School Accreditation Standards and the Structure of American Legal Education," 515, 517.

15. Reed, *Present-Day Law Schools*, 37.

16. The executive committee had not appropriated any funds for the council, so it was suffering severe financial problems. Reed, *Present-Day Law Schools*, 39. Stolz argues that the ABA was facing "schoolmen" forces who thought they were riding high and were in control of what the A.B.A. was likely to do with respect to legal education. Stolz, "Training for the Law," 15.

17. As Dean Vance of Minnesota put it: "We have got to connect up and connect up closely with the American Bar Association. We have got a job to do, if we want to accomplish the purpose we set for ouselves; we have to go to the American Bar Association Meetings. . . . We have got to recognize facts—that we were beaten in the last contest, and we have got to do better next time." Cited in Lee, *The Study of Law and Proper Preparation*, 14.

18. The report had aroused controversy. Charles Carusi responded by saying, " . . . I protest in the name of 111,000,000 people against so reactionary, so narrow, so unfair a position as says: 'It matters not what your competency in every particular; if you did not acquire it in one of about a half dozen great endowed universities, then, not *prima facie*, but conclusively, you are unfit to represent your fellow citizens or to advise them upon their legal rights.'" 4 *American Law School Review* 682 (1921). James Andrews added, "This report proceeds from the AALS by way of the eminent committee of the ABA, for adoption. I will say with all deference, that is a mere camouflage." Ibid., 695.

George Price responded by asking, "[D]oes the ABA want to let down the tests simply to let in uneducated foreigners? Do we propose to erect a simple standard that will accommodate these people?" Ibid., 689.

The question of intentional exclusion of foreigners was probably an inevitable result of the Root Report. William Howard Taft loftily claimed that the recommendations involved nothing less than "saving society from the incompetent, the uneducated, and the careless ignorant members of the bar." *Handbook of the Association of American Law Schools, 1921*, 143. The night school operators attacked the report as being aimed at immigrants and as "dangerous, uncalled for, unnecessary and un-American." Root himself felt sure that two years of college would insure that prospective lawyers "will be taking in through the pores of their skin American life and American thought and feeling." Ibid., 155. With respect to the exclusion of the poor, Taft put his conscience at rest by arguing that "the opportunities for college education are not confined to the great eastern endowed universities, or the great state universities, now flourishing in every state. The whole country is dotted with collegiate institutions of learning near the home of every young man anxious to come to the Bar, with facilities for supporting himself through his college course if he has the courage and tenacity and self-restraint to avail himself of them. There are thousands of young men doing this now." 47 *ABA Reports* 498–99 (1922).

19. Stolz, "Training for the Public Profession of the Law," Appendix II to Appendix A, Packer and Ehrlich, *New Directions in Legal Education*, 235–45. For an example of one result of this conference, see Vold, "Improving North Dakota Bar Association Requirements," 59.

20. Reed felt that Smith had "annexed some of the ingredients of his own cake." He was also slowed down by the refusal of some law schools, "with memories of Flexner's exposé of medical education," to cooperate. Pritchett fumed at Reed's delay. Savage, *Fruit of an Impulse*, 150–51. Reed was not an easy man. He feuded vigorously with Hastings Law School. Barnes, *Hastings College of Law*, 216. It is arguable that he mellowed somewhat after his marriage, at the age of 47, in 1921.

21. Reed, *Training for the Law*, 92.

22. Stolz, "Training for the Law," 247–48. At the joint meeting of bar examiners and the ABA Section of Legal Education in 1915, Charles Griffin of New York pointed out "that our neighboring state of New Jersey . . . still maintain(s) the distinction between attorneys and counselors. When a man is admitted to the bar in New Jersey he is sworn in as an attorney and he cannot attain the rank of counselor at law until he has practiced three years as an attorney and satisfied his brethren of the bar that he is worthy to have the rank of counselor conferred upon him." 4 *American Law School Review* 35 (1915).

23. First argued, "It made better economic sense for the law schools (and the profession) to shut off a differentiated bar trained in 'below standard' law schools. Such schools would be a possible substitute product for elite model education; substitute products weaken a seller's market power." First, "Competition in the Legal Education Industry," 357, n. 267.

24. Reed's motives in allowing the Root Committee to see the draft of his report are unclear. Probably it could be attributed to the fact that Root was a close friend of Pritchett's and "took a keen interest in the Project." Jessup, *Elihu Root*, 2:468. First attributed the move to "tactics" without explaining what he meant, noting that it allowed the Root Committee to "gain the initial advantage in the debate."

25. Stolz, "Training for the Law," 247.

26. Corbin, "Democracy and Education for the Bar," 143. Reform of bar admission requirements, Corbin noted, "cannot properly take the form of dividing the bar into

two classes, an inner and outer bar, the competent and the incompetent, or the sheep and the goats. It would be enough to say of this suggestion that it is quite inconsistent with our history and our accustomed modes of action. . . . No reasonable suggestion has been made to the principle on which law business can be divided. . . . There is therefore no place for two kinds of legal education in two kinds of law schools for two kinds of lawyers." Ibid., 147, 150.

27. Stevens, *American Medicine and the Public Interest*, passim.

28. Auerbach, *Unequal Justice*. Auerbach qualified his statement about state legislatures by adding, "Yet the fight for higher standards had tangible significance for the organized bar and for law teachers." Ibid., 118. Ironically, Reed's reaction to the reunion of the ABA and the AALS was one of high praise: "The AALS and the ABA for years, whoever may be to blame, have been playing at cross purposes. Now, finally, you have come together and it is a magnificent thing, in my opinion, a thing of great promise for the future of legal education." 4 *American Law School Review* 761 (1921).

29. For reactions to Redlich see, especially, Beale, "The Law School as Professor Redlich Saw It," 617; Stone, "Dr. Redlich and the Case Method in American University Law Schools," 262; Baldwin, "Education for the Bar in the United States," 437; Kocourek, "The Redlich Report and the Case Method," 321; Venny, "The Case Method of Teaching Law," 182; 15 *Handbook of the Association of American Law Schools* 77 (1915).

For the most vigorous reviews of Reed's first report, see Albert M. Kales, review of Reed's *Training for the Public Profession of the Law*, 35 *Harvard Law Review* 96 (1921), and reply by Reed, "Scholarship or Opinion?," 355; Stone, "Legal Education and Democratic Principle," 639; and reply by Reed, "Criticism of Carnegie Foundation Bulletin," 114; and rebuttal by Stone, "Dean Stone's Rejoinder to Mr. Reed's Reply," 187; Lewis, "Agreements and Differences between the Report of the Committee on Which the Action of the Association Was Taken and the Carnegie Foundation Report," 39; Nilsson, "Legal Education and Admission to the Bar," 104; and Reed, "The Lawyer as a Privileged Servant of Democracy," 154.

30. Redlich, *The Case Method*, 35, 50.

31. He would have preferred to see even more use of treatise materials ("Institutes"). Ibid., 41 ff.

32. The Pow Wow Club was begun at Harvard in 1870 with the main purpose of holding weekly moots. Sutherland, *Law at Harvard*, 344. Similar clubs developed at Columbia, although Columbia's early experiments were not a success. The official Columbia historian has described the student apathy in Dwight's time as "a symptom of decadence." Goebel, *School of Law, Columbia*, 103–4. Even after Columbia allowed the moots to be run by students, interest did not improve at once. Eventually, however, the moots became very popular, drawing 250 participants by 1912–13. But unlike Yale and Michigan, at neither Harvard nor Columbia was moot court part of the early curriculum. Goebel, *School of Law, Columbia*, 179, 471; *Report of the Dean, Yale Law School, 1903–04*, 161, 164; Brown with Blume, *Legal Education at Michigan, 1859–1959*, 505–11.

33. The *Centennial History* suggests that at least one professor, James Barr Ames, was able to transmit to his students a much broader interest through the force of " 'his social conscience, his lofty conception of personal obligation, his legal ideals.' " Appendix 1, 179, quoting Professor Kirchwey of Columbia.

34. The law reviews were usually separate from the curriculum, often (especially at the "better" schools) under total student control; yet there was then, as later, general faculty agreement that the law review was unexcelled as a teaching device. See,

especially, Llewellyn, *The Bramble Bush*, 107. Redlich went so far as to say that law reviews "undoubtedly count for a great deal in the practical success of the case method of teaching." Redlich, *The Case Method*, 33. Harvard's was the first law review, founded in 1887. Warren, *History of the Harvard Law School*, 2:440. Yale followed with the *Yale Law Journal*, in 1891. Hicks, *Yale Law School, 1869–1894*, 65. In 1896, Pennsylvania's Law Department took over the existing *American Law Register* as its journal. Goebel, *School of Law, Columbia*, 430, n. 97. The *Columbia Law Review* was founded in 1901. Ibid., 183–84. Others followed rapidly—some, of course, in a gambit for prestige. See Rodell, "Goodbye to Law Reviews—Revisited," 279. Reed counted forty-two law school journals that were or had been in existence by 1927. Reed, *Present-Day Law Schools*, 566. By 1970, there were over one hundred law reviews published by law schools.

35. Redlich, *The Case Method*, 40.
36. Cited in Goebel, *School of Law, Columbia*, 144.
37. Redlich, *The Case Method*, 49–50.
38. Ibid., 46. The response of law teachers to this aspect of the Redlich Report was interesting. Although most of the leaders of the academic profession were outraged, there were maverick voices. Dean Frederick Woodward argued that "it is no secret that a phonographic record of the so-called case method exercises in the classes of some of the most devoted disciples of Langdell would sound suspiciously like an old-fashioned lecture." 4 *American Law School Review* 99 (1915). Albert Kocourek noted: "The case method is simply one of a number of expedients for learning the law; and in a special way and for a limited object, it is such an efficient expedient that there is danger of coming to think that no other method is possible, or at any rate desirable, for learning anything connected with law." Ibid., 103.
39. He was obviously attracted by Judge Baldwin's characterization of the casebook and the case method: "It is in substance a series of fragmentary portions of opinions from reported cases. . . . No science can be learned purely from particulars. The universals must be studied to discover what the particulars mean and whence they sprang." Cited in Redlich, *The Case Method*, 41.
40. Ibid., 16.
41. Ibid.
42. Overall, the reaction to the Redlich Report showed that the establishment was not willing to listen to criticisms of the case method. Although the Redlich Report said many flattering things about the case method, it was not fulsome enough to satisfy the leaders of the AALS. As would the postwar establishment in response to Reed, the pre-World War I establishment reacted with fury to Redlich's report. The president of the AALS dismissed the critical portions of the report by saying Redlich must have listened to gossip, and others were highly critical of Redlich's conclusions. See "Minutes of the AALS Convention," 4 *American Law School Review* 90 (1915). Harlan Stone, then dean of Columbia Law School and later Supreme Court justice, noted that, "My observation and experience lead me to believe that Redlich lays too great stress on the apparent confusion of the law student in beginning his law study by the case method, and too little stress upon the capacity of instructors in subjects usually taught in the first-year classes in our schools." Ibid., 93. Dean Frederick Woodward claimed that he once participated in a serious attempt to do what Redlich recommended and concluded that it did the first-year student more harm than good. Ibid., 100. Many critics also pointed out that a four-year curriculum, as suggested by Redlich to provide room for more courses, was too long. Similarly, Redlich's criticism of large classes was deemed unreasonable by many. Joseph Beale noted: "The principle of mob psychology in its

best form you will find in a big class; that psychology which leads to our giving to every man added power to think and to reason and to reach individual conclusions." Ibid., 108.

43. 2 *American Law School Review* 312 (1909).

44. E.g., Prof. Dudley McGovney of Tulane, 3 *American Law School Review* 17 (1911).

45. Ibid., 462–74 (1913).

46. "Except in the sense of practicability there was nothing startingly original in this idea." Reed, *Training for the Law*, 371.

47. Ibid., 373–74.

48. Ibid., 374–77.

49. Ibid., 379.

50. "There was no provision for practical training in advising clients or in conducting litigation, but only for the acquisition of theoretical knowledge; . . . no attention paid here to government or borderland subjects, but only to technical private laws; no interest here in the statutory enactments of legislatures, but only in the decisions that judges had made; and within the field of judge-made law only the generalized principles of the so-called national law were to be studied, to the exclusion of concrete local rules that might be quite inconsistent. The omitted portions were relegated to after life. The product of any educational system must continue to grow intellectually, to keep up with the development of his specialty after his student days. But a lawyer has to do more than merely keep up with the development of the law; he has to catch up with the law as it was even when he was in the law school." Ibid., 379–80.

51. Ibid., 388.

52. Ibid., 380.

53. Ibid., 382.

54. "Either, on the one hand, the method is none the less attempted, and something which is neither a good case method nor a good textbook or lecture school results. Or the method is not employed, but the school, whether through ignorance or from motives of expediency, misleads prospective students as to the type of education it provides. . . . The vogue that Harvard methods now enjoy, especially among college presidents who wish their law schools to conform to prevailing styles, is by no means an unmixed blessing." Ibid., 381.

55. In 1915, Pope noted during the AALS convention that "it seems to me that the practicing lawyer and the professor have been getting further and further apart all the time." "Minutes of the AALS Convention," 4 *American Law School Review* 90, 108 (1915). In 1929, during his attack on the elite schools of the ABA, the dean of the John Marshall Law School in Chicago unequivocally stated: "I do not believe that the law should be taught only . . . by professional law teachers who have never tried a case in court or had a single client. I do not believe the American Bar Association should directly or indirectly endorse any system of legal education, or method of instruction, or dictate the number of 'full time' professors that should teach in a law school." Address by Edward T. Lee before the ABA Section of Legal Education, 10 October 1929. John Marshall Law School Archives, Chicago, Ill.

56. See Redlich, *The Case Method*, 49–50:

> Undoubtedly this work of making from out of the almost incalculable mass of published cases . . . a continually better selection of those which are to be used in teaching, and of arranging these again systematically in the case-books, has been performed admirably. But, on the other hand, it is equally certain that this kind of literary activity has prevented many forceful writers among American law teachers

from cultivating the fields of legal history and dogmatic literature as fruitfully as they might otherwise have done.

57. Johnson, *Schooled Lawyers*, xvii.
58. Robinson, *A Study of Legal Education*, 15.
59. Holmes, "The Use and Meaning of Law Schools, and Their Methods of Instruction," 919, 922.
60. Ibid., 920.
61. Ibid., 921.
62. Edward T. Lee was born in Connecticut in 1861, the son of Irish immigrants who had emigrated during the potato famine. After his father, a small businessman, was ruined in the panic of 1873, Edward worked his way through Hartford High School and then Harvard College. As a result of the need to earn money, he was twenty-five when he graduated from Harvard. He then became legal secretary to Senator Platt of Connecticut and while he held that appointment he was a night student at Columbian (George Washington) Law School. Graduating at the age of thirty-three, he began practice in Buffalo and then in 1898 moved to Chicago, both practicing and working for the *Chicago Legal News*. In 1899, he was among a group of lawyers who founded the John Marshall Law School, which was intended to be a day school catering to clerks in law offices who had "release time" to study law. When the first executive (dean), Webster, left shortly after its founding, Lee took over the school, turned it into a night school, and by 1904 had 137 students. The core of Lee's seven principles was that "the processes of the administration of justice can be open to all only if all persons, regardless of race, language, economic status, etc., can avail themselves of these processes through advocates of their own kind." "In Memoriam Edward T. Lee, 1861–1943," 7 *Alumni Docket* 2 (1944). John Marshall Law School Archives, Chicago, Ill.

8 / The Legal Culture and
Legal Theory: The Social Sciences
and All That

As the legal practitioners and academics fought to define the structure, style, and method of legal education over the years, a more subtle change was taking place in American law. The view of what the law itself was, its logic and structure, went through a series of metamorphoses in the course of the nation's development. In the period of Jacksonian Democracy, there had appeared in this country an essentially indigenous legal culture and, arguably, a conscious break with the English past. This break proved to be, as might have been expected, only temporary. By the latter part of the nineteenth century, as Dwight and Langdell helped restore formal training to the legal profession, there was a subtle shift back to a much more English approach to the law, despite the fact that the English legal culture had itself changed in the previous half century.[1] In the 1880s and 1890s, American judges seemed to be imitating the increasingly formalistic English approach to law, with its heavy emphasis on the law as a series of interrelated objective rules motivated exclusively by an internal logic of their own.[2] This approach, casting the judges as the guardians of preexisting neutral rules of law, was blessed by the new breed of academics from Harvard,[3] especially men like Eugene Wambaugh[4] and Joseph Beale.[5] Certainly there were increasing links between England and North America at this time. Holmes and at least some of his fellow judges were in frequent touch with leading English lawyers and judges. The English idea of the common law as a self-sustaining body and even as a mystical force in its own right had reappeared in America.

In England, however, there was a tiny bench (in 1900, there were only twenty-five High Court judges), a small and tightly organized bar (in 1900, there were about one thousand active barristers), a highly centralized legal system (all the judges, most of the barristers, and most of the important litigation were in London),[6] and a highly selective method of law reporting.[7] Moreover, as collectivism began to replace laissez-faire as the dominant English political philosophy, the judges and lawyers were increasingly excluded from sensitive and important aspects of the decision-making process.[8] None of these features applied in this country, and the flirtation with re-Anglicizing the American legal culture, at least in doctrinal terms, was doomed to failure. There was a limit to the influence of even the Harvard Law School.

By 1880, when the population, at 50,155,783, was only twice the size of England's, there were 64,137 lawyers in the United States. By 1910, with a population of 91,972,266, there were no fewer than 122,149.[9] The extraordinary number of jurisdictions and judges in the United States made highly unlikely the same kind of manageable case law as in England; the establishment of the National Reporter System by the West Publishing Company in 1879, designed to produce exhaustive rather than selective reporting, assured that anything like the English approach was bound to perish.[10] English judges found it relatively easy to appear to select precedents only from a clear-cut stream of cases, whereas American judges had a wide area of selection, which emphasized their creative discretionary role. Moreover, at the very moment English judges were being denied a role in public law (for instance the Trade Disputes Act of 1906 put labor law beyond the reach of judges), American judges were increasingly called on to handle quasi-political issues.

By early in the twentieth century, there was little doubt that, despite ABA rhetoric to the contrary, the legal cultures of the two countries had diverged noticeably.[11] Although some of the implications for the judiciary of parliamentary democracy were not clear at the time, it was not difficult to chronicle the changes in such things as legal publishing.[12] In 1915, Harlan Fiske Stone argued that "unless courts set some restraints on the length and number of published opinions, it is inevitable that our present system of making the law reports the chief repository of our unwritten law will break down."[13] In 1924, Benjamin Cardozo suggested that "the fecundity of our case law would make Malthus stand aghast."[14] The courts did not impose restraints, and the publishers of law reports remained both unselective and overfertile. With numbers of lawyers and reported cases both far in excess of those in England, any attempt to emulate the English legal culture was doomed to failure irrespective of social and political differences. Indeed, during this very period these same conditions subtly altered the American approach to legal reasoning.

The strict approach to common law, characteristic of the Harvardizers of the late nineteenth century, was fading away. In its place, American law became associated with precedents rather than principles and with ad hoc rationalizations, as the judges moved from case to case.[15] Instead of attempting to discover "the underlying theory of law," the American lawyer looked "for cases 'on all fours,'" cases whose facts duplicated as closely as possible the ones from the case at hand.[16] Some writers point to the West Publishing Company, with its indiscriminate publication of cases, as the leading assassin in this passing of the strict approach to the common law.[17] It may well be, however, that the case method of teaching was an equally important conspirator. Redlich certainly thought so, although Reed, who was no uncritical admirer of the method, was more skeptical.[18] Redlich's claim that guilt lay with the case method was repeated both by a special ABA committee in 1916[19] and by Arthur Goodhart in 1930.[20] Despite the efforts, beginning in the 1890s, of the National Conference of Commissioners on Uniform State Laws to produce statutes (especially in commercial areas) that might be adopted in all states, and, despite the work of the American Law Institute early in this century to codify basic common-law principles in its series of doctrinal "Restatements," the United States was becoming the most common of the common-law countries.

Whether or not the case method was a major contributor to the atomistic approach to the common law—which is peculiarly American at least in its intensity—the law schools were certainly the major beneficiaries of the breakdown of a monistic theory of law. Although they had done little to develop legal theory, the leading law schools generally appeared as the entity most likely to save the system and the profession from the confusion into which it had been thrown by the gradual collapse of formal legal reasoning. Prodded by the interest of business and commerce, academic lawyers had joined practitioners in the formation of the American Law Institute;[21] together, they produced the Restatements, which it was hoped would replace "the wilderness of single instance" that the American common law had become.[22] Academics like Samuel Williston were also at the center of the work of the Uniform Commissioners. In the process, and partly for want of competition from the bench or from a narrow elite of barristers, the leading academics strengthened their position of intellectual leadership in the legal life of the country.[23] Writing in 1922, Max Weber differentiated "legal honoratiores" in Germany and in England: in Germany, the intellectual leaders of the legal profession were the legal educators; in England, they were the leading advocates.[24] In America the Continental patterns of prestige had reappeared.

Arthur Goodhart, an American who became professor of Jurisprudence at Oxford in 1930, highlighted the contrast by explaining that "the English teacher emphasizes what the judge has said: the American professor explains what the judge should have said."[25] Typical of this vacuum and the way the academics seem destined to move into it was Herman Oliphant's presidential address to the AALS in 1927. Republished under the title, "A Return to *Stare Decisis*," it became particularly important in the intellectual debates of the following decade. In Oliphant's words, "not the judges' opinions, but which way they decide cases, will be the dominant subject matter of any truly scientific study of law. This is the field for scholarly work worthy of [the] best talents."[26] The law professors, not the judges, liked to feel they were the final arbiters of "the law."

Intellectually, in the period after 1870, the law schools had attempted to embrace a kind of Germanic "scientism" while retaining an Anglophilic and Anglophonic facade. By the 1920s, not only had the facade cracked but its base of scientism was also facing the challenge of indigenous intellectual developments. Only certain schools recognized this change. Those that did, however, used the impact of new developments and their potential power to raise themselves to positions of prominence. These institutions were to have the dominant influence on the remaking of the American legal culture.

World War I veterans, returning to the so-called national law schools, found that a flirtation with the new "soft" sciences was underway. This flirtation, together with the only serious attempt to rework the whole of the law school curriculum and the rise of an amorphous state of mind known as the "Realist Movement," formed the three strands woven into the fabric of the intellectually stimulating decades of the twenties and thirties.

To pretend that all this was a total break with the past is to misunderstand the evolution of legal cultures. After all, the ABA owed its existence at least in part to the prompting of the American Social Science Association. Although Harvard and its followers had initially rejected the importance of the social sciences for the sake of a "pure" and "scientific" law, it had long since been clear to the rising generation of young academics that the Langdellian claims that all law could be found in the books and that law was a series of logically interwoven objective principles were, at most, useful myths. As early as 1880, Holmes had talked of "the necessary instability and inconsistency of any given state of the law."[27] In 1910, Roscoe Pound was already repeating fears about legal educators being "legal monks" and pleading for training in sociology, economics, and politics to "fit new generations of lawyers to lead the people."[28] Moreover, the work of Walter W. Cook, Arthur Corbin, and Wesley Hohfeld at Yale[29] (together with Cardozo's Storrs lectures at that school)[30] in the second dacade of the twentieth century had underlined in a more scholarly way the need for a broader scholarship and, by implication, a revised curriculum.

The year 1916 provides a useful date for suggesting that the social sciences were beginning to affect the increasingly ivory-towered law school. It was in that year that Thomas Swan became dean of the Yale Law School. By November of that year the Law School had presented to President Theodore Woolsey of Yale a printed proposal for expanding the Yale Law School into the Yale School of Law and Jurisprudence.[31] The purpose of this change was to emphasize the threefold purpose of the Law School: "the study of law and its evolution, historically, comparatively, analytically, and critically, with the purpose of directing its development in the future, improving its administration and perfecting its methods of legislation." Much of the document appeared to reflect the views of Arthur Corbin,[32] but it may also have been influenced by the hand of a precocious student—Karl Llewellyn.

The details of the proposal expounded the need to achieve the "scientific and constructive purpose." In addition to calling for a $2,500,000 endowment, the paper recommended heavy scholarly emphasis on criminology, administrative law, international law, Roman law, and in such courses as "Historical Comparative Analytical and Functional Jurisprudence" and "The Science and Art of Legislation."[33] Such goals highlighted the potential conflict between the scholarly and the professional. By promoting courses outside Harvard's vision of pure law, Yale was once again overtly presenting legal education with the dilemma that it had always been reluctant to face directly. Was the law school essentially a professional school, or was it instead an academic area of the university? Or was it both?

Dean Swan would have responded that a law school had a moral duty to fulfill both functions. In 1920, he made this clear:

> A university law school has two functions. It aims by the case
> method of instruction to train its students so that they may become
> successful practitioners in their chosen profession. It aims also or
> at least it should aim, though too few schools have recognized this
> obligation, to aid in improving the law by scientific and analyti-
> cal study of existing laws, by comparative study of the jurisprudence
> of other countries, by criticism of defects and suggestion for im-
> provement in the administration of law and in methods of legisla-
> tion, and by relating law to other institutions of human society. . . .
> It is the duty of a university law school to emphasize through re-
> search and publication by its faculty and through the character of its
> instruction, this broader base of legal education, as well as to give
> the merely professional training.[34]

A Yale Law School with such a broad mandate, however, seems to have been at least a somewhat premature vision. Despite Swan's "Harvardization" and an increasingly impressive list of faculty members, the Yale Law School in the early 1920s was still to all intents and purposes a Connecticut school with out-of-state students, and it was intellectually overshadowed by Harvard and Columbia.[35] It is to these latter two institutions, therefore, that one has to look for new waves in legal scholarship during the era of prohibition and unfettered capitalism.

In 1916, the same year that Swan came to Yale, Roscoe Pound became dean of the Harvard Law School. Although he had never earned a law degree (he attended Harvard Law School for one year), he had practiced in Nebraska while earning a Ph.D. in botany. He then taught botany at the University of Nebraska before his move to the Harvard Law School. Universally considered one of the enigmas of American legal education, Pound's beliefs defy consistent analysis.[36] His claims to the deanship rested partly on his "Causes of Discontent" speech.[37] No one wrote more about the "emergence of the Law,"[38] the "spirit of the Law," "social engineering," and the like.[39] He was considered the leader of "the revolt against formalism" in the field of law, and some would say he was the harbinger of legal Realism.[40] He, however, concurrently presided over the Harvard Law School in its full flight of formalistic Hessian training, and later he would be attacked by the Realists as "an arch-reactionary."[41]

The author of "The Scope and Purpose of Sociological Jurisprudence"[42] was in many ways a strange man.[43] Intellectually, he attacked the legal Realists when—insofar as they took a single approach—they appeared to be putting flesh on the bones of "social engineering."[44] A man hired as a progressive, in the sense that he was committed to the reform of the legal system, turned out to be a coward when, as dean, he was asked to stand up for civil liberties. He would not support Felix Frankfurter when the latter was accused of left-wing leanings primarily in connection with the Sacco-Vanzetti defense, nor did he respond to President Lowell's public anti-Semitism.[45] Pound's lack of courage alienated Frankfurter, and his authoritarian running of the Law School lost him the support of other faculty members as well.[46] Pound became an admirer of Hitler, calling him "a man who can bring them [the central Europeans] freedom from agitating 'movements,'" as well as a critic of the New Deal,[47] and by 1936 most were relieved to see him give up the deanship.

To pin down Pound intellectually is almost as difficult as trying to pin him down politically. He was an ardent supporter of the American Law Institute and its work with the Restatements, regarding it not merely as an effort to produce a national legal system but also as an effort to beat back the Realist movement. Despite all the calls for reform in legal education, a number of which he made early in his own career, Pound was apparently wedded to large classes[48] and saw no reason to make changes in the curriculum.[49] Indeed, his successful fund-raising as dean was in part the result of his implicit promise to leave Langdell's LL.B. untouched. Instead, his increases in the endowment went into institutes[50] and the graduate program, which Edward H. ("Bull") Warren thought would be the death of the Harvard Law School.[51] In response, the LL.B. students soon began to rebel against the conventionality of this otherwise unconventional man. Not only did graduates flock to Washington to serve the New Deal[52] but, by 1935, the Harvard student body attacked the case method as well as the overall blandness of the Law School during the curriculum study of that year.[53]

If Pound himself is difficult to categorize or if his views are difficult to define, so is his impact on legal education. Although he inspired ideas of reform, he did little to advance change himself. Pound's writings supplied a terminology for advocates of a broadened law school curriculum,[54] yet his actions so alienated others, especially Frankfurter and his followers, that they could only succeed in their reform measures by rejecting him. As for innovations at Harvard itself, Pound advocated the study of extra-legal topics but only by prelaw students or graduate law students. The curriculum for the LL.B. was seen as sacrosanct. Although Yale achieved no radical reform in the 1920s, neither did the nation's most prestigious school, which in most ways remained Langdell's school.

Despite Swan's naive hopes and Pound's pretensions, the frontier of legal scholarship during the 1920s was at Columbia. At the end of World War I, Columbia's curriculum had been a conventional one.[55] But in 1922–23, functionally organized courses[56] began to appear in legal economics and trade regulation. "It was the development of [these courses], with their challenge to the accepted taxonomy of the law and their disturbing impact on the unity and the proportions of the curriculum, which was directly responsible for the extensive studies which the faculty undertook four years later."[57] A faculty group, led by Herman Oliphant, and emphasizing economics, began the process of rethinking the curriculum. The dean of Columbia, Harlan Fiske Stone, was at least somewhat sympathetic to "sociological jurisprudence." In discussing the problems of legal education in his *Dean's Report* for 1923, he noted that "we have failed to recognize as clearly as we might that law is nothing more than a form of social control intimately related to those social functions which are the subject matter of economics and the social sciences generally."[58] Soon the pace and approach to reform were changing. By 1926, the faculty was prepared to take the plunge,[59] and it called in an outside Curriculum Committee chairman, Leon Marshall, professor of political economy at the University of Chicago.[60] The whole of the curriculum was to be organized along functional lines, and for two years the faculty labored in ten groups[61] to produce an entirely new law school curriculum.

Today the idea of "functional" held by the Columbia faculty may seem dated, but the scope of the attempt was indeed remarkable. An outline of the results of the work by the various groups and committees under Marshall was put together by Oliphant, and it appeared in 1928 under the title *Summary of Studies in Legal Education by the Faculty of Law of Columbia University.* In an introductory essay, Oliphant explained the background of the report and then went on to summarize the problems of legal education as perceived at Columbia.[62] Analysis of these problems had led the Columbia faculty to recognize that

> the time has come for at least one school to become a "community
> of scholars," devoting itself to the non-professional study of law,
> in order that the function of law may be comprehended, its re-
> sults evaluated, and its development kept more nearly in step with
> the complex developments of modern life. This means not merely a
> broadening of the content of the legal curriculum, and not merely
> a graduate school in law added to the regular course; it means
> an entirely different approach to the law. It involves critical, con-
> structive, creative work by both faculty and students rather than
> a regime devoted primarily to the acquisition of information.[63]

The body of the report went on to describe the structure and approach of a law program designed to meet these criteria.[64] Overall, it was a courageous document, facing many of the inherent conflicts in legal education posed by the immense success of Langdell's method, and although it was slanted toward the needs of business, the Columbia study must still rank as the most important ever made in American legal education. Although the grand design failed, interesting by-products emerged, including case books organized around functional themes and including material far broader than appellate decisions. If most of the recommendations of the study were never implemented, in 1937, Dean Smith was able to conclude that the study had "presented the most pervasive analysis and challenging discussion of legal education that had been put forth up to that time. While many of the proposals contained in that document have since been modified or rejected by the Columbia faculty, it nevertheless served as a basis for experimentation during the succeeding years by our own Faculty and it stimulated similar inquiries and activities in other schools."[65] Translating from the decanal prose, it may be safely said that, though the report was generally admired as an elegant idea, Columbia had returned to a state that would have appealed more to Dwight or Keener than to Oliphant or

Douglas. The first (and most serious) attempt to turn a law school into a scholarly institution had failed.

At least two major reasons for the failure must be distinguished.[66] The first was the conflict, generated by the study, about the purpose of legal education, a conflict that inevitably led to a violent faculty split.[67] Second, the new approach assumed not only that the traditional categories of law were irrelevant but also that law could only be taught as an integral part of the social sciences: "It is both feasible and desirable for Columbia Law School to pursue both the 'community of scholars' objective and the 'training for public service in the law' objective. There should be set up a 're-search school' at Columbia University, to be operated in conjunction with a 'training school,' only the latter to be financed out of the University's funds."[68]

Whatever the merits of those two concepts, it was early seen that they could not help but undermine Columbia's efficiency in producing practicing lawyers. Nor were the advocates of the new approach prepared to hide their light under a bushel. Many of them were attracted to the idea of Columbia as an institution devoted predominantly, and perhaps even exclusively, to research. This was too much for Dean Smith. Although he was willing to have a few full-time researchers, "whatever may be said in favor of establishing elsewhere a school or institute devoted exclusively to research in law, the present important position now occupied by Columbia Law School in the field of legal education, coupled with the fact that it is outstanding as a first-grade professional school in the state of New York, makes it socially desirable that it should not relinquish its hold upon prospective members of the Bar."[69] The die was cast. Was it possible to be both legal scholar and scholar of the law? Was all the important work to be done on the borderline of law and the other social sciences? Hessel Yntema, William O. Douglas, Herman Oliphant, and Underhill Moore thought so; they resigned. The Johns Hopkins Institute for the Study of Law and the Yale Law School became the frontiers of legal education.[70]

There was another reason, however, in addition to the clash between responsibilities to the profession and to scholarship, that caused the Columbia experiment to fail. In truth, the social sciences had been oversold. They proved to be of far less help to the legal scholar than had been expected.[71] Columbia's attempt at an interweaving of social sciences data about the family with family law, for example, revealed that little data was available about the modern family; extensive research would have to precede any possible reorganization. Dean Smith spent much of his report for 1930 explaining that the integration of law and social science was easier said than done: "It has not been an uncommon experience for the dissatisfied legal scholar, who has made excursions into the realm of economics, or philosophy, or of psychology, to return with a feeling of relief to the more settled and orderly domain of the law."[72]

Dean Smith was not alone in his skepticism about the value of the integration attempts. At Yale, curriculum changes in the 1920s were initiated during the deanship of Robert M. Hutchins (1927–29)[73] while Hutchins engaged in interdisciplinary research on the basic principles of evidence with members of the Institute of Human Relations.[74] In 1934, however, Hutchins, by then president of the University of Chicago, recalled that "what we actually discovered was that psychology had dealt with very few of the points raised by the law of evidence; and that the basic psychological problem of the law of evidence, what will affect juries, and in what way, was one psychology had never touched at all."[75] Even by the time he wrote this, the lamp had already been handed on.

Those members of the Columbia faculty who saw the need for an institute of research had set off on a new venture. Oliphant and Yntema joined Walter W. Cook and Leon Marshall in founding the Johns Hopkins Institute for the Study of Law. As the founders continued their own projects and began studies of judicial administration in Maryland, New York, and Ohio, the institute slowly took shape.[76] It had, however, been funded in 1928 for only five years, during which time the depression and other problems dashed its founders' hopes.[77] As a result, it represented a somewhat unfair test of whether an empirically oriented research institute was needed, justified, or supportable in the American legal scene.[78]

Meanwhile, two of the Columbia faculty—Douglas and Moore—headed off to Yale.[79] Underhill Moore became involved not only in his studies of banking[80] but in what appeared in retrospect to be faintly unrealistic empirical studies of parking offenses in New Haven.[81] For a while he was joined in such empirical work by Charles Clark, by then dean of Yale Law School, who worked on judicial administration in Connecticut[82] and on an abortive attempt to conduct a national survey of the bar.[83] More typical of what made Yale famous in the 1930s was the work of William O. Douglas. Before leaving for the Securities and Exchange Commission and ultimately the Supreme Court, Douglas had joined with others to establish Yale as the enfant terrible of legal education.[84]

No cow was too sacred to be attacked. Inferiority feelings about the Harvard Law School and analytical scholarship were turned to good advantage in the form of often violent attacks on unsuspecting victims.[85] The work of Charles Clark, William O. Douglas, Abe Fortas, Walton Hamilton, Wesley Sturges, Edward Robinson, and others during these years poured scorn on centuries of doctrinal scholarship.[86] Much of the scorn was justified. American legal thought had been dominated by a pedestrian search for certainty, a misguided urge to emulate the English bench and bar, and an obsessive belief in the ability to contain doctrines within written rules. There was a legitimate revulsion against many aspects of Langdell's case method of teaching.[87] The Yale critics, however, were themselves often unconstructive. Straw men were set up with careless abandon. Much of what the Restaters—a favorite target of the Yale faculty—were trying to do, by way of consolidating basic principles of the common law in different areas, was indeed naive.[88] Harking back to medieval precedents, when that occurred, was not relevant to an America beset by the depression. Across the Atlantic Wittgenstein was demonstrating the absurdity of attempting to put language in a straitjacket, yet the Restaters pressed on. The alternatives offered by the Yale critics, however, whether in terms of intellectual or pedagogical goals, were largely nonexistent. The Yale faculty's "general attitude was against dogma of all kinds."[89] At times the intellectual base seemed no more than rebellion against Harvard and what legal education had stood for during the previous seventy-five years.

Current research is elucidating some aspects of the puzzle. Working from the Yale Law School archives, John Henry Schlegel has traced the gradual disillusionment of Deans Hutchins and Clark with the fact-gathering aspects of the interaction of law and the social sciences.[90] He has also stripped away fact from fiction where the indefatigable Underhill Moore is concerned.[91] To a large degree, his research has chronicled the failure of empiricism and social science to fulfill the Yale faculty's desire to create a "sociological jurisprudence." In the face of the shortcomings of their new approach, many turned to new interests. The government agencies of the New Deal were particularly attractive, and Yale lost a number of its faculty through their defection to FDR.[92] There appeared to be a symbiotic relationship between Realism and the New Deal. Even by the mid-1930s, although the rhetoric remained shrill, the reality of Yale's commitment to research and innovation had worn thin. The Yale Law School of those days, contrary to the mythology, was a socially (and increasingly intellectually) elite institution.[93] Although the school trimmed a little financially, it continued to pay its professors well and actually increased the size of its student body steadily throughout the depression.[94] There was a great deal of partying (even before the repeal of the eighteenth amendment), and *Yale Law Journal* editors were regarded as social outcasts if they spent the weekend in New Haven rather than socializing in New York.[95] It was an atmosphere that was sympathetic to an intellectual trend away from principle and toward manipulation.

NOTES

1. Oliver Wendell Holmes' review of Langdell's first edition of *Cases on Contracts* was largely complimentary. 5 *American Law Review* 539 (1871). By the time of the second edition, Holmes still viewed Langdell positively but with a more questioning eye. "Mr. Langdell's ideal in the law, the end of all his striving, is the *elegantia juris* or logical integrity of the system as a system. He is, perhaps, the greatest living legal theologian, he is less concerned with his postulates than to show that the conclusions from them hang together." 14 *American Law Review* 233 (1880). Holmes would later say:

> What has been said will explain the failure of all theories which consider the law only from its formal side, whether they attempt to deduce the *corpus* from *a priori* postulates, or fall into the humbler error of supposing the science of the law to reside in the *elegantia juris*, or logical cohesion of part with part. The truth is, that the law is always approaching and never reaching, consistency. It is forever adopting new principles from life at one end, and it always retains *old ones* from history at the other, which have not yet been absorbed or sloughed off. It will become entirely consistent only when it ceases to grow. [Holmes, *The Common Law*, 32]

2. Later American writers were to describe this as a case of Grand Style giving way to the Formal Style. See Dawson, *The Oracles of the Law*, 88–89. Gilmore notes the transition as one from an "Age of Discovery" to an "Age of Faith." Gilmore, *Ages of American Law*, chaps. 2, 3. Karl Llewellyn attributes the height of the Formal Style to the period between Wambaugh's publication of *The Study of Cases* and its reissue by Cooley in 1909. Karl Llewellyn also attempted to show that things became "better" after 1909 as American judges returned to the Grand Style and ignored the formalism of Wambaugh. Some of the contrast between the modern English and American styles of jurisprudence may be gained by noting the comments on the *Study of Cases* by a leading English scholar fifty years later: "The book appeared in the United States as long ago as 1894 but it is still of great value even to an English reader." Cross, *Precedent in English Law*, 50.

3. For Holmes' early travels in England, see Howe, *Justice Oliver Wendell Holmes*, vol. 1, chap 7; vol. 2, chap. 6. For his later familiarity with the English scene, see Howe, ed., *Holmes-Pollock Correspondence*, passim (1961), and Howe, ed., *Holmes-Laski Correspondence*, passim (1953). Meanwhile, in 1898, Lord Coleridge began the tradition of English lords chief justice and lords chancellor visiting the United States, normally in connection with meetings of the American Bar Association. Heuston, *Lives of the Lord Chancellors, 1885–1940*, 124. The Oxford law faculty (e.g., Pollock, Maine) was well known to the federal judiciary and both Dicey and Bryce dedicated books to President Eliot of Harvard. Anson's *Law of Contracts* went through several American editions, including one edited by Arthur Corbin. One example of the exchange of information between the countries was the publication in the English *Law Quarterly Review* (edited by Frederick Pollock) of Langdell's speech at the quarter millennial celebration of Harvard University in 1886. See 3 *Law Quarterly Review* 123–26 (1887).

4. See Wambaugh, *The Study of Cases*, especially pp. 17–18.

5. On Joseph Beale, see especially Cohen, *American Thought*, 154, describing Beale as a "legal fundamentalist." Cohen puts Samuel Williston into essentially the same class.

6. There were of course more lower court judges and solicitors, but their influence on the legal culture at that time was relatively insignificant. See Abel-Smith and Stevens, *Lawyers and the Courts*, pt. 2.

7. Sir Frederick Pollock was editor of the official English *Law Reports* from 1894 until the 1930s. He edited the judges' prose ruthlessly and, more important still, published only select cases on appeal and very few at first instance. See, for example, *Holmes-Pollock Correspondence*, 2:145, 183. Pollock allegedly kept a drawer of "bad law"—cases where judges had failed to apply the law scientifically. In this way he did more effectively for English law what Langdell originally had hoped for as a goal of his system.

8. For an analysis of the growing formalism of the English legal culture, see Abel-Smith and Stevens, *Lawyers and the Courts*, chap. 6; and Stevens, *Law and Politics*, passim.

9. Reed, *Training for the Law*, 442.

10. The West Publishing Company's National Reporter System published all United States Supreme Court reports, all Circuit Court of Appeals cases, some inferior federal court reports, and all cases in state courts of last resort. Eventually it would also publish intermediate court reports, at least in the larger states.

11. This was as evident in legal education itself as in the broader field of American law. In 1886, the *Albany Law Journal* was enthusiastically reporting, in an article containing some considerable inaccuracies, that Queen's College, Cambridge, was opening a law school that would teach by the case method. A general interest in law programs, especially those of England, was manifested around the turn of the century in such articles as Walton, "Notes on the Early History of Legal Studies in England," 601–6. Such articles raised the hopes that the system contained enough similarities that each might be able to adopt to advantage the different aspects of the other.

12. See, for instance, the writings of Arthur L. Goodhart, an American who emigrated to England in the 1920s. Writing in 1930, he noted: "It has become almost traditional for lawyers who deal with the subject of Anglo-American relations to emphasize the fact that one of the fundamental bonds between England and the United States is the common law. It is my purpose to suggest that this bond is a weakening one and that even at the present time there is a marked divergence between the English and the American attitude to the most characteristic doctrine of the common law—the doctrine of *stare decisis*." Goodhart, "Case Law in England and America," 173. See, especially, 186, where he noted that in the United States there were 350 volumes of law reports published annually; in England, there were 6.

13. Stone, *Law and its Administration*, 214.

14. Cardozo, *The Growth of the Law*, 4.

15. Morris Cohen opined: "Though American experience in law-making has been extraordinarily rich in novelty and diversity, our contributions to legal philosophy have been impressive neither in quality nor in quantity." Cohen, *American Thought*, 135.

16. Reed, *Training for the Law*, 370; Gilmore, "Legal Realism," 1027, 1041–42.

17. Gilmore, *The Ages of American Law*, 59. Strangely little has been written about the West Publishing Company; but see Mayer, *The Lawyers*, chap. 12 (1967).

18. Reed, *Training for the Law*, 369–70. He too attributed the American view of the common law to the exhaustive reporting of decisions and to "a corresponding deterioration in their quality. . . . [T]he confusion of obsolescent law in the older decisions was increased by the confusion of bad law in the newer decisions. . . . Case law, which had always been chaotic in its arrangement, now became illogical in its substance as well. . . . Yet still the theory was preserved that all this mass of material was relevant and authoritative, that a new case could not be decided on its merits, but only in the light of previous decisions made upon a similar state of facts. Hence arose the eager search for the case 'on all fours'—the case, that is to say, in which the state of facts was precisely the same. . . ."

"This degradation of the old common-law theory was an evil that, once started, was bound to become steadily worse. The more logically inconsistent became the decisions, the stronger became the temptation to conceal this inconsistency by accentuating the letter rather than the spirit of the case. The greater the number of decisions that had been rendered, the greater the likelihood that one could be found precisely in point. The more needful it seemed to find this closest possible parallel case, the greater was the demand for access to the largest and most up-to-date collection of decisions. . . . The low educational standards of the bench and bar have contributed to this shift of attention from principles to precedent, but the mere bulk of the law is the dominant reason." Ibid., 374–76.

19. 2 *American Bar Association Journal* 623 (1916).
20. "A moot court in the Inns of Court or at Cambridge University . . . is . . . bound by English precedents, and it must follow the principles laid down in these whether it believes them to be correct or not. The American law student, having been taught not the law of a single jurisdiction but the principles of a number of jurisdictions, is less inclined to believe in the authority of precedents than is his English brother. His critical faculty has been sharpened to such an extent that he regards every judicial opinion with suspicion. With such a background, his devotion to the doctrine of *stare decisis* must be far weaker than is that of the English student who has been taught to accept the doctrine contained in a case as laying down the law. It is only natural that in later life, when the student has become a practicing lawyer or a judge, he will be profoundly influenced by his early training." Goodhart, *Essays in Jurisprudence and the Common Law*, 70–71.
21. Samuel Williston of Harvard was the drafter of the Uniform Sales Act, promulgated in 1906. He later became the chief reporter for the *Restatement on Contracts* of the American Law Institute. The founder of the institute itself was William Draper Lewis, then dean of the Law School of the University of Pennsylvania.
22. In speaking of his early judicial career, Cardozo depicted the results of this confusion graphically:

> I was much troubled in spirit, in my first years on the bench, to find how trackless was the ocean on which I had embarked. I sought for certainty. I was oppressed and disheartened when I found that the quest for it was futile. I was trying to reach land, the solid land of fixed and settled rules, the paradise of a justice that would declare itself by tokens plainer and more commanding than its pale and glimmering reflections in my own vacillating mind and conscience. [Cardozo, *The Nature of the Judicial Process*, 166.]

23. "Statutes like the Uniform Sales Act were not statutes at all. . . . Drafted in terms of loose and vague generality, they were designed to provide access to the prevailing academic wisdom. The rules for decision in sales cases were to be found, not in the Uniform Sales Act . . . but in Professor Williston's treatise on the law of sales. . . . [T]he courts—and counsel—paid no attention at all to the Sales Act; they paid enormous attention to Professor Williston's treatise." Gilmore, *Ages of American Law*, 71–72.
24. Max Weber, *Law in Economy and Society*, chap. 7, especially 203.
25. Goodhart, *Essays in Jurisprudence and the Common Law.*
26. 14 *American Bar Association Journal* 71 (1928).
27. Gilmore, *Ages of American Law*, 52.
28. Cited Auerbach, *Unequal Justice*, 82–83.
29. Schlegel saw this trio, working together under Dean Swan, as the nucleus of "a respectable and even promising law school attached to what was otherwise an unintellectual, overgrown college." Schlegel, "American Legal Realism," 464–65. William

Twining credits Corbin and Hohfeld with the following convictions, articulated in an editorial in the *Yale Law Journal*:

"The first of these is that the rules of human action that we know as law are constantly changing, that no system of human justice is eternal, that law forms but a part of our ever-changing social *mores*, and that it is the function of lawyers, of jurists and of law schools to cause the statement and the application of our legal rules to be in harmony with the *mores* of the present instead of those of an outgrown past. The second matter upon which emphasis has been placed, and the one perhaps which has been most obvious in recent pages of the *Journal* has been the necessity of a more exact terminology leading to a more accurate legal analysis." [Cited in Twining, *Karl Llewellyn and the Realist Movement*, 27]

Cook was a firm believer in "scientific empirical research into legal processes":

"Underlying any scientific study of the law, it is submitted, will lie one fundamental postulate, viz., that human laws are vices, tools which society uses as one of its methods to regulate human conduct and to promote those types of it which are regarded as desirable. If so, it follows that the worth or value of a given rule of law can be determined only by finding out how it works, that is, by ascertaining so far as that can be done, whether it promotes or retards the attainment of desired ends. If this is to be done, quite clearly we must know what at any given period these ends are and also whether the means selected, the given rules of law, are indeed adapted to securing them." [Cited in Twining, *Karl Llewellyn and the Realist Movement*, 38]

30. Cardozo, *The Nature of the Judicial Process*.
31. In the 1960s, President Martin Myerson of SUNY at Buffalo renamed the Buffalo School of Law. Its name became the Buffalo School of Law and Jurisprudence, and its dean became provost of the "new" institution.
32. Corbin, "The Law and the Judges," 234.
33. *Yale Alumni Weekly*, 23 March 1917. Two years earlier, Dean Rogers had requested money to expand Yale into a school for the comparative study of the world's legal systems. *Report of the Dean, Yale Law School, 1914–15*, 319, 321. See also Hohfeld's call for the establishment of a "Vital School of Law and Jurisprudence." Hohfeld, *Fundamental Legal Conceptions*, ed. Cook, 332.
34. *Report of the Dean, Yale Law School, 1919–20*, 393–94. See also his view that "in all the universities closer connection should be established between the schools of law and the departments of social sciences, political science, economics, history, and psychology." See also Swan, "Reconstruction and the Legal Profession," 794. "In these years," the official Yale historian George W. Pierson has written, "the Law School completed its rise to pre-eminence." *Yale College*, vol. 2, *1921–1937*, 259. Before this rise, Yale had been a local and semiproprietary law school. Pierson, *Yale College*, vol. 1, *1871–1921*, 222. In his 1921–22 report, Dean Swan wrote that his scholarly faculty was "generally recognized as placing this school among the leading law schools of the country." *Report of the Dean, Yale Law School, 1921–22*, 255. There were, however, at this time only three full-time faculty members in addition to the dean. Dean Clark would later date the turning point as about 1924. *Report of the Dean, Yale Law School, 1930–31*, 3.
35. Schlegel dates the starting point of Yale's innovative period with the 1927 appointment of the twenty-eight-year-old Robert M. Hutchins as dean. With the support of Charles Clark, who would later take over Hutchins' post when the latter left to become president of the University of Chicago in 1929, Hutchins brought "academic respecta-

bility, scientific distinctiveness, competitiveness, . . . a certain notoriety" (due to his age), and a "whirlwind" of activity to Yale. Schlegel, "American Legal Realism," 477. Hutchins created committees, made innovative appointments, was instrumental in the founding of the Institute of Human Relations, and brought social scientists on to the faculty. Summarizing these years, Schlegel wrote:

> In considering Hutchins' career at the law school, one can almost hear him yell, "Do something!" And his style reflects that command. The pace was frenetic, as he constantly pushed, jostled, and probed both law in general and legal education in particular for ways to make them better, more sensible, more reputably a subject of academic inquiry. At times, as in curriculum reform toward which he made three starts in little over a year, the style could verge on a kind of educational guerilla warfare. Then, movement, keeping the enemy—old, tired ways of thinking and teaching—off balance, became more important than the careful planning that may be essential to any success at the endeavor, if the Columbia experience may be taken as a guide. [Ibid., 489]

Schlegel argued that Hutchins got Yale started; it would take someone else to keep it moving. Ibid., 466–91.

36. All too often authors willing to write at length about other legal personalities avoid discussion of Pound, or, as with Auerbach (*Unequal Justice*), merely touch on certain actions of his without attempting to draw them into a consistent pattern. Even Gilmore (*Ages of American Law*), almost overready to wreak havoc on the reputations of Langdell and Holmes, has relegated Pound to his footnoes. Twining (*Karl Llewellyn and the Realist Movement*) complained, "Less easy to explain is the relationship of Roscoe Pound to Langdellism and to the realist movement." Ibid., 22. Even in his own time, Pound was a mystery. Learned Hand wrote to Charles E. Clark in 1933, "You know what a curious person Pound is, and how little you can tell what attitude he is going to take." Cited in Schlegel, "American Legal Realism," 505, n. 225. For one of the more coherent, or at least more courageous, attempts to deal with Pound, see Seligman, *The High Citadel*, chap. 3.

37. E.g., Roscoe Pound, "The Formative Era of American Law" (1938). These lectures, delivered at Tulane, contain a good deal of unreliable history.

38. E.g., Roscoe Pound, "The Spirit of the Common Law" (1921). These lectures, delivered at Dartmouth, contain a good deal of superficial legal theory.

39. See, generally, Sayre, *The Life of Roscoe Pound*.

40. Twining, *Karl Llewellyn and the Realist Movement*, 22–23; Wigdor, *Roscoe Pound*, passim.

41. See Gilmore, *Ages of American Law*, 59, n. 4 and 78, n. 25, for his view of Pound's "sadly comic" confrontation with the Realists.

42. Pound, "The Scope and Purpose of Sociological Jurisprudence," 591.

43. Holmes and Pollock obviously shared some of this skepticism. Howe, *Holmes-Pollock Correspondence*, vol. 1.

44. Roscoe Pound, "The Call for a Realist Jurisprudence," 697. On this point, see Twining, *Karl Llewellyn and the Realist Movement*, 24, 72–73, 77–81, and Gilmore, *Ages of American Law*, 69, n. 4 and 78, n. 25.

45. Seligman, *The High Citadel*, 58–59. Another of the many paradoxes connected with Pound is that he signed an earlier publicized report condemning Attomey-General Palmer's Red Scare. For an attempt to defend Pound's behavior, see Sayre, *Life of Roscoe Pound*, 218–23. Although Auerbach has in one place dismissed Pound as an

elitist (*Unequal Justice*, 84–85), in another he credits Pound with having "stood firmly by" Frankfurter during the Sacco-Vanzetti controversy. Ibid., 147.

46. Seligman, *The High Citadel*, 60–61.

47. Ibid., 59–60. "Felix Frankfurter complained that Langdell Hall was being turned into a Nazi holiday." Ibid., 60.

48. Sayre denied this. *Life of Roscoe Pound*, 231–32.

49. Seligman, *High Citadel*, 62.

50. Institutes of legal history, criminal law, comparative law, and international law. Sayre, *Life of Roscoe Pound*, 235.

51. Warren, *Spartan Education*, 55–56.

52. Auerbach, "Born to an Era of Insecurity," 12.

53. For a picture sympathetic to the students, see Seligman, *The High Citadel*, 64–67. For a more defensive view, see Sutherland, *The Law at Harvard*, 283–86.

54. Twining, *Karl Llewellyn and the Realist Movement*, 22.

55. A minor attempt at reform around the turn of the century had made no progress. In the 1920s, the leadership in the curriculum reform movement has been conceded to Columbia because "no other school undertook the application of [reform] ideas so systematically nor left such an explicit record of the educational policy involved." See Currie, "The Materials of Law Study, Part III," 2. Although Yale made some curriculum changes at this time, they were on a much less formal basis; revisions proceeded course by course under the direction of the faculty member in charge. Hutchins, "Modern Movements in Legal Education," 32. Schlegel, after discussing Columbia's reforms, admits, "In contrast, no one would call Yale's attempts at curriculum reform either sustained or major." Schlegel, "American Legal Realism," 479. Agitation for change had begun at Columbia even before 1922 through Walter Wheeler Cook, who had left Yale for Columbia in 1919 (but would return to Yale by 1923), and Underhill Moore. Herman Oliphant, leader of the radicals, joined the faculty in 1922 and by 1923 was ready to remake the curriculum. Columbia's president, Nicholas Murray Butler, however, preferred to wait for faculty support. Goebel, *Columbia Law School*, 299. See, generally, Currie, "The Materials of Law Study, Parts I and II," and Currie, "The Materials of Law Study, Part III."

56. "Functional" was defined as arguably "related to the areas of social life affected by law." The functional movement had begun at Berkeley. It was for this reason that O. K. McMurray and Alexander Kidd were brought from Berkeley to Columbia and why Underhill Moore taught summer school at Berkeley in 1924. Epstein, "Law at Berkeley."

57. Currie, "Materials of Law Study, Part III," 3–4.

58. Ibid., 10–11. Stone had written about the importance of sociological jurisprudence for legal education as early as 1915. As early as 1917, a faculty member, Thomas Reed Powell, had written, "Since law is a rule to govern human relations, the wisdom of any rule of law is essentially dependent upon its effect on human relations. But this effect is necessarily forecasted and evaluated by a process of ratiocination rather than of experimentation. And the ratiocination is all too seldom controlled or guided by any special and exact knowledge of the social and economic conditions which create the need for law, and which are in part the product of the particular rules of law which are chosen." Powell, "Law as Cultural Study," 336.

59. The extended curriculum studies were based on four major dissatisfactions with the existing situation: failure of general and of legal education to present insights into the structure of society, including the law school's persistence in ignoring statutory law; the

law school's concentration on concepts at the expense of essential facts; failure of the law school to consider preparation for the actual work involved in modern law practice as a basis of curriculum organization; the difficulty of teaching large classes of students with uneven ability. Powell on Columbia in *Modern Movements in Legal Education*, 35–36.

60. A good sense of the working of Marshall's mind may be obtained from his standard business-school treatise, *Business Administration*, first published in 1921.

61. Labor; Finance and Credit; Marketing; Form of Business Unit; Risk and Risk Bearing; Law Administration; Criminal Law; Family and Familial Property; Legislation; Historical and Comparative Jurisprudence. Currie, "Materials of Law Study, Part III," 22.

62. These included "Methods of Instruction and Study": "By and large, the average student of the case method does not devote enough time and energy to his work and he continues to expect and to get much 'spoon-feeding' from his instructor." Oliphant, *Summary of the Studies on Legal Education by the Faculty of Law of Columbia University*, 11; "A Survival of Belief in Natural Law": "Human relations are now too largely classified for legal treatment in categories too broad to give intimacy of view and too old adequately to disclose contemporary problems and contemporary practical considerations which should be weighed in solving them." Ibid., 14; and "Research": "The total of productive scholarship in American law schools needs to be increased and something should be done to stop our present extemporizing in the matter of the selection and training of law teachers." Ibid., 17.

63. Ibid., 20–21.

64. A working classification of major areas of law study was agreed upon. Substantive law was divided into Familial Relations, Political Relations, and Business Relations (subdivided into Marketing, Business Organizations, Finance and Credit, Labor Relations, and, tentatively, Risk and/or Production); Law Administration served as a general category for procedural and administrative law. The objective of the new classification was the selection of categories that would reflect the connections between law and modern life; the aspects of life to be selected were to be those for the law school course of study that emerged from the 1928 *Summary* and were based on these categories, balanced by introductory and synthetic materials at the beginning and end of the curriculum. Of overall importance would be historical and comparative studies in each of the functional areas. The field of "law administration" was to be treated with greater comprehensiveness in the revised curriculum, through the inclusion of such neglected areas as administrative boards and commissions and nongovernmental administrative agencies, along with greater emphasis on training in all areas of procedure. In the substantive law fields, political relations would deal with "inter-group relations and the individual versus the group." Included would be areas of law dealing with protection of the individual, spheres of action within the structure of government (including municipal corporations), some parts of constitutional law including public finance and taxation, and criminal law. "Familial relations" would include materials from domestic relations courses and from much of the property field; continued social science investigations were expected to reveal other areas for inclusion. The "business relations" category was discussed in depth. Marketing was to be approached primarily through the presentation of the economic facts, with the integration of facts and law as a later consideration. "Business associations" subjects were expected to point up the basic functions necessary for the coordination of specialists—functions common to any business organization; labor relations was regarded as a specialized aspect of that subject area. Finance and credit studies would be largely centered on the commercial bank. Historical, comparative, and analytical jurisprudence were dismissed as of

importance only in training and research and as means to other ends, while teleological jurisprudence was valued for the purpose of presenting law in its practical application to social and economic life. "Synthesis studies" were to follow at the end of the curriculum as a means of providing a comprehensive view of law and its workings in society. The final suggestion was a concentrated survey of bar examination courses at the end of the third-year work to insure the essential professional training and to free the rest of the curriculum from that pressure. Ibid., passim.

65. Cited in Currie, "Materials of Law Study, Part III," 70. Dean Smith was not always so conventional. In 1928, he was reported as believing that "the case method of legal education developed at the Harvard Law School . . . has been found unsuited to the demands of modern life . . . and is to be abolished at Columbia." *New York Times*, 10 December 1928.

66. Currie catalogs the many other practical difficulties of attempting to carry through so extensive a program. The obstacles were "typical of those that usually beset reform movements." Currie, "Materials of Law Study, Part I," 337. There was a financial problem in the need for expensive research staffs and libraries. Currie, "Materials of Law Study, Part III," 23. The original goal of simplifying course offerings turned out to be an impossibility: the course on corporations, for instance, was split into three parts, each a separate course, and family law seemed likely to require at least as many branches. Ibid., 26, 32, 73. It was also realized that some areas of law were not suited to functional handling (e.g., property, ibid., 38); "any thoroughgoing functional organization would have threatened duplication on a scale far beyond anything suggested by the superimposition of a few special courses on the traditional curriculum." Ibid., 73. These problems seem in large part attributable to what Currie calls "the inverted procedure of defining courses first and searching for content later"—a product of the sense of haste and need for immediate change, which pervaded the Columbia faculty. Ibid., 73–74.

67. Twining describes in some detail the faculty reaction to the report, but he attributes its failure less to the contrasting ideological disagreements with the report than to the concurrent crisis over the appointment as dean of Young B. Smith, a man opposed to the research institute model. Twining suggests that if it had not been for the deanship crisis, a research institute might have been set up. Twining, *Karl Llewellyn and the Realist Movement*, 50–55. This seems unlikely; it also downplays the importance of the opposition to the research model by those who feared the economic and status losses likely to result from downplaying professional training.

68. Oliphant, "Return to Stare Decisis," 23.

69. Columbia University, *Report of the Dean, School of Law, 1928*, cited in Currie, "Materials of Law Study, Part III," 65. Dean Smith's was, in 1928, the prevailing view of legal education at the fifty-five AALS member schools. The only objective of legal education on which all were agreed was the preparation of students for professional practice in the common-law system. *Summary of Studies on Legal Education*, 18. The Carnegie Foundation's *Annual Review of Legal Education, 1919* praised Harvard and Michigan for reserving research work for the graduate year and thereby avoiding a common error among research-oriented law schools of cultivating legal science "somewhat at the expense of their primary function as professional training schools" (13).

70. See Twining, *Karl Llewellyn and the Realist Movement*:

> The first statements about the programme of the institute contained few surprises. Its professed philosophy rested on three familiar ideas: "scientific method," "social engineering," and "community of scholars." The principal function was to be

research, training being ancillary and directly related to the major objectives of the institute. The clearest statement of education aims was expressed in negative terms: "It seems clear that the Institute must not now (and, so far as we can now see, should never) commit itself to maintaining an orthodox professional school for training of practitioners." [Ibid., 60]

71. Currie, "Materials of Law Study, Part III," 29.
72. Columbia University, *Report of the Dean, School of Law, 1930*, 5–6.
73. When Robert Hutchins was acting dean in 1926–27, he noted in his report the beginnings of course revisions and commented (like Oliphant) that current formal course divisions were too artificial for modern law study. *Report of the Acting Dean, Yale Law School, 1926–1927*, 118. Unlike the Columbia studies, curriculum revisions at Yale proceeded course by course through the group of faculty members directly involved. Hutchins emphasized the mood of experimentation and tentativeness that prevailed, and he also gave credit to Columbia for having provided leadership in the area of curriculum study. Hutchins, "Modern Movements in Legal Education," 32–33.
The introduction of an honors program in 1926 was one early result of the studies. Another change was the introduction of social science, psychiatric, and psychological materials into the criminal law course; without such materials, the existing course had become "an historical survey of crimes that no longer exist." *Report of the Acting Dean, Yale Law School, 1926–27*, 117–18. In his report for the following year, Hutchins commented that the curricular study had advanced only as far as discussions of the existing curriculum, which had revealed too much duplication of areas of study and too little correlation among the subjects offered. A further plan (which looked like an imitation of Columbia's) was outlined, but Hutchins did not indicate whether that was carried through: a member of the faculty of the Department of Economics, Sociology, and Government, who was also a lawyer, was to head a general review committee planned for the fall of 1928. *Report of the Dean, Yale Law School, 1927–28*. By 1929, work in family law was planned, business organization was being developed, but criminal law was regarded as still unsatisfactory and in need of further work. *Report of the Dean, Yale Law School, 1928–29*, 6, 10. Credit transactions, business units, and new procedure courses had been developed by 1930, all formed by reworking previous courses. *Report of the Dean, Yale Law School, 1929–30*, 10.
74. See Hutchins and Slesinger, "Some Observations on the Law of Evidence," 432. In fact, the institute had been developed and funded largely through Hutchins' initiative. Begun in 1928–29, it was administered by representatives of the Graduate, Medical, and Law Schools and by natural and social science professors from the college. Carnegie Foundation, *Annual Review of Legal Education, 1929*, 37.
75. Hutchins, "The Autobiography of an Ex-Law Student," 511, 513. This is, in some ways, unfair. Edward Robinson, a Yale psychologist, who also taught at the Yale Law School, published *Law and Lawyers* in 1935, a book that still makes stimulating reading.
About the series of Hutchins-Slesinger articles, Schlegel has said: "The articles were of a generally high quality, although their effectiveness varied directly with respect to the quality and relevance of the underlying psychological literature: where good quantitative, behavioral studies were available, the articles were crisp and the criticism effective; where older, introspective psychology or new Freudian psychology provided the studies, the articles tended to be less well focused and their criticisms weak." Schlegel, "American Legal Realism," 482. He also pointed out that the social sciences were not always to blame; often the legal academics made poor use of, or misunderstood, the quantitative and statistical methods developed by the social scientists. Ibid.,

519–45, especially at 544–45. Finally, insufficient funding prevented the acquisition of the proper personnel, facilities, and tools. Ibid., especially 545–52.

76. The Law School of Case Western Reserve University was particularly excited about the institute and established a joint program with it as a way of aiding the development of both Case Western and Johns Hopkins. Case Western's graduate law program was thus severely crippled by the failure of the institute. Cramer, *The Law School at Case Western*, 50–51.

77. During the 1920s, foundation funds for research had poured into the leading law schools. There were never enough funds, of course: "Money for research in the social sciences generally, and in the law in particular, has not been plentiful at best." *Report of the Dean, Yale Law School, 1931–32,* 20. When the depression undermined this source of revenue, the schools expressed some bitterness. Dean Clark quoted a 1931 study entitled *American Foundations and Their Fields* for statistics on foundation grants during the previous fiscal year: to medicine and public health—$16,509,734 (additional special grants, such as over $900,000 for psychiatry, were not included); to the physical sciences—$2,803,239 (also with additional special grants); to law, including international law, criminology, and penology—$589,143. *Report of the Dean, Yale Law School, 1931–32,* 20n. Expectations had risen during the 1920s as the result of several sizable bequests to the law schools. The University of Michigan Law School apparently received something under $11,000,000 in the 1920s and early 1930s. Compiled from figures listed separately in Brown, *Legal Education at Michigan,* 323, 325. The Sterling bequests to the Yale Law School apparently totaled about $5,500,000. Compiled from *Report of the Dean, Yale Law School, 1928–29,* 6; *1929–30,* 14. The bequests provided primarily for new buildings, although there was a provision of over $2,000,000 for legal research at Michigan. *Report of the Dean, Yale Law School, 1929–30,* 14; Brown, *Legal Education at Michigan,* 323.

78. "The Johns Hopkins Institute for the Study of Law," 6 *American Law School Review* 336 (1928). The Columbia and Yale studies inspired other research groups, including (in addition to Yale's Institute of Human Relations) Columbia's Foundation for Research in Legal History, begun in 1930, and institutes of criminal law and of comparative law begun by Pound a year earlier at Harvard. Carnegie Foundation, *Annual Review of Legal Education, 1929,* 37. Even more extensive at Harvard were the concurrent informal empirical research studies, beginning with a 1922 survey of the administration of criminal justice in Cleveland, followed by a study of Boston. Sutherland, *The Law at Harvard,* 229. Projects at Yale and elsewhere are described in Hurst, *The Growth of American Law,* 192 ff. Probably the most extensive of the Yale undertakings was a field study of court administration ranging over several states, described in detail in the dean's reports for the 1920s and 1930s. But see also Clark and Shulman, "Jury Trial in Civil Cases—a Study of Judicial Administration," 867; U.S., National Commission on Law Observance and Enforcement, *Progress Report on the Study of the Federal Courts* (Washington, D.C., 1931). No great amount of empirical research was done at Columbia in the 1930s. "The library and the armchair were still more attractive than the marketplace and the courts." Twining, *Karl Llewellyn and the Realist Movement,* 58. Research professorships date from 1926 at Michigan. Brown, *Legal Education at Michigan,* 339, 773.

79. For a detailed account of the Yale experience during the 1930s, see Schlegel, "American Legal Realism," 491–596.

80. See Moore and Sussman, "Legal and Institutional Methods Applied to the Debiting of Direct Discounts," 381, 555, 752, 928, 1055, 1219.

81. Moore and Callahan, "Law and Learning Theory," 1. "Moore's work was to the last

degree specific, precise, limited, and as objective as it could conceivably be made. [This was] indicated by the selection of the field of his chief investigation, . . . [including] the effect of city parking ordinances on the actual duration of parking on city streets." Clark, "Underhill Moore," 192.

82. Clark and Shulman, *A Study of Law Administration in Connecticut: A Report of an Investigation of the Activities of Certain Trial Courts of the State.* Published in 1937, this was the report of a study begun in 1926. For an amusing and somewhat cynical view of these studies, see Arnold, *Fair Fights and Foul,* 62–63.

83. See Schlegel, "American Legal Realism," 558–59.

84. In later years, Douglas recounted his skepticism upon his arrival at Yale in September of 1928:

> By the time I had reached Yale and had time for reflection, I was, in a way, sorry that I had turned to law. I had seen enough in New York City and in the State of Washington to realize that the practice of law required predatory qualities. . . . Finance was predatory and many men who managed it had predatory proclivities. . . . I had seen that Wall Street had its Augean stables, and many of the caretakers were lawyers. The great names in the law were, with few exceptions, attached to men who exploited the system but brought very few spiritual or ethical values to it. Those who reached 65 might be wealthy, but as I observed in New York, they were mostly shriveled men with no interests beyond the law. Few had rendered public service, and those who did used that front merely to get more business.
> . . . [Lawyers] of New York City were . . . suave, sophisticated and deft. . . . Teaching was only a stone's throw away. Why spend one's life teaching bright youngsters how to do things that should not be done? Why teach them to be cleverer than their fathers? Or, on the other hand, why not practice and use the new-found finesse for one's own benefit? [Douglas, *Go East, Young Man,* 162]

85. See Thurman Arnold's review of Arthur L. Goodhart, *Essays on Jurisprudence and the Common Law* in 41 *Yale Law Journal* 318 (1931); Arnold, "The Restatement of the Law of Trusts," 800.

Perhaps this attitude should not be presented as confined merely to professors. Even by 1926, a Yale graduate wrote to the *American Bar Association Journal* to relate, perhaps with some glee, his story of how Langdell visited Yale and was confused by the quick repartee and questions of students in Corbin's class. See "Letters to the Editor," 12 *ABA Journal* 869 (1926).

86. See Clark, *Real Covenants and Other Interests Which "Run with Land."* Although Clark was able to show various historical confusions in the area and to add some of his own, his solutions were even less valuable than those of the Restaters.

Douglas lists some of the projects of the period, which also give a sense of the feeling and energy of the participants:

> Charles Clark was pioneering in Procedure, and his activities had ended, by 1938, with the Federal Rules of Civil Procedure, drafted by his committee for the U.S. Supreme Court and Congress. Thurman Arnold was teaching and writing his "Folklore of Capitalism." Hutchins, to enliven the subject of Torts, brought Walton Hamilton, an economist, to the Law faculty. . . . Hammy had never studied law but he had a wonderfully creative mind and put old principles into brand-new bottles— not only in Torts, but in Business Regulations, Patents, and related fields. . . .
> Another Yale law professor who was opening up new vistas was Wesley Sturges. His field was arbitration. Harry Shulman was doing the same with labor. Richard J. Smith was bringing common sense and the British experience to bear on public

utility rate regulation. . . . Harold Laski of the London School of Economics was
there off and on. The Yale Law campus was filled with a fervor that no other law
faculty experienced. . . .

Walter Nelles, brilliant but little known, was on the faculty, and he was probing
delicate areas of civil rights in the late 20's and 30's. Edwin Borchard claimed
international law; but two of his outside interests made enduring impressions.
Borchard was almost a one-man lobby to push through the federal Declaratory
Judgement Act, and he also wrote *Convicting the Innocent*—case histories of
innocent men found guilty of major crimes. It was a book which quickened the
conscience of America in regard to legal injustice. [Douglas, *Go East, Young Man*,
163–64]

87. "No more time wasting system of studying law has ever been devised." Arnold, *Fair
Fights and Foul*, 263.

88. Ibid., 58: "The law was a separate science, apart from other human institutions. . . .
That faith had given us comfort and stability for the preceding half-century. It had been
responsible for the growth of our great law schools. Of course, the search for certainty
in the law was not producing certainty. The cases pouring off the presses were
increasingly in headlong arithmetical progression. Some central institutions had to be
created to reconcile them. And thus was born the American Law Institute. Professors
were recruited from all over the United States—principally from Harvard, which was
then the high church of abstract legal theory."

89. Ibid., 35.

90. Schlegel, "American Legal Realism," 33.

91. Schlegel, "American Legal Realism and Empirical Social Sciences: The Singular Case of
Underhill Moore," 191.

92. For example, during the summer of 1933, Thurman Arnold, Wesley Sturges, Abe
Fortas, and Howard Marshall all worked in Washington. Fortas and Marshall became
so involved in their work that they stayed once the fall semester started. Schlegel calls
this only "a preview of what was to come." Schlegel, "American Legal Realism," 559, n.
524.

93. In 1929, there were 274 applicants, of whom 100 were accepted. See J. Burke Zen,
"Yale Law School and the Thirties" (paper presented at the Yale Law School, 1976). In
that year, of the 296 students in the school, 134 were Yale College men, 18 were from
Princeton, 7 were from Cornell, and 6 each were from the University of Pennsylvania
and Columbia. Ninety-seven of the 296 were still Connecticut residents. Of the 392
students in 1938–39, Yale provided 115, Princeton 45, Harvard 30, Dartmouth 25, and
Amherst 18; the number of Connecticut residents had dropped to 63.

94. From 296 in 1929 to 394 in 1939. In 1927, Yale had been the fourth most expensive
law school in the country, charging $310 for tuition. By 1928, the figure was $360 and
by 1932 at the height of the depression, Yale was the country's most expensive law
school, charging $460. Although the number of students dropped that year, over the
years increases in tuition were not always followed by a decline in enrollment; in 1930,
the number of students had increased along with tuition costs. See First, "Competition
in the Legal Education Industry," 365, n. 323.

95. Zen, "Yale Law School," passim. See also Justice Douglas' remarks about the law
school at which he arrived in 1928:

New Haven was a relaxed, easy-going college town. Its physical beauty and
intellectual grace made it an ideal habitat. People were intimate and friendly.
Although there were undercurrents of a minor antagonism between Town and
Gown, Yale produced a lively social atmosphere and in some departments a lively

intellectual climate. Yale College, however, was filled with sons of the elite who lived in a warm glow of easy scholarship, easy living, easy work. They were the "chosen" who in time would man the nation. The college professors dealt kindly with them; they were spoonfed, coddled, pampered. I early discovered that they were unused to intellectual discipline, for the Yale College men in my law classes were waiting for someone to fill their heads with knowledge. Yale, in those days, was notorious for being that kind of filling-station. [Douglas, *Go East, Young Man*, 161]

9 / Intellectual Excitement for the Few: Realism and Reality

ACED with what they believed to be a stagnating approach to law and legal education, law professors at Harvard, Columbia, and Yale had attempted individually or collectively to carry out an assault on the status quo. These attempts had failed to bring about any definable institutional change, whether for financial or political reasons or for reasons having to do with prestige or faculty competence. Rather than regarding the controversies of this period only in the light of immediate, concrete results, however, it is fairer to attempt to assess the contributions in terms of long-term results and those elusive "changes in attitude" that are, unfortunately, less easy to define than "concrete" manifestations.

At least some of the participants in the Yale, Harvard, and Columbia scene during the 1930s may incidentally be included as members of that eclectic group known as Realists. That Realism represented at most a general outlook rather than a single school of thought is now widely accepted. The outlook was, in part, a lineal descendant (or perhaps a collateral relative) of the skepticism of Holmes and the social engineering of Pound. It may also be said to have built on the functionalism of the 1920s evident in the work of Cook, Oliphant, and Yntema, and its functional view of law became closely associated with the political "can-do" spirit of the New Deal. It is, however, hazardous to attempt to define too carefully the predecessors or beliefs of this "group." It was, if anything, an amorphous skeptical movement, which ultimately did for law what Russell and Wittgenstein did, with appreciably more intellectual elegance, for philosophy.[1]

It was not, perhaps, until Roscoe Pound attacked "our younger teachers of law" in the *Harvard Law Review* of March 1931 that a rather disparate group, frustrated by the then current approach to law, acquired any sense of unity. Ironically, Karl Llewellyn's reply in the June issue of the *Review*, denying that there was "any such school,"[2] merely served to strengthen the sense of unity among the disjointed collection of thinkers. The situation was further complicated by the fact that Leon Green's *Judge and Jury*, Karl Llewellyn's *Bramble Bush*, and Jerome Frank's *Law and the Modern Mind* had all appeared within a period of a few months in 1930. The Realist "movement" thus gave the impression of being more firmly established than in fact it was. The distance between Frank at his most extreme and Llewellyn at his most constructive could not have been greater. It is little wonder that the "movement" has proved difficult for scholars to analyze.[3]

The major contribution of the Realist movement was to kill the Langdellian notion of law as an exact science, based on the objectivity of black-letter rules. When it became acceptable to write about the law as it actually operated, legal rules could no longer be assumed to be value-free. This change inevitably caused the predictive value of doctrine to be seriously questioned. The vantage point of American legal scholarship was finally established as being process rather than substance. The Realist movement was a crucial, and probably necessary, force in the development of the American legal culture. England, for instance, has suffered serious intellectual stultification from having had no such revolution.[4] At the same time, the effect of the Realists was much like the role that Carlyle pronounced for Matthew Arnold: "He led them into the wilderness and left them there." There had already been a tendency for American jurisprudence to abandon the apparent certainty of a series of inter-related principles, in the ever widening search for cases "on all fours." The Realists went a long way toward killing the idea of "the system" altogether. All legal logic came under suspicion. American law became increasingly purposive, increasingly secularized,[5] and increasingly atomized. Whatever enhanced value this instrumental approach gave to social and political causes of the right and left as they sought to enlist "the law" on their side, law became less valuable as an objective force binding together different elements in the community. It was one thing to agree that legal objectivity and neutrality were myths; it was another to destroy such myths, providing as they do vital elements of social control, without offering any alternatives.[6] Such an undermining of legal sinews proved to be the Realists' lasting monument.[7]

Although the work of the Realists may have been less constructive than that of others, the value of their capacity to question accepted tenets of law and legal education cannot be denied. Although one may dismiss much of Jerome Frank's legal philosophy as immature, his pleas for "lawyer schools" were an attack on the heart of the Langdellian assumption that the case method was both practical and in the intellectual tradition of German scientism.[8] Frank argued powerfully that law schools had become both too academic and too unrelated to practice:[9]

> The Law student should learn, while in school, the art of legal practice. And to that end, the law schools should boldly, not slyly

and evasively, repudiate the false dogmas of Langdell. They must decide not to exclude, as did Langdell—but to include—the methods
of learning law by work in the lawyer's office and attendance at
the proceedings of courts of justice. . . . They must repudiate the
absurd notion that the heart of a law school is its library.[10]

Frank's call for a return of the lawyer-school touched few chords in the
1930s but would become, in a sense, the basis for the return to respectability of clinical education in the 1960s. Frank and other Realists recognized that, by the 1930s, law teaching was predominantly in the hands of
those who had had little or no contact with practice and that the case
method by itself could not teach practical skills, or at least those not
inculcated by the Socratic method. Although the Realist School, if it may
be called that, did not survive beyond the beginning of World War II, its
ideas had a permanent impact on legal thought. As the 1930s gave way
to the 1940s, the work of Harold Lasswell and Myres McDougal provided an intellectual link between the Realists and the process schools of
the later decades.[11]

The 1920s and the 1930s, then, were an occasion of considerable
intellectual excitement for the faculty members within a few law schools.
At many law schools in the country, however, legal education consisted,
at most, of preparation for the local bar examination.[12] Teaching at such
schools took the form of a lecture-and-text system or, more frequently, a
modified version of the case method, sometimes modified more because
of the professors' or students' lack of competence than because of intellectual doubts about its desirability. A possibly larger group of schools—
the average state universities and smaller private schools—espoused the
Harvard case-method model and continued to imitate it on a lesser
scale.[13] The imitation was lesser both quantitatively and qualitatively
because money was generally short, the faculties miniscule and generally undistinguished, and libraries in most cases modest. Moreover,
students were interested in learning the law in order to pass the bar
examinations. To many of them, especially those with poorer educational
backgrounds, the Harvard method of teaching seemed designed to im-
pede the learning process. Although it was possible to adapt some aspects
of the case method under such circumstances, any research on the part of
faculty required perseverance. Teaching experiments were largely unheard of.[14] At best, developments in legal education slowly percolated
down to these schools from the leading national schools and the better
state universities.[15]

All this should not be taken as implying that the intellectual ferment,
even among the faculty at the leading schools, directly stimulated their
own students. Although the 1929 Carnegie Foundation *Review of Legal*

Education noted that Yale and Columbia were at work on studies in social problems and added that both "permit activities of this sort to be offered, under certain restrictions, in partial satisfaction of requirements for their first law degree,"[16] the statement was misleading. At Yale, Dean Clark, after complaints by the alumni, observed that "the field projects must necessarily remain somewhat separated from the teaching division of the school."[17] He later added, "in fact, one of our problems is to bring this body of material into the ordinary day-to-day bounds of knowledge of the student."[18] Only in some situations, such as Underhill Moore's first-year course in commercial bank credit, was the new wave of research directly available to the student.[19]

Although the direct benefits of faculty projects were negligible, students at the better schools profited in indirect ways. One result of the reform movement was that a few schools—again notably Yale and Columbia—added social scientists to the law faculty.[20] Probably the most significant result of the attempts to integrate law and the social sciences was the development of new teaching materials. As new casebooks appeared during the 1920s and 1930s, the typical title changed from "Cases on X" to "Cases and Materials on Y," Y sometimes being a totally new category like securities or business corporations.[21] The new books did not always vary greatly from the old ones nor was original research always evident, yet there were a few real departures from the old patterns. Karl Llewellyn's *Cases and Materials on the Law of Sales* is normally singled out as the most original of these.[22] By 1930, the prominent schools had scores of new casebooks (Yale listed a dozen newly published in 1931),[23] and the 1930s saw a rapid increase in the number of schools interested in spreading the new gospel of functionalism through casebook production.

A third major development of the interwar years—the seminar[24]—was largely an extension of the elective principle. Fairly widespread by the mid-1920s,[25] electives provided a base for the gradual introduction of seminars well down in the hierarchy of the law schools,[26] providing an opportunity for the breakup of the curriculum. Indeed, the establishment of electives was in itself an acknowledgment that, even substantively, the law was rather more than the limited number of principles and subject areas that Langdell had been talking about in the early years of his deanship. When carried to its logical conclusion, the idea of electives seemed to suggest that both principles and subject matter could be multiplied indefinitely as society became more complex. Was the law still one field, or should it be viewed as a limitless terrain?

To those who viewed it as one field, the solution to its expanding scope was to extend the length of law school. Thus, during the 1930s, the idea of a four-year law degree became increasingly popular.[27] The concept was first pushed by John Henry Wigmore in a dissent from the AALS Curriculum Committee report in 1920.[28] Against the wishes of the president of the university he then established such a program at Northwestern.[29] By 1935 it was seen as a losing idea and was abandoned. The concept was not, however, dead. Chicago's optional four-year curriculum, begun in 1937, was perhaps the most innovative of the experiments along these lines. Part of a reorganized curriculum designed to introduce "an evaluation of the social workings of the law" and to "attempt to deal more articulately with the question of what law is and what is involved in the criticism of rules of law,"[30] the program included courses in psychology, English constitutional history, economic theory, accounting, political theory, and ethics.[31] A required course designed to occupy half of the fourth year was particularly striking; called Law and Economic Organization, it dealt with distribution of income and the business cycle, economic theory, statistics, legal aspects of competition, control devices, and bankruptcy and reorganization.[32] The Chicago program was maintained until 1949; only Minnesota, however, was to have long-term success with the four-year curriculum, and it was not finally dropped there until 1958.[33]

Variants of the four-year programs, and as transient, were the combined law-business courses, apparently most ambitious and extensive at Yale. The Yale program in cooperation with Harvard's Graduate School of Business Administration began in 1933.[34] The hope for the program was that it would provide a "real gain in scientific knowledge and in methods of control of our intricate social organizations."[35] The first students reported their Harvard experience as valuable and interesting, but lack of enrollment forced the program's discontinuation in 1938.[36] At least another model for legal education had, however, been established—a four-year "law and" program.

Even more than business subjects public law dominated substantive curricular growth in the 1920s and 1930s. Perhaps it was natural that the elite schools, building on an earlier history of public law teaching, introduced the new courses.[37] Administrative law had first been taught at Columbia in 1892, and it was introduced for second- and third-year students when the University of Chicago began its law school in 1902. It was moved from the graduate to the LL.B. program at Yale in 1918–19 (although not at Harvard until 1941–42).[38] By the time Reed wrote his second report in 1925–26, the leading schools were branching into other areas related to public law. Labor law was by then offered at Harvard and Northwestern; Michigan and Harvard both offered taxation; trade regulation or restraint of trade was offered by Michigan, Harvard, Chicago, and Northwestern.[39] The law schools had at last taken cognizance of the legal implications of the Progressive movement.

The New Deal was to have a profound effect in all these areas.[40] Work in Washington attracted many established members of the legal profession, but it was an even stronger magnet for recent law graduates and law professors.[41] Changes in the law school curricula reflected this fascination with the burgeoning federal government. The 1930s saw the development of first-year courses in administrative law at several schools, although not until the 1940s did the emphasis in such courses shift from the study of judicial review of administrative action to the study of administrative agencies and their work.[42] After faculty members returned from service in the New Deal, courses with such enticing titles as "Modern Social Legislation" or "The TVA" began to appear.[43] Moreover, the use of faculty members from the law schools in running the New Deal was itself significant.[44] Just as the idea of a full-time faculty was spreading from national schools to the less prestigious schools, it became accepted that public service was a major part of the law professor's role. Such an aspect may have been good for federal, state, and university administration; it was scarcely likely to strengthen legal scholarship,[45] if legal scholarship were to have any connection to the scholarship by then accepted in other areas of the liberal university.

Graduate programs also felt the effects of the times, the most notable reaction being the establishment in 1938 of New York University's Graduate Division of Training in Public Service, which stressed administrative, labor, and tax law.[46] Significant efforts to improve the quality of the student body were made at the leading schools. "All the institutions which offered graduate work are dissatisfied with the caliber of the men to whom it appeals. . . . With a few notable exceptions graduate study appeals to second-class men who must have some decoration to make them attractive."[47] There seem to have been few concrete suggestions for the improvement of graduate students, but Yale, at least, found the quality more satisfactory after the early 1930s when admissions to the graduate program were made selective.[48]

In the long run, even more significant was the introduction of selectivity into the LL.B. programs. Harvard had an open admissions policy, at least for affluent males. If he had a B.A. and could pay his way, anyone might enter the first year of law school. This resulted in about 250 of a first-year class of nearly 700 being failed in 1926–27.[49] Yale attacked the problem in that year, announcing that entering classes were to be limited to 100 students.[50] No student was to be admitted to the first-year class unless he or she[51] was considered able to make a C average; transfer students were to have a B average.[52] Yale's admissions procedures were in an experimental stage until about 1930, but after 1926 a transcript of the applicant's college record, recommendations, a personal interview, and a classification test were all required.[53] An aptitude test was introduced in 1928—the first to be used at any law school[54]—and it became a standard part of the admissions procedure.[55] Columbia introduced selective admissions in 1928–29, also using an aptitude test, one of its own devising that was successful in keeping out the worst risks but that in no way separated the very good from the average.[56] Yet the elite schools had solved the problem that had first been posed when it was clear that the case method was best adapted to the analytically outstanding student. Rather than cut back on the case method, the schools cut back on the average student.

Yale and Columbia added academic selectivity to what was already an elitist tradition based on the ability to pay and a college degree.[57] Such selectivity perhaps meant little at Yale in the 1930s with its comfortable endowments, its well-paid professors, and well-heeled students.[58] As the idea of selectivity spread to other schools, however, it had more impact. As Harvard slowly moved toward some additional tests of ability beyond the college degree,[59] new student expectations became apparent. In 1935 a student evaluation listed various defects in the Harvard LL.B. After the first year the case method allegedly lost its value; the students thought it should be dropped or modified in the second and third years. Lectures should be reintroduced; discussion should replace the existing Socratic method, which consisted of a dialogue between the professor and a handful of students in a large class; something should be done to discourage the decline of interest in the third year; and all students should have an experience akin to law review. Selectivity might be seen by faculty as shoring up the case method, but it did not mean the case method was sacrosanct in the eyes of students.[60]

Lest it be thought that only the select of Harvard dared to criticize, it is worth remembering that Reed reiterated many of his earlier complaints about American legal education when he delivered himself of his second report in 1928. He continued to have no doubt about the "superiority" of the case method; he found that it wasted time, excluded coverage of many important areas of law, and also deemphasized "the amount of immediately available information." He was still worried about the intellectual state of American law, the decline of jurisprudence and legal theory, and the excessive time required for entry into the profession.[61] He was equally worried about the condition of legal scholarship, again partially attributed to the case method and, at the structural level, was unenthusiastic about the substitution of the J.D. degree for the LL.B., a fad begun by Chicago in 1902.[62]

In terms of later developments, however, perhaps the most significant of Reed's observations concerned clinical studies. In his first report, Reed had begun the chapter, "Inadequate Provision for Practical Training," with the observation that "the failure of the modern American law school to make any adequate provision in its curriculum for practical training constitutes a remarkable educational anomaly."[63] In his second report, he remained concerned that, in the laudable task of taking over legal education from the practitioners, law schools had underplayed the need for some clinical experience:[64] "There is probably no other practical calling the preparation for which is so unrelievedly academic as that which is provided for American lawyers by most American law schools."[65]

The 1920s and 1930s witnessed a limited redressing of the balance between the academic and the practical. Although in 1916 Wisconsin had begun requiring six months of office work from candidates for a degree,[66] Reed felt the best line of development would be for students to gain clinical experience through legal aid work rather than office work. The University of Pennsylvania had incorporated some legal aid work into its program as early as 1893, and Denver followed in 1904. By 1925, Harvard, Cincinnati, Northwestern, and a few other schools had some form of legal aid program. John Bradway's work, in setting up clinical legal aid programs at the University of Southern California and at Duke, was a particularly significant development in this pattern, and clinical legal studies received some encouragement from the 1933 Frank article, "Why Not a Clinical Lawyer-School?" Such developments were, however, deceiving. The legal establishment, particularly the AALS, displayed little enthusiasm for clinical programs,[67] and Frank's article was not as supportive as its title indicates. He was basically calling for law faculties composed of those with extensive experience in practice and for more emphasis on teaching the way judges, particularly at first instance, decided cases. Although he wished to get students out of the library, he was interested primarily in getting them into the moot court room or to listen to trials at first instance,[68] and, in this respect, he had relatively little impact on the way clinical programs ultimately developed.

The intellectual momentum, if not the immediate goals, of the 1920s had carried through, in a limited way, to curricular discussions in the next decade. Columbia's attempt to develop a functional organization had faltered,[69] but Yale and Northwestern in particular had notable success in using parts of the original classification.[70] Yale was especially successful in handling business categories functionally. Yale's new courses and programs, and its continued attempts at original research, resulted largely from efforts to take advantage of the promise of the 1920s. Moreover, in challenging vocational training as the primary function of a law school, Columbia and Yale set an example that at least influenced a few other schools. Michigan's Dean Bates, for instance, wrote in his 1933 report, "Law should be treated as a means of social control, to be employed . . . with a view of using it to harmonize clashing interests, and for the welfare of society as a whole."[71] Developments in casebooks, seminars, graduate work, public law, extended and extension programs, clinical programs—innovations prompted by the questionings of this period—may not have had a powerful or immediate impact on legal education nationally, but they set a precedent for developments over the course of the next decades.

These early developments were in most cases, however, restricted to perhaps two dozen of the leading schools at most,[72] and the atmosphere elsewhere was quite different. Preparation for the local bar exam, the primary purpose of many—perhaps most—schools, did not require innovative offerings or allow faculty time for research. The 1933 bulletin of one university law school stated it simply: "The faculty has in mind no radical experiments in legal education. The subjects offered are found in the course of study of accredited schools. The method of instruction has been in use . . . for many years. . . . We stick to fundamentals. No member is inclined to convert his classroom into an expensive laboratory in which to experiment with novel, radical, or untried theories."[73] The developments of the 1920s, although likened by Harold Laski to Langdell's innovations in degree of importance,[74] were not to be nearly as pervasive as the Harvard developments of the 1870s had been.

Moreover, the late 1930s saw disillusionment and a corresponding loss of initiative at schools that had been at the forefront of the earlier efforts. Between 1939 and 1941 Esther Brown visited twenty-three schools in preparation for her study of legal education sponsored by the Russell Sage Foundation. Afterward she wrote, "leadership in legal education was no longer centered primarily on the Atlantic seaboard. 'The great Eastern schools' were, in fact, momentarily weary or disorganized and were waiting to get their breath for a renewed effort."[75] Perhaps like the New Deal they had run out of steam. If, however, the bulk of law schools had been left untouched by curricular reform, they had been rapidly overtaken by changes in the structure of legal education.

NOTES

1. White, *Social Thought in America*, passim.
2. Llewellyn, "Some Realism about Realism," 1233.
3. The nearest approach is Rumble, Jr., *American Legal Realism*. An outsider's view comes from Twining, *Karl Llewellyn and the Realist Movement*.

4. On this, see Goldstein, "Research into the Administration of Criminal Law," 27, 37.
5. See, generally, Woodard, "The Limits of Legal Realism," 689.
6. Not all Realists were unaware of the social advantages of political myths. Thurman Arnold, for example, despite his cynicism, looked at the law as a cultural anthropologist and was more interested in change through the system. Arnold, *The Folklore of Capitalism.*
7. Gilmore would disagree with this statement:

> . . . the revolution may have been merely a palace revolution, not much more than a changing of the guard. My own thought has come to be that the adepts of the new jurisprudence—Legal Realists or whatever they should be called—no more proposed to abandon the basic tenets of Langdellian jurisprudence than the Protestant reformers of the fifteenth and sixteenth centuries proposed to abandon the basic tenets of Christian theology. These were the ideas that "law is a science" and that there is such a thing as "the one true rule of law."
> At the hands of the Realists, the slogan "law is a science" became "law is a social science." Where Langdell had talked of chemistry, physics, zoology, and botany as disciplines allied to the law, the Realists talked of economics and sociology not merely as allied disciplines but as disciplines which were in some sense part and parcel of the law. [Gilmore, *Ages of American Law,* 87–88]

8. See Patterson, *Jurisprudence*; Rosenberg, *Jerome Frank.*
9. Frank complained about Langdell's obsession with the library and noted that "students trained by the Langdell method are like dog breeders who only see stuffed dogs"; he saw a link between "stuffed dog study and overproduction of stuffed shirts in the legal profession." Frank, "Why Not a Clinical Lawyer School?," 908–12.
10. From "What Constitutes a Good Legal Education?," a speech to the Section of Legal Education in 1933. Cited in Lee, *The Study of Law and Proper Preparation,* 29.
11. See Lasswell and McDougal, "Legal Education and Public Policy," 203. For the apparent conversion of Lasswell and McDougal to the value of the process school, see their "Jurisprudence in Policy-Oriented Perspective," 486, 506. For an analysis of the place of process in American legal philosophy, see Morrison, "Frames of Reference for Legal Ideals," in Kamenka et al., eds., *Law and Society.*
12. See, for instance, one school's statement of its ideal: "If the professional school would realize its own ideal and do the work it is able to perform, it must be localized, and confine itself to instruction in the art of law as understood and practiced in its own locality. Every state should have its own law schools, whose professors are selected from its own practitioners, and should bring its law schools into such close relations with its courts and bar that every possible advantage in observing practice and in practical training may be afforded to their students." *John Marshall Law School Catalog* (1933).
13. One result of this was a proliferation of law reviews, all largely based on the Harvard model. The number of reviews went from 0 in 1887 to 50 in 1937. Although the *Harvard Law Review* boasted that it is a "perfected, efficiently operating machine serving an educational need, . . . we ought not to be disturbed to find it constructed and operating according to certain standard specifications which experience has proved to produce the best results" (50 *Harvard Law Review* 873 [1937]), not all agreed with this. Joseph Werner stressed the need for law reviews that emphasized local law, suggesting that these would be the province of the state schools. Werner, "Need for State Reviews," 49. David Cavers admitted that some specialized periodicals were published (giving as examples the *George Washington Review of Public Law* and

Air Law Review), but he found that there were far too few of those and advocated more and better publications of this type. Cavers, "New Fields for the Legal Periodical," 1. In "Goodbye to Law Reviews," 38–41, Fred Rodell launched a spirited attack against the existing law reviews, arguing that the "average law review writer is peculiarly able to say nothing with an air of great importance" and suggesting that this was a common feature because they all copied Harvard. He also objected to the lack of humor, their limited appeal, and explanatory footnotes, which are "an excuse to let the law review writer be obscure and befuddled in the body of the article and then explain it at the bottom of the page; . . . these huge chunks of small type . . . are what make the legal article very, very learned."

14. Innovations were not entirely missing outside the East. In the 1930s, Northwestern had an untraditional curriculum structure of two years of formal classes followed by one or two years of lab studies with concentration in two or three areas. At the end of the lab studies, the student was required to submit a written work about the studies. See Green, "A New Program in Legal Education," 299.

Most significant, perhaps, was the work of John Bradway at the University of Southern California and at Duke University. Bradway instituted a legal aid clinic at USC, starting in 1928, which was so successful that he was invited to set up a similar program at Duke. Throughout the 1930s and into the 1940s, Bradway developed and propagandized the legal clinic program, producing a series of influential articles. See "The Beginning of the Legal Clinic of USC," 3 *Southern California Law Review* 36 (1932); "Legal Aid Clinic," 7 *St. John's Law Review* 236 (1933); "Clinical Preparation for Admission to the Bar," 8 *Temple Law Quarterly* 185 (1934); "Objectives of Legal Aid Clinic Work," 24 *Washington University Law Quarterly* 173 (1939); "Classroom Aspects of Legal Aid Clinic Work," 8 *Brooklyn Law Review* 373 (1939); "Education for Law Practice: Law Students Can be Given Clinical Experience," 34 *American Bar Association Journal* 103 (1948); and "Case Presentation and the Legal Aid Clinic," 1 *Journal of Legal Education* 280 (1948). See Lindsay, "John Saeger Bradway—the Tireless Pioneer of Clinical Legal Education," 6.

The establishment did not respond with enthusiasm to Bradway's evangelism. Despite efforts to establish standards for the clinics in the 1940s, in 1948, the AALS Committee on Legal Aid Clinics found that "the original belief that Legal Aid would provide sufficient material for a broad program of in-school clinical training was too optimistic." "Report of the Committee on Legal Aid Clinics," *AALS Proceedings, 1948*, 188. By 1950, the AALS felt that the issue was decided and that it could do no more work in the area of clinics. "Report of the Committee on Legal Aid Clinics," *AALS Proceedings, 1950*, 123.

15. One observer noted that there had been "movement and much talk of movement in the field of legal education" but "of the few efforts which have proceeded from print to action . . . almost none have ventured far from the curriculum of the national . . . institutions," and he hoped that local schools would attempt to raise their standards toward those of the national schools. Brosman, "Modern Legal Education and the Local Law School," 517. From a different point of view, B. F. Boyer noted the differences between the local and national law schools, which were still patent just as World War II began. He argued that the smaller schools should accept their financial and size limitations and stop trying to emulate the more prestigious schools. Boyer, "Smaller Law Schools," 281.

16. Harvard, the *Review* continued, had "a more conservative policy" toward student participation in research projects. Carnegie Foundation, *Annual Review of Legal Education, 1929*, 37.

17. *Report of the Dean, Yale Law School, 1929–1930*, 21. Robert Hutchins began his law degree "out of boredom" while still an undergraduate. He managed to finish the degree in two and a half years by taking courses at odd hours of the day and in the summer and getting credit for his work as research assistant to Clark. He ran into considerable faculty disapproval for this program and was advised to take "some of the fundamental subjects given in the regular course." When Hutchins became a member of the faculty, he and Clark wrote up a proposal for honors courses based on the program Hutchins had followed, but the faculty only accepted it after it had been "watered down." Schlegel, "American Legal Realism," 467–70, nn. 39, 57.

18. *Report of the Dean, Yale Law School, 1930–31*, 24.

19. Ibid. Students referred to the course as "The Sex Life of a Check."

20. Temporary collaboration with teachers from other university departments was a related development with a similar history. From the 1920s, various short-lived experiments followed one another at the leading schools without ever becoming part of the regular curriculum. Examples from the era under discussion included federal administration, offered in the 1930s at Harvard for students of both law and administration programs, and joint seminars in labor relations and trade practices, offered at Wisconsin by the Law School and the Department of Economics. These and various similar experiments are chronicled in Brown, *Lawyers, Law Schools, and the Public Service*, 124–31. What characterized many of these interdisciplinary courses and seminars was their ephemeral character and their habit of reappearing as "major innovations" in later decades.

21. These new casebooks were to come into wide use; by 1937 the new Columbia casebooks alone were being used in 117 of the 190 law schools in the country. Goebel, *School of Law, Columbia*, 500.

22. This was the first casebook extensively to violate "the classical principle" of full reprinting of cases. Ehrenzweig, "The American Casebook," 235. Although based on the business transaction, the book was not purely functional. Llewellyn wrote in his introduction, "Legal technique . . . moves into the foreground, and an understanding of the business situation becomes not a primary object, but a means of making the job intelligible." Another landmark was Leon Green's functionally organized torts casebook, published in 1931. "To advocates of doctrinal organization the maddening feature of Green's *The Judicial Process in Tort Cases* (1931) was that he denied the legitimacy of a doctrinal approach. Green's organization . . . abandoned the tripartite scheme and arranged concepts 'functionally' by reference to the 'interests' affected. Green seemed to be saying (to many reviewers) that the participants in a case, the atmosphere it created, and the interests at stake were what determined its outcome, quite independent of rules or principles." White, *Tort Law in America*, 85.

23. *Report of the Dean, Yale Law School, 1930–31*, 22.

24. The distinction between courses and seminars is, unfortunately, clear only to those who have spent many years in the law school culture. But a seminar generally presupposes smaller numbers and written work. Furthermore, professors normally sit to teach seminars and stand (possibly in honor of Langdell?) for case classes.

25. The 1920s saw the rise of the seminar at the leading schools as one way of addressing the criticism of large classes. Columbia found seminars useful for experimenting with the new courses suggested by the Marshall reorganization. Goebel, *School of Law, Columbia*, 234–35. There were seventeen honors seminars for the best second- and third-year students at Columbia in 1928–29. *Summary of Studies in Legal Education*, 190. Harvard held sporadic seminars by the early 1920s, and they seem to have come into regular use at Yale about 1930–31. Sutherland, *The Law at Harvard*, 341; *Report of the Dean, Yale Law School, 1929–30*, 11.

26. This process was just beginning by World War II: a 1939 survey of forty-five smaller law schools showed only four, at most, offering seminars. Leflar, "Survey of Curricula in Smaller Law Schools," 259–61. The post-World War II era saw the spread of seminars—even then, rarely more than a few—to the middle-grade schools. Moreland, "Legal Writing and Research in the Smaller Law Schools," 53–54.

27. "The four-year course of study is not a product of the thirties, but it stands out as one of the most popular experiments of the decade." Harsch, "The Four-Year Law Course in American Universities," 244. The earliest experiments with the four-year course dated from 1919 at California and Northwestern: neither had been successful. Ibid., 250–53.

28. Wigmore, "Minority Report on Committee on a Four-Year Curriculum," *AALS Handbook, 1920*, 215–19.

29. It was, however, supported by the ABA. Roalfe, *John Henry Wigmore*, 169–70.

30. Katz, "A Four-Year Program for Legal Education," 530.

31. Ibid., 529. *The Preliminary Statement of the Committee on Legal Education of the Harvard Law School* noted that Chicago had done most among interested law schools in the offering of nonlaw courses within the local school itself (113).

32. Katz, "A Four-Year Program," 533, 536.

33. Minnesota's four-year curriculum was first adopted in 1930 (for a few years after 1938 it was the only option). Based on two years of required prelaw study, the program could assume student familiarity with the subject matter of the prescribed college courses, largely in government, history, and the social sciences. (Seventy percent of the undergraduate program was prescribed.) The program was highly successful at first; in 1936, over 60 percent of the entering students opted for this program instead of the three-year one. But changing demands diminished its viability. The drop in admissions during the war necessitated the return of the three-year program dropped in 1938, and students became increasingly less willing to devote four years when three would suffice. The four-year option itself was dropped in 1958. Lockhart, "The Minnesota Program of Legal Education—the Four-Year Plan," 234–55; *Bulletin of the University of Minnesota Law School, 1958–1960*, 5; and Stein, "In Pursuit of Excellence—a History of the University of Minnesota Law School, Part III," 1187–1200. There were also experiments with four-year programs at Louisiana State, Stanford, the University of Washington, and Washington University during this period.

34. *Report of the Dean, Yale Law School, 1932–33*, 5. Nine completed the course, and about the same number took the combined program in the next few years. Ibid., *1933–34*, 7; ibid., *1934–35*, 9; ibid., *1935–36*, 7; ibid., *1937–38*, 7.

35. Ibid., *1932–33*, 16.

36. Dean Clark wrote of its failure, "This promising venture in legal education is, I fear, somewhat ahead of the times." Ibid., *1934–35*, 9; ibid., *1938–39*, 6–7.

    Yale was not the only school to maintain a law-business program in the 1930s. For various other ventures, see, especially, Harsch, "The Four-Year Course," 254–55, 270; Brown, *Lawyers and the Promotion of Justice*, 88; Brown, *Legal Education at Michigan*, 299–300; Brown, *Lawyers, Law Schools, and the Public Service*, 131.

    The abandonment of the combined programs was explained by Leon Keyserling on the ground that the law-business studies actually attempted were made "from the point of view of the practicing lawyer rather than from that of the economist. As a result, the real rapprochement has been between the law school and the business school." Keyserling, "Social Objectives in Legal Education," 455.

37. Even these schools did not all react at the same rate. Although Columbia by 1934 was requiring every student to take at least twelve semester hours in public law, Harvard's 1938 revised curriculum still concentrated heavily on private law (two hours of

criminal law was the only public law requirement). Goebel, *School of Law, Columbia*, 327; Harvard Law School, *Statement of the Committee on Legal Education*, 80.

38. Comment, "Ernst Freund—Pioneer of Administrative Law," 29 *University of Chicago Law Review* 755.

39. Taken from Reed's study of Michigan, Harvard, Chicago, and Northwestern as four typical schools of the "widely elective type." Reed, *Present-Day Law Schools*, 231, 234.

40. See, especially, Garrison, "Developments in Legal Education at Michigan, Illinois, Chicago, Northwestern, Minnesota, and Wisconsin," 28–30; Handler, "What, If Anything, Should Be Done by the Law Schools to Acquaint Students with the So-Called New Deal Legislation and Its Working?," 164. Even the small schools were feeling the pressures for change by the end of the decade: a survey of forty-five small law schools in 1939 showed twenty-three offering administrative law and twenty-two giving a course in public utilities; in addition, six offered labor law and six trade regulation. Various other public law courses were common. Leflar, "Survey of Curricula," 262. Even the unapproved (generally proprietary) law schools had begun to include public law in their regular curricula. A survey of half a dozen such schools in the late 1930s found all of them offering at least one public law course, usually constitutional or administrative law. See, for example, the catalogs of Portia, University of Baltimore, Balboa, Atlanta, Cincinnati YMCA, and Southwestern University law schools, and the Northwestern College of Law (Oregon) for 1939–40.

41. See Auerbach, "Born to an Era of Insecurity," 12, n. 56, and Auerbach, *Unequal Justice*, 158–230.

42. Brown, *Lawyers, Law Schools, and the Public Service*, 178–79, 81. One of the first to reflect the change was Columbia's "Legal Problems of Governmental Administration," begun experimentally just before World War II. Ibid., 191–92.

43. Leach, "Property Law Taught in Two Packages," 35.

44. Often these law professors played major roles. Adolf A. Berle, Jr., one of the members of Franklin D. Roosevelt's "Brain Trust," had graduated from Harvard Law School and was a professor at Columbia. Rex Tugwell, another member of the trust, explained Roosevelt's use not only of law professors but also of professors in general in these terms: "Roosevelt preferred to keep our present discussions among those of us who had no contact there [Wall Street]. We were merely university people; we might not be practical, might not even be expert in procedures, but we had the virtue in his eyes of being free, and also of being bright enough, he thought, to bring him the stuff policies could be made from. Adolf [Berle] was questionable from this point of view; he had an office in the financial district, but it was a law office and this evidently cleared him." See Tugwell, *The Brains Trust*, 167. Harvard's Felix Frankfurter was another major figure, serving both as adviser to the president and as perhaps the most enthusiastic encourager of the migration of law students to Washington. Although Frankfurter was probably never as influential as he believed himself to be, he became powerful enough so that Hugh Johnson raged about his being "the most influential single individual in the United States" and about his "boys [having] been insinuated into obscure but key positions in every vital department." Auerbach, *Unequal Justice*, 170. For some statistics on the migration of students, see ibid., 181.

45. Frank's attitude about working for the New Deal, as interpreted by Auerbach, is particularly, if unconsciously, revealing about how Frank and his colleagues became wrapped up in this work to the exclusion of other more traditional scholarly duties:

> Frank personified the affinity between legal Realism and the New Deal. Realists, he declared in the thinly veiled autobiographical statement, easily became New Dealers because they were less Procrustean and more flexible in their techniques

and because they judged legal institutions by their human consequences rather than by their platonic essences. As experimentalists they were skeptical of their own notions but not paralyzed by inaction. The lawyer who believed in "undeviating fixed legal principles," Frank's "Mr. Absolute," would be repelled by the New Deal. His adversary, "Mr. Try-It," could run social experiments for sixteen hours each day without strain or fatigue. [Auerbach, *Unequal Justice*, 29, 178]

46. Brown, *Lawyers, Law Schools, and the Public Service*, 188–89.
47. *Report of the Dean, Yale Law School, 1927–28*, 115–16.
48. *Report of the Dean, Yale Law School, 1932–33*, 18. Graduate programs grew during these years. Columbia's graduate program, dominated by functionally organized seminars even before the undergraduate reorganization, was, by the late 1920s, "probably the most highly regarded and vigorous" of any law school's. Currie, "The Materials of Legal Education, Part I," 8. The graduate programs were largely designed for prospective teachers, and nearly all the fellowships went to students planning to teach. Reed, "Legal Education, 1925–28," 771; Smith, "Training the Law Teacher through Graduate Work," 93–94; Yale received $250,000 for Sterling Fellowships in 1928–29. Harvard by 1931 had over twenty fellowships available from $250 to $3,000, and Columbia had nine, offering between $1,200 and $3,000. *Report of the Dean, Yale Law School, 1928–1929*, 6; Smith, "Training the Law Teacher," 92–94. In-depth studies in comparative law were stressed at Harvard, and the functional orientation at Columbia and Yale provided encouragement for graduate study in nonlegal matters. *Report of the Dean, Yale Law School, 1931–32*, 18; "Notes and Personals," 5 *American Law School Review* 424 (1924); *Report of the Dean, Yale Law School, 1925–26*, 112.
49. Sutherland, *The Law at Harvard*, 277.
50. *Report of the Dean, Yale Law School, 1926–27*, 116. By 1928–29, Yale was rejecting over two-thirds of its applicants to maintain this limit, and the overall student quality had improved markedly. *Report of the Dean, Yale Law School, 1928–29*, 7. "There was a certain amount of fraud in the initial application of this policy, because even previously there had never been more than a hundred in each class. Nevertheless, it was a bold announcement to the world, and particularly to Yale's competitor, the Harvard Law School, that Yale intended to remain a small school, not because few students applied, but because it had voluntarily resolved to remain small. Under the leadership of Dean Clark, it was not long before applications increased so heavily that the selective-admission policy became reality instead of a false front." Arnold, *Fair Fights and Foul*, 35.
51. Yale had admitted women in 1918.
52. *Report of the Dean, Yale Law School, 1926–27*, 116. By 1940, students normally had to have a predicted B average before acceptance.
53. Ibid., 117; *Report of the Dean, Yale Law School, 1930–31*, 13.
54. Yale's experiment initiated a number of similar ones in other schools. Using the word "psychopoyemetrology" to define the "science of measuring mental achievement," John Henry Wigmore decided after experiments with a Stoddard-Ferson test that this test had no substantial value in predicting success in law studies. Wigmore, "Juristic Psychopoyemetrology—or How to Find Out Whether the Boy Has the Makings of a Lawyer," 454. For four years, the University of Tennessee experimented with a test but concluded that it had no particular usefulness, because although it could demonstrate inherent ability to some degree, it gave no indication of the "will to work." See "Letters to the Editors," 25 *Illinois Law Review* 446 (1931). The University of Southern

California concluded a few years later, after a study of 520 of its first-year students, that their test could only be used with extreme caution. Cormack and Hutcheson, "Relations of Pre-Legal Studies and Intelligence Tests to Success in Law School," 35. It was not until 1947 that the College Entrance Examination Board in Princeton developed the "Law School Admissions Test," which was first administered in February 1948. Crawford, "Use of Legal Aptitude Test in Admitting Applicants to Law School," 151; Gorham and Crawford, "Yale Legal Aptitude Test," 1237; Reese, "The Standard Law School Admission Test," 124.

55. Carnegie Foundation, *Annual Review of Legal Education, 1928,* 26; *Report of Dean Clark, 1930–31,* 13.

56. *Summary of Studies in Legal Education,* 184; Reese, "The Standard Law School Admission Test," 125. Minnesota also experimented with aptitude tests in the 1930s and was unsuccessful in finding a reliable one. Stein, "In Pursuit of Excellence," 1195.

57. First argued that Yale's decision to limit enrollment was a primary example of how "[t]he stronger individual schools were . . . able to express their elitist preferences without concern for competition from the profit maximizers." Although First is correct in noting that Yale could probably not have succeeded in its selective admissions policy were it not relatively wealthy and prestigious, this argument ignores the fact that Yale, though perhaps no longer in conscious competition with part-time schools, was seriously competing with other elite schools, Harvard and Columbia in particular, and any decisions on policy could not be made at will but had to take into consideration the actions and policies of these schools.

58. Yale Law School's endowment in 1931 was a little over $2,000,000. $150,000 was received yearly as income from the general funds of the university. *Report of the Dean, Yale Law School, 1930–31,* p. 33.

59. Sutherland, *The Law at Harvard,* 249–50, 306–7. In 1937–38, just under 19 percent of the applicants for the first-year class were rejected, reducing the size of the class between 15 and 20 percent. Simpson, "Developments in the Law School Curriculum and in Teaching Methods," 1040.

60. Sutherland, *The Law at Harvard,* 283–86. See also Seligman's description of the student complaints, *The High Citadel,* 64–67; and note, in general, the remarkable similarity to contemporary complaints about curriculum teaching methods and orientation, ibid., pp. 95–200, passim.

61. Reed, *Present-Day Law Schools,* 223–29.

62. In fact, the Harvard Law School had asked the corporation in 1900 to allow a J.D., in place of the LL.B., at the time when it was restricting admission to college graduates: "That is to say, the Harvard law faculty had originally created the anomaly in question, by being the first to utilize the English baccalaureate for a course of purely professional training divorced from cultural studies. It now proposed to rectify the anomaly by utilizing the Continental doctorate for purposes equally at variance with its traditional significance. The training that was to be represented by this degree contains, in its collegiate portion, cultural work of a kind that no Continental university provides, and lacks that emphasis upon research work not pursued for professional ends that specially characterizes these universities." Ibid., 78.

63. Reed, *Training for the Law,* 281.

64. Reed, *Present-Day Law Schools,* 199–200, 213–21. "The admission directly into practice of applicants who have received no training outside the college and professional school cannot be justified on the ground that they are adequately prepared to practice law. It can be justified, if at all, only on the ground that the mission phase of their preparation cannot be supplied under existing conditions. . . . On the other hand,

because these institutions cannot provide this sort of training within their own walls, it does not follow that they might not do something to restore this vanishing *element* to legal *education*."

65. Ibid., 215.
66. Ibid., 216.
67. Jerome Frank, *Courts on Trial*, 232–36.
68. On this, see Brown, *Lawyers, Law Schools, and the Public Service*, 234–39.
69. "The new era had not arrived. . . . There are still courses in Contracts, Torts, Property, and Trusts, retaining their old names and shapes; and even in those courses which have been revamped and renamed the appellate decision is the focus of study still. Law and the social sciences remain unintegrated." Currie, "The Materials of Law Study, Part I," 337.
70. Currie, "The Materials of Law Study, Part III," 26, n. 99. Esther Brown has suggested that Northwestern carried the functional approach further than any other school; she cites the 1946 curriculum revision as evidence. Brown, *Lawyers, Law Schools, and the Public Service*, 101, 104.
71. Cited in Brown, *Lawyers and the Promotion of Justice*, 86.
72. Ibid., 86.
73. Ibid., 86–87.
74. Cited in *Report of the Dean, Yale Law School, 1930–31*, 4.
75. Brown, *Lawyers, Law Schools, and the Public Service*, 10.

10 / Rising Standards for the Many

THE changes from 1922 to 1945 outside the elite centers of legal education reflected the economic and social pressures being exerted at a national level. The intellectual ferment of the Realists may have left the bulk of these schools unaffected, but the ever-rising commitment to higher standards did not. The story of the ABA–AALS and their fight to "raise standards" became, if anything, more complex in the 1920s and 1930s. While the elite schools worried about whether or not to develop institutes for advanced legal study,[1] the professional organizations were concerned that most law students were not getting adequate legal education in their first degrees. In 1922, there was not one state that required attendance at law school. Proprietary schools were as vigorous as ever.[2] The 1920s were to begin with the ABA and the AALS moving vigorously to raise standards from the bottom up.

In 1921, the ABA put its seal of approval on the requirement of two years of prelegal college work for all prospective law students while approving either four-year part-time or three-year full-time programs in law schools. As an entirely voluntary body, the ABA's only weapon in promoting conformity to its standards was in theory logic but in practice the art of persuasion. This did not always work,[3] although there were some successes. In 1922, the ABA-sponsored meeting of local and state bar associations (the Conference of Bar Association Delegations) generally approved these decisions.[4] At the conference, however, certain variations from the ABA model, as envisaged by the Root Report, surfaced. Although the delegates did not accept the basic two years of prelegal college training (which the Reed Report had also called for), they approved a requirement of "equivalent training" as an alternative. There was other evidence that the conference was more "democratic" than the ABA convention, which had discussed the proposals. States without such facilities were encouraged to establish colleges and law schools, so that economic considerations would not prevent the less affluent from entering the profession.[5] The conference also passed a resolution deploring the commercialization of legal education but stressing the desirability, for ethical reasons, of close contact between the law students and practicing lawyers.[6]

The 1921 and 1922 meetings had given some added legitimacy to the part-time and evening schools[7] by establishing the four-year requirement in addition to the full-time schools' three-year one. In the long run, though, the resolutions gave even greater legitimacy to the middle-grade schools. As their spokesman, the AALS joined the ABA in pressing for ever-increasing "standards" each year. It is true that by 1922 membership in the AALS had again been opened to part-time schools,[8] but concurrently the requirements for full-time study were raised.[9] In 1923, the criteria for part-time education were increased, and the AALS formally added one year to the prelegal college education requirement for member schools.[10]

The early 1920s were to see close cooperation between the ABA and the AALS,[11] as they each established new regulations. In 1923, the ABA issued its first list of approved schools.[12] In 1924, the AALS established a requirement of one full-time teacher for each one hundred students,[13] tightened the definition of part-time education yet again, and raised the library requirements that had originally been set in 1912.[14] The next year, the AALS requirement of two years of prelegal education went into effect;[15] the ABA in its turn adopted the AALS faculty requirement[16] and dropped its category of provisionally approved schools.[17] In 1926, the ABA again adopted an earlier AALS requirement by demanding two years of prelegal college work, and the AALS rescinded the rules allowing law students to take limited college work concurrently with their law studies.[18]

An even more significant rapprochement between the two associations occurred in 1927 when the ABA appointed its first full-time adviser on legal education, Claude Horack,[19] who was at that time also the secretary of the AALS. His primary assignment was to raise the standards of law schools and of bar admissions. In keeping with this goal, the two associations continued to press on relentlessly with heightening requirements. The ABA extended its concerns beyond legal education and, in addition to demanding more public colleges, called for an examination to test whether alternatives to college education were, in fact, "equivalents."[20] The AALS, having set new library standards only three years before, raised them once again in 1927, establishing a minimum of 7,500 volumes with an annual minimum maintenance of $1,000.[21] At the same time, it shook off virtually all alternatives to two years of prelaw college work.[22] In 1928, the ABA followed the AALS once more and demanded of its members a minimum of three full-time instructors and 7,500 volumes in the library.[23]

During the 1920s, the legal profession had grown by 38,000, and the number of law schools rose from 142 in 1921 to 173 in 1928. There had been at the same time a rapid rise in the standards required by the ABA and AALS. Moreover, as the result of their close cooperation, by 1927 the ABA list of approved schools was almost identical with the membership of the AALS.[24] All of this was, however, "like the action of acid on metal." ABA standards were met by only about half the country's law schools (there were 65 ABA-approved schools in 1927) and only about one-third of law students were in AALS schools (34 percent in 1928),[25] representing a rapid drop since the beginning of the decade. More important, however, was the fact that, in 1927, of the forty-nine jurisdictions (the forty-eight states and the District of Columbia), thirty-two states still had no formal legal requirement for prelaw studies, and eleven required merely high school graduation or its equivalent. Only six required two years of college or its equivalent.[26] In 1927, none required attendance at law school.

On the other hand, during the 1920s, there had been a significant rise in the requirement for some formal legal training. By 1928, every jurisdiction except Indiana had a compulsory bar examination.[27] Nine jurisdictions still had no requirements for any law training,[28] but the tide had turned. By 1930, four states had come to require attendance at law school (three years in West Virginia, two years in Colorado, one each in Kentucky and Wyoming). Moreover, in the remaining forty-five jurisdictions, law school and law office training had become alternatives, and only four states still insisted on some office training for all students. All other states allowed the alternative of a preparation exclusively done at a law school, and a few—including Illinois, Michigan, Minnesota, New York, Ohio, Washington, and Wisconsin—were actually ready to offer three years of law school as an alternative to four of apprenticeship.[29]

It was in this atmosphere of rising standards and increasing conformity that Reed's second report appeared.[30] His major concern by 1928 was the rapidly accelerating homogenization of law schools,[31] which pressures from the ABA and the AALS were promoting.[32] The only major exception to the pattern was the "four-year part-time" proviso that had saved the "better" evening schools.[33] In all other areas, the mark of the professional elite was clear, and the effects of the ABA–AALS drive were particularly evident in the increasing demands for prelegal training. Such requirements were forcing the smaller law schools into the mold of the elite, and Reed feared that eventually the standards would be applied to all schools, even those catering to the least affluent sections of the population. "The profession already is divided . . . in the worst of all possible ways. The recent effort to abolish the division by the method of abolishing evening law schools has been abandoned. The current effort to abolish the division by the method of making evening law schools the equivalent of the orthodox type cannot . . . succeed."[34] Reed was indeed back to his perennial theme—the misleading assumptions underlying the supposed homogeneous bar in America. This time he called for only two types of law schools, with his model by then more clearly the English barrister and solicitor. He still thought that the profession would be driven to his position, but he offered a caution about the suggestions in his earlier volume: "The reception accorded to these parts of the volume convinced its author that little sympathy with this idea can be expected from the present generation of lawyers. They dismiss it as a vision, and not even an attractive vision."[35]

The potential conflicts between the different types of law schools were abundantly evident at the meeting of the ABA Section of Legal Education in 1929. That year's meeting of the section was probably one of the most unpleasant on record. All the questionable aspects of the policy of raising standards were brought to the surface and expounded upon at length. The supporters of ABA–AALS policy were no less vocal in their defense of their point of view. The two approaches were typified, on one hand, by William Draper Lewis, the chairman of the section, and on the other, by Gleason Archer, the dean of Suffolk Law School, the largest in the country. The former was able to boast that "progress" had been so rapid that fourteen states were "now" complying with ABA regulations.[36] When Archer's turn came, he announced his address under the title, "Facts and Implications of College Monopoly of Legal Education,"[37] and the content matched its title. After noting that the ABA had given the section $15,000 to use during Lewis' chairmanship, Archer asked: "Now, what is the Section of Legal Education doing with this lavish contribution from our treasury? . . . The present Chairman of this Section, but for twenty years the guiding spirit of the Association of American Law Schools, and in 1924 its President, has hired H. Claude Horack, the present President of the Association of American Law Schools, at a $10,000 a year salary as field agent to capture the various states of the Union for the college monopoly."[38] James Brennan of Massachusetts backed Archer's charges of the suppression of the nonelite: "this great big organization now is attempting to divide our schools into groups, using, may I say, the blacklist—one of the most damnable and dangerous things in American life—the blacklist and the boycott."[39] Edward T. Lee, the dean of the John Marshall Law School in Chicago, also refused to back down before the section: "A group of educational racketeers—deans and professors in certain endowed and university law schools of the country—have used the American Bar Association as an annex to the Association of American Law Schools, a close corporation of 'case law' schools, entirely irresponsible to the American Bar Association, and . . . they have been boring from within our Association in the interest of their own, unmindful of two fundamental objects of our Association, to uphold the honor of the profession of the law and encourage cordial intercourse among the members of the American Bar."[40]

At least within the organized bar, however, the forces of "standardization" and "progress" were in the ascendant. The idea of a legal profession without standards was as unacceptable as a hospital without asepsis. Henry Drinker from Philadelphia said the majority of complaints received by the grievance committee of that city's bar association concerned "Russian Jew boys" and that requiring a college education from such people would "allow" them to "absorb American ideals."[41] Xenophobia, economic concerns, and professional vanity, coupled with a genuine concern for the public interest, were more than strong enough to resist Archer's and Lee's spirited attacks. Pluralism was apparently on the wane and all the ABA standards were reaffirmed at the 1929 meeting.

The 1930 meeting was almost as tense. Archer prefaced his remarks this time with the query: "Is this to be a deliberative meeting, or are we to have shock troops rushing in at the last minute and outvote those who have heard the debates?"[42] The ABA responded by passing a resolution against commercially operated schools. Archer was not to be cowed into submission, and he renewed the attack by proposing that one-half of each law school faculty be composed of practicing lawyers. The resolution caused a storm and, although it received considerable support, was ultimately defeated handsomely. The scholar-lawyers could still rely on the support of successful practitioners. Archer and Lee managed only to have a vague recommendation passed calling for personal contact between law students and established practitioners.[43]

In this and other ways the ABA managed to overpower the forces of the nonelite during the 1930s. The AALS, too, boosted standards. It decided that by 1932 all its member schools should have at least 10,000 volumes in their libraries and spend at least $2,000 a year in library upkeep. By the same deadline, member schools would have to employ four full-time instructors.[44] The incessant push for higher standards had led to a showdown between the professional "establishment" and the part-time schools. The establishment had emerged, largely unscathed, as the victor but only in terms of ABA and the AALS membership requirements. For all the friction between the ABA and the AALS there was far more community of interest between leading practitioners and full-time professors than there was between the big firm lawyers and the typical solo practitioner. The typical solo practitioner, however, was more likely to have rapport with state legislators than were members of the legal establishment. Thus it still remained for most states to pass legislation bringing their requirements up to those of the ABA and the leading law schools. The ABA's concern with standards and control of the legal profession would therefore continue into the 1930s.

Despite higher standards promulgated by the association, in 1928 part-time and mixed schools contained 60 percent of the total number of law students,[45] but the net was closing. In 1930 the ABA sponsored a new organization—the National Conference of Bar Examiners[46]—led by Will Shafroth, who had succeeded Claude Horack as adviser to the ABA Section of Legal Education. Some saw this new organization as a way of maintaining educational diversity. Reed, for instance, was optimistic.[47] The initial list of objectives of the conference, however, indicated a different orientation, namely toward standardizing legal education and admissions to the bar nationally.[48] The National Conference of Bar Examiners rapidly became part of the vehicle of the middle-grade AALS law schools' march toward uniformity,[49] and a major effort was launched to convince bar examiners that, as far as possible, they should set exam questions that looked like exam questions in the "better" law schools.[50]

If the Horatio Alger myth made legislatures reluctant to demand a higher education background of their lawyers, they marched more willingly to the beat of economic collapse. Not only Wall Street took notice of 1929. By 1932, no fewer than seventeen states required two years of prelegal college training[51]—nearly three times the number four years earlier. Moreover, thirty-three states required at least three years of law study, although that was generally allowed either in law school or by way of apprenticeship. Symbolically, Indiana in 1933 changed its constitution to allow the formal reestablishment of the legal profession, and it at once adopted many of the ABA requirements. This consolidation was materially aided by the depression, although, in one sense, the economic collapse had less effect than might have been expected. Numbers fell but not dramatically. There were 46,397 law students at the high-water mark in 1928. The number fell by about 15 percent to 39,417 in 1931 and then rose again to 41,920 in 1935.[52] Meanwhile, the number of law schools actually increased from 173 in 1928 to 182 in 1931 and to 195 in 1935. What did change, however, was the distribution of students. Between 1928 and 1935, the number of students in ABA schools actually increased by 5,000, represented only partly by an increase in the number of such schools from 66 to 68; the enrollment in unapproved schools fell by 10,000, and the number of such schools remained constant at 107. In percentage terms, the approved schools' share of the student body rose from 32.2 percent to 48.8 percent.[53] The marginal law schools were finding it economically difficult to survive.[54] Elitism appeared to be an advantage in times of financial crisis.[55]

Just how much the decline in the number of unaccredited schools during the 1930s was due to the depression, and how much to the establishment's continued raising of standards, still remains unclear, although one clearly fed on the other. Although leading members of the bar and law professors from prestigious law schools were at the center of the New Deal, the typical member of the bar was badly frightened by the depression and its effect on the legal profession.[56] State bars spent these years discussing overcrowding and trying to find an "acceptable" way of limiting numbers.[57] Proprietary schools were seen as the major cause of the overcrowding in the profession, and it was argued that having states raise standards would not only improve the quality of education by eliminating such schools but would also decrease the quantity of graduates and thus the number of those admitted to the bar. In addition to higher standards, another recommendation that only graduates of qualified schools be permitted to take bar exams also flourished as a way of driving the proprietary schools out of the market.[58] Despite the accusations that only selfish and undemocratic reasons motivated such suggestions,[59] the bar continued to argue that it was protecting the public from the incompetence and corruption that an overabundance of lawyers would inevitably engender.[60]

Worries about overcrowding,[61] however, involved more specific issues, including concern over lawyers' incomes, standards for bar examinations, and unauthorized law practice. Lloyd Garrison showed that in Wisconsin there was actually a need for more legal services but that many lawyers failed to make an adequate income.[62] Rather than seek to expand legal services, however, the ABA urged state legislatures and state supreme courts to prosecute unlicensed practitioners and competing professionals.[63] Such an approach was in keeping with the association's attitude toward legal education.

By the mid-1930s, the ABA was scenting victory in its efforts to eliminate unaccredited schools. It was not without significance that, in 1935, when the ABA took over from the Carnegie Foundation the publication of the *Annual Review of Legal Education*, the main article was by Will Shafroth, the new adviser to the ABA Section of Legal Education.[64] After discussing "overcrowding" and the importance of "good moral character," Shafroth noted, without complete condemnation, that the Philadelphia Bar Association had voted to limit the number of practicing lawyers in its jurisdiction: "Limitation on admission to the bar is opposed to the democratic traditions of this country and to our theories of equal opportunity, and it seems safe to say it will not be adopted on any wide scale except as a last resort. If we are in fact licensing too many lawyers, there are other ways of cutting down the supply."[65]

Perhaps Shafroth was not overly worried about the action of the Philadelphia bar because the organized bar, in fact, did have other methods in mind. Once again the medical profession, as it had in the time of Flexner, provided the precedent for the two-pronged attack: "This control has been accomplished by securing the adoption of rules and regulations in forty-four states requiring the applicant for a medical license to be a graduate of a school approved by the American Medical Association. Substandard medical schools have been eliminated and in the last thirty years the number of medical schools have been cut in two."[66] The ABA was determined to emulate this achievement. By 1937, it adopted the requirements of two years of college study, and three years of full-time or four years of part-time study at a law school that had a library of at least 7,500 volumes, a minimum of three full-time professors, and a student-faculty ratio of no more than one hundred to one.[67]

The response of the AALS to overcrowding was more hesitant than that of the ABA. Assuring the bar that the law schools were "not engaged in the bootlegging of embryo lawyers across the borders defended by bar examiners,"[68] the AALS at first "reacted skeptically to complaints of overcrowding."[69] Karl Llewellyn pointed out that, in reality, the bar was not overcrowded; it was just restricting its services to more elite groups and ignoring the less affluent majority of the population. There was merely an appearance of overcrowding because everyone was trying to enter the same sector of the market;[70] the same point that had been made by Lloyd Garrison in his Wisconsin survey.[71] Such hesitation, however, did not affect the AALS's commitment on higher standards.[72]

Despite this disagreement over the provision of services, the associations finally began to be more effective in their influence over state governments. Although the number of law schools rose, lawyers slowly emulated the physicians in persuading the states to raise their educational requirements. In his 1935 article in the *Annual Review of Legal Education*, Shafroth was able to report that "within the past two years the rapidity of the movement has increased, eleven states having adopted the two-year college requirement since January 1, 1934."[73]

The change was indeed remarkable. Each year during the 1930s, three or four states moved to a requirement of two years of prelegal college education. Isolated states went so far as to require three years of prelegal work. Pennsylvania, among other states, used stiffer character requirements as a means of curbing the number of lawyers, and other boards of bar examiners steadily raised the minimum passing grade.[74] Increasingly, the states required law school training and required that training to be in ABA schools; and, increasingly, the students went to those schools. In

1937, California, for instance, delegated the accrediting of law schools to the state bar and required students in unaccredited schools to take a special qualifying exam after one year.[75]

By 1938, there were 101 ABA-approved schools with 63.7 percent (23,827) of the national law school student body. By that year there were only eight states that did not require two years of college education before law school, and the ABA cheerfully noted a drop in the number of law students: "This decline is likely to continue as the effect of the adoption of the two-year college requirements in Massachusetts, California, and the District of Columbia, as well as in other states, continues to be felt."[76] Overall numbers were falling.[77] In 1939 there were 34,539 students, 3,000 less than there had been the year before, "undoubtedly . . . due in most instances to the increased entrance requirements."[78] The following year the president of the AALS referred to his organization as an "accrediting agency" and announced that "in the competition between schools for students the non-member carries a heavy handicap."[79] Either the depression or the AALS appeared to have become the savior of legal education.

NOTES

1. See, for example, Schlegel's description of the creation of the Institute of Human Relations at Yale. Schlegel, "American Legal Realism," 482–88, 545–58. See also Pound's concern with graduate work at Harvard. Seligman, *The High Citadel*, 60–61.

2. One state that saw a number of unaccredited schools emerge in the period was Virginia. Most were operated by ambitious entrepreneurs—practicing lawyers or businessmen—hoping to earn a profit. From 1911 until sometime in the 1930s, the Norfolk Law School ran evening courses, often functioning with a single professor. Norfolk College, a business school, operated a law department from 1924 until the late 1940s, or possibly the early 1950s—records are scanty. In 1922, William and Mary, home of the first law chair in the country, finally reopened its long closed law department and, perhaps ironically, faced hard going for many years. See Bryson, "The History of Legal Education in Virginia," 14.

3. State legislatures did not respond quickly to the ABA measures of 1921. Four years later, only one state required two years of college for law school applicants. Even by 1928, only West Virginia required graduation from an AALS-approved school, and, in 1929, in all the states but three an applicant to the bar still did not need to have graduated from a law school. First, "Competition in the Legal Education Industry," 361.

West Virginia's march toward mandatory law school may well have been typical of the road followed by other states. After the Washington conference in 1922, John W. Davis was invited to address the state bar association. In a speech complete with references to Communists and "parlor Bolsheviki" and worries about the increasing number of immigrants, Davis clearly carried considerable influence. Although John Boman pointed out that "every time you raise the standard you exclude some good young man and you are creating a sort of monopoly," and a Mr. Neal thought the proposals favored "the boys whose parents have been able to send them to colleges to get their equipment," these were not the majority sentiments. The majority shared the view of J. W. Vanderport: "We need not worry about the poor boy. If he has the aspiration to acquire an education, to improve his standard of living, and to improve the standard of the profession, there is little question of his achieving his ambition." The 1921 proposals passed by voice vote. West Virginia Bar Association, *Proceedings of the 37th Annual Meeting*, 38, 40, 105–38 (1922).

There was still disagreement in the West Virginia Bar Association, but in 1924 the association persuaded the Supreme Court of the state to accept the 1921 ABA proposals. Thus effective in 1928, two years of college and three years of law school were mandatory for admission to the bar. West Virginia Bar Association, *Proceedings of the 40th Annual Meeting*, 13–15 (1925).

4. The 560 delegates met in Washington, D.C., and, at the end of the second day of their deliberations, were subjected to a vigorous speech from Elihu Root, who had chaired the ABA committee making the recommendations. It was probably largely as a result of that speech that the delegates accepted virtually all the ABA resolutions.

5. A law school education was undeniably expensive: tuition charges in 1925 averaged between $100 and $250 a year. Harvard, Yale, Columbia, and a few others were already charging over $300, and Pennsylvania had reached $400. Reed, *Present-Day Law Schools*, 405–513. Scholarships and loans were scarce even at the well-endowed private schools. Yale's Dean Swan recorded the necessity of even the best students having to support themselves. *Report of the Dean, Yale Law School, 1923–24*, 124.

Ironically, these same law schools had become so successful financially that William Draper Lewis revealed in 1929 his belief that "the case is not uncommon . . . [in which] more than 70 percent of the money taken from the law student in fees is diverted to other than law school purposes." The law schools had "ended up subsidizing the university." See also First, "Competition in the Legal Education Industry," 363–64.

6. Earlier, such contact had been established through law office study, but the dramatic decline in this type of legal education was evident from the statistics of the 643 applicants taking the bar exam in New York in 1922. Only 9 out of the total number had not been to law school at all, and of these 9, 3 had graduated from college. Ibid., 361, n. 295. Ironically, as concern for lack of practical skills increased in the years after this, one suggested solution to the problem was that law offices should start "taking in" law students. See Weaton, "Law Teaching and Pragmatism," 338. See also Harno, *Legal Education in the United States*, 108–12; Seavey, "The Association of American Law Schools," 3, 163; and Sullivan, "Professional Associations," 415.

7. The number of students at part-time schools exceeded the number at full-time schools for the first time in 1923–24.

8. Part-time was defined as instruction given largely after 4:00 P.M. or involving less than twelve hours credit a term. Seavey, "The Association of American Law Schools," 158.

9. From 900 to 1,080 classroom hours. Ibid., 163.

10. Reed, *Present-Day Law Schools*, 124–26.

11. First, "Competition in the Legal Education Industry," 362.

12. Sullivan, "Professional Associations," 416. Thirty-nine schools were held to comply with ABA standards and were put into Class A. Nine schools, who hoped to comply, were put into the provisional Class B.

13. In 1925, Harvard had one full-time instructor to every 78 students (the ratio was 17:1,320), Yale one to 70 (6:418) and Columbia about one to 103 (7:721). Most smaller schools were in better shape. For example, at Cornell the ratio was 1:27,

182 / Law School

Nebraska 1:37, Kansas 1:18, Washington 1:25, Texas 1:26. But note that at Dickinson the ratio was 1:112, at Albany 1:150, and at Buffalo 1:283. Reed, *Present-Day Law Schools*, 262. The earliest standard on faculty had been an 1892 ABA recommendation of at least one full-time faculty member. By 1919, the AALS was requiring three. Carnegie Foundation, *Annual Review of Legal Education, 1921*, 7–8.

14. Reed, *Present-Day Law Schools*, 102, 124–25.
15. Sullivan, "Professional Associations," 416. In 1925, 62 of 168 law schools were AALS members. Reed, *Present-Day Law Schools*, 263–64.
16. Carnegie Foundation, *Annual Review of Legal Education, 1925*, 18.
17. Stolz, "Training for the Public Profession of the Law," 23. At this time, the ABA had approximately 8,000 members. Rogers, "The American Bar Association in Retrospect," 1:166.
18. Reed, *Present-Day Law Schools*, 133.
19. He became president of the AALS in December 1928. Harno, *Legal Education in the United States*, 114.
20. Sullivan, "Professional Associations," 417–18; Smith, "History of the Activity of the American Bar Association in Relation to Legal Education and Admission to the Bar," 5. In fact, pressures were beginning to mount. The 1927 meeting of the ABA Section of Legal Education was an acrimonious one. "Proceedings," 6 *American Law School Review* 168–70 (1927).
21. Some sense of the de facto hierarchy of law schools may be gained by contrasting these minimal requirements with the holdings of the leading law schools. The 1920s was a time of expansion in the great libraries: in 1916, Harvard had 290,000 volumes. Sutherland, *Law at Harvard*, 278. In 1928, Columbia had 147,000 volumes. *Yale Library Report, 1928–29*, 14. Yale had 107,000 volumes and the total was growing at about 8,000 volumes a year during the late 1920s. Ibid., *1927–28* through *1929–30*.
22. Reed, *Present-Day Law Schools*, 149, 552.
23. Carnegie Foundation, *Annual Review of Legal Education, 1928*, 48.
24. Reed, *Present-Day Law Schools*, 43.
25. Ibid., 378. In 1900–1901, 52 percent of law students were at AALS schools; in 1920–21, 43 percent. Ibid., 29.
26. Colorado, Illinois, Kansas, Ohio, and West Virginia. New York had agreed to demand two years of college as of 1929. Ibid., 52.
27. Some thirteen states still had a form of the diploma privilege. The controversy over this "right" seemed never ending. In 1932, the ABA still felt the need for further vociferous attacks against it. Goodrich, "Law Schools and Bar Examiners," 101. In 1937, the privilege still existed in twelve states (Kinnane, "Recent Tendencies in Legal Education," 563), although Texas would abolish it as of June of that year. Shafroth, "Recent Changes in Bar Admission Requirements," 304. Even into the 1940s and beyond, the dilemma continued. In 1941, the Supreme Court of South Dakota voted to abolish the privilege, but the action met with so many objections that it was restored. 10 *Bar Examiner* 4 (1941). In 1947, 628 of the total national bar admissions were by means of the diploma privilege that still existed in Alabama, Arkansas, Florida, Louisiana, Mississippi, Montana, South Carolina, South Dakota, West Virginia, and Wisconsin. *AALS Proceedings, 1948*, 167.
28. Arizona, Arkansas, Florida, Georgia, Indiana, Mississippi, Missouri, Nevada, and Virginia. Reed, *Present-Day Law Schools*, 49.
29. These changes in the direction of stricter formal requirements by the states may have been accelerated by the movement, begun in the 1920s, to have state legislatures make it compulsory for lawyers to join the state bar association. The so-called integrated bars

frequently found it easier to obtain extensive rights of self-government, and ABA influence could thus be felt more strongly and directly in state regulation.

The movement began when the American Judicature Society published a model state bar act in December 1918. The first integrated bar was in North Dakota in 1921, followed by Alabama in 1923, and New Mexico in 1925. Finally, in 1927, California passed a state bar act. For a study of the politics of its passage and its impact on the legal profession in California, see Gilb, "Self-Regulating Professions and the Public Welfare." Some twenty-eight state bars were integrated as of 1970. Johnstone and Hopson, *Lawyers and Their Work*, 42–43.

30. Reed, *Present-Day Law Schools*. In terms of theoretical approach, this report was not appreciably different from the first one.

31. In 1919–20, there were still 1 one-year and 18 two-year law schools, in addition to 127 law schools of three years and more. By 1927 and 1928, there were 166 law schools with courses of three years or more, 8 two-year, and 2 one-year schools. Short-course schools survived only in the southern states and Indiana. Ibid., 111.

At the same time the number of students undergoing part-time instruction had risen rapidly during the 1920s (from some 13,318 in 1919 to 26,430 in 1926–27)—far faster than full-time students. Moreover, of the 176 degree-granting law schools, only 111 had any serious contact with a university. Ibid., 120. In 1926–27, roughly 43 percent were full-time students, 33 percent were evening students, 8 percent were early morning or late afternoon students, and 17 percent were late afternoon students.

32. Reed put it tactfully: "There has finally been formulated a definite programme, one which, because of the combination of influential and worthy elements that support it, must be respectfully considered by the authorities of all law schools, and by the legislatures, courts, and boards that are responsible for the admission of applicants to the practice of law." Ibid., 43.

33. They increased from 69 in 1919 to 86 in 1927–28. Ibid., 128. There were in all 70 exclusively part-time schools, offering a four-year course. One of them—Suffolk Law School—had over 2,000 students, while another—Boston YMCA (Northeastern)— had, in its various branches, 1,600. New York Law School had over 1,000 and 5 others had between 500 and 1,000: National (D.C.), Detroit YMCA, Cleveland, Chicago-Kent, Kansas City. Ibid., 287 ff.

34. Ibid., 305–6.

35. Ibid., 109.

36. 54 *ABA Reports* 57 (1929).

37. Archer referred to this monopoly as the "Educational Octopus." See Archer, *The Educational Octopus*. In 1919, Archer wrote the following in the introduction to the history of Suffolk:

> The writing of this chronicle of a school for the training of sons of working men, and how it encountered the Educational Octopus that controls all things educational in Massachusetts, has rendered necessary the projections of the personality of the author to a greater degree than would be called forth by the ordinary history. As in the case of the historian of ancient days, I am describing events all of which I saw and a part of which I was, for as the founder and Dean of the School the brunt of things necessarily devolved upon me. [Archer, *Building a School*, 11]

38. 6 *American Law School Review* 583 (1929).

39. Cited in First, "Competition in the Legal Education Industry," 363.

40. He had entitled his speech, "*In re* The Section of Legal Education and the American Bar Association: Is the Association to be Controlled by a Bloc?"

41. Drinker readily linked the raising of college requirements and racial attributes:

Is a two-year college course preliminary to the three-year course of the law school, as conducted by the efficient law schools there are nowadays, calculated to produce a better type of lawyer, the type that this Association would be in favor of, than without that advantage? Are we going to take full advantage of the wonderful efficiency of the modern system of legal education that has been devised in modern times, or aren't we?

Was John Marshall—the great Marshall—was Blackstone, was Tilghman, was Black, were they great lawyers, and did one of those great lawyers have a telephone in his office? Not one. Therefore you would all be better off, you would have more effective offices, if you threw away your telephones.

Now, this discussion heretofore has been devoted primarily to the educational feature of this matter. I want to direct your attention to another aspect of it, which seems to me to be at least of equal importance. I happened to be Chairman of the Committee on Grievances of the Law Association of Philadelphia. I was on that committee for three years, and in that way I came in contact, more than the average lawyer would, with the type of lawyer that this Association wants to keep from studying law, if it can, ...

... when you take a man who has done something that he ought not to have done as a lawyer, ... the man who has the law school training and the college training ... knows he has gone wrong, he is immoral, he is consciously doing wrong, ... but over and over again I have found these fellows, that came up out of the gutter and were catapulted into the law, have done the worst things and did not know they were doing wrong. They were merely following the methods their fathers had been using in selling shoe strings and other merchandise, that is the competitive methods they use in business down in the slums. I think, that on the average, the fellows who did not have this college training, who did not associate with the American boys, were not apt to realize they were doing anything wrong.

Another thing I noticed ... [was] that of the men who came before us who had been guilty of professional abuses, an extraordinarily large proportion were Russian Jew boys, young fellows who had been at the Bar a few years, and I could not understand why that was. I have known so many splendid Jewish lawyers and judges and had such great admiration for them, I could not see why such a large proportion were this way. I asked some of my good friends among the Jewish lawyers why this was, and they told me the Russian Jews, and the other foreign Jews too, who come over to this country, are all afire with a tremendous ambition that somebody in their family shall make good, and that if they have four or five boys and two or three girls, when they get big enough they pick out the one that is the smartest, and they all make a sacrifice to let that boy get an education, and they put him through school and try to get him to be a professional man, and lots of them become lawyers and doctors. Well, the boy comes on, works in a sweat shop or somewhere in the daytime and he studies law at odd times mostly—some of them send them through college, but most of them cannot; and he comes to the Bar with no environment at all except that out of which he came, and, with the tremendous pressure back of him to succeed, he has to make good; the whole family have been sacrificing themselves so he can. He does not have a chance—he has not had a chance to absorb the American ideals. There are any number of foreign boys to whom that situation applies. [*ABA Proceedings*, 1929, 622–23]

42. "Proceedings," 7 *American Law School Review* 33 (1930).

43. Ibid., 37–43.
44. Ibid., 176.
45. Kinnane, "Recent Tendencies in Legal Education," 559, 561. This reflected a steady increase since 1910, when enrollment at full-time schools was at a high of over 43 percent. McGuire, "The Growth and Development of American Law Schools," 91, 101.
46. This was not the first time that an attempt had been made to establish a national organization of bar examiners. Such efforts had been made in 1898, 1904, 1914, and 1916. Shafroth, "National Conference of Bar Examiners," 134. The success of this last effort may be attributed partly to the higher quality of state bar examining committees by 1932. All the states except Indiana had a state board of bar examiners. Shafroth, "Bar Examiners Take Steps toward Permanent Organization," 699. The committees, however, still had a long way to go in their development. Almost all of them were still at the amateur bar-examiner stage, meaning that the examining committee consisted of state court-appointed, elderly practicing lawyers, who were not professionally trained to give a bar examination. The average length of an examiner's term was 3.8 years, and most received less than $200 a year in compensation. Shafroth, "Training for the Bar," 21; Shafroth, "Bar Examiner and Examinees," 375.
47. "It may, should it see fit, help to develop those portions of a complete preparation for legal practice that lie outside the province of some, and possibly of all, law schools. In addition to these considerations of greater concern, it will of course not fail to discuss the less fundamental, but important, problems of bar examination technique." Reed, "Cooperation for the Improvement of Legal Education," 51–52.
48. The immediate objectives of the first National Conference were: the improvement of general education and legal education standards; the development of a more thorough character investigation process; the development of a better method of evaluating the fitness of bar candidates already admitted in another state; and the improvement of bar exams as a whole. See Shafroth, "Bar Examiner and Examinees," 134.
49. The bar exam was a continual source of worry both to ABA and to AALS members. One problem with most committees was considered to be that the examiners, usually the older members of the bar, were not always familiar with "modern" techniques and gave examinations on "out-dated" lines. Graduates of AALS schools might still pass, but it was just as likely that those from non-AALS schools could pass too. Green, "Legal Education and Bar Admission," 105; *AALS Proceedings, 1936*, 60. Another question was whether or not a bar exam could ever weed out the good from the bad. Leon Green did not think so, and Claude Horack questioned this as well. Green pointed out that bar examinations encouraged those proprietary schools offering cram courses (and may have implicitly promoted the validity of the diploma privilege as a way to avoid this), and Horack, in words reminiscent of Eliot's judgment on the lecture method, later added that "no amount of improvement can make them function properly; . . . [bar examinations] try to do the impossible—try to dip water with a sieve." Green, "Who Shall Study Law?," 578–79; Horack, "Securing Proper Bar Exams," 89.
    Just as the ABA and the AALS had trouble cooperating when they first tried to work together, so did the AALS and the bar examiners. "[E]ach group has been so intent on its own objectives that the common objectives of sound preparation and discriminating selection as a joint responsibility have been largely lost in the shuffle. . . . [T]his failure is due in some part to a lack of machinery for cooperation and coordinated effort, but more seriously it's . . . due to misconceptions about independence of functions, which in some instances has resulted in apparent hostility." *AALS Proceedings, 1936*, 97. A bar examiner from Minnesota conceded it would be "helpful to the examiners to have exam questions drafted by a sub-committee of law teachers." Ibid., 116. By 1939, one

commentator could note the "marked tendency toward cooperation between examiners and law schools in recent years." Kinnane, "Recent Tendencies in Legal Education," 563. By this date, twenty states had procedures for bringing together bar examiners and law professors in accredited schools. There was already a clearer sense of the unity of interest in reducing the number of lawyers and getting rid of the "poorer" lawyers and law schools. Maggs, "How the Common Objectives of Bar Examiners and Law Schools Can Be Achieved," 147. For further evidence of "raising the sights" of bar examiners in the 1930s, see Horack, "Securing Proper Bar Exams," passim.

A description of the first Annual Conference of the National Conference of Bar Examiners in Atlantic City in 1931 was provided by Biener: "Its objects shall be to increase the efficiency of State Boards of Law Examiners and Character Committees in admitting to the bar only those candidates who are adequately equipped from the standpoint of knowledge, ability and character to serve as lawyers, and also to study and cooperate with other branches of the profession in dealing with problems of legal education and admissions to the bar." Biener, Jr., "Retrospect and Prospect," 1. By 1939, the same author, in a speech replete with racist jokes, reported that "we have worked hand in hand with the officers and members of the Section of Legal Education and Admission to the Bar of the A.B.A. and with officers and members of the A.A.L.S. and our common efforts have undoubtedly resulted in marked improvement in bar admission methods in this country since our organization and have placed us in position to go forward to much greater accomplishments." Biener, Jr., "Address of Chairman to Ninth Meeting of National Conference of Bar Examiners," 390. Note also Bartlett, "Report of Committee of the Section on Legal Education on Co-operation Between the Law Schools and the Bar," 32.

50. Harno, *Legal Education in the United States*, 116.

51. Standards were proposed that included the following: "No Bar Examiner shall be appointed who does not have such scholarly attainments as are necessary, which accurately reflect the law school training that is now being offered in law schools approved by the A.B.A." *ABA Proceedings, 1940*, 50; Box 3, Stanford Law School Archives, Stanford University, Stanford, Calif.

52. Despite the optimistic signs, however, the impact of the depression was lasting, and World War II made matters worse. Enrollment did not reach the 1928 level again until the veterans returned from the war. In 1947, there were 51,015 law students. American Bar Association, *Annual Review of Legal Education, 1947*, 19. First, "Competition in the Legal Education Industry," 370.

53. American Bar Association, *Annual Review of Legal Education, 1935*, 64. The figures, however, can be deceptive. Although from 1928 to 1931 numbers at AALS schools fell by less than 2 percent, after this point the smaller AALS schools experienced serious difficulties. A 1934 Executive Committee report showed that, on average, members' budgets had been cut 17 percent between 1931 and 1933, library funds had fallen by 23 percent, and faculty salaries were lower by 14 percent. The report added, "Some reductions were very much larger. It was only by virtue of the fact that the larger schools suffered small reductions that the average was kept as low as herein shown." First, "Competition in the Legal Education Industry," 370–71.

Sutherland has noted of Harvard that the "depression did not materially diminish the number of students seeking the school's education." Sutherland, *Law at Harvard*, 282. Although Yale claimed to have been "very badly hit by the Depression," that seems to have been true mainly in terms of the availability of funds for research, even though there were some losses of funds for other things. Schlegel, "American Legal Realism," 444, 545. Yale's difficulties were probably typical of those faced by other leading schools: library purchases were cut back; new field research studies could not be undertaken, and it became difficult to find financing in order to complete the older projects; competition for professors from private firms grew harder to meet. *Report of the Dean, Yale Law School, 1931–32*, 6, 20–21. Ibid., *1932–33*, 4. Scholarship funds were reduced at precisely the time they were most needed. Ibid., *1931–32*, 33; ibid., *1933–34*, 8; ibid., *1935–36*, 15. By the mid-1930s, however, the National Youth Administration was supplying funds for employing students thus relieving financial pressure on students and, at the same time, providing otherwise unavailable research assistance for the faculty. Ibid., *1935–36*, 16; ibid., *1936–37*, 16. The depression seems to have caused no immediate problems in placing students graduating from leading schools. Yale graduates were placed with little difficulty throughout the depression, although the pattern of employment altered; by 1938, an increasingly large number of graduates was entering government service. Of the major schools, only Columbia seems to have suffered significant losses; enrollment had fallen 13 percent by 1931. First, "Competition in the Law School Industry," 370 and n. 349.

54. Non-AALS schools in the areas of Boston and New York were particularly affected by the depression. Enrollment in Boston went down by a third; in New York, by nearly one half. Meanwhile, similar schools in Chicago and Washington showed total increases of 26 percent and 23 percent, respectively. Ibid., 370 and n. 347.

Even here the patterns may have been changing. In the Class of 1918 at the John Marshall Law School in Chicago, 7 out of 40 members reporting their birthplace had been born abroad: 3 were born in Russia, 1 in Rumania, 1 in Poland, 1 in Asia Minor, and 1 in Sweden. In the Class of 1928, 5 out of 53 reported being born abroad: 3 were born in Russia, 1 in Austria, and 1 in Italy. In the Class of 1938, none reported being born abroad, and the vast majority had been born in Illinois. John Marshall Law School, *Alumni Directory, 1899–1967*, passim. Copies of the student yearbook (*The Abstract*) showed 2 blacks in the Class of 1928 but virtually none in the classes of the 1930s. John Marshall Law School Archives, Chicago, Ill.

55. First has offered a partial explanation for these phenomena:

> Legal education in the mid-1930's was not an industry in distress. Apparently at the same time that lawyers were complaining of overcrowding and cutthroat competition, people were still interested—indeed, increasingly interested—in entering the legal profession. An information lag may explain the continued demand, but our model of student as consumer provides a more plausible explanation. The question for the student is whether the expected return on an investment will likely be higher than that on alternative investments. Thus, if the returns on comparable investments had declined at least as much as the return on legal education, demand would not be adversely affected. So long as students had funds to invest, demand might continue strong despite the appearance of poor prospects on graduation. It is not surprising, then, that law school education continued to be an attractive investment during the Depression. ["Competition in the Law School Industry," 374–75]

Although this explanation has a certain validity, it ignores the fact that the smaller, less expensive schools were fairly hard hit, whereas the large, expensive schools balanced out the statistics by maintaining steady admissions.

56. The average lawyer across the country was seriously affected by the depression. In 1933, almost half the practicing lawyers in New York City had earnings below the minimum subsistence level for American families. In Missouri, about the same proportion of "country" lawyers lived at subsistence level. In California, statistics for lawyers

admitted to the bar from 1929–31 showed that 51 percent did not earn enough to support their families during their first year of practice; by the second year, this was still true of 37 percent and by the third year the figure was 33 percent. Auerbach, *Unequal Justice*, 159. See also MacDonald, "Bar Admission and Legal Education," 69–70; and "Limitations on New York Bar Admissions Recommended," 5 *Bar Examiner* 115 (1936).

57. In 1931, Shafroth predicted dire consequences if the projection of 240,000 lawyers in 1940 were to come true. Shafroth, "The Part of the Bar Association in Fixing Standards of Admissions," 512. Local jurisdictions worried too. In Mississippi, it was alleged that there were "a number of men now practicing law in Mississippi that ought to be out plowing." Stone, "The Greatest Good for the Greatest Number," 290. Tennessee was particularly concerned over the fact that it had a disproportionately high number of bar admissions compared with other southern states and that from 1930 to 1936 eleven new law schools opened there. Respondents to a questionnaire from the Missouri bar indicated serious overcrowding, and 44 percent of young lawyers in California said that overcrowding was affecting their opportunities on the job market. Kennerly, "299 a Year!," 224; Arant, "Survey of Legal Education in the South," 182; *AALS Proceedings, 1934*, 75; Brenner, "A Survey of Unemployment Conditions among Young Attorneys in California," 175.

58. See Ethridge, "Unjust Standards for Law Practice," 276, 277.

59. The "proposition is undemocratic and tends to create by law a favored class of professional aristocracy to consist alone of those who have the good luck to be born well off financially, or who have rich friends who will let them have the means to take up these long years of study." The same author suggested that class warfare could result from such policies: "Let's not kindle the fire of revolution and class hatred by establishing class privilege and by taxing the poor for the support of special and favored institutions of learning." Ethridge, "Unjust Standards for Law Practice," 284. The National Association of Law Schools, consisting of non-AALS members, demanded that a man be judged not by his law school education, but by his "reputation, knowledge and experience as a lawyer." 4 *John Marshall Law Quarterly* 544 (1939). Some invoked the frontier experience of the early years of the nation as an argument against high standards. The hard-working were entitled to be admitted to the bar. Rogers, "Democracy versus High Standards," 1.

60. "Primarily, then, we must answer, not whether some deserving boy may find it more difficult . . . to gain admission to the bar because he must first secure some college education, but rather whether the public will be better served if every lawyer is required to have an adequate general education as well as a technical training in the study of law." *Statement of the A.B.A. Council on Legal Education and Admissions to the Bar*, 28 September 1937, 11. A bar member in Tennessee argued somewhat illogically: "The name and character of the great Lincoln have been slandered and libelled by those who have used him as an argument for the toleration of disgracefully low standards in legal education. If Lincoln had grown up in the last forty years, he would certainly have had college and law school degrees." Arant, "Survey of Legal Education in the South," 184. The same author put forth a more common argument (showing a strong dose of Horatio Alger mythology): "Opportunities are too common and there is too much subsidization of education for any young man of reasonable ability and strength of character to be without as much education as is required by those states in this country which have the highest educational standards for admission to the bar. . . . The fact that a young man is stupid, lazy, or even poor is not a reason to bestow upon him a license to practice law." Ibid., 184–85.

61. Much was written in this period about overcrowding. See Shafroth, "The Problem of the Lawyer's Qualifications," 268; "Report of the Chairman," 2 *Bar Examiner* 181 (1933), where a familiar analogy was invoked: "Like Alice in the White Rabbit's house, the legal profession will soon be bumping its head against the ceiling with one leg up the chimney, and one arm out of the window, but there seems to be no little cake marked Eat Me which will even stop its prodigious growth much less reduce its size." For a general review of the literature, see Hurst, *The Growth of American Law*, 255, 314–17. See also First, "Competition in the Legal Education Industry," 371–75.

62. Garrison, "Address," 165. On incomes during this period, see "Income of Lawyers, 1929–1948," U.S. Department of Commerce, *Survey of Current Business* (1949), 18. See also ABA, Special Committee on the Economic Conditions of the Bar, *The Economics of the Legal Profession* (1938); Wickser, "Law Schools, Bar Examiners, and Bar Associations—Co-operation versus Insulation," 734. The literature on the economics of the law during this period is reviewed in Brown, *Lawyers and the Promotion of Justice*, 150–69. On the bar during the 1930s, see Laski, *The American Democracy*, 572–80.

63. Concern about unauthorized practice should not be underrated. See Swaffield, "Unlawful Practice of the Law," 181–87. For other aspects of the problem, see also "Notes—Unauthorized Practice of Law," 15 *Nebraska Law Bulletin* 164–66 (1937); Stecher, "Unauthorized Practice and The Public Relations of the Bar," 278; McCoy, "Unlawful Practice of the Law, Some Recent Prosecutions," 294; Houck, "The State Acts to Suppress Unauthorized Practice," 235.

64. Shafroth, "The Next Step in the Improvement of Bar Admission Standards," 13.

65. Ibid., 21.

66. Ibid.

67. See *Statement of the A.B.A. Council on Legal Education and Admissions to the Bar*, 28 September 1937.

68. Wilson, "Preparation for the Bar Exam," 128.

69. First, "Competition in the Legal Education Industry," 375.

70. "I don't know whether there are too many lawyers or not, . . . as the profession is organized there's too little business for half of them. Maybe that's because we have too many lawyers, and maybe it's because some of those we have are paying $200,000 in income taxes. . . . I say that the honest ambulance chaser does what the 'better' bar does not do. He brings legal services to the man who needs legal services a lot more than the blue stocking man does." *AALS Proceedings, 1933*, 64.

71. Although including statistics that showed that lawyers, doctors, and engineers all suffered about a 40 percent drop in income between 1929 and 1932, Garrison had attributed the loss more to an uneven distribution of legal services than to actual overcrowding. Garrison, "Results of Wisconsin Bar Survey," 58–68.

72. First argued that the AALS had reason to oppose raising the standards of law school admissions as high as the ABA seemed willing to go. Its own weaker members had been in trouble since the beginning of the depression, and a change in standards could mean a drop in membership. In addition, at a time when almost all AALS schools were experiencing at least some decline in applications, they could not afford to raise admissions requirements so high that admittable candidates would have to be rejected and go to more understanding accredited schools. The AALS therefore suggested alternative solutions including bar admission quotas, agreements between the law schools in each state to reduce admissions, and limitations on advertising. These devices were, however, unsuccessful and in the late 1930s admissions began to fall in AALS as well as non-AALS schools. Fearing major losses and under pressure from the ABA, the

AALS in 1939 voted to admit certain night schools. By widening the cartel, at least it had been possible to avoid reducing standards dramatically. The pressure of the market had been too great; much as the AALS and the ABA wished to restrict admissions, members of the AALS simply could not afford to face the threat of increasing competition from outsiders. First, "Competition in the Legal Education Industry," 373–85.

   Despite the evidence, it is difficult to accept the First theories in their entirety. In 1937, the AALS standards were still higher than those of the ABA and, however one looks at it, pressure from the ABA cannot have been a push for *higher* standards.

73. Shafroth, "The Next Step," 15.

74. American Bar Association, *Annual Review of Legal Education, 1936*, 35.

75. Gilb, *Hidden Hierarchies*, 59. This drove several California schools out of business. The worst of these were described in a 1933 report by Shafroth to the California bar: "The weakest type is a one-man institution, dominated by a single individual who makes the important decisions and, as a rule, does a large part of the teaching. This school has as its highest ambition mere preparation for the bar examinations and as its worst the collection of as much money as possible from its students. Usually it is without financial resources, admits any kind of student, whatever his qualifications or lack of them, graduates practically all who remain the required length of time and pay up regularly for their tuition and books, and has only the lowest standards of scholarship." State Bar of California, *Report of the Survey Committee* (1933).

   On the California bar examination, see also Brenner, "Bar Exam Research in California," 29; Brenner, "Post Exam Appraisal of California Bar Exam System," 89; and Clarke, "Some Random Comments by a Former Member of the Committee of Bar Examiners," 5.

76. American Bar Association, *Annual Review of Legal Education, 1938*, 7. 1938 saw the end of law schools at Southwestern University (Long Beach Branch), the University of the West (Los Angeles), South Bend University, Grand Rapids College of Applied Science, the National College of Law and Commerce in Tennessee, the Dallas YMCA, and Norfolk College in Virginia.

77. By 1938, 9 law schools required students to have a degree before admission, 32 schools required at least three years of college, and a further 109 required two years of college; 30 others had lower standards.

78. American Bar Association, *Law Schools and Bar Admissions Requirements in the United States for 1939*, 10.

79. *AALS Proceedings, 1940*, 14.

11 / The Rush to Excellence:
The Worm's-Eye View

MUCH of the history of legal education, in the years between World War I and World War II, has been written from the perspective of the law school establishment. From this perspective what was achieved was, indeed, remarkable, both in intellectual and structural terms. Yet the leaders of the ABA and the AALS had, perhaps, relatively little sense of what they had wrought in terms of the hopes of immigrant and racial groups, nor in terms of the overall context of legal theory.

The case method marched inexorably on. Its continuing appeal was summarized by President Woolsey of Yale in 1924: "The old way bred great lawyers, but like the caste mark of the Brahmin, the case system is the cachet of the crack law school of today."[1] The same, however, might equally have been said of the requirement of a three-year law degree and the ever-increasing demands for prelaw work. Wherever one looked, at least in "upwardly mobile" law schools, the change was on. Any university president wishing to have a first-rate law school had to subscribe. At the University of Montana during the 1920s there was a battle between the president who wanted to appoint Harvard men to the law school faculty and the State Board of Education who wanted local practitioners. The compromise was a local dean, a "Harvard" faculty, and the case method.[2] At Alabama the transition was more gradual. The case method arrived during the long deanship of Albert J. Farrah (1913–44) as part of an overall process of change, including the founding of a law review and moving to a three-year curriculum.[3]

Meanwhile, the "progress" continued elsewhere. The University of Southern California, for instance, moved to the case method in the 1920s as did Notre Dame,[4] and the large state universities in the South began to succumb. In 1923, President Harry Woodburn Chase of the University of North Carolina announced that modernization of his university's law school was necessary to prevent the school from becoming a "coaching school" for bar examinations. The governor of North Carolina opposed Chase's suggestion for two years of college before law school, while another opponent complained, "I know that most of the law schools follow the case system. This, I think, is due not so much to any merit in the system as to the fact that it is a system adopted by Harvard University." At the same time, President Edwin Anderson Alderman of the University of Virginia urged President Chase not to appoint faculty or deans because they were experienced practitioners: "Our successes have not been practitioners—our failures have been, or rather our mediocrities as teachers."[5] Quite why the president of Virginia felt able to offer the slightly patronizing advice to the president of North Carolina is unclear. As late as 1921, Dean William Minor Lile of Virginia was still arguing against the case method: "The natural tendency of the system is to develop a race of case lawyers. But the most serious objection is the slowness with which the course goes forward, and the gaps that the method must leave in the continuity and completeness of the topics pursued. If the student had six years to devote to his law school course, instead of three, the case method might prove ideal."[6] Indeed, in this atmosphere, the case method was only introduced at Virginia in 1922, when Armistead Mason Dobie returned there with an S.J.D. from Harvard, and it was not totally victorious until his deanship of the school, from 1932 to 1939.[7]

The case method even spread into some of the unaccredited schools. In 1930, the educational activities of the District of Columbia YMCA were "hived off" as Southeastern University.[8] The new Southeastern Law School began recruiting a different type of faculty member who, although part-time, was to teach by the case method.[9] The school claimed that the new image led to more students.[10] Even earlier, Northeastern—the old Boston YMCA—had boasted of being "An Evening Law School with Day School Standards," meaning the "Case Method of Instruction, Competent Instruction, Compulsory Attendance and Rigorous Examinations."[11] In practice, Northeastern merged the case method with the lecture method.[12] For most unaccredited schools, however, the lecture method was the only method of instruction. For evening students, the case method of teaching had even less attraction than it did at the elite schools. Passage of the bar examination rather than "thinking like a lawyer" was their criterion of success. Moreover, for most schools outside the narrow elite, these were years when changes or innovations in curriculum and teaching methods paled into insignificance when compared with the energy needed to cope with the national efforts to "raise standards."

In the cause of intellectualism and protection of the public, the structures demanded affected a wide range of schools in the period between 1922 and 1945. Leading schools were on the march in tandem with the states and the bar associations. The University of Montana began to require two years of college work from students,[13] and the University of

Southern California began to require three years.[14] The University of North Carolina, which moved to a three-year law program in 1919, initiated the requirement of one year of college in 1923 and then raised it to two years in 1925.[15] In 1921 Toledo began requiring two years of college before law school, although it went out of business for a while the following year.[16] By 1919, Northwestern had joined Harvard and Pennsylvania in requiring a college degree before law school from all students, and during the 1920s Pittsburgh and Stanford joined the list. Others required a degree from all those who had not done their undergraduate work in the same university,[17] and the number of schools requiring at least three years of college grew.[18]

It was the unaccredited schools, however, that bore the brunt of the effort to raise standards. Reed had seen the part-time school as a democratizing phenomenon, "whose existence, like that of similar institutions in other education fields, is justified by the democratic desire to extend the privileges of education to the many—a desire that is particularly potent when this privilege carries with it that of admission to our governing class."[19] After the battles in the House of Delegates in the late 1920s, however, John Kirkland Clark, chairman of the ABA Section of Legal Education and Admission to the Bar, had no problem in seeing things rather differently. In 1934 he said, "we must direct our efforts toward a campaign to create public sentiment which will put unworthy law schools out of business, and which will induce or force the schools which are worthy and capable of improvement to raise their standards to the level which has been set for us by our organization."[20] As if to drive home his point, in December 1934, Clark published a survey of 152 schools, entitled "A Contrast: The Full-Time Approved School Compared with the Unapproved Evening School," a document in which it was concluded that "until something is done either to improve these schools, or eliminate them, there seems little hope of attaining the goal of a better bar in this country."[21] It became increasingly clear that, although in 1922 the law school establishment had publicly welcomed the idea of the part-time law school, the goal of both the ABA and AALS was that "in the interest of the individual student, the legal profession and the public, there should be assurance that part-time instruction shall come as close as possible to full-time instruction in point of effectiveness."[22]

The individual responses of law schools as they sought to meet pressures—normally imposed by local legislatures or bar examiners[23]—were fascinating. When Illinois demanded graduation from high school before studying law, the John Marshall Law School established its own high school for prelaw students.[24] When Colorado decided to require one year of college before law school, the state's largest (and unaccredited) law school—Westminster University School of Law[25]—responded by opening its own one-year junior college, available only to potential law students.[26] When the state increased the requirement to two years in 1927, the junior college offered a second year. All was not easy for Westminster in the 1930s; it was hit badly by the depression and the faculty went unpaid, but it survived.[27]

In Boston the situation was aggravated by the division, which emerged earlier in the century, between those schools that were looked on as catering to the worthy poor and those that were seen as catering to the unworthy poor. Among the latter, MacLean's Portia Law School and Archer's Suffolk Law School were financially successful by the 1920s, Archer's appreciably more so because he had the lucrative male market. In 1923, Northeastern (YMCA) had admitted women, and, in 1929, MacLean sought to admit men to Portia, a move rejected by the state commissioner of education because its standards were too low for men. Yet they both had to respond nimbly as Massachusetts moved to raise standards. When the state moved to demand high school before admission to the bar, Portia established its own prep school in 1921 to provide high school equivalency. This arrangement continued until 1938 when the regulation allowing the taking of high school and law school courses concurrently was abandoned. Indeed, in that year, the Massachusetts requirement of two years of college before law school came into force. Faced with this threat, in 1935 both Portia and Suffolk established colleges, open only to those who planned to attend those law schools. Portia College, shortly to be renamed Calvin Coolidge College, soon became open to men and women, as MacLean opened his law school to men to compete more effectively in the marketplace.[28]

Not all schools were in this fortunate position as the states moved in. In the 1930s the state bar of California conducted its first major raid on unaccredited schools.[29] Tennessee conducted its own studies. Will Shafroth and Claude Horack, who were the consultants chosen by the Tennessee bar, were not prepared to see the continuation of such schools as the John Randolph Neal College of Law in Knoxville and the Andrew Jackson Business University School of Law in Nashville.[30] Tennessee, which in the 1920s had required only a "fair general education" and one year of law study, was slowly being whipped into shape.[31] During the 1930s, the League of Ohio Law Schools worked to drive out the unaccredited,[32] and the Dallas Bar Association, working with the ABA and AALS, forced the Dallas YMCA to let itself be absorbed by Southern Methodist.[33]

In 1938, Westminster still had 90 students, the John Randolph Neal College of Law had 74, and the Andrew Jackson Business University

School of Law, with 32 students, was still functioning. In the meantime, however, there had been some important casualties. Of the four black law schools mentioned by Reed in his 1928 study, three—Freylinghuysen, Simmons, and Virginia Union—had either disappeared or were about to.[34] This is what the constant calls by AALS presidents to "remedy this unfortunate situation by whatever means are available"[35] had wrought. Legal education—as one of the by-products of rising standards —was moving out of the reach of minorities,[36] and in some cases the stories were pathetic.

Freylinghuysen University, for instance, had been founded in Washington, D.C., in 1906 by Jesse Lawson as a university for "colored working men and women."[37] The John M. Langsten Law School was a part of the university from the beginning and produced a trickle of lawyers until 1927, when Congress gave control over the awarding of degrees in the District to the D.C. Board of Education. That board refused to give Freylinghuysen the right to award an LL.B., although the law school required two years of college and had a part-time faculty of eleven.[38] Although the school hoped the degree-granting privilege would ultimately be restored, it desperately sought to keep up with the dictates of the ABA and AALS. The commencement for 1932 noted that "owing to the advancing of standard requirements from three to four years, there are no graduates for 1932 from the Department of Law." While the dean and law faculty continued to teach nondegree candidates, the university was producing graduates from its Jarvis School of Embalming and the Carson School of Practical Nursing.[39] Yet, although Freylinghuysen suffered under the rule of the D.C. Board of Education, Congress exempted the Washington College of Law—primarily for white women—and Southeastern—the YMCA school and the least elite of the white schools—from this control.[40] Even such successful nonelite schools might, however, have succumbed to the concerted efforts of the organized bar had the AALS not weakened in 1939 and agreed to let in the solely part-time schools once again. Respectability at last came to the YMCA schools: Southeastern was offered tentative ABA approval in 1942 (although the parent YMCA would not accept the terms),[41] and Northeastern in Boston was to be accredited in 1945.

This was all a far cry from the early self-policing of the AALS during this period. In 1926, both the University of Mississippi and Vanderbilt University were expelled from the AALS for refusing to require two years of college work.[42] Others were only too willing, however, to fight to be admitted into (or remain in) the AALS. The majority of schools in D.C., for instance, saw elitism as worth striving for. Howard had had only an evening program until 1923, but, as the law department developed itself into a school of law, it sought membership in the AALS and took the appropriate steps to make that possible.[43] In 1922, the school demanded the equivalent of high school education for admission and in 1923 demanded two years of college work. Tuition had been increased in 1921 (at that time both the ABA and AALS judged quality partly by tuition), and, in 1923, three full-time professors were appointed. There was a vote to pay them $1,500 a year, if possible. The library reached 1,000 volumes (then the AALS requirement) and an LL.M. was established (to be abandoned two years later). Claude Horack visited the school in 1928, and the part-time program was expanded to four years. Finally, in 1930–31, Howard received ABA accreditation and, in 1931, was elected to the AALS.[44] Although there was no doubt rejoicing in the Howard faculty, the real availability of the most obvious black law school was dramatically curtailed. Potential minority students found it difficult to meet the education requirements and tuition costs. In 1923–24, Howard had had 135 students; in 1926–27, it had 82.[45]

Catholic University Law School achieved membership in the AALS in 1921, when the school had 97 students. When the two years of college requirement was implemented in 1925, the total student body fell to 16.[46] Fortunately for Catholic, its law faculty also taught in the Knights of Columbus Law School, which opened the year after Catholic joined the AALS.[47] The Knights of Columbus School prospered as Catholic withered. By 1924, the night school had 212 students, and it proved to be an effective bar examination cram course.[48] Not only did the official Catholic University go respectable, so did the Jesuits. Until 1925–26 Georgetown had operated as an evening law school with few admission requirements. In that session Georgetown began a day program and required two years of college. The student body dropped from 1,130 in 1923–24 to 489 in 1926–27.[49]

There was yet a fourth school in the swamps of Washington determined during the 1920s to increase its status. George Washington established a day program in 1924–25 and began to demand two years of college work in 1925–26. The student body, which had been 1,063 in 1923–24, dropped to 717 in 1926–27 and to 685 in 1928–29. When the school began to require one year of college, the *Alumni Bulletin* had proudly announced that 'this step has been taken by the University with a feeling of assurance that in this way it can render a greater service to the public and its students. From the public the demand is for better-trained lawyers than for a larger number; from the individual student the demand is for a training such as is essential to succeed in a crowded and scholarly profession."[50] A moot court program, postgraduate degrees, and a law review followed. In praising the moves, the *Alumni Bulletin* explained the "great strides" made since 1922 and concluded that "we may confidently look forward to a time when vastly improved standards for admission will ensure to our society a legal profession adequate to its needs."[51]

Yet more was in store. In 1935, George Washington announced the requirements of a B.A. or B.S. degree for admission to the LL.B. program. The *Alumni Bulletin* was beside itself:

As far as entrance requirements are concerned the Law School is now in the first rank. There is no institution in the country higher. There are only seven others with entrance requirements as high.

This action was taken in order to give the school a place among other law schools which the prestige of the University requires. From the point of view of institutional progress it was a very desirable action. The broader purpose however behind it was public service. The growing realization of the public nature of the work of the lawyer, as judge, administrator, legislator and as advocate and legal advisor has brought home to our law schools and bar examiners the tremendous responsibility that is theirs in recruiting the bar of the future. . . . The George Washington University therefore in placing its law school on a graduate basis is performing a real service to the bar of the future and to the country.[52]

The auguries were so favorable that even Princeton once again considered establishing a law school. In 1924, a trustee committee unanimously reported in favor of the idea of a law school.[53] Edward W. Sheldon, one of the trustees, corresponded with Roscoe Pound and noted in the trustees' copy of the report that the "country is governed by lawyers and Princeton's duty [is] to train for public service."[54] Poor Princeton, however, could never quite work it all out. By 1929, it looked as if the board might be prepared to move, provided that establishing a law school would not interfere with building a chapel. All that was changed by the fortunes of the stock market in October of that year. The 1920s and 1930s were indeed a period of fluctuation in the course of legal education.

If one needed further evidence of this, the Bay area provided fascinating evidence. In the early 1920s there was vigorous competition among the three most elite schools—Berkeley, Stanford, and Hastings— all of which required two years of college before law school.[55] With the depression, the elite private schools, ignoring the threats of classical economics, raised their fees to survive (Stanford's went from $285 in 1928 to $360 in 1937). The leading state schools like Berkeley and Hastings were able to freeze their fees because the state subsidy was kept at a stable level. A new element had been added to the competitive situation

—a rapidly widening gap between tuition at the leading state and private schools. As a result, Berkeley increased its enrollment 179 percent between 1928 and 1937.[56]

Of the private schools, however, Stanford was in the most favored position in the Bay area during this period. It was actually able to become selective and limit enrollment in 1933–34 at the very height of the depression. Although Berkeley and Hastings could do the same, the position was very different for the less distinguished private schools. Of the nine Los Angeles law schools founded between 1924 and 1932, four did not make it through the depression. Others, like the universities of San Francisco and Santa Clara in the Bay area and Loyola in Los Angeles, would have failed but for financial support from the Jesuits, who felt it was important to keep open law schools for Irish and Italian immigrants.[57] During World War II, some private schools, including Loyola, Santa Clara, and McGeorge, closed, while the state of California actually increased its subvention to Hastings tenfold.[58] Not only had the balance of power tipped toward the accredited schools but the state schools had become heavily favored.

In the East the state schools were far less important. Even today only Connecticut and Maine of the New England states provide law schools. Thus, in Massachusetts, the market was open, with the YMCA competing with Suffolk and Portia at the lower end of the market. The YMCA school, as it transformed itself into Northeastern, saw itself as at the top end of the lower half. Not only did it favor the case method, but it also saw itself as the working man's alternative to the elite schools.[59] Although its numbers did not compete with Archer's claim of 4,000 students at Suffolk, there was no doubt that Northeastern played an important part in bringing immigrants into the mainstream,[60] and, by 1929, at Boston and in the three branches at Worcester, Springfield, and Providence (Rhode Island), there were over 1,400 students. The depression produced the first blow. By 1932–33, the combined student body was down to 1,091, and the Providence branch had been closed. Although the other branches continued to have strength during the mid and late 1930s,[61] eventually they too were closed in 1942. Their closing had, however, nothing to do with either demand for them or their success. Northeastern was anxious to join the AALS, and the AALS insisted that the Worcester and Springfield branches be closed before admission.[62] The establishment had insured that there would be no legal education in western Massachusetts.

World War II merely underlined the directions taken in the 1930s. Even before the outbreak of the war, the numbers of law students fell rapidly because of the selective service law, and by the academic year

1943–44, there were only 6,422 students in the schools, of whom a quarter were women.[63] Several unaccredited schools closed, never to reopen.[64] What the ABA and the depression had begun, Hitler helped to complete.[65] Moreover, although, for the most part standards were waived for the emergency,[66] the ABA established library standards for approved schools for the first time in 1942 and in 1944 moved to inspect all schools.[67] The postwar path was clear. Law was supposed to be an "intellectual" profession. To the leaders of the profession, it also was evident that law schools were training for a homogeneous profession rather than providing a gateway qualification for diverse careers.

NOTES

1. Hicks, *Yale Law School, 1895–1915*, 45.
2. Montana State University, *Dedication and History: School of Law*, 26–27. Lest anyone should question the lessons to be drawn from history, an almost identical scenario was acted out in choosing a new dean for the University of Texas Law School in 1979. Powerful alumni persuaded the president of the University of Texas to reject the panel of four "eastern" candidates recommended by the faculty because they were "insufficiently Texan." *Chronicle of Higher Education*, 4 September 1979, 2.
3. The three-year course began in 1921; the law review began in 1925. McKenzie, "Farrah's Future."
4. In 1919–20, the *Bulletin* reported, "Excellent as the case method is for imparting a knowledge of the particular principles of the law applicable in the cases analyzed, a general idea of the law as a whole, its main features and universal concepts cannot be learned without the aid of the textbook. Therefore, the law is taught here by textbook assignments as well as cases, both explained and illustrated by classroom talks of the instructors." By 1928–29, the *Bulletin* announced that the case method was the "primary method of instruction." Moore, *A Century of Law at Notre Dame*, 57, 67.
5. Coates, "The Story of the Law School at the University of North Carolina," 45–49.
6. Ibid., 57.
7. Ibid., 74.
8. The D.C. YMCA had begun law courses in 1919–20, and by 1926–27 there were 100 students in the LL.B. program. Reed, *Present-Day Law Schools*, 424–25; *Washington Star*, 12 January 1930.
9. For example, the appointment of Fred J. Eden as lecturer in Bankruptcy was announced in a press release: "Mr. Eden is lecturing to senior students in morning and evening classes by the case-book method. The subject has been taught only by lecture—in the past." *Washington Post*, 22 February 1931.
10. *Washington Star*, 9 September 1937.
11. Northeastern University Law School, *Catalog, 1913*. The muscular Christianity of the YMCA infected the approach to law. See, for instance, the *Catalog* for 1920–21: "The study of law requires close application, a clear head, and persistent effort. In order to do the work successfully, pass the examinations, and finish the four years in good physical condition, one must find time for physical exercise and a reasonable amount of recreation and social enjoyment. We impress all our students with the necessity of a well-balanced program, mental, physical and social."

12. Successfully, too. The passing rate for the Massachusetts bar in 1924 was 86 percent. Northeastern had continued to attract an excellent faculty. Of thirteen attorneys who taught regularly in the Boston division between 1916 and 1924, nine were either undergraduates or law graduates of Harvard, Yale, Columbia, Williams, Colby, Oberlin, or Boston University. Of the thirteen, Arthur Willis Blackman was counsel to the New Haven Railroad and William Edwin Dorman was counsel to the state of Massachusetts. Of the eleven instructors at the Worcester division, ten held Harvard degrees, and the pedigrees at Springfield and Providence divisions were similar. Boston YMCA, *Annual Report, 1924* (1925).

The Springfield branch of Northeastern proudly announced that it used the case method: "The law is a science, the only approved and effective method of teaching which, as is true of all sciences, is the inductive method. . . . For these and many other incontrovertible reasons all the leading law schools, following the Harvard Law School, use the case system." Northeastern College, School of Law, Springfield, *Catalog, 1927–28*, 29.

13. Montana State University, *Dedication and History: School of Law*, 46.

14. University of Southern California, *Dedication Ceremonies: School of Law Building*, 45.

15. Coates, "The Story of the Law School at the University of North Carolina," 38–41. The Salmon P. Chase College of Law in Ohio, as yet unaccredited, was doing its best to become accredited during the 1920s. In 1926, it introduced the requirement of one year of college work; by 1927, it had already raised that to two years. Dieffenbach, "The Salmon P. Chase College of Law," 19.

16. First, "Legal Education and the Law School of the Past," 146–47.

17. Western Reserve, Yale, Cornell, Illinois. Reed, *Present-Day Law Schools*, 137.

18. California (Berkeley), Chicago, Columbia, Northwestern, William and Mary, Southern California, Michigan, Notre Dame, Syracuse, and Wisconsin. Ibid.

19. Reed, *Training for the Law*, 56.

20. Clark, "Qualifications for Bar Admission," 3.

21. Among other things Clark reported were the following: (a) most full-time schools were affiliated with a larger institution; only 1 out of 7 part-time schools were; (b) full-time schools averaged libraries of 150,000 volumes; part-time schools averaged 25,000 volumes; (c) full-time schools had an average tuition of $200; part-time schools charged an average of $150; (d) 4 out of 5 full-time schools used the case method, but only 1 out of 6 part-time schools did; (e) scholarship standards were "lower" in the part-time schools. For a more sympathetic approach, see Snyder, "The Problem of the Night Law School," 109.

22. Kirkwood, "Requirements for Admissions to Practice Law," 18, 34. Kirkwood also admitted that "there is a proper place for the part-time school. There are a great many mature people with family responsibilities who cannot avail themselves of an education in a full-time school. It does not seem that they should be deprived of the opportunity to become lawyers, and the part-time school is the only proper answer to their needs." Ibid.

23. The pressure was on the part-time schools to move to four years. In 1919–20, there were 9 two-year, 38 three-year, and 21 four-year, part-time programs. By 1927–28, there were 7 two-year, 22 three-year, 50 four-year, and 1 four-and-a-half-year programs. Reed, *Present-Day Law Schools*, 126.

In 1919–20, 28 of the 70 full-time schools, none of the 8 part-time schools and full-time schools, and only 2 of the 68 part-time schools required two years of college. By 1927–28, 70 of the 77 full-time schools, 13 of the 20 full- and part-time schools, and 17 of the 79 part-time schools required two years of college. Ibid., 120, 134.

24. Later expanded, when the state regulations changed, to include college courses. The prelaw college was finally abandoned in 1951. John Marshall Law School Archives, Chicago, Ill.

25. The Law School was all that survived after Westminster University (or college) went bankrupt. The Law School began in 1912. It was to produce a governor of Colorado and a member of President Truman's cabinet. It had a proud tradition. The yearbook, for instance, was called *The Lamplight*. Its name was explained in the 1926 edition (2): "Westminster is a night law school. Throughout the day the students toil for their daily bread, and in the shadow of the evening gather at the fountain of legal learning to quench their thirst for judicial knowledge; . . . by lamplight they are guided onward. While their comrades sleep, they toil upward through the night." Westminster Archives, Western Collection, Denver Public Library, Denver, Colo.

26. Westminster University Law School, *The Lamplight*, 1924, 22.

27. Ed Lehman, "Attorneys by Midnight Oil," *Denver Post*, 11 June 1956, mag. sec., 2.

28. In 1935, of the thirty-five students graduating from Portia (all women), only four were college graduates. One was black. *The Legacy*, 1936 (yearbook of Portia Law School). New England Law School Archives, Boston, Mass.

29. See *Report of the California Survey Committee* (1933), a committee headed by Horack and Shafroth. Of unaccredited schools, they noted:

> The high pressure method by which the original enrollment is secured in some of these schools is deserving of the severest censure. Solicitation of law students by the low grade schools in California presents a condition, which, it seems safe to say, is worse than any other state in the Union. A practice analogous to ambulance chasing has grown up where commissions are paid to law students for each new victim they may bring to the school and where solicitors are not only regularly paid to hunt out and sign up prospects but are further compensated as long as their students stay in school. Instances were found where a dean was engaged for a school and was paid a certain amount for each student whom he brought with him or induced to come over from another school. Naturally this leads to misrepresentation to the students. [Ibid., 3]

30. "Law Schools in Tennessee, Report of the Survey Committee," 15 *Tennessee Law Review* 354 (1938).

31. By 1935–36, Tennessee required the equivalent of a high school education and two years of legal education, either in a law office or at law school, or a mixture of the two. American Bar Association, *Annual Review of Legal Education, 1935*. The process worked. The East Tennessee Law School apparently went out of business in 1938 and the Andrew Jackson Law School in 1939 (although it reappeared fleetingly in 1947). 1940 saw the demise of the Kent College of Law in Nashville and 1942 both the Nashville YMCA and the Chattanooga College of Law.

32. First, "Single Firm Study," 148–49.

33. First, "Competition in the Legal Industry," 381n.

34. Freylinghuysen had disappeared from the listing of the *Review of Legal Education* as early as 1929. See Carnegie Foundation, *Annual Review of Legal Education, 1929*. Virginia Union was still listed in 1930, though it was noted that attendance had not been reported since 1926, and by 1931 it too was gone. Ibid., *1930, 1931*.

Virginia Union was run by Peter James Henry (a Howard graduate) and Clarence McDonald Maloney (a Dalhousie graduate). The school had a four-year evening program and between 1922 and 1931 graduated twenty-three students, but only six passed the bar. "The law school was a well-intended undertaking, but it was ambitious beyond the resources of the university and the needs of the community." Bryson, "The History of Legal Education in Virginia," 201. Simmons University in Kentucky, having reported attendance figures erratically from 1928, was dropped from the list in 1932. Carnegie Foundation, *Annual Review of Legal Education, 1932.*

35. Herschel Arant, president of the AALS, in *AALS Proceedings, 1938,* 10.

36. In fairness, it should be recorded that even during the era of "separate but equal," black applicants sued and were admitted to the law schools of Maryland and Missouri, because there was nothing that might be mistaken for "equal." *University of Maryland v. Murray,* 169 Md. 478, 182 A. 590 (1936). *Gaines v. Canada,* 305 U.S. 337 (1938). The latter case moved Missouri to create Lincoln Law School. Washington, "History and Role of Black Law Schools," 385, 398.

37. Lawson was a black U.S. Patent examiner, who named his school after Sen. Frederick Freylinghuysen of New Jersey, a supporter of rights for blacks. Freylinghuysen University Archives, Washingtoniana Collection, Martin Luther King Library, Washington, D.C.

38. The Board of Education was apparently influenced by its first black member who was associated with the Robert H. Terrell Law School, a commercial black law school that, from 1931 on, was able to award degrees. Radney, "History of Schools for Negroes in the District of Columbia." For a more sympathetic view of the Terrell School, see Washington, "History and Role of Black Law Schools," 396.

39. The Law School was nominally in existence as late as 1947. *Afro,* 7 June 1947.

40. H.J. Res., 582, 1938.

41. "Diploma Mill Charge Hurled at Southeastern," *Washington Star,* 17 May 1946. Southeastern Archives, Washingtoniana Collection, Martin Luther King Library, Washington, D.C.

42. *AALS Proceedings,* 1926, 6–7, 80. Two years after imposing the two-year college requirement Mississippi's numbers dropped from 110 to 88 and Vanderbilt's from 212 to 136.

43. Logan, *Howard University,* 121, 151.

44. The real power behind these moves was William Hastie, dean from 1939 to 1946 and later a judge of the Third Circuit Court of Appeals. Ibid., 266.

45. Reed, *Present-Day Law Schools,* 422. In 1929, that number had dropped even further to 68 (Carnegie Foundation, *Annual Review of Legal Education,* 1929); by 1932, it was 44 (ibid., *1932*), but by 1935 it had climbed back to 64 (American Bar Association, *Annual Review of Legal Education, 1935*) and by 1938 it was at 71 (ibid., *1938*).

46. Reed, *Present-Day Law Schools,* 423.

47. Its announcements actually carried the subheading "Catholic University Extension Courses." Knights of Columbus Archives, Washingtoniana Collection, Martin Luther King Library, Washington, D.C.

48. "The Law School was organized four years ago. It has now over a hundred students. Its first graduating class made a very remarkable record in the local bar exam, a larger percentage of those taking the examination from this school being successful than from any other school." *Book of Washington,* 1927.

49. Reed, *Present-Day Law Schools,* 423.

In 1929, it was at 477 (Carnegie Foundation, *Annual Review of Legal Education,* 1929) and by 1932, it was at 455 (ibid., *1932*). But by 1935, having gained ABA approval, it had a total of 649 students (American Bar Association, *Annual Review of Legal Education, 1935*) and by 1938, it had grown slightly to 654 (ibid., *1938*).

50. *George Washington Law School Association Bulletin,* 1921.

51. Ibid., *1933.*

52. Ibid., *1935*.
53. Princeton Archives AM 3177, Princeton University, Princeton, N.J. For a record of the discussion of the trustees, see the minutes of their meetings of 14 April and 29 September 1924; 29 September 1925; and 12 April and 28 September 1926. The proponents of establishing a law school also published a pamphlet, *The Princeton Law School* (1926).
54. Letter from Roscoe Pound to Edward W. Sheldon, 4 May 1923, Princeton Archives AM 3177, Princeton University, Princeton, N.J.
55. In 1924–25, Hastings had 112 students of whom 21 (19 percent) had degrees. In 1925–26, Stanford had 314 students of whom 115 (37 percent) had degrees. In 1926–27, Berkeley had 195 students of whom 181 (93 percent) had degrees. Barnes, *Hastings College of Law*, 228.
56. Ibid., 232–33. Hastings actually had a rough time in the 1930s, not economically, but from the ABA and AALS for its failure to have an adequate library and a large enough cadre of full-time faculty. Ibid., 239–43.
57. Ibid., 234. The University of San Francisco, begun in 1912 as a night school, added a day program in 1932 for college graduates, when it changed to university status. By 1935, it was accredited by the ABA. University of San Francisco Archives, San Francisco, Calif. See also McGloin, S.J., *Jesuits by the Golden Gate*, passim.
    The University of Santa Clara had also begun a Law School in 1912. It was a two-year program open only to those who had had two years of college. This was part of President James Peter Morrissey's plan for "a great Catholic University of the West." By 1938, athletic receipts were being used to support the school, which had received ABA approval the previous year. McKevitt, S.J., *The University of Santa Clara*, 172, 256, 278.
58. Barnes, *Hastings College of Law*, 251. In general, the leading private schools stayed open during the war, but some, such as Vanderbilt, closed.
59. Harvard and Boston University "have not been able to reach a very large group of highly intelligent and ambitious employed men who desire advancement either through preparing for the legal profession or through a law training which ought to be applicable in their business careers." Northeastern College, School of Law, *Catalog 1921–22*, 10.
60. In a historical article about the Springfield branch, the *Springfield Republican* attributed a significant influence to diversifying Springfield to the YMCA school. In 1919, the year the school was founded, "the so-called Yankees ran Springfield City Hall and foreigners such as Italians, Jews and Irish couldn't get near the place. . . . A major Springfield employer hung out a sign that said 'No Catholics Hired!' " *Springfield Republican*, 1 October 1978, sec. B, 1. Law School Archives, Western New England College, Springfield, Mass.
61. At the Springfield branch numbers dropped from 157 in 1927–28 to 75 in 1932–33; they were back again to 167 by 1937. They dropped to 120 in 1938 when the state required two years of college. Herman, *Western New England College*, appendix. At least half those who graduated from the law school passed the bar examination. *Nor'Eastern* (Springfield, Mass.), December 1942, 5. Law School Archives, Western New England College, Springfield, Mass.
62. "The above reasons were responsible for the closing of the evening law school and not any stiffened requirement for the state bar examination." *Nor'Eastern* (Springfield, Mass.), December 1942, 5. Law School Archives, Western New England College, Springfield, Mass.
63. American Bar Association, *Annual Review of Legal Education*, 1944, 19. Harvard was

still not accepting women (a situation that survived until 1950), but 40 percent of Columbia's and over 25 percent of Yale's wartime students were women. Sutherland, *Law of Harvard,* 319; Goebel, *School of Law, Columbia,* 506; *Reports of Dean, Yale Law School,* 1942–43, 4; and ibid., 1943–44, 4.

64. First, "The Legal Education Industry," 386–88.

65. For example, Jones University, Alabama; Oakland College of Law, California; Peabody Law School, Portland; North Texas School of Law.

66. For details, see Sullivan, "Professional Associations," 420–21.

67. Ibid., 222.

12 / The Law Schools after 1945: Paradigmatic Structure and Reinvention of the Wheel

I N the years after 1945, the legal education movement entered a new phase. In the 1870s, legal education essentially meant a requirement for some period of law study followed by a bar exam. The second stage of growth had been recognition of law school as an alternative to apprenticeship. The third stage was the requirement of law school without the alternative of office study, and the fourth was recognition solely of ABA-approved law schools coupled with the requirement of attendance at college as well. The third and fourth stages in the movement had begun in the 1930s and were to come to fruition in the postwar years.

The return of the World War II veterans temporarily swelled the depleted ranks of law students. By 1947, there were 51,015 law students, far more than in any earlier year. The G.I. Bill had made legal education possible for many who would never have had the opportunity before, and, even more important to the ABA and the AALS, the majority of new students were choosing to exercise this right at approved schools. There was no incentive to attend the cut-price or marginal school. No fewer than 36,999 of the law students in 1947 were full-time day students at accredited schools; a further 407 were afternoon students, and some 6,313 evening students attended approved part-time schools (111 such schools in all).[1] The forty-seven unapproved schools had only 14.3 percent of the total student body—7,296, of whom 6,082 were evening students.[2]

Although the accredited schools were bursting at the seams and the state schools were making still further gains,[3] many private unaccredited schools did not reopen after the war. The president and alumni of Southeastern in D.C., for instance, were anxious to reopen as an accredited school after the war. The YMCA was reluctant to give up its control of the board and the moneymaking potential of the school. The alumni sponsored a congressional hearing aimed at taking the school away from the YMCA.[4] The result was that the president was fired and the law school folded. Of course, depending on geography, a few proprietary

schools did benefit from the G.I. Bill. From 1947 to 1959, William Par-
ham Martin ran the Smithdeal-Massey College of Law in Richmond,
Virginia. The school shared its name and premises with a successful
secretarial school. Seventy-five of the school's graduates applied to the
Virginia bar, "many" were successful, and "the school was a great financial success."[5]

In general, however, although a few existing schools were still being
received into the ABA and AALS, the founding of law schools slowed.
One exception was the founding of black law schools in the South in an
effort by the state governments to maintain segregation.[6] Vestiges of the
establishment's wartime panic about numbers[7] were evident in the ABA's
vigorous opposition to the extension of the G.I. Bill to correspondence
schools, but it soon became evident that such concern was misplaced.[8]
The economic effects of the war followed by the federal subsidy through
the G.I. Bill had finally and irrevocably given the approved schools the
upper hand in the marketplace, and within that approved group the
power of the public institutions was growing rapidly.

The phenomenal influx of students into accredited schools after the
war rapidly restored the confidence of the ABA and the AALS. In the
years after 1945, standards leaped and structures hardened. The list of
requirements adopted during the course of these years shows a striking
similarity to those of the 1920s, 1930s, and early 1940s, except possibly
for the ambiance of more self-confidence and complacency. The competition of the 1920s, the economic gloom of the 1930s, and the patriotic
duties of the 1940s were no longer threatening the stability of law schools.
State governments were also coming into line. Not only were they more
willing to appropriate funds for law schools in the state universities, but
they were legislating to conform to the profession's standards even more
rapidly than before.[9]

Once again, it was the AALS out in front pacing the ABA, which in
turn was the pacemaker for the state bars and legislatures.[10] Each year
the ABA's *Annual Review of Legal Education* recorded the "victims";[11]
the states could never quite catch up with the pacemakers. Progress was
to be marked in terms of the "standard": a three-year ABA school following four years of college. The idea that the bar was unitary was taken
to be an "irrebuttable presumption."[12] The contention that the public
might be adequately protected by bar examinations alone was apparently
not mooted; only accreditation of law schools was acceptable. That the
new scheme might make it more difficult for minority groups to obtain a
legal education,[13] or might hold back those wishing to specialize,[14] was
immaterial. The American bar, as everyone knew, was unitary. "Higher"

standards meant "better" lawyers; the public must be protected at all costs,[15] and that protection was clearly best arranged by the existing members of the profession.[16]

The standardization movement became increasingly specific. In 1948, the AALS voted to require a full-time dean in every school.[17] The following year an even more important movement began. The Section on Legal Education recommended to the ABA that the prelegal college requirement be raised from two to three years.[18] In 1950, the ABA accepted the recommendation, to be effective by 1952,[19] for once pulling ahead of the AALS in the demands it made on approved schools.[20] Meanwhile, the AALS had been battling since the end of World War II with the issue of size of faculty and faculty-student ratios. Eventually in 1952, the AALS decreed a minimum faculty-student ratio of one full-time teacher to every seventy-five students (the resolution had originally called for a ratio of one to fifty and had been watered down in debates spanning five years) and a minimum of four full-time faculty members and a librarian, in addition to the dean.[21] The move, important for the future, also underlined the modest minima of even accredited schools in the pre-World War II era.

The 1950s and 1960s saw a continuation of the drive for stiffer standards.[22] State legislatures finally overcame their concern that Lincoln had not been to law school. "Such an argument overlooks the fact that there was no law school in Illinois at the time Lincoln studied law and that there was then only one law school west of the Appalachians."[23] They continued to cooperate in the ever-upward trend.[24] Even by the late 1950s, from the point of view of the ABA what had been achieved was remarkable. In 1949, 11,114 of the 57,579 students were in unapproved schools. By 1958, apparently only 3,502 of the 42,646 students were in such schools.[25] Unaccredited schools had either been driven out of business or had "raised their standards." In any event, the market had been closed to a number of possible applicants. In 1951, the John Marshall School of Law (Lee's old school) was accredited by the ABA[26] and, in 1953, the Suffolk School of Law (founded by Archer). In D.C., Washington College of Law was absorbed by American University, and, in 1954, George Washington Law School absorbed National Law School. Also in 1954, Catholic absorbed (or reabsorbed) Columbus Law School, as the Knights of Columbus School was by then known. In Colorado, Westminster, after unsuccessfully seeking ABA accreditation, was absorbed by the University of Denver in 1957.[27] The leaders of the proprietary movement—or at least their schools—had been absorbed by the establishment. By 1958, only thirty unapproved schools existed. They were in fourteen jurisdictions—those few remaining states that had not at that point accepted the test of graduation from an ABA-approved school as a basis for taking the bar examination.[28]

One difficulty faced by the AALS as a result of this success was serious questioning of what its purpose and functions would be now that its standards had been reached by so many schools. Even as early as 1952, the incoming president of the association criticized its pedantic concern with standards for "washrooms, floor space, and record keeping." Setting standards, however, gave the group a purpose, and thus the process continued. By 1961, Karl Llewellyn would grumble that concern over such minute details was "the damnedest waste of time that any intelligent organization ever indulged in."[29] Another result was continuing demands that the AALS justify what it had done. With respect to that, the AALS leadership of the time had few hesitations. In 1958, Dean Erwin Griswold of Harvard justified AALS actions in purely elitist terms:

> It has long been true in this country, I think, that there have been too many lawyers—and not enough good lawyers. This has not been due to inadequate education in the law schools, but it is more directly referable to standards for admission to law schools which may be too low. . . . And it might be that we should eventually conclude that those who are not endowed by nature with a reasonably high quantum of intellectual ability should not be given the facilities to study law.[30]

Ultimately, both the AALS's worries about its purpose and Dean Griswold's confidence about the intellectual caliber of law students would appear to have been premature. The very year of Griswold's statement, 1958, proved to be a turning point. After that, the percentage of law students at unapproved schools remained roughly static, or may even have grown. By 1967,[31] Maryland had over 1,000 students at two unaccredited schools, while Massachusetts had 500 at three such schools. Georgia, which demanded only graduation from a law school "requiring classroom attendance for three academic years," had no fewer than five unaccredited schools with an unknown number of students.

The most active growth area in unaccredited schools was California, with fifteen such schools apparently enrolling several thousand students[32] and new ones continually appearing. California had the most generous provisions of all the states for those who wished to take its bar exams. Not only did it allow graduates of correspondence schools to take the bar examination,[33] but the graduate of any unaccredited law school might take the bar after studying even part-time for four years, providing he or she had passed the special bar-run exam at the end of the first year.[34] The rapid growth of this new industry worried the leaders of the California bar, who in 1969 offered a solution whereby students in approved schools might take their bar examinations after two years. The leading law schools in this state, although seriously concerned about the unaccredited schools' encroachment on the "unitary" bar,[35] turned down this opportunity to drive out their competitors, apparently because they feared demoralization and dissidence during the required third year of law school from those students who had already passed the bar examination. One of the first opportunities to break down the monolithic national structure in American legal education had been rejected.

Despite the modest resurgence of the unapproved schools, the ABA and AALS had come close to achieving their goal of nationwide standardization by 1970. By 1950, three years of college became the norm,[36] and by the 1960s, four years of college. The two-year law school had long since evaporated; in its place were three-year full-time schools and four-year part-time schools. The ABA–AALS minimum standards had rolled ever on, requiring increasing numbers of volumes in libraries and even fuller full-time faculties. The clerkship route to the bar had become a rarity. The success of the crusade had taken a long time, but the movement had had the effect desired by its leaders. A law student of 1970, thoroughly indoctrinated in the unyielding standards of his time, would probably have had difficulty believing that it was not until roughly 1950 that the number of lawyers who had been to college exceeded the number of those who had not.

The emphasis on standards in the years after 1945 was symptomatic of a wider attitude, betaking a little of blandness, among the leading members of the academic legal profession. The intellectual ferment in the so-called national schools had in fact died down before World War II. After the war, educational standards remained high, but, in terms of offerings, faculty-student ratios, libraries, budgets, quality of students, and similar matters, the standards enforced by the ABA and the AALS had brought other, less nationally known, schools to a comparable or almost comparable level. There was less to distinguish the elite from the nonelite than there had been in previous decades. In so many ways the triumph of the AALS was to prove the triumph of the good second-level schools at the expense of the elitist institutions.

Bergin has described the Yale of the late 1940s and early 1950s as a basically "Hessian training" (i.e., trade school) operation.[37] Although the famous Harvard curriculum study of 1947 made some interesting suggestions, they were relatively limited, and the changes implemented were small. As if to emphasize the situation, while the elite law schools stood still, or inched forward only slowly, their student bodies were becoming increasingly selective and better prepared.[38] Caught between the fire of ever-brighter and better-prepared students and the structural inhibitions of professional schools, the lot of the leading schools in this period was far from enviable.

If, by the late 1940s, the major schools were suffering from a kind of intellectual ennui, the state of the schools outside the elite and middle-level circles was even less enviable. In 1947, one law school dean described the typical AALS school in these terms:

> The run-of-the-mill member school is, under ordinary circumstances, relatively small in size, is located in a provincial university, is geared currently to the production of lawyers for the local private practice, tends to be insecure from a budgetary standpoint, is manned by an ill-paid and frequently overworked faculty of sometimes modest performance potential, operates on a too narrow pre-legal educational margin, and is virtually dependent for its very existence on the professional approval of the community in and for which it functions.[39]

In terms of curricula, the ABA's Survey of the Legal Profession, which included an inspection of nearly all of the country's law schools in the late 1940s, reported:

> The curricula are fairly well standardized. The vast majority of schools are either local or regional and the curricula have been fashioned largely around the subjects in which the graduates of the school must be examined for admission to practice. By and large, the law students have pressed for the "bread and butter" courses and the subjects specified in the rules for admission to practice. The law schools have tended, because of limited funds, inadequate facilities, and lethargy, to yield to the pressures.[40]

To record the development of curricula in the post-1945 era is thus, in so many ways, disheartening. Perhaps, having achieved unification of standards, the schools had little incentive to encourage intellectual experiments. No doubt, too, the returning veterans were not interested in novelty. When examining developments in the curriculum, there is an overwhelming sense of déjà vu. So many of the suggestions for curricular reform in the 1940s, 1950s, and 1960s had already been made, and often tried, in the 1920s and 1930s. Earlier experiments had frequently failed because of the remarkable underfunding of legal education manifested in poor student-faculty ratios, the lack of student interest in scholarly endeavors, and a strong tradition of faculty independence. Similar postwar experiments normally met similar fates for similar reasons. The actual changes in the curriculum, such as they were, generally represented additions or further fragmentation. At most, changes were marginally incremental. Possibly wisely, and certainly understandably, there was no such thing as radical reform.

One of the most noticeable features of this period was the cyclical approach to changes in the curriculum. In the late 1940s, the innovations in substantive course offerings at Yale were "Recent Scientific Developments and the Law," "Legal Aspects of Public Health," and "Welfare Administration." In the late 1960s, similar courses mysteriously reappeared, this time emphasizing the legal control of science and technology, law and medicine, and poverty law. Other developments to be seen repeatedly after World War II were even less innovative, going back to well before the war. Such long-standing "experiments" as combined law and business or arts and law programs returned.[41] Popular subject areas— international law,[42] the law relating to government agencies, or anything with "policy" in its title—were emphasized at any school able to afford to be "fashionable." Stress on the need to integrate law with the social sciences had not diminished, but, except for a few productive fields, little effective progress was made.[43] Some schools resorted to the time-honored tradition of consolidation and rearrangement of existing courses,[44] or discussed once again lengthening the curriculum to four years—a suggestion that was soon rejected.[45] Of these postwar carry-overs from the 1920s and 1930s, most noticeable was the growing concern with public law.[46]

At the leading schools, which were concomitantly dealing with increasing disenchantment with the case method,[47] there was some rise in the number of electives, usually taught as seminars.[48] This "success" mainly served to emphasize the accuracy of Reed's judgment of the American law school curriculum as a "mere aggregate or conglomerate of independently developed units."[49] A look at Harvard's experience is enlightening. The curriculum report of 1947[50] confirmed the strengths and weaknesses in that school that the student surveys in the 1930s had noted; and, if further evidence were needed, the same weaknesses and strengths were faithfully recorded in the 1960 curriculum report.[51] Large classes, the case method, and the absence of written work were still the chief complaints. Almost every school that attempted to restructure the curriculum could report similar experiences. Yet none of these reports led to any fundamental changes. Perhaps such stability was desirable, but it contrasted dramatically with the emphasis on innovation that filled the annual reports of the deans of the leading law schools.

It is probably accurate to say that the structural changes suggested and the curricular development proposed during the period, at least at the leading law schools, had one common goal: the hope of making a law school education more programmatic or sequential.[52] The approaches varied from plans for patterning elective choices to redesigns of whole programs. Ultimately, these attempts at reorganization backfired as new structures fell apart or innovative course work failed to find its niche. The changes produced, if anything, greater fragmentation. As a result, it became difficult to find major or continuing trends in structural changes or curricular development; rather, an amorphous picture of diverging pathways is presented by the data.

Introductory law courses, the use of teaching fellows for first-year tutorial assistance, legal skills courses, the problem method, and clinical legal education were some of the most prominent innovations of the 1950s and 1960s.[53] Not all, of course, were based on novel ideas, but as foci of attention each had reached a different level of commitment. In connection with the increasing analysis of legal skills, there had been a realization that there were important skills other than those inculcated by the case method, outstanding as it undoubtedly was for teaching analytical skills. Discussions of curricular reform increasingly centered on skills such as negotiation, drafting, and counseling—legal skills that had had no place in the Langdellian scheme of things.

Such realization did not help the fragmentary nature of the curriculum. Introductory courses appeared in response to arguments challenging the "value of unrelieved confusion" in the first semester,[54] generally with an extenuating assertion such as "the student needed to understand the purpose of what he was doing in law school and its relation to his professional goal."[55] Since an attempt was frequently made to teach these introductory courses through the case method—such was its all-pervasive influence—they often lacked intellectual coherence. Thus, although in 1950 they had been regarded as standard, by 1970 such introductory courses were on the decline, a decline exemplified by Harvard's demolition of its previously compulsory "Development of Legal Institutions."

Closely related to these introductory courses were the tutorial programs. Chicago used recent law graduates in its ambitious writing program,[56] and, between 1947 and 1949, Yale, Harvard, and Columbia all adopted this approach.[57] The tutors held discussion groups for ten or twenty students at a time, designed to introduce the students to the study of law, to the use of the library, and, at Yale, to the organization and ethics of the profession.[58] They soon dropped out of use at some schools —including Yale—although they were in turn introduced at others, including some less elite institutions. By 1970, a fairly wide range of schools used such fellows. Sectioning the first-year courses and providing separate introductory work in small groups were other experiments begun in this period in schools that had the least inadequate faculty-student ratio.

At the same time it is easy to overestimate the breadth of student interests even at the more fashionable schools. As a professor at the University of Virginia Law School opined: "It also seems reasonably evident to me, based upon a brief survey of the catalogues of a number of first-rank law schools, that the core program—that is, the program which the students are not obliged to take, but which they *will* take—is pure, old-fashioned Hessian-training, leavened presumably with a dash of what Dean Dillard calls 'exuberant skepticism.'"[59] Whether at Yale,[60] Berkeley,[61] or other of the prestige schools, this analysis still appeared to be correct, with limited exceptions, as the 1960s drew to a close. Although the "national" schools remained stationary and the typical AALS school saw its role as a strictly limited one, the better state universities moved up dramatically in the pecking order. Berkeley, Wisconsin, Minnesota, and Virginia were already seen as national law schools by the 1930s. In the 1950s, other state schools came closer to the leaders. Such schools as UCLA, Illinois,[62] Indiana, Iowa, and Texas gained increasing respect. In the 1960s, schools as varied as Alabama, Arizona State, Connecticut, SUNY–Buffalo, and the University of Washington came into national prominence. It is not without significance that the two most perceptive studies of legal education skills during the 1960s came from Ohio State[63] and North Carolina.[64]

Slowly what had been thought of as the hallmarks of the major school came to be regarded as increasingly common in the middle-grade-school, even if they were totally alien to the small, night, or proprietary institutions.[65] Although most small schools were still not offering seminars in the mid-1950s, the seminar movement was spreading out from the elite schools.[66] This was a natural result of the rapidly increasing number of full-time faculty members.[67] Administrative law and labor law were by then accepted at almost every school, no matter what its status, while land planning and poverty law, or their equivalents, were widely distributed. Similarly, whereas the idea of bringing in psychiatrists and sociologists to join in the teaching of family or criminal law, or the economist in connection with antitrust laws, had originally been the preserve of one or two schools,[68] by 1970 it was accepted by a significant number of institutions. By the late 1960s, the seminar and elective had become the staple of all accredited schools.[69]

The triviality of many of the so-called developments, however, was enshrined in the *Journal of Legal Education*. Concern with skills training was evident among an increasing number of schools. One attempt to utilize the case method to teach skills more directly was the "adversary method," used by Howard Oleck at New York Law School. Students were randomly chosen to represent sides of a case as it came up in class and then argue it out. "Almost invariably, most of the contentions are cancelled out by this process, leaving unrefuted the principle or rule which is the basic idea intended to be illustrated by the particular case."[70] UCLA offered a course called "Methods of Proof" during its summer session, intended as a course in fact-finding, which included such teaching skills as eyewitness testimony, detection of deception, confessions, ballistics, fingerprints, blood chemistry, and general investigative procedures. Erle Stanley Gardner, the creator of Perry Mason, gave the introductory lectures.[71]

Less flashy, but probably more generally practical, were the various legal clinic programs. John Bradway had continued his long-standing program at Duke[72] without much support for many years, but in the 1950s other schools started to follow his lead. Tennessee had a legal clinic similar to that at Duke,[73] and the Louisville Law School offered a variation on clinical education by instituting a "Briefing Service."[74] Colorado had a particularly ambitious clinical program involving actual cases and witnesses,[75] and Connecticut offered a three-week summer "Seminar on Connecticut Practice," another variation of clinical work, inspired by a comparable course at Wisconsin.[76]

Ever since legal apprenticeship had first started to fall into disfavor, the ability of the law school to teach legal skills, other than purely analytic ones, had been questioned. The era after World War II brought some serious attempts to prove that law schools could and should expand the range of skills taught. The 1944 report of the AALS Curriculum Committee, written primarily by Karl Llewellyn, was apparently the first organized attempt to isolate legal skills and so to articulate the rationales underlying legal education. That report noted, first of all, that with the increasing complexity of the law the regular case course was no longer, except for the best students, an adequate vehicle for indirect conveyance of the basic legal skills—"current case-instruction is somehow failing to do the job of producing *reliable professional competence* on the by-product side *in half or more of our end-product,* our graduates."[77] Outside analytic skills, however, there was little agreement as to what were legal skills.

Llewellyn's indignation provided some responses. A curriculum organized around legal skills appeared at Ohio State in 1950. The core of the program was the allotment of specific skills to each course to be taught along with the regular subject matter,[78] and as the 1944 AALS curriculum report (the inspiration for Ohio's reform)[79] had pointed out, the instructor thereby assumed responsibility, no matter what else he did, for teaching the assigned legal skills.[80] The approach did not survive. In the 1960s, some of the most interesting developments were plans, at best only partially implemented, for a functional curriculum at Southern California[81] and for a legal skills approach at North Carolina.[82] Again, the long-term effect of these changes appears to have been small.

The problem method, as an alternative to traditional case discussions, was another experiment that attempted to provide close faculty-student relations and also emphasized skills rather than substance. The study of problems rather than appellate cases met an objection to the case method that had been pointed out by David Cavers: "In the casebook study of cases, the student is studying solutions of problems, not how to solve problems."[83] Although the problem method was not widely used, there were several experiments along these lines,[84] and, at one time, Notre Dame attempted to build its syllabus around the problem method.[85] Again, the approach had limited long-term effects.

One major reason why the problem method was not more widely used was the lack of well-prepared problems or the existence of problem books; preparation of problems was a skill requiring both specialized knowledge and abilities in problem-construction. Good library facilities and small classes allowing for individualized attention were probably also essential for successful problem teaching.[86] A variation on the problem method was use of the problem case, planned to meet the objections to regular case teaching. The problem case omitted either facts, or the opinion or the decision, referring the student elsewhere for the omitted materials.[87] It was not a success.

Of all aspects of the renewed interest in skills, the particular interest in the skills embraced in the concept of clinical legal education was to prove the most important. Although definitions of "clinical" were as diverse as its proponents, "practical experience" enjoyed a considerable vogue in the 1960s. This was certainly not the first time that clinical work had been discussed or attempted.[88] Its antecedents went back to the 1920s and 1930s, when Bradway was establishing clinical programs and Jerome Frank was publishing "Why Not a Clinical Lawyer-School?"[89] Clinically conducted courses did not really begin to appear, however, until the 1940s.[90] The most elaborate of these was probably Yale's short-lived "Case Presentation," begun after World War II.[91] More important, however, was the increasing interest in clinical programs dealing with real clients and problems. Many of the law school legal aid clinics date from the 1940s, although eleven already were in successful operation by the beginning of that decade. There were twenty-eight clinics available for student participation in 1951 that were maintained by the law schools or by independent legal aid societies or public defender offices. Participation in legal aid work was a degree requirement in five schools by the 1950s; more usually it was an elective, or, if there were many applicants, it became selective among interested students.[92] Only rarely was it given for credit.

It was on the basis of these legal aid clinics, however, that, in the late 1960s, a new and much stronger clinical law movement began.[93] Growing student demands for relevance, and the increasing sense of boredom felt by the elite schools' carefully selected students in their second and third years,[94] fueled the demands for clinical studies. In 1968, the Ford Foundation put a foot in the door with CLEPR (Council on Legal Education for Professional Responsibility) whose funds encouraged all types of law schools to experiment with a limited form of clinical studies.[95] Within a few years almost half the law schools in the country had some kind of clinical studies program, normally closely related to a legal service office,[96] and a new breed of law faculty member—the clinical professor—was beginning to appear.[97] Vital in this new crusade was the possibility of credit for clinical studies.

The 1960s brought significant advances in the use of clinical work in law schools. Clinical programs inspired experiments in related areas,[98] and there were high hopes for the future. Although the use of the problem method, the viability of introductory law courses, and the effectiveness of other general "legal skills" approaches appeared to be in doubt, clinical legal education had acquired funding and an external lobbying group. Simultaneously there was increasing evidence of hostility on the part of more sophisticated academics toward the less sophisticated clinical approaches.[99] The 1970s were to prove a serious testing time for clinical legal studies.

NOTES

1. On part-time law schools, see Tinnelly, *Part-Time Legal Education*; Kelso, ed., *Study of Part-Time Legal Education*.
2. American Bar Association, *Annual Review of Legal Education*, 19 (1948).
3. For instance, between 1946–47 and 1948–49 the Veterans Administration paid Hastings Law School $740,000, although its expenses were only $343,000. Barnes, *Hastings College of Law*, 265–66.
4. "Diploma Mill Charge Hurled at Southeastern," *Washington Star*, 17 May 1946. The president sided with the alumni and was fired. "Dr. James Bell Is Ousted as Southeastern University President." Ibid., 2 August 1946. Although one class did apparently graduate in the postwar period, the law school effectively did not reopen. In 1966, Southeastern finally severed any connection with the YMCA and charted a course as a conventional proprietary business school. Southeastern University Archives, Washingtoniana Collection, Martin Luther King Library, Washington, D.C.
5. Bryson, "The History of Legal Education in Virginia," 202–3.

6. South Carolina created a law school at the State College of South Carolina rather than admit John Wrighten to the University of South Carolina. *Wrighten v. Board of Trustees of University of South Carolina*, 72 F. Supp. 948 (E.D.S.C., 1947). Texas pressed on with the creation of Texas Southern Law School in 1947 rather than admit Herman Sweatt to the University of Texas Law School. *Sweatt v. Painter*, 339 U.S. 629 (1950). Jones, "Texas Southern University School of Law—the Beginning," 197. *Brown v. Board of Education of Topeka*, 347 U.S. 483 (1954) saw the beginning of the end of these schools. Washington, "History and Role of Black Law Schools," 401–5. Predominantly black law schools now exist only at Howard, North Carolina Central (Durham, N.C.), Southern University (Baton Rouge, La.), and Texas Southern.

7. The decrease in the numbers of both law students and faculty members was dramatic during World War II, but it was only temporary. By 1947, the statistics showed that not only had the law schools survived the crisis, but also that they were flourishing and surpassing prewar figures. In 1938, there was a total of 28,000 students in 109 ABA-approved schools. By 1943, there had been 4,800 students in these same schools. Wicker, "Legal Education Today and in the Post-War Era," 700. In 1944, the number of full-time law teachers had fallen to 138 and part-time teachers to 229. *AALS Proceedings, 1944*, 115. Less well-known law schools saw a dramatic improvement upon the return of veterans. The Buffalo Law School, whose number had fallen to 23 in 1944, had an entering class of 136 in 1946. Conditions became so overcrowded that, by 1948, the LSAT was introduced as an admissions screen. See Pedersen, *The Buffalo Law School*, 85.

8. Sullivan, "Professional Associations," 425.

9. By 1947, by way of prelegal education, three states (Delaware, Kansas, and Pennsylvania) added the requirement of graduation from college; South Dakota and Wisconsin required three years of college; and all but Arkansas, Georgia, Mississippi, and Louisiana required two years. Earlier efforts to specify the nature of prelegal work had been largely abandoned. Of the twenty-three schools Esther Brown visited for her 1948 study, only Minnesota had prelaw course requirements. Brown, *Lawyers, Law Schools, and the Public Service*, 127. In no fewer than fifteen jurisdictions, it was no longer possible to enter the profession through apprenticeship. (They were Alabama, Arizona, Colorado, D.C., Florida, Indiana, Minnesota, New Mexico, Ohio, Oklahoma, Oregon, South Dakota, Utah, West Virginia, and Wisconsin. In Wyoming it was possible to qualify after two years of office work following a year at an approved law school.) Moreover, only four states required some apprenticeship, and the law school route to bar admission could be followed in every jurisdiction. In addition, at least seventeen jurisdictions gave credit only to "approved" law schools, and "approved" almost invariably meant "ABA-approved." Another two jurisdictions gave more favorable treatment to students from "approved" schools. American Bar Association, *Annual Review of Legal Education, 1947*, passim.

10. "In perspective, the American Bar Association and the Association of American Law Schools have been and are mighty forces for the advancement of legal education. We are apt to fret over the tardiness with which improvement comes about, but viewed over the long reach of the years, it is clear that much progress has been made, and it is equally clear that the tempo of progress was materially accelerated when those two great protagonists entered the arena of legal education. Even so, major problems remain and one of them is the unapproved law school. The Association of American Law Schools is unable to solve this problem. . . . The program of the American Bar Association is broader and has been effective in mitigating the disruptive implications of the unapproved schools." Harno, *Legal Education in the United States*, 120.

11. In 1948, Connecticut began to require three years of college before law school and

abolished entry to the profession through clerkship in an office, while Tennessee abolished entry through office practice and substituted attendance at an ABA law school. American Bar Association, *Annual Review of Legal Education, 1948*, 26. In 1949, Indiana and Nevada began to require attendance at an ABA school, and Nevada joined Indiana in closing off the law office route. In the same year, Arkansas joined the states requiring two years of prelaw-school college work. American Bar Association, *Annual Review of Legal Education, 1949*, 26.

12. This view of the bar was evident in some of the standards proposed at this time. In 1948, the Committee on Aims and Objectives of the AALS suggested that a school not be admitted to the AALS unless "the standards of legal education in the area in which the school is located are being promoted by the existence of such school." With the AALS determining such standards, it was likely that only those schools would be admitted that would prepare students for the "unitary bar" in which the AALS so firmly believed. Dean Gant of Indiana said of the proposal, "[T]he general background, I suppose, is to facilitate the elimination of some of the smaller schools." First, "Competition in the Legal Education Industry," 390.

13. As a result of the Flexner reforms and the pressure on the marginal medical schools, the eight black medical schools that had existed in 1910 had shrunk to two by 1923. Morais, *The History of the Negro in Medicine*, 89–90. The number of black physicians dropped between 1900 and 1950. For the efforts by the ABA to keep black lawyers out of the organized bar, see Hurst, *Growth of American Law*, 255. For the efforts in the 1960s to compensate for earlier discrimination, see Gellhorn, "The Law School and the Negro," 1069.

14. For an analysis of the conflict between the increasing de facto specialization of the bar and the "egalitarian ethic," see Christensen, *Specialization*, 18–24.

15. There were some who objected to this. Dean Charles Fornoff of Toledo Law School was one. Comparing the legal profession to the medical profession, he noted: "I suspect there is in the minds of a good many people a suspicion that the medical profession have [sic] solved their problem on the financial side but that the public suffer from the lack of really competent physicians, that might be produced with a little more competition." Fornoff feared similar results for the legal profession, which was so clearly attempting to follow the lead of the medical schools. First, "Competition in the Legal Education Industry," 390.

16. Law, of course, was not alone in its urge to strengthen its formal structures. A professor of law at Columbia examined barbers: "Of eighteen representative states included in a study of barbering regulations in 1929, not one then commanded an aspirant to be a graduate of a 'barber college,' though apprenticeship was necessary in all. Today, the states typically insist upon graduation from a barbering school that provides no less (and often much more) than 1,000 hours of instruction in 'theoretical subjects' such as sterilization of instruments, and this must still be followed by an apprenticeship." Gellhorn, *Individual Freedom and Governmental Restraints*, 146.

17. *AALS Proceedings, 1951*, 382.

18. Sullivan, "Professional Associations," 425.

19. An alternative of two years of college and four of law school was allowed. American Bar Association, *Annual Review of Legal Education, 1951*, 27.

20. The AALS passed a similar resolution, but only as a "standard" and not a "requirement for membership."

21. *AALS Proceedings, 1950*, 84.

22. In 1951, the ABA increased its library requirements to a minimum outlay of $3,000 a

year and, from 1955 on, the AALS required a minimum annual expenditure of $4,000, coupled with a minimum holding of 20,000 volumes and extra requirements for all students in excess of one hundred. *AALS Proceedings, 1952*, 224, 228. Meanwhile, the AALS had begun issuing standards (not requirements) about faculty teaching loads, which were not to average more than eight hours a week in member schools. *AALS Proceedings 1951*, 382. By 1958, the AALS would add the somewhat bizarre requirement that faculty members of AALS schools should be "competent." *AALS Proceedings, 1958*, 305. The ABA soon followed the lead of the AALS in library standards. By 1963–64, there had to be a minimum of 15,000 volumes and an annual expenditure of $4,000. American Bar Association, *Annual Review of Legal Education, 1956*, 27. By 1963, the ABA joined in the AALS standard of one faculty member for every seventy-five students. Ibid, *1959*, 22. More leapfrogging was in store. In 1968, the AALS moved to a minimum of $30,000 expenditure during 1968–71 and a total of $10,000 a year for acquisitions (or, more correctly, $40,000 for the inclusive years between 1968 and 1971). The regulation also provided a minimum volume count, for a member school, of 60,000 volumes by 1971. *AALS Proceedings, 1968*, 54.

23. Crotty, "Who Shall be Called to the Bar?," 86. For a contemporary statement of the reasons why it was thought that law office study was unsatisfactory, see remarks of Nighswander, "Should Study in a Law Office Be Abolished as a Qualification for Admission to the Bar?," 31.

In 1952, for instance, Virginia, while preserving the clerkship route, cut off the unapproved law school route. This led to the demise of the Virginia College of Commerce and Law, associated with the Richmond Business College. It had been founded by a group of businessmen and lawyers in 1937.

24. By 1966, only thirteen jurisdictions even allowed admission exclusively through office study, with a further five states allowing some mixing of law school and office practice. One source gave an intriguing reason for the survival of apprenticeship this long: "With the increasing reluctance of law schools to accept students dropped for poor scholarship by other schools, some states have retained law office study as the only remaining hope for such students." National Conference of Bar Examiners, *The Bar Examiner's Handbook* 41 (1968). In fact, the AALS regulations against admitting students dropped by other schools were modified during the 1960s. Until 1965, the rule was that a student dropped by one AALS school could not be admitted by another member school. By 1969, it was possible for the other school to admit such a student "provided that (a) the admitting school has reason to believe that the prior performance of such student does not indicate a lack of capacity to complete satisfactorily his law study in the admitting school, and (b) such students do not constitute a substantial portion of the admitting school's enrollment." *AALS Proceedings and Reports, 1965*, pt. 2, 103–5. Even those modified rules were subject to a test case as to their constitutionality. American Bar Association, *Annual Report, 1968*, 138 (1969).

Each year after 1966 there were assaults on apprenticeship, and by 1969 only fourteen states even contemplated any part of legal training taking place in a law office. American Bar Association, *Annual Review of Legal Education, 1969*, 27–31. In addition, by 1970, the demand for three years of college before law school was well on its way to universal acceptance. Eight jurisdictions actually required a degree or four years of college, and thirty more had, for all practical purposes, adopted the three-year requirement. Delaware, New Jersey, Pennsylvania, and Rhode Island still retained a requirement of a brief law office experience, and every state accepted basic law school training in lieu of clerkship. All states except Montana—which allowed two—required three years of law school. American Bar Association, *Annual Review of Legal Education, 1969*, 29. In no less than thirty-three jurisdictions the de facto requirement was graduation from an ABA-approved school. Ibid., 27–31.

25. American Bar Association, *Annual Review of Legal Education, 1969*, 20. The statistics, however, are not entirely reliable.

26. The school also began a day program in the 1950s, and by the 1960s this had become the main focus of the school. The *Announcement* for 1969–70, however, still advertised that "the student body is composed of young men and women, many of whom support themselves in whole or in part by daily employment and who desire to avail themselves of the opportunities for service to their fellow men that a legal education affords." The *Announcement* for 1976–77 had abandoned any mention of Lee's original aspirations for the school.

27. *Denver Post*, 2 September 1957, 15.

28. In 1956, Milton Friedman, in expressing economic disapproval of the success of the Flexner reforms, noted: "The lawyers have never been as successful as the physicians in getting control at the point of admission to professional school, though they are moving in that direction. The reason is amusing. Almost every school on the American Bar Association's list of approved schools is a full-time day school; almost no night schools are approved. Many state legislators, on the other hand, are graduates of night law schools. If they voted to restrict admission to the profession to graduates of approved schools, in effect they would be voting that they themselves were not qualified. Their reluctance to condemn their own competence has been the main factor that has tended to limit the extent to which law has been able to succeed in imitating medicine. I have not myself done any extensive work on requirements for admission to law for many years but I understand that this limitation is breaking down. The greater affluence of students means that a much larger fraction are going to full-time law schools and this is changing the composition of the legislatures." Friedman, *Capitalism and Freedom*, 151–52.

29. Cited in First, "Competition in the Legal Education Industry," 393.

30. Ibid., 399.

31. In 1967, there were thirty-four unapproved schools in twelve jurisdictions. American Bar Association, *Annual Review of Legal Education, 1967*, 17–19. By 1969, there were twenty-seven such schools in eight jurisdictions. American Bar Association, *Annual Review of Legal Education, 1969*, 17–18. Unfortunately, no accurate statistics exist for such schools during this or more recent years.

32. After suffering various defeats in the 1930s, proprietary law schools began gaining once more in California in the 1940s, perhaps because of the slow growth of law schools within the University of California system—at least in terms of the population growth of that state. There is no reason to think that their intellectual quality was any higher than that of their predecessors. They were not necessarily even good trade schools; one school, with 470 students at the time of the 1949 survey, had not produced any graduates able to pass the California bar examination in eight years. Prosser, "Legal Education in California," 197. See also State Bar of California, *Legal Education and Admission to the Bar of California* (1949).

In 1968, Western State University had 481 students; the University of West Los Angeles, 313; California College of Law, 82; Pacific Coast University, 94; Southwestern, 656; Van Norman, 52; Kennedy, 40; McGeorge, 508; San Fernando University, 580; and Humphrey's, 114. 21 *Journal of Legal Education* 323 (1969).

33. A provision shared with no other state, Montana having in 1970 withdrawn permission

for correspondence students to take the bar exam. 1 *Legal Education Newsletter* 3 (June 1970).

The performance of correspondence graduates on the California bar exam was poor. Their pass rate for 1936–41 was 11.2 percent, compared with the 8.7 percent for office students and in contrast to 59.9 percent for law school graduates. Prosser, "Legal Education in California," 192. The national bar examination "pass" average at about that time was 50 percent (i.e., roughly 7,000) yearly. Blaustein and Porter, *The American Lawyer*, 229. See also Brenner, *Bar Examinations and Requirements for Admission to the Bar*.

34. This was a compromise after a long battle between Homer Crotty of the state bar and Dean David Snodgrass of Hastings. The bar's establishment had wanted a passing rate of 60 percent in the state bar as a requirement for accreditation. Barnes, *Hastings College of Law*, 310–14.

35. William L. Prosser, the dean of the University of California Law School at Berkeley, declared: "The first fact about legal education which strikes any reader of the report is that there is far too much of it." Prosser predicted that of the 5,000 students then studying law, over one-half would never make it to the bar exam and that of those who did make it as far as the exam, about one-half would fail. Prosser believed that there were only two things that saved the California bar from the hordes of poor lawyers. Those were an exam that weeded out the worst of the students in the unaccredited schools after their first year and the regular bar exam itself. Prosser, "Legal Education in California," 186.

36. McDougal, "The Law School of the Future," 1353.

37. Bergin, "Law Teacher," 637–42.

38. The Law School Admissions Test (LSAT) was a postwar addition to the admission process. The Educational Testing Service had begun work on a new test in 1947, at Columbia's suggestion, with the cooperation of a dozen other schools who agreed to share the cost. An experimental version was tried at seven schools that same year, and a standard LSAT was ready for general use in 1948. It made possible far greater selectivity in the admissions process. Reese, "The Standard Law School Admission Test," 125–26; Goebel, *School of Law, Columbia*, 371–72.

During the 1950s, the selectivity of schools increased dramatically. In 1954, Berkeley accepted 70 percent of those who applied (248 out of 352); in 1968, 34 percent (675 out of 1,988) were accepted. In 1967–68, Columbia accepted 713 out of 2,269; Harvard, 843 out of 3,247; Illinois, 514 out of 1,129; Iowa, 284 out of 412; Minnesota, 281 out of 657; Yale, 331 out of 1,698; and Hastings, 575 out of 1,773. Stolz, "Training for the Law," appendix.

Nevertheless, in 1961 it was made clear that even a number of accredited schools operated at a marginal intellectual level: "too many of the less well-known schools are unable to attract the superior students needed to supply intellectual leadership and tone." *Report of the ABA Special Committee to Study Current Needs in the Field of Legal Education*, 6.

In 1952, Dean O'Meara had been able to say: "There are two schools of thought. One, the so-called Harvard approach, tends to admit all with degrees and fail only those with real inadequacies. The other, the so-called Yale approach, favors selectivity in admission and anticipates few failures." Moore, *A Century of Law at Notre Dame*, 109. Although O'Meara said, "I favor the Harvard approach," by 1970 there was really only one approach at Harvard, Yale, and Notre Dame: selective admissions with rare exclusions for failure. For the efforts by Minnesota to end the "revolving door" approach to admissions and dismissals, see Stein, "Pursuit of Excellence," 834.

39. Nicholson, *The Law Schools of the United States*, 2, quoting Judge Paul Brosman (formerly dean of the Tulane Law School).

40. John G. Hervey, quoted in Nicholson, *Law Schools of the United States*, 21. Another inspector commented, "Of the nine schools I inspected, six showed no impact of the modern world, whatsoever." Quoted in Harno, *Legal Education in the United States*, 163. A Detroit study compared the curricula of forty-eight smaller schools with the state bar examinations and found a strong correlation in thirty-six cases. Pemberton, "Report on Legal Education," pt. 1, 88. See also *1947 AALS Handbook*, 135; and Fuller, "Legal Education and Admissions to the Bar in Pennsylvania," 250–51: "While some of this pressure could be lifted from the undergraduate law program if the law schools were to develop better continuing legal education programs, few have chosen to do so."

41. The University of Denver announced a letters-business-law program in 1946, and Michigan briefly revived a similar program beginning in 1947. University of Denver, *Report of the Committee on Curriculum* (1946), 116–17; Brown, *Legal Education at Michigan*, 115. Harvard was offering a combined law-business program at this time. *Preliminary Statement of the Committee on Curriculum of the Harvard Law School*, 111 (1947). Minnesota maintained a law and business administration course leading to degrees in both fields, and in 1950 it planned to begin a combined program with the university's Engineering School "shortly." Lockhart, "The Minnesota Program," 259. At Michigan in 1950, a seven-year letters and law combined course replaced the previous six-year course, continuing in existence until 1958. Brown, *Legal Education at Michigan*, 301–2.

42. At the larger schools, there was also a postwar emphasis on international and comparative law. Cornell, under pressure from veterans, arranged a program of specialization in international affairs, considerably strengthened by a $390,000 grant from Ford in 1956. Henn, "The Cornell Law School—Its History and Traditions," 146. By 1950, Harvard's Institute of International Legal Studies had begun to offer courses. Sutherland, *Law At Harvard*, 333–34. Yale had such an institute under consideration as early as 1938–39. *Report of the Dean, Yale Law School, 1938–39*, 17. After World War II, Yale added a new division of graduate studies, a two-way fellowship program for the exchange of American and foreign graduate students interested in international and comparative law and jurisprudence. *Report of the Dean, Yale Law School, 1946–47*, 7, 11. Columbia's 1950–51 list of seminars included half a dozen in comparative and international law. Goebel, *School of Law, Columbia*, 150, n. 118. Columbia's stress on comparative law dated back at least to the establishment, in 1930, of the Parker School of Foreign and Comparative Law. Ibid., 330.

43. By about 1950, commercial law, labor law, government control of business, and especially criminal law were said to be making the greatest advances in the use of the social sciences. Brown, *Lawyers, Law Schools, and the Public Service*, 117, 121. Other areas—such as family law—were added to the list as relevant research appeared.

44. For example, one of the debates during the 1940s and 1950s was whether administrative and constitutional law—by then staple courses—should be moved into the first year. See Freeman, "Administrative Law in the First-Year Curriculum," 225–26.

45. Oliver Morse, "Let's Add Another Year," 252. Cf. Prosser, "The Ten-Year Curriculum," 149. In 1950, there was talk of restoring the prewar mandatory four-year law degree at Minnesota, but it was decided to retain it as optional. In 1957, the four-year program was reduced to three and a half years, and in 1965 the three-and-a-half-year course was

reduced to three. Stein, "In Pursuit of Excellence—a History of the University of Minnesota Law School," 310–11, 840, 842.

46. This was also the era for insisting on a public emphasis in private law courses. In the property field, the change was sparked by Yale's Myres McDougal. His dissatisfaction with property teaching at Yale led to a rearrangement of the property course and to the 1948 publication by McDougal and David Haber, of a first-year casebook entitled *Property, Wealth, Land: Allocation, Planning and Development*, nearly half of which dealt with the public aspects of property law. Brown, *Lawyers, Law Schools, and the Public Service*, 165; Leach, "Property Law Taught in Two Packages," 36–37; Percy Bordwell, review of McDougal and Haber's *Property, Wealth, Land: Allocation, Planning and Development*, 1 *Journal of Legal Education* 326 (1948).

47. The analyses in the 1940s were no kinder than some of their predecessors. Karl Llewellyn said, "[I]t is obvious that man could hardly devise a more wasteful method of imparting *information about subject matter* than the case-class. Certainly man never has." Llewellyn, "The Current Crisis in Legal Education," 215. Most critics also agreed with Cavers that "after the first year, the system is not exacting in its demands on any but the morbidly conscientious student." Cavers, "In Advocacy of the Problem Method," 453.

48. "To take a stroll through the Elective Courses of a modern law school catalogue is a treat that should be kept for Christmas Day. Why, it is a veritable gift shop of ideas, and certainly proof of the fact that law school can be fun and relevant at the same time. But I am afraid that all the glitter—the courses on poverty, urban development, social legislation and civil rights, or those challenging seminars on law and psychiatry or the law of developing nations—is the glitter of paste. And I ought to know, for I teach one. These courses and seminars are, in reality, only further symptoms of the law teacher's schizophrenia." Bergin, "The Law Teacher," 647–48.

49. Reed, *Present-Day Law Schools*, 252.

50. *The Preliminary Statement of the Committee on Legal Education* appeared in March 1947, suggesting not sweeping changes but various specific reforms. The suggestions included the possibility of offering parallel three-year curricula, one traditional and one experimentally organized around problems of legal planning; the moving of foundation public-law courses—constitutional law, taxation, and administrative law—from the third year into the first or second, and requiring students to take one or all of them; a reading program to survey the legal profession; and a summer reading program in private-law subjects that might otherwise be crowded out of the curriculum.

A revision followed this report in 1949, but actual changes were cautious. The first-year courses remained prescribed, and wide election was still allowed only in the third year. First-year introductory work using teaching fellows was introduced. "A significant beginning towards an adequate training in draftsmanship" was expected from drafting work being done in the property courses. Some extralegal subject areas would be covered; a course in accounting was offered and a certain amount of work given in the Graduate School of Business Administration would be open to law students. Further integration of legal and nonlegal matters could be undertaken by individual instructors within their own courses; a new course, international organizations, for instance, incorporated economics by focusing on the economic functions of agencies of world government. Administrative and constitutional law were moved to the second year and required. Sutherland, *Law at Harvard*, 323, 337; Cavers, "The First-Year Group Work at Harvard," 39.

51. Casner, "Faculty Decisions on the Report of the Committee on Legal Education," 10.

52. Adding structure to previously free course elections was one move designed to get rid of random choices, or worse, choices based on reputedly easy A's. A plan of required election of subjects within designated groups was adopted at California (Berkeley) and Columbia, and to a lesser degree, at Michigan. The Columbia plan put into effect in 1949–50 restricted the student's choice of electives by establishing minimum requirements from each of five groups. "Thus was recognized the fact that the average student is unable to plan for himself a balanced program of studies." Goebel, *School of Law, Columbia*, 370. Under these new requirements, at least thirteen hours had to be taken in a group of business, property, and family law subjects; at least six hours from listed procedure subjects; and at least two hours each from a jurisprudence group and from a group including international and comparative law and the legal profession. Ibid., 509–10.

Perhaps the most noteworthy of these attempts, however, was Yale's Divisional Program. The original design was that work of the fourth and fifth terms would revolve around one area of the law and include major research involving several seminars and a thesis seen as the equivalent of a law journal comment. "It is emphatically not a program of specialization." *Report of the Dean, Yale Law School, 1956–57*, 7. The program went into effect in 1957–58, and within a year problems were apparent; by 1965, the whole arrangement was dissolving. The faculty, Dean Eugene V. Rostow noted with regret, was finding the divisional structure "rigid" or "cumbersome." *Report of the Dean, Yale Law School, 1963–64* and 64–65, 6–7. See also Freilich, "The Divisional Program at Yale," 443. In contrast to Yale's asserted rejection of the idea, a few schools attempted to focus their second- and third-year programs on a particular specialty, at least for some students, and that experiment was by no means always limited to the so-called national schools. See, for example, Temple's program in forensic medicine and Detroit's program in urban law. Introductory courses of this era included legal method (used at Columbia and elsewhere), Chicago's "Elements of Law," and Notre Dame's "great books" in jurisprudence. Pemberton, Jr., "Report of the National Law Student Conference on Legal Education—Conference Report," pt. 1, 87; Jones, "Notes on the Teaching of Legal Method," 22.

53. There were a few genuine efforts to restructure whole curricula, but they were not to cause as much stir as Columbia's efforts had in the 1920s. In the 1940s, there were new curricula at Northwestern and Nebraska, based on lengthened degree programs, and with an emphasis on innovation. The Northwestern program, begun in 1946 under the rubric "Reconversion in Legal Education," adopted a group unit plan covering seven terms in twenty-nine months. A unit of related work occupied each term. The first three units were concerned with basic concepts; the fourth unit consisted of procedure courses, the fifth was called "Corporate Industry"; the sixth unit was entitled "Trade and Finance"; and the seventh was called "Government and Public Services." Seminars designed to cut across the entire field of the unit were a required part of each term's work. After the first three terms, lectures, readings, and writing exercises replaced the case system as the basic teaching method. Compromises in the plan, however, began almost immediately as the more demanding program proved unattractive to applicants. The group unit plan had to be abandoned totally in 1952–53. Although Northwestern failed to achieve its ultimate goal, the experiments were said to have "not been without profound and beneficial effect both within the law school and upon the efforts of legal education everywhere to improve the techniques of law today." Rahl and Schwerin, *Northwestern University School of Law*, 175–86. See also "Report of Committee on Curriculum," 46 *AALS Proceedings* 116 (1946).

Louisiana State University was influenced by Northwestern's 1946 program and adopted two of its basic elements for 1946–47: a group unit plan of course offerings and the use of the summer session as a regular part of the school year. That reform did not survive either. Ibid., 115. The Nebraska program, begun in the same year, suffered a similar fate. Basically a four-year program, it was divided into two parts: two years of nonprofessional studies in basic law subjects, political theory, and social science (leading to a Bachelor of Science in Law, which did not entitle the student holding it to practice) were followed by two years in technical law for the professional degree. Nearly all the work was prescribed, and, although more work in private law was required, one-quarter of the curriculum had to be taken in public law. Two extensive skills laboratories constituted the major innovation of the program—the legislative laboratory and the practice laboratory—both designed to prepare Nebraska graduates for the usual employment pattern—entry into private practice directly from law school. Beutel, "The New Curriculum at the University of Nebraska College of Law," 117–89; Brown, *Lawyers, Law Schools, and the Public Service*, 218–19.

54. Sutherland, *Law at Harvard*, 323.

55. Brown, *Lawyers, Law Schools, and the Public Service*, 228; Weihofen, "Education for Law Teachers," 427. Redlich's ghost must have smirked with satisfaction.

56. The program was designed for 100 to 125 first-year students each year, and, by 1948, required a staff of one faculty member and four teaching fellows. By 1948, about three hundred hours of student time and an output of about twenty-five thousand words were required. Eight hours credit, in a forty-hour first-year curriculum, was given for the writing program. Kalven, "Law School Training in Research and Exposition," 108–9; Pemberton, "Report of the National Law Student Conference on Legal Education," pt. 2, 223. Once again, however, a program was destined to collapse under its own weight, or at least as the result of inadequate faculty-student ratios in law school. The concern with student ability in writing (and perhaps even scholarship) was not limited to undergraduate programs. After 1933, the J.S.D. at Yale required the preparation of a thesis. *Report of the Dean, Yale Law School, 1931–32*, 19. Harvard had added a thesis requirement for the doctorate in 1928; both Harvard and Columbia demanded a "publishable" dissertation. Sutherland, *Law at Harvard*, 234; Goebel, *School of Law, Columbia*, 510–11, n. 124.

57. Kalven, "Training in Research and Exposition"; *Report of the Dean, Yale Law School, 1947–48*, 17; Sutherland, *Law at Harvard*, 323; Goebel, *School of Law, Columbia*, 371. Columbia had tried a similar experiment in 1933–34, without success. Ibid., 502, n. 132.

58. *Report of the Dean, Yale Law School, 1947–48*; Sutherland, *Law at Harvard*, 323; Goebel, *School of Law, Columbia*, 371.

59. Bergin, "Law Teacher," 643.

60. At Yale, for instance, despite the breadth of the electives permitted, courses in traditional areas occupied 75 to 90 percent of the average student's program. Yale University Council, Committee on the Law School, *Report*, 1966. See also Harvard Law School, *Preliminary Statement of the Committee on Curriculum* (1947), 157.

61. A study of the California law schools found that the curriculum tended to freeze on the twenty required bar examination subjects, all based on the traditional curriculum of the previous generation. Even at Berkeley, courses on labor law, creditors' rights, corporation finance, federal jurisdiction, insurance, legislation, government regulation of business, restitution, or a second year of taxation were not widely elected because of the bar examination "cramming." Prosser, "Legal Education in California," 201–2.

62. John Cribbet, describing the University of Illinois's Law School as typical of local law schools at large state universities, noted that the largest growth courses at Illinois

between 1948 and 1958 had been in public law. Tax law courses, too, increased from two to five (including two seminars); labor law increased from one course to two courses and a seminar. Cribbet, "The Evolving Curriculum—a Decade of Curriculum Change at the University of Illinois," 230–31.

63. Strong, "A New Curriculum for the College of Law of the Ohio State University," 44–56. A detailed inventory of the ideal legal capacities of a good lawyer was made, and the law school courses were then shaped to provide adequate training in all the areas listed. See also Strong, "Pedagogical Implications of Inventorying Legal Capacities," 555.

64. University of North Carolina Law School, "Educative Elements in Legal Training," mimeographed (1968).

65. There were, of course, variations in the degree to which schools were able to respond: a few schools could still afford to offer two or three times as many courses as the average school. Jones, "Local Law Schools vs. National Law Schools," 287.

66. In 1953–54, fifty seminars were offered at Harvard and twenty-six at Columbia; in that year, Illinois offered five seminars, Ohio State fifteen, Iowa more than twelve, Indiana eighteen, Utah ten, North Carolina, Louisiana State and Alabama two or three each, and New Mexico and Vanderbilt one each. Moreland, "Legal Writing and Research in the Smaller Law Schools," 49. Ten years later the list was much larger. See a survey of 115 schools in Del Duca, "Continuing Evaluation of Law School Curricula," 309.

67. For instance, the Salmon P. Chase School (to become the law school of Northern Kentucky) had two full-time faculty in 1952; by 1971 it had ten.

68. The acceptance of the relevance of social science to the law school curriculum was materially aided by grants made by the Russell Sage Foundation during the 1960s to Berkeley, Northwestern, Wisconsin, and Yale. The Walter E. Meyer Research Institution of Law aided considerably in stimulating empirical work related to law. See, especially, Harry Kalven, Jr., "The Quest for the Middle Range: Empirical Inquiry and Legal Policy," in Hazard, ed., *Law in a Changing America*, 56.

69. Courses introducing the student to the study of law and basic concepts were popular. These included a special project in legal writing at Drake, a course in legal bibliography, and panel discussion groups at Kansas. Mandelker, "Legal Writing—the Drake Program," 583; Speca, "Panel Discussions as a Device for Introduction to Law," 124. The University of Pittsburgh attempted to promote cooperation between the law school and other professional schools by having law and chemistry students collaborate on studying additives to oleomargarine. Nutting, "An Experiment in Intraprofessional Education," 44.

A concern with professional standards led Southern Methodist to offer a course on the legal profession. Dean Robert Storey explained, "We think so much of the course that it is not only required but we would not consider graduating our students without the course." Harris, "The Inculcation of Professional Standards at Southern Methodist University School of Law," 823. The University of Illinois also offered a course on the profession. Harno, "Professional Ethics at the University of Illinois," 821. In this same area, Berkeley, among the elite schools, felt that the best way to learn about the profession was to have the students meet its members. First-year students were therefore offered a course based on a panel of lecturers: seven judges and six attorneys. The class was held as an informal discussion over dinner, followed by a presentation. Robert Kingsley, "Teaching Professional Ethics and Responsibilities," 84. Such was the level of discussion of curricula "reform" during the period.

70. Oleck, "The 'Adversary Method' of Law Teaching," 104.

71. Houts, "A Course in Proof," 418.

72. See, for instance, Bradway, "Legal Clinics and Law Students," 425.

73. Miller, "Clinical Training of Law Students," 298.

74. Dobie, "An Approach to 'Clinical' Legal Education," 21.

75. Storke, "Devices for Teaching Fact-Finding," 82.

76. Stephenson, "Academe To Agora," 163. Some sense of this changed approach to professional responsibility may be gleaned from the announcement in the 1968–69 *Bulletin* for Notre Dame Law School: "The School believes that the lawyer is best served, and the community as well, if he pursues not only legal knowledge and legal skills but also a profound sense of the ethics of his profession—and something else which the curriculum is likewise designed to cultivate: pride in the legal profession and a finer partisanship for justice. To that end the Law School participates in a local program to provide legal services, mainly in civil cases, to persons unable to pay counsel. This activity is part of the Legal Services Program of the Office of Economic Opportunity." Cited in Moore, *A Century of Law at Notre Dame*, 111.

77. *AALS Proceedings, 1944*, 168. Among the recommendations of the report were that law faculties should decide what legal skills ought to be taught and that these skills should be allocated among the first-year courses, so that each first-year instructor would be primarily responsible for the teaching of a certain skill. The 1947 AALS Committee on Teaching and Examination Methods, chaired by Weihofen, attempted to carry Llewellyn's suggestions further. That report analyzed the skills implied in the phrase "thinking like a lawyer" and found five distinguishable skills: the ability to determine the holding of a case (legal analysis); the ability to form principles from the study of separate cases (legal synthesis); the handling of complex fact situations (legal diagnosis); the ability to interpret statutes and regulations; and the ability to apply legal principles to the solving of problems (legal solution). *AALS Handbook, 1947*, 76–79. David Cavers introduced the distinction between "skills" and "skillfulness," pointing out that the schools could not expect to train students to exercise legal skills *skillfully* and recommending that legal skills be emphasized simply as an approach to problems from the lawyer's point of view. Cavers, "Skills and Understanding," 396, 399.

78. Information, insights, skills, and practice were the major headings of an inventory of legal capacities developed for Ohio's curriculum study. The information category included basic substantive and adjectival (procedural) rules, principles, concepts, and standards. Insights to be stressed were a comprehension of theories of law and an awareness of the institutional structure of the law, together with an understanding of legal method and an awareness of policy issues. Legal skills included the dialectic skills of fact discrimination, case analysis, and issue disposition, and the technical skills of adjective and argumentative advocacy, draftsmanship, research, and writing. Practice was to be provided in the areas of legal counseling, negotiation, "contestation," and planning. Strong, "A New Curriculum for the College of Law of the Ohio State University," 45–48, 52. The skills approach apparently had some success at Ohio; at least the *Catalog for 1968–69* still stressed the development of legal skills as a primary objective.

79. "The Place of Skills in Legal Education," *AALS Handbook, 1944*, 159.

80. Drafting, when taught, was usually covered in a legislation course or as an extracurricular subject; more frequently, it was just ignored. Another irregular opportunity for drafting practice was provided when a state requested drafting assistance from its state law school. A more substantial attempt to teach drafting was the legislative laboratory established at Nebraska as part of the major curriculum revision in 1946. Law review editors at North Carolina were given similar experience through biennial critiques of state legislation. Wisconsin included drafting practice in a summer clinic for training in

legal skills held in 1948, and Michigan began a full course called "Drafting and Estate Planning" in 1947–48. A Minnesota course in legislation and drafting was particularly successful: the emphasis of the course was on the lawyer as draftsman and counselor. See Brown, *Lawyers, Law Schools, and the Public Service*, passim. Although most of these projects withered, there was a revival of interest in drafting in the late 1960s. See, for example, the Yale Legislative Services Program.

81. "Law Language and Ethics" was introduced as a compulsory first-year course, adding a new dimension to the standard first-year syllabus. Mayer, *The Lawyers*, 91–92; Riesman, "Some Observations on Legal Education," 63.

82. "University of North Carolina Reports," mimeographed (1968).

83. Cavers, "In Advocacy of the Problem Method," 455. The problem method, Karl Llewellyn commented, simply applied the essence of proper case teaching, namely, the study of problem-raising situations, rather than the study of judicial decisions in settled areas. Llewellyn, "The Current Crisis in Legal Education," 217. Problems also provided a convenient form for combining legal and nonlegal materials.

84. Cavers taught conflict of laws at Duke using the problem method, and Charles Carnahan's conflicts casebook (Washington University) combined cases and problems for simultaneous use. The University of Colorado's prewar constitutional law and Albert Kocourek's security transactions at Northwestern were both problem courses. Brown, *Lawyers, Law Schools, and the Public Service*, 231; "Report of the Committee on Teaching and Examination Methods," *AALS Handbook, 1942*, 89.

Harvard began reworking its course in government regulation of business, labor law, and legislation in the 1940s, incorporating problems in planning and negotiations. *Preliminary Statement of the Committee on Legal Education of the Harvard Law School*, 119. That idea was revived again at Harvard in the late 1960s. Columbia's seminar in governmental administration, begun before the war and revived in 1946, used hypothetical problems. Another Columbia experiment was the seminar in selected legal problems, introduced in the spring of 1940 and revived in 1946–47. Practicing lawyers submitted current problems to the class once a week; the students were to write memoranda outlining their approaches to the problem at hand. Brown, *Lawyers, Law Schools, and the Public Service*, 191–204; Goebel, *School of Law, Columbia*, 338–39. Michigan, besides using problems in several courses, taught some courses through problems without cases, including corporate organization, drafting, and estate planning. *AALS Handbook, 1947*, 109. Harvard Law School's *Preliminary Statement of the Committee on Curriculum* (1947) commented that estate planning and business organizations were areas particularly amenable to problem teaching; these two, together with security and creditors' rights, were isolated as the fields in which the use of problems had been most successful (65–66).

85. See, for instance, Ward, "The Problem Method at Notre Dame," 100; Moore, *A Century of Law at Notre Dame*, 112; Volz, "The Legal Problems Courses at the University of Kansas City," 91.

86. Brown, *Lawyers, Law Schools, and Public Service*, 232.

87. Ehrenzweig, "The American Casebook," 236. Larson used such an approach at Cornell (which he labeled "inductive") in torts and agency. Each student wrote an opinion based on the facts of the case and "common sense," with the opportunity of later comparing his opinion to the actual one. Larson, "An 'Inductive' Approach to Legal Education," 287–88. Where the problem case was used without such a specific system, however, difficulties arose. Better students did not like the indefiniteness of a problem approach and tended to ignore unanswered questions: a Yale questionnaire indicated

that only rarely did students study problem cases with care. Ehrenzweig, "The American Casebook," 236.

88. It should be remembered, too, that "clinical" education at this time had a broad meaning. The long-familiar moot courts were one type; these flourished in the 1930s and 1940s, and of the forty-two schools represented at the National Law Student Conference in 1948, nearly all maintained (frequently student-run) appellate moot courts. Pemberton, "Report on Legal Education," Part I, 73; Pemberton, "Report on Legal Education," Part II, 224. Trial-court programs were less frequent, largely because verisimilitude was difficult. For experiments, see Green, "Realism in Practice Court," 422–23; Hunter, "Motion Pictures and Practice Court," 426–29. The law reviews, which some still included in the category of clinical education, had flourished since their origins in the late nineteenth century; by 1955, seventy-eight were being published, and work on a law review was still regularly assumed to be the best educational experience the law schools could provide. Mewett, "Reviewing the Law Reviews," 188; Cavers, "In Advocacy of the Problem Method," 451–52.

89. Frank, "Why Not a Clinical Lawyer-School?"

90. By the 1950s, such programs were receiving significant positive support in legal periodicals. Frank was still arguing in their favor. Frank, "Both Ends against the Middle," 20–47. Finn advocated adding a fourth year of clinical work to law programs in order to bring the young lawyer up to the standards of the better-trained young doctor. Finn, "The Law Graduate—an Adequate Practitioner?," 84–89. Not all agreed. Andrew W. Clements, dean of Albany Law School, objected to clinical work on the prophetic ground that it would require the "dean . . . to be a juggler and a lion tamer" to deal with both theorists and practical men. Another problem, in his opinion, was that "an overemphasis upon practical training, or know-how, could dull our sense of moral values and make of the law schools little more than vocational institutions." Clements, "Law School Curricula—a Reply," 36–42. Another long-time advocate of clinical education, however, was still fighting in the face of what then appeared overwhelming opposition. John Bradway claimed, "The problem of providing practical legal training has already been substantially solved by some of us in the law school field." Bradway, "Practical Legal Training," 52–55.

91. Taught as a three-credit seminar for twelve students at a time, the course provided the experience of carrying several cases from their first stage to their conclusion. During the course, the students obtained practical experience in interviewing, negotiation, arbitration, and the conduct of trials. Mueller and James, "Case Presentation," 129, 134. Although Columbia had attempted a moot arbitration and Chicago had a prewar program in which students sat in on pretrial conferences and on arbitration proceedings, there were few opportunities besides Yale's case presentation course for students to obtain experience in negotiation and arbitration. Ibid., 129; Pemberton, "Report on Legal Education, Part 2," 229–30. Other new clinical courses in the late 1940s included the University of Washington's course in trial technique, taught with the use of films, and a Columbia seminar on trial advocacy, introduced in 1949–50, which stressed the arts of advocacy rather than procedural rules. Ibid., 225; Goebel, *School of Law, Columbia*, 370.

92. What the students were allowed to do varied from clinic to clinic. At Harvard, Yale, and Colorado, experienced students did most of the supervising; at Harvard, students handled about fifteen hundred cases each year and did nearly all the work themselves. In nine schools, students could carry cases into court. Johnstone, "Law School Legal Aid Clinics," 535, 541–44, 551. Critics of students' participation in legal clinics argued

primarily that clinic work was irrelevant to the average student's later law practice. John Bradway argued equally vehemently in favor of clinics. Bradway, "Some Distinctive Features of a Legal Aid Clinic Course," 469. Perhaps the most persuasive defense of clinical work came from the practicing profession: "The group that seems to be most solidly in favor of legal aid clinics is made up of lawyers in practice who did clinic work as students." Johnstone, "Law School Legal Aid Clinics," 540. Such arguments are summarized ibid., 539, and in Brown, *Lawyers, Law Schools, and Public Service,* 238.

93. Several of these clinical programs are described in Conference of California Law Students, "Student Internship Programs: A Memorandum," mimeographed (1967).

94. Gellhorn, "Second and Third Years of Law Study," 1; Kelso, "Symposium on Legal Education," 26; David Currie, "Our Students Have Outgrown Our Curriculum: The Third Year," mimeographed, University of Chicago Law School (1968).

95. The AALS developed the Council on Education for Professional Responsibility. It succeeded the National Council on Legal Education when the latter suffered a financial death. The AALS obtained a $950,000 Ford grant to continue the council's work. "The new entity made eleven grants totaling approximately $76,000 in its first nine months of operation . . . and twenty-three grants totaling nearly $251,000 in the succeeding twelve months." Steigler, "Reconstruction of NCLE," 279; "Report of the CEPR," AALS *Proceedings, 1966,* pt. 1, 285–89. The Ford Foundation announced the establishment of the Independent Council on Legal Education for Professional Responsibility (CLEPR) in June 1968, to be funded with a grant of approximately $6,000,000 in the first five years of its projected ten-year life. Ford Foundation press release, 12 June 1968. The CLEPR program gave priority to clinical work and fieldwork in criminal and juvenile law, with an injection of the clinical element "into civil areas of law such as landlord-tenant and creditor-debtor relationships, city planning, zoning, mortgage banking, title insurance, and the operation of insurance companies and administrative agencies." Ibid., 3. CLEPR was to work "intensively" to make clinical programs a regular part of the curriculum in ABA-approved schools on the ground that "exposure to real problems reinforces the conscientiousness of the activists and develops in others a sensitivity and perspective that prepares them for careers as professional men and public policymakers. The public and its agencies of justice will benefit in the long run. But even during the training process, society will be served directly by the participation and assistance of law students and their faculty supervisors." Ibid., 2. Smith, "Is Education for Professional Responsibility Possible?" 509. For the further statements about the status of clinical education during this period, see Edmund W. Kitch, ed., *Clinical Education and the Law School of the Future.*

96. For descriptions of the programs at Denver, Minnesota, Michigan, Boston, Harvard, New York University, and Notre Dame, see Kitch, *Clinical Education,* 138 ff.

97. The passage of Title XI of the Higher Education Act gave some support to clinical legal education by authorizing up to $7,500,000 a year (with a maximum of $75,000 to each school) for such programs. The title was added in 1968, but no appropriations were voted until late in the 1970s.

98. One of these was the return, albeit in a slightly different guise, of apprenticeship, this time, however, in the programs carefully designed and controlled by a law school. An early and notable example was Yale Professor Walton Hamilton's experiment in the spring semester of 1942: seven second-year students spent the term in Washington, each assigned to a particular government official. The students were under Hamilton's general supervision and met with him regularly for group conferences. The experiment was pronounced relatively successful: "The program has provided an exposure somewhat different from that which the classroom gives. It develops an awareness and brings

out skills which complement and underwrite those developed in New Haven. It should enrich the work of the third year. In its difference, it seems to provide more than adequate compensation for what is surrendered in regular courses. All the more so, since it provides a new stimulus and a fresh attack in the second year, when the law school has the least of novelty to offer and the morale of the student body is at its lowest." "Experiment in Training Students by Assignment to Government Agencies, Part II: Report of Walton Hamilton to the Dean of the Yale Law School," *AALS Handbook, 1943*, 124.

Although the innovation was not repeated at Yale, it was not the end of the internship form of apprenticeship. In 1970, the Center for Law and Social Policy was established in Washington, D.C. Under the supervision of full-time attorneys, students from a number of schools were enabled to spend a clinical term at the center. It was to have considerable success—at least from the students' point of view—during the 1970s. Stanford's Extern Program, begun in the 1960s with similar hopes, apparently did not achieve its goals. Ehrlich and Headrick, "The Changing Structure of Education at Stanford Law School," 452, 461–63.

Smaller schools encountered difficulties, as had Yale and Stanford, when they started clinical programs on their own or through a government agency. The Washington College of Law created its School of Public Law in 1946. Its aim was to provide "clinical" training in Washington, D.C., and it was open to students from any interested law school as well as to others interested in comparative governmental procedures. Brown, *Lawyers, Law Schools, and the Public Service*, 189–90. Other schools tried state and local government apprenticeship plans: the University of Cincinnati experimented briefly with apprenticeship in local law offices just before Pearl Harbor. Wisconsin had a prewar program that placed students in local public and private law offices for two summers. Wisconsin also provided three graduate fellowships for state government apprenticeships. Ibid., 238–39. None of these programs seems to have had major or lasting success.

99. Expressed most articulately by Kitch, *Clinical Education*, 5.

13 / The Profession and the Law Schools: Radicalism, Affluence, and OPEC

ACED with mainly subsidized competitors, by the mid-1960s even one or two of the previously prominent private schools sensed that chill economic winds were blowing, and for some private schools the situation was becoming difficult.[1] In this situation, even funded state schools had to be conscious of economic roadblocks. Although the sudden surge of interest in the profession during the late 1960s was to reverse the increasingly threatening financial situation at least for the next decade, the long-term financial future of at least the less fashionable part of the private sector was in serious doubt. By the early 1980s it looked as if, when the unaccredited schools were gone, the underendowed private schools would be the next to disappear.[2] Fiscal and professional pressures were underlining the homogeneity of legal education, but the intellectual pressures inhibiting permanent change, as opposed to frenetic and fragmentary experimentation, were, if anything, even greater.

Legal education by the mid-1960s had found itself caught in the web of its own history. There had been much talk of change, but little change had occurred. Although legal education had remained relatively static, changes were occurring outside the law school that threatened to encroach upon its sacred walls. The mid to late 1960s was the era of civil rights activism, Vietnam, the escalation of the women's movement, and "radical" agitation in general. None of these could be entirely ignored by the legal profession. Many of the issues involved new and complex legal questions, and although perhaps only a small percentage of the practicing bar might deal directly with these, legal educators were brought face to face with all aspects of the student revolution.

The future of legal education was not certain. It seemed to have had only limited ability to adapt in the years leading up to the 1960s, but some professed to see silver linings in the storm clouds. Most significant among these were the remarks suggesting that a greater flexibility in the structure and purposes of law school, even possibly a differentiation in their functions, would be more appropriate to American society. There was even, somewhat euphemistically phrased, a demand for a far more clearly defined hierarchy of law schools.[3] Reed's fifty-year-old assertion that the bar was not homogeneous but pluralistic was finally attracting some vocal adherents.[4] There was talk of increasing specialization as well as of research projects reminiscent of the ill-fated Johns Hopkins Institute.[5]

Just as there were demands to open up more scholarly tracks, something dear to the hearts of academics, there was for the first time a willingness to discuss a two-year law degree.[6] Nationally, there was a growing feeling that structured higher education went on too long. Nowhere was this more vividly stated, with respect to law schools, than in the report of the chairman of the AALS Curriculum Committee for 1968. He argued that "fundamental changes must be made soon. It is not only that law students over the country are reaching the point of open revolt, but also that law faculties themselves, particularly the younger members, share with the student the view that legal education is too rigid, too uniform, too narrow, too repetitious and too long."[7] Bergin concurred: "To be mercifully brief, law school is unmercifully dull because the only skill gained after the first year is the skill of feigning preparedness for class. To be sure, we pack our second- and third-year students with rule knowledge; but the energy output which the student must use to gain a knowledge of law becomes so high (or seems to) that the very thought of getting ready to put out the required energy is fatiguing in the extreme."[8]

In a slightly different way, there were moves to remove law, at least partially, into the more scholarly areas of the university. The idea of teaching law in the undergraduate degree as a liberal subject—stressing its historical, philosophical, and social science aspects—achieved a new respectability. (For the most part, up to that time such law as had survived in the undergraduate curriculum had consisted of business law courses whose intellectual reputation was low, and they were eschewed by most respectable institutions.) Hampshire College, a new experimental liberal arts college, developed an area of concentration in law with emphasis on empirical research, and there was talk of similar moves elsewhere. Brandeis floated the idea of developing a law department in the Graduate School.[9] An increasing number of schools offered a J.D.–Ph.D. program. At the same time, there was a growing willingness to develop more professional tracks. Northeastern refounded its law school, and, in so doing, required its students to alternate periods in practice with periods of academic study. All of these experiments, if pushed far enough, would face head-on all the issues of structure that had been building up for a century. They might even undermine the image of the law professor as predominantly a nonscholar generalist.

The law schools, however, had little time for thinking about educational reform, because they were about to be enmeshed in the social ferment of the period. In 1963, women had comprised only 2.7 percent of the profession.[10] In the academic year 1969–70, only 6.35 percent of the degree candidates at law school were women,[11] despite the arrival of the women's movement.[12] In 1969, blacks, although constituting about 12 percent of the national population, only accounted for 1 percent of the bar, a situation reflected in low statistics in the law schools as well.[13] A study of selected elite and semi-elite schools for the classes of 1970 and 1972 showed that the majority of students came from relatively high-status economic groups, and the figures generally represented a larger percentage of such high-income groups than ten years earlier.[14] These statistics for the more prestigious schools were not necessarily statistically reliable nationwide, but it was clear that minority students had limited chances to get into the upper stratum of the profession. Despite a decade of civil rights, women's rights, and antipoverty agitation, the law schools had been little influenced by these developments in society.

This failure to be responsive to the times would not have been so hazardous had the attitudes of the students in the law schools remained as committed to the past as were the structure and curriculum of legal education. By 1970, it was evident that this was not the case. Law students had caught the bug; civil rights and poverty law were the popular topics of the day. Students at least in the elite law schools at the end of the 1960s claimed a dramatically greater interest in serving the underprivileged and restructuring society than had students at the beginning of the decade.[15] When questioned about their political philosophies, they showed a decided shift to the left.[16] Perhaps even more important to the law schools themselves was that students were becoming openly hostile to legal education,[17] especially to the case and Socratic methods.[18]

Yet the situation was complex; these same students showed contradictory tendencies. Professing to envisage a career for themselves as civil rights lawyers, they nevertheless expected to earn as much, or often more, than their predecessors.[19] Although many students would refuse to admit that they planned to work on Wall Street, there was some evidence that some desire to do so had influenced their decision to attend law school.[20] Once in law school, many students seemed to have been confused about their attitude toward the experience, exhibiting almost a love-hate relationship to their studies.[21] If legal educators were showing schizophrenic tendencies in their approach to law and legal education, the same could be said of law students.

The contrasts in the minds and actions of law professors and law students was, perhaps, not inappropriate for a profession as fragmented as that of law. Although a study of elite schools showed 70 percent of Yale 1960 graduates and 87 percent of Iowa graduates working as partners in a firm,[22] nationwide the majority of lawyers were solo practitioners.[23] A study of Chicago's black bar in the same period emphasized a sharply stratified profession with a number of struggling solo practitioners at the bottom with those who did work in firms being given the lowest status positions.[24] Not only did minorities have a hard time: although the horseback-riding circuit lawyer of the nineteenth century no longer existed, his equivalent in status could be found in any of the nation's cities. The stratification was not limited to the contrast between wealthy corporate lawyers on Wall Street and poor solo practitioners in the cities; the American legal profession existed at many different levels of the economy and encompassed large numbers of different, though traditional, areas of legal work.[25] American law students might dream of civil rights work, but the realities of the profession indicated that their career paths would be dramatically different.

Law students, law professors, and the legal profession faced the decade of the 1970s as both the victims and perpetrators of intellectual confusion. Law schools did not seem to be adapting to changing political times, although innovations were frequently mentioned; law students, while parroting radical rhetoric, seemed at heart to retain many of the goals of their predecessors; and the profession, while offering increasing opportunities for wealth,[26] at its "lower levels" remained, to a considerable extent, the profession that had been shaped by or had survived Jacksonian Democracy.

In the student revolution that coincided with the height of the Vietnam War, there were obvious changes at the elite law schools. At Yale, students were given voting rights on committees and a place in faculty meetings. Grades had disappeared—at least in the first semester. It seemed as if this was only a beginning. Student disciplinary cases appeared to put the faculty on trial. At Harvard Law School, the scene was little different, although there students were probably less successful than at Yale in producing change.[27] It was clear, however, that the elite law school had become part of the student revolution.[28]

In the 1970s, student radicalism declined, but the bull market in legal education did not. Interest in going to law school had grown dramatically in the late 1960s, as students decided, probably using as a role model a handful of civil rights lawyers, that law was where the action was. Between 1968–69 and 1971–72 the number of persons taking the LSAT doubled from 60,000 to 120,000.[29] The law school industry grew. It has been estimated that the income of law schools rose from $17 million in 1948 to $275 million in 1976.[30] The encouragement was considerable;

new law schools appeared. Princeton, as in the 1920s, dipped its toe in the water but decided not to swim.[31] Claremont, UC–Santa Barbara, and Brandeis made similar decisions.[32] Many universities, however, as well as groups unrelated to colleges or universities, showed little restraint. Only the activities of the ABA and AALS, which made it difficult to enter the market, prevented an even more dramatic increase in the number of law schools.[33] The financial and social appeal of establishing a law school was attractive. The talk was bullish. Typical was the statement by the president of the American Civil Liberties Union, Norman Dorsen, an NYU law professor, who publicly insisted that "we need more lawyers."[34] Already, however, two things were happening. First, even before the end of the war in Vietnam, the radicalism of students was declining;[35] second—and the cynic might see this as related—the demand for lawyers was declining.[36] Yet the pressure to get into law school, and especially the leading law schools, did not slacken.[37]

As in the 1930s, there was increasing talk of a surfeit of lawyers.[38] The number of law students, rising from 68,562 in 1962 to 95,943 in 1971, leapt to 105,245 in 1972 and to 114,800 in 1973.[39] Indeed, this was the period when para-professionals, who were going to add still further to the lawyer-ridden society, came into their own.[40] It was also the period when there was a revival in academic undergraduate programs in law.[41] It should be remembered, however, that even today, statistics on legal education are still surprisingly amateur, and reported numbers largely exclude the unaccredited schools. The press continued to report that the boom in law schools was over[42] and that the market for lawyers was overcrowded.[43] Yet the number of law students crept up slowly until it reached 126,000 in 1977, from which point onward it appears to have leveled off.[44] The Bureau of Labor Statistics predicted that between 1976 and 1985 the legal profession would need to grow from 396,000 to 490,000, a 25 percent increase. This increase could be met by 23,400 law graduates per annum, 10,000 fewer than were produced in the summer of 1981. Nevertheless, to have the number of one's customers double in a decade, as legal education had done, would not be thought unsuccessful in other industries.

While expanding, however, legal education continued to be subject to much of the public questioning that characterized the late 1960s. At one level this was inevitable. Tocqueville's natural aristocracy does not fit comfortably into a society that resounded to the rhetoric of equality. Yet the skepticism of the decade—fueled by the civil rights movement, Vietnam, the women's movement, and Watergate—saw lawyers attacked from right[45] and left.[46] Not only did it become chic to work for legal services, it became positively antisocial in the eyes of some to represent

General Motors.[47] Yet even in this area there was evidence that at least the radical commitment, if not the rhetoric, was evaporating early in the 1970s.[48] Later studies have questioned how deep this commitment had been as well as confirmed the reversion to the norm.[49]

The role of lawyers was perhaps more questioned in the 1970s than at any earlier time. As some of the conventional areas of practice were scrutinized, there were corresponding developments in the legal profession itself. The Legal Services program of the Office of Economic Opportunity (OEO) grew into the Legal Services Corporation.[50] The idea of legal insurance (prepaid programs) just got off the ground.[51] Economists were busy developing models to test the demand for lawyers.[52] Faced with the competition and reluctantly accepting that an allegedly intellectual profession had about it an element of a trade, the bar agonized publicly for a long period about whether it would allow advertising,[53] only to be told by the Supreme Court that it was in restraint of trade for not doing so.[54] The Supreme Court had already in 1975 slaughtered another sacred cow of the legal profession—the professional minimum fee—in the *Goldfarb* case.[55]

The organized bar sought to undo much of this alleged misfortunate and poor public image. Indeed the bar—led by the American Bar Association—had probably never seemed so public spirited or well led. If the ABA dragged its feet on no-fault compensation, it supported the Legal Services Corporation, stressed legal ethics, and encouraged research.[56] Indeed, after Watergate, legal ethics became almost an industry in itself. No one stopped to remark that attendance at law schools had been made mandatory, at least according to the rhetoric of many, in order either to make the bar available only to those who could stay the course intellectually or to socialize all into a sense of high professional standards.

On this occasion, the bar reacted to criticism by tightening its disciplinary procedures, although they remained ludicrously loose compared with those in other common-law countries.[57] The bar, however, attempted to make it more difficult to become a lawyer by raising the level of the character and fitness requirements, which, with the exception of a period in the early 1950s when they were used to exclude those thought to harbor left-wing sympathies,[58] had been largely honored in the breach. Nevertheless, for the most part the bar expected the law schools to be the primary channel for instilling legal ethics. It was not an unreasonable assumption given the history of legal education, but the law schools did not view the new task with any particular pleasure. They felt that the basic moral values of their students were more likely to be molded in homes, high schools, and colleges than by the Socratic method.[59] This was perhaps why much that passed under the rubric of legal ethics in law school had traditionally been concerned primarily with unauthorized practice. By the late 1970s this assumption changed dramatically.[60] The bars were demanding that the study of ethics be made compulsory,[61] yet most observers assumed that ethics were unlikely to subfuse law school teaching in the way the leaders of the bar hoped.[62]

In a similar vein, the bar began to consider the relicensing movement, which was increasingly discussed among physicians, and thus to make continuing legal education mandatory rather than voluntary. This movement, which began in Minnesota,[63] showed signs of spreading,[64] although it appeared to be occurring almost entirely outside the law schools and their spheres of influence. The suggestion of legal specialization, again carrying overtones of medical practice, grew much stronger.[65] Beginning in California,[66] the idea, which in its early stages emphasized upgrading professional standards, seemed[67] increasingly to be little more than a form of advertising,[68] and critics of the profession assumed the primary purpose of specialization was to exploit the legal monopoly more effectively.[69] Certainly, after the Supreme Court struck down the prohibition on advertising the specialization movement showed signs of running out of steam.[70]

As the fundamental way of upgrading the bar, however, the profession continued to look to the law schools, which, by the 1970s, had effectively become the only portal of entry to the profession.[71] Increasingly, the leaders of the bar expressed concern that the law schools were not living up to their expectations. Chief Justice Burger's oft-articulated concerns about the quality of advocacy in the federal courts were symptomatic.[72] What went on in law school had always interested the organized bar, which frequently criticized what its members saw, but the new interest on the part of the bar was seen, especially by the law schools, as having about it a sinister element of anti-intellectualism.[73] The bar, having achieved the structure of legal education it had been working toward, was apparently ready to transfer its interest from structure to what actually went on in law schools. The bar was irritated by an apparent reluctance on the part of leading schools to be concerned with those skills that the profession regarded as important;[74] leaders of the profession also felt that the broadening of legal education had gone too far. By the 1960s at most schools, the second and third years had become largely elective, and the course titles bore little resemblance to the courses taken by leading lawyers when they had been in law school. The implications of this were to come to the fore in the friction between practitioners and academics during the 1970s.

This clash of cultures appeared in different areas and arenas. One battle was over the so-called Clare Proposals, in which a Second Circuit

Committee called for those lawyers who wished to practice in its courts to have studied evidence, civil procedure, criminal procedure, professional responsibility, and trial advocacy. To one outside the profession, such modest requirements might not have seemed extreme. Yet to the law schools—and especially to the deans of the elite schools[75]—the report threatened to reverse the power balance established over the previous one hundred years. Michael Sovern, dean of Columbia, complained that the move would reduce law schools to "technical schools."[76] Although the new rules were set to come into effect in 1979,[77] they remained in a state of suspended animation, as federal districts within the circuit refused to accept them.[78]

The Rule 13 controversy in Indiana had, for legal education, some of the connotations that California's Proposition 13 concerning property taxes had for politicians.[79] When, in 1973, Indiana adopted a rule requiring some fifty-four hours of designated course work from potential Indiana practitioners, the action underlined the inherent schizophrenia in legal education, as well as the differing visions of legal education held by different types of law schools.[80] In this case, the solution to the dilemma, presented to legal educators from an outside source, was increasing emphasis on what the leaders of the bar viewed as practical.

Yet such disputes, despite their superficial academic-versus-practical rhetoric, in reality appeared as disputes between the AALS and their allies, who argued that law schools be allowed to run their own show, and leading practitioners, who were anxious that law students be exposed to an educational system with a greater emphasis on doctrine and practical experience. History was at work, too. When the bar in the last part of the nineteenth century allowed time spent in law school to count in lieu of time spent in the law office, it saw the two methods of education in similar terms and had not intended to abandon its watching brief over the training of the legal profession. Indeed, the chief justice of Indiana gave, as one of his rationales for Rule 13, the growth of "social awareness" courses at the expense of lawyering skill courses, opining that "war is too important to be left to the generals."[81]

In 1981, South Carolina emulated Indiana. A committee chaired by Mr. Justice Cameron Bruce Littlejohn of the state supreme court left no doubt where that state was headed. Littlejohn announced that "you can't divorce lawyer competence from law school education; they're tied too tight." With this in mind, South Carolina began to require students to have taken fourteen subjects in law school, including trial advocacy, before being eligible to take the bar examination. The committee also admonished students to take English, U.S. history, accounting, political science, and philosophy in college. Littlejohn also warned that "we're toying with the idea" of requiring an internship in a law office before admission to the bar.[82] The legal establishment seemed as suspicious of innovative educational developments as it was of an emphasis on teaching skills whatever the rhetoric of the debates implied.

Meanwhile, the Devitt Committee continued the work of the Clare Committee and fourteen federal district courts were poised, in 1981, to require an examination in certain "practice" courses from those wishing to be admitted to practice before them. Rule 13 remained in force, Georgia talked of emulating South Carolina, and the tension between academics and practitioners persisted.[83] During the year, the president of the AALS, Harvard Law School dean Albert Sacks, talked of fears of "balkanization" as states around the nation made an effort to control curricula.[84] The new wave of standardization suggested that any "filial" relationship between the ABA and the AALS was at an end.[85]

The report from the ABA's special task force on lawyer competence chaired by Roger Cramton, dean of Cornell,[86] was, however, expected to ease the situation. The Cramton proposals, emerging in the summer of 1979, emphasized the need of law schools to stress ethics and lawyer skills; the proposals went far beyond both advocacy training, which had been the crux of the Clare Report, and basic subject matter, the rationale of Rule 13. The panacea was to be clinical legal education. It seemed that the legal education establishment was offering to shape up its commitment to clinical legal education in return for being left in peace by the practicing profession with respect to the more conventional areas of the curriculum.[87] Yet when, in 1980, the council of the ABA Section of Legal Education voted to require all accredited schools to offer instruction in special professional skills, the AALS complained its autonomy was threatened.[88] Once again the ABA backed off and the AALS breathed a sigh of relief.[89]

If clinical legal education were to be used to bail out conventional legal education in the 1980s and to protect it from the ire of the practicing profession, it would be ironic but not novel. The push and pull of clinical legal education was intriguing. The push had been increasingly clear in the attitude of students, especially during the 1960s. Even at the height of the radical phase on campus, students who intended to practice even if their career goals may have been somewhat different from earlier generations still complained of the "theoretical" rather than the "practical" orientation of legal education.[90] The time was ripe for promoting clinical legal education and if William Pincus and the Council on Legal Education for Professional Responsibility (CLEPR) had not been in existence, someone would have had to invent them. CLEPR's predecessors had been at work during the 1960s, propping up the marginal legal aid clinics that existed in various law schools and attempting to relate them, after 1964, to the OEO legal services program. It was only with the $6 million grant from Ford in the spring of 1968, however, that the newly created CLEPR achieved the leverage it needed to push even powerful law schools into undertaking serious clinical legal education. Between 1970 and 1976 the number of programs grew from 169 to 494.[91]

Pincus, the vocal president of CLEPR, made no apology for his assault on the conventional academic content of law school, arguing that "academic work should contribute eighty percent of the first-year curriculum; and a very small percentage, no more than twenty percent, of the third-year curriculum."[92] Although, in 1975, only 24 percent of second- or third-year law students had had any clinical experience, the strength of the movement was undeniable. Conventional law teachers reacted with noticeable ambivalence to the CLEPR enticements. Few could deny the alienation of many students or that many students seemed drawn to clinical programs. Few also could deny that a well-supervised clinic with feedback into the classroom and the curriculum provided a historically acceptable model of legal education.[93] Yet in most schools the clinical faculty members remained second-class citizens,[94] and the core faculty saw clinical programs neither as an opportunity for experiencing nor for examining social issues and generally not as an integral part of the academic programs.[95] Perhaps the most significant reason advanced for the ambivalence toward CLEPR and student efforts was a familiar one— clinical programs were expensive. CLEPR funds were exhausted in 1980, but federal funds had slowly come in to replace them,[96] although the support seemed unlikely to continue under a Reagan administration. The absence of such funding might well threaten the compromise implied by Cramton.

Of course, some law schools were different in the sense that they merged comfortably with the expanding clinical movement. Growing out of the Boston YMCA School, Northeastern made use of "cooperative education" by mixing classroom work with experience in law jobs.[97] More innovative, still, was the Antioch School of Law in Washington, D.C., founded in 1972. It saw itself as a "law school–law clinic–public interest law firm,"[98] and its founding and accreditation were achieved amid a blaze of publicity.[99] The school undoubtedly achieved much in freeing up admissions and bringing law practice to the center of a law school curriculum. At the same time, the school appeared to be in a constant cultural revolution.[100] Similar experiments, however, continued, encouraged by student interest and the political activism of some law teachers.[101]

Not all members of the professorate by any means were anxious to loosen the structure of the three-year law schools. Demands for some structural change—especially from a handful of reformers in the elite law schools—were, however, a continuing phenomenon of the 1970s. The structural changes being advocated at the end of the 1960s, especially the two-year law school, for a while seemed close to being accepted early in the new decade. The well-funded and visible AALS Curriculum Committee, chaired by Paul Carrington of Michigan, argued, in its 1971 report, for a basic standard two-year J.D. degree, followed by a series of post-J.D. alternatives designed to respond to the different types of legal practice.[102] From a more elitist perspective, Bayless Manning, the dean of the Stanford Law School, called for a two-tiered system of legal education,[103] although who belonged to which tier was a matter of doubt.[104] The 1972 Carnegie Commission report suggested the two-year model, again as part of an overall freeing up of the alternative structures of legal education.[105]

In light of this, the Section of Legal Education and Admissions to the Bar recommended to the mid-year meeting of the ABA in 1972 that Rule 307 of the law school standards be modified to allow the two-year law school. Many assumed the change would go through. They could not have been more wrong. In his witty article, "The Day the Music Died,"[106] Preble Stolz chronicled what actually happened. The deans of the leading law schools extolled the virtues of the three-year law school. Dean Albert Sacks of Harvard, arguing a position redolent of the longest traditions of academic life, suggested that the "time was not yet ripe," since Havard was apparently about to make the great breakthrough in legal education. Dean Bernard Wolfman of Pennsylvania, reflecting the follow-my-leader view of legal education, opposed the idea because, he argued, if one school went to two years, all schools would follow. Dean Michael Sovern of Columbia rejected the scheme on the ground that it would increase the supply of lawyers at the very moment there was a glut, and at a local level he noted that his students would have to sacrifice $20,000 to stay on for the third year at Columbia. Dean Abraham Goldstein of Yale, emphasizing that lawyers had to be trained as generalists, opposed shortening law school at the very moment that law was becoming more complex and students needed to be trained in history, philosophy, and the social sciences. Only Dean Thomas Ehrlich of Stanford supported the proposals.

The two-year law school may have been dead, but the debate about the lockstep of seven years of higher education continued. Dean Sovern of Columbia proposed the 2–1–1 idea—the three-year law school with a year of practice after the second year[107]—and Columbia had already developed a six-year B.A.–J.D. program with a group of elite colleges.[108] Sniping, however, continued. Justin Stanley, president of the ABA in 1975–76, continued to argue for a two-year law school,[109] and once again the profession's heightened interest in professional competence kept the pressure on. In 1978, Chief Justice Burger called for a two-year conventional law school followed by a year of clinical work.[110] Again the law school establishment was not amused.[111] The two-year law school movement, which had seemed so vigorous in 1970, seemed virtually dead by 1980.

Yet the fact that even at elite schools the students were increasingly working in law offices during their second and third years,[112] together with the professional pressure for competency, insured that the issue would not die. During the 1960s and 1970s, students had voted with their feet. Many states changed their rules to allow students, at least after their first year, a limited right of audience in the courts. This, coupled with the growth in demand for lawyers' services, saw many firms increasingly relying on law students to work part-time in law offices. The pressures from the "practical" side of the profession slowly became clearer. Somewhat reluctantly, in 1979, Harvard accepted a large grant from the Legal Services Corporation headed by Thomas Ehrlich (former dean of Stanford and the only supporter of the two-year law school at the New Orleans meeting) to allow some Harvard students to finish the conventional Harvard Law School in two years and to spend the third year exclusively in a clinical program. Even at Mecca, the religious structure had developed a fissure.

The structural discussions of the 1970s proceeded amid increasing public and political confusion about the role of accreditation.[113] The process irritated radicals for being elitist and market economists for being anticompetitive. The Bureau of Competition of the Federal Trade Commission attacked the AMA's Liaison Committee on Medical Education, and Millard Ruud, the AALS's executive director, conceded that "the American Bar Association is more vulnerable than the Medical Association."[114] Meanwhile, the bull market for lawyers—at least in the early 1970s—encouraged the growth of unaccredited schools while the increasing bear market of the later 1970s brought back the profession's fears of "overcrowding." The night school, which was going out of business in the 1960s,[115] had also reappeared, sometimes in connection with an accredited school.[116] There was still no accurate count of how many students were enrolled in unaccredited schools, because these schools did not willingly share their data with the ABA–AALS accrediting bodies. Officially, the number of students in unaccredited schools rose from 3,646 in 1969 to 8,698 in 1973.[117] Although the official statistic for 1979 was only 4,055, that figure was based on the seven unaccredited law schools that had replied, but it ignored the fifty that had not. There could have been as many as 20,000 students in unaccredited schools.

Little was known about these schools. By then they were primarily in Georgia and California, although they existed in other states.[118] Unaccredited law schools came packaged in various forms. Some looked back to the 1920s, as in the case of the Nashville YMCA Night Law School.[119] Some emphasized the radical, as did the National Conference of Black Lawyers Community College of Law and International Diplomacy in Chicago and the People's College of Law of the National Lawyers Guild in Los Angeles.[120] Paul Savoy, a radical law professor of the 1960s, was dean of John F. Kennedy Law School in Orinda. Some of the unaccredited schools were effectively defunct while others were vibrant—the Fullerton Branch of Western State University had 632 full-time students and 1,115 part-time ones, and its San Diego branch had 975 students. Some schools were in storefronts and walk-ups; some were library-less; others had reasonable facilities and provided a useful resource for local communities.[121]

The forty-two unaccredited schools in California attracted the most attention. With the decision of the state in 1973 to have no more law schools in the University of California system,[122] the inevitable tension between the demands of students and the bar's professional pride increased. Although the "better" schools such as La Verne and San Fernando Valley were approved by the State Committee of Bar Examiners, the bar as a whole waged war on what it regarded as the dangerous unaccredited schools. By the mid-1970s, the special consultant to the California bar, John Garfinkel, referred to a dozen of the unaccredited schools as a "horror story." At the Ocean College of Law it was revealed that although the students had paid their tuition, the faculty had not been paid, and the dean had been convicted of "pimping and pandering." Once again the state bar proposed minimum standards for such institutions, standards which by the beginning of the 1980s looked as if they were about to be enforced.[123]

The problem was that by 1980 no one was quite certain who was the gamekeeper and who was the poacher. Accreditation had become something of a dirty word. During 1976, one speaker at the ABA annual meeting suggested that perhaps accreditation might be abandoned in the interests of social justice, diversity, and competition, with the Federal Trade Commission being left to protect the public from fly-by-night operations.[124] The idea was not well received, but at that very moment the ABA was getting its fingers burned in its efforts to discourage accreditation of Western State University College of Law.[125] That institution, which was a serious unaccredited but profit-making school, sought approval from a regional college-accrediting agency. The ABA opposed accreditation because the school made a profit. Maxwell Boas, the dean of the school, argued that many university law schools were profitable but that the parent university siphoned off the profit,[126] an argument that both hit home and undercut the ABA–AALS position.

The ABA was in trouble with the United States Commissioner of Education and his advisory committee on accreditation as a result of its attempt to organize a boycott of the regional accreditation of Western State. That activity resulted in the ABA's being served with an order to show cause why it should not cease to be recognized as an accrediting agency.[127] The ABA shaped up. The council of the Section of Legal Education and Admissions to the Bar voted in 1977 to accept profit-making schools for provisional approval. Although the exception was apparently renewed on an annual basis, no "proprietary" school had been accredited by 1980. The climate, however, had clearly changed. When an ABA inspection report noted that "the intellectual spark is missing in the faculty and the students" at the Delaware Law School, the ABA's consultant on legal education was successfully sued for libel, paying $50,000 in damages.[128] Accreditation was being subjected to the same kind of skeptical public scrutiny that had been lavished on objective tests, including the LSAT. It came as no real surprise when, in 1980, there was serious discussion about the AALS, at least, going out of the accrediting business. That association was *functus officio* as far as accreditation was concerned. Its main rationale for staying in the business may well have been the felt need for academics to keep an eye on the ABA.[129]

Meanwhile, the movement toward stricter accreditation in California brought allegations of racism and social elitism. A spokesman for Glendale University College of Law saw the California moves to strengthen accreditation as aimed at the "ethnic minorities, working class, physically handicapped and foreign students." The National Conference of Black Lawyers predicted there would be fewer minority lawyers as a result of the change.[130] How true these claims were for California was not clear. Certainly nationwide, as far as minority lawyers were concerned, there had been important changes from the paternalistic pontifications of ten years earlier.[131] The Council on Legal Education Opportunity, a head-start program for minority law students, and other programs had worked. The number of minority students in accredited law schools rose from 2,933 in 1969–70 to 10,008 in 1978–79,[132] although it still did not reflect the percentage of minorities in the population.[133] Some of the selection processes through which these students came to law school appeared to be questioned by the Supreme Court's decisions in *De-Funis*[134] and *Bakke*,[135] although the decision in *Weber* partly quieted these fears.[136] Of greater concern by 1980 was the allegation of cultural bias not only in the LSAT but in bar exams. In California the situation was particularly acute;[137] various studies were conducted and a commission with black and Hispanic members investigated the charges.[138] Its report found minorities experienced serious problems in taking the bar exam but no evidence of cultural bias. Meanwhile, the Georgia bar examiners were taken to court for alleged racial bias,[139] and concern grew nationwide that although the large law firms were taking black associates, few were promoted to partners.[140]

Other minorities, however, had fared better. In the 1930s and 1940s, Jewish students were heavily channeled into government service, teaching, and the nonelite or predominantly Jewish law firms.[141] There was still a hint of anti-Semitism among the large firms in the 1960s.[142] By the 1970s, no such discrimination was generally thought to exist; moreover, the majority of law students at many elite schools were Jewish.[143] Women, too, had emerged from the era of "we'd like to take them but we have no separate washroom." The women's movement had become strong enough to prevent women being satisfied with the profession of legal assistant, and women moved into the law schools in large numbers. In 1968, 3,704 of the 62,000 law students in approved schools were women; by 1979, there were 37,534 women out of 117,279 students in approved schools. In short, during a ten-year period women moved from less than 10 percent of law students to more than one-third of the total.[144] Such an increase was important because there was evidence that, as was the case with other minorities, women needed a critical mass to perform well.[145] Perhaps less surprisingly, there was still evidence that women were being tracked into the less elite parts of the profession.[146]

Certainly during the 1970s, the public came to know far more about law students than they had, indeed, more than some might have wished. *One L*[147] was graphic; *The Paper Chase* was popular, finding its way from movie house to television serial.[148] Perhaps most significant was the number of studies of law students[149] culminating in the related series of ABA studies.[150] Although studies of the socialization and professionalization of law students were still inadequate, empirical studies blossomed in the 1970s. They confirmed that law students wanted to be lawyers, not scholars, and that the first year of law could be both exhausting and terrifying, even though the better students—at least those who did not make law review—could avoid excessive work during the later years when their energies were often siphoned off into clinics or part-time jobs that might or might not be in a legal setting.

In the early 1970s, there was extensive evidence that outside those working on law review there was a dramatic falloff in energy levels and work at the end of the first year, if not in the first semester.[151] Later studies suggest that that trend has been reversed, but some saw the matter as more of a stalemate. Although few law students were activists in the late 1970s,[152] the dissatisfaction level was still high. Thus although Harvard announced a new curriculum study in 1979, it was not unrealistic to expect that many of the students' concerns would be similar to those found in the curriculum studies of 1946 and 1960 and the student evaluations of 1935.[153] Hence, although many claimed some frustration with the case method, no other method of teaching was considered to be its peer. That, in so many ways, was the enigma of American legal education, but it explained why law schools—or at least the better ones—could reasonably expect to be left in peace "to do what we do best."

NOTES

1. On this, see Bowen, *Economics of Major Private Universities.*
2. Such schools proliferated most in Washington, D.C., New York City, and Chicago, where there had been a minimum of competition from the good public schools. By 1970, it was becoming increasingly clear that if a federal or district-funded law school in addition to Howard, a predominantly black school, were to be established in the District of Columbia, this might pose a severe financial threat to at least some of the local private schools. If the state or city university were to establish law schools in New York City, the fate of Fordham, St. John's, and New York Law School might well have been in the balance. The decision by Queen's College, CUNY, to open a law school in the early 1980s may, in this sense, be especially significant. More problematical still were the 1982 Reagan budget cuts, particularly those affecting student loan programs in professional schools. "Law School Students Face New Loan Plan," 67 *ABA Journal* 550 (1981).
3. Cavers, "Legal Education in Forward-Looking Perspective," in Hazard, ed., *Law in a Changing America*, 139. One of the results of the obsession with turning every law school into a center for producing policymakers was an increasing demand for legal technicians, politely known as paralegal personnel. A controversy arose about whether law schools should develop programs for such paralegal personnel or should leave such programs to state colleges and commercial enterprises.
4. For example, it was suggested that "the present uniformity of the major law schools in structure and purpose is wasteful." Dworkin, "There Oughta Be a Law."
5. Abraham S. Goldstein, "The Unfulfilled Promise of Legal Education," in Hazard, ed., *Law in a Changing America*, 157.
6. At least the length was reflected in the J.D. degree replacing the LL.B. as the standard law degree during the 1960s. See American Bar Association, *Annual Review of Legal Education*, 1969, 22–25. In August 1964, the Section of Legal Education and Admissions to the Bar of the ABA approved a resolution recommending "for all approved law schools favorable consideration of the conferring of the degree of Juris Doctor (J.D.) by such schools on those students who successfully complete the program leading to the first professional degree in law." All schools did give this "favorable consideration" and decided to adopt the degree. When Michigan announced in 1967 that it would award the J.D. to all students, the assistant dean explained, "In this regard, it seemed appropriate to recognize that the degree offered by the Michigan Law School was recognition for post-baccalaureate work, although not a graduate degree in the traditional sense.

The Juris Doctor degree was selected." Cavers et al., "Issues in Legal Education," 9–10.

7. "Report of Charles J. Meyers," *AALS Proceedings, 1968*, 8. "[I]n any given law school most of the students are doing the same things; exactly the same thing in the first year, much the same in the second, and only marginally different things in the third year." Ibid., 9.

8. Bergin, "Law Teacher," 648–49. In keeping with the theory that demands for reform in legal education are cyclical, compare Karl Llewellyn's view, expressed thirty-five years earlier, that education in American law schools was "blind, inept, factory-ridden, wasteful, defective and empty." Llewellyn, "On What Is Wrong with So-Called Legal Education," 653.

9. *New York Times*, 22 December 1969. There was academic support for such a view. It was suggested that there should be a distinct department of law in the university, offering "scholarly" law courses at both the undergraduate and graduate level. See Hall, "An Open Letter Proposing a School of Cultural Legal Studies," 181. Dean Abraham Goldstein of Yale observed that "advanced work in a legal field is less likely to profit from the study of other law courses than from fields which are not legal at all, in any conventional sense." Goldstein, "Unfulfilled Promise in Legal Education," in Hazard, ed., *Law in a Changing America*, 162. Some put it rather more melodramatically: "Who is talking your language, my friend from the tax department? It's not the guy who teaches forms of actions. No. It's an accountant, a business manager, a welfare worker, a G-man, an actuary, a social engineer, a banker. And who is talking your language, my friend in international law? It's a geo-physicist, a geo-politician, a diplomat, a trader, an economist. And yours, my friend in Municipal Corporations I or II? An urban planner, a public health planner, an architect, an engineer, a sonar physicist. And yours, brother in criminal law? A sociologist, a psychiatrist, a psychologist, an economist, a statistician." Mueller, "Pre-Requiem for the Law Faculty," 413.

10. American Bar Association, *The American Lawyer: Statistical Report* 15 (1968).

11. The Association of American Law Schools and the Law School Admission Test Council, *Pre-Law Handbook: Report on Law Study and Practice in the United States, 1970–71* (1970). In the South, the statistics were even more disproportionate; only 5.36 percent of the law students were women. For analysis of sex discrimination on the job market, see, generally, White, "Women in the Law," 1051, 1048–88. See also Johnstone and Hopson, *Lawyers and Their Work*, 19; Barnes, "Women and Entrance to the Legal Profession," 276.

12. On the other hand, Harvard had finally admitted women in 1950. In 1966, even Notre Dame moved to admit women. As the official history put it: "The Old Order changes, yielding place to the new, and God reveals Himself in many ways." Moore, *A Century of Law at Notre Dame*, 123.

13. See the statement of the Association of American Law Schools. *Hearings on S. 3474 before the Subcommittee on Education of the Senate Committee on Labor and Public Welfare*, 91st Cong., 2d sess. (1970). As with other issues there had been extensive rhetoric in the 1960s advocating minority admissions, but with limited results. See, for example, Committee on Minority Groups, "Report on the Law Schools and Minority Group Students," *AALS Proceedings, 1970*; "Report of the Advisory Committee for the Minority Groups Study," ibid., *1967*; "Report of the President," ibid., *1963*. See also Askin, "The Case for Compensatory Treatment," 65; Bell, "In Defense of Minority Admissions Programs," 364; Gellhorn, "The Law Schools and the Negro," 1069; Brooke, "Introduction to the Symposium: Disadvantaged Students and Legal Education—Programs for Affirmative Action," 277.

14. Stevens, "Law Schools and Law Students," 571–74. The schools included were Boston College, Connecticut, Iowa, Michigan, Pennsylvania, Stanford, Southern California, and Yale. As of 1972, only Yale had more than 10 percent minority students. Ibid., 572.

15. Ibid., 583–86. By 1970, the total of Yale first-year students responding to a questionnaire who described themselves as "far left" or "liberal" was 92 percent; for alumni who had graduated ten years before, the figure had been only 56 percent. At Iowa a total of 15 percent of the 1960 alumni described themselves as "far left" or "liberal" upon their entry to law school, while the total for first-year students at the school in 1970 was 40 percent.

16. Some believed that the structure and methods of the law students sapped both the creative urge and concern with social issues: " 'Most of the time when I've seen my fellow students at the beginning of the year make really interesting comments about the relationship of the course to outside problems, to social problems, or to larger philosophical questions, they were usually ignored, or put down or bypassed. . . . There is a conscious desire to mold our thinking into being more precise and more legalistic.' " Ibid., 640.

17. Ibid., 645:

> "You go from that [college] atmosphere where you are encouraged to do a lot of writing, you do a lot of independent work, making a continual effort, particularly in class; you are encouraged to; and so you come in here and bang, you are thrown into a big class where you sort of stick your neck out when you say something, you don't know very much about the law, so intellectually you are sticking your neck out, more than physically; and some of these guys boo me; chop it off. So what happens to a lot of people—I sort of have been looking at this lately; I see this happening—you learn not to open your mouth. Many people—that's how they react. They don't open their mouths because they see they are going to get their heads chopped off."

18. Ibid., 570–71. The study found "the continuing expectation by students in the age of 'radical chic' that law is a potentially lucrative profession. While the rhetoric of the 1960s emphasized the need either to restructure, or to replace, the system, students still expected it to provide generous rewards." Ibid., 571.

19. Ibid., 577. During the 1960s, the importance of money as a reason for entering these schools apparently increased.

20. "[F]ew students conceded that a desire to work on Wall Street drew them to law school, even though more students in the Class of 1972 indicated that a desire to work on Wall Street influenced their decision than did members of the Class of 1960." Ibid., 580.

21. Ibid., 638–39:

> "In one class I don't feel he's catching me with my pants down or that I've been bad by not having read it. I do feel, however, I've let him down personally. It's a terribly personal kind of relationship with every student in that class, which he conveys. . . . I've never heard him demean anyone for an answer, no matter how negative, I mean wrong, the answer might be. He invariably—first of all, he says, 'good'—just as the standard mechanism—you know, 'good—you've said the answer.' Now, I think you're wrong—or 'now,' you know—'let's look at it this way.' And consequently in that class people feel that they sort of are compelled to be honest—terribly honest— and he's honest with them. And a few times he has apologized for misunderstanding what someone said, or just themselves misleading someone, you know, by a question. He is also terribly fair."

22. Ibid., 564. Figures in the same categories for other schools were Boston College, 79 percent; Connecticut, 78 percent; Pennsylvania, 64 percent; and Southern California, 79 percent.
23. The exact figure was 56 percent. American Bar Foundation, *The American Lawyer: 1964 Statistical Report* 32 (1965). In the Colorado study, with a 47 percent response rate, 35 percent of the respondents were partners, 29 percent were in solo practice, 13 percent were associates, 9 percent were in government service, 7 percent were house counsel, and 7 percent were judges, law professors, etc. Colorado Bar Association, *Report of the 1967 Economic Survey of the Colorado Bar* (1968). In Florida, in 1963, 3,295 lawyers were solo practitioners, 2,369 were partners, and 568 were associates. Florida Bar, *1966 Survey of the Economics of Florida Law Practice* (1966). By the time of the 1966 survey, which had a 45 percent response rate, those reporting included 646 solo practitioners, 229 space-sharers, 469 associates, and 1,174 partners. In 1969, the South Carolina Bar Association's study reported that 78 percent of South Carolina lawyers were in private practice, with 40 percent of those being solo practitioners, 32.5 percent partners, and 6 percent associates. South Carolina Bar Association, *Economic Study of the Lawyer of South Carolina* (1970). Income figures were also sharply differentiated by type of practice. See Stevens, "Law Schools and Law Students," 567–68.
24. Goldman, *A Portrait of the Black Attorney in Chicago*. The author concluded: "The latent racism which has accumulated in all major American social institutions also pervades the legal profession. While the ethics of the profession support the ideal of equal justice for all, black Americans meet both direct and indirect discrimination when they seek to obtain legal training and later attempt to establish themselves within the metropolitan bar. Although overt discrimination has decreased in recent years, aspiring black attorneys still encounter many obstacles because of their race." Ibid., 49.
25. In 1970, over a quarter of the 1960 graduates of Yale, Southern California, Pennsylvania, and Connecticut were earning between $30,000 and $40,000 annually. Stevens, "Law Schools and Law Students," 566. The average practitioner in Florida earned $16,000; in Wisconsin, $22,900; in Texas, $13,500. Ibid., 568–69.
26. See, for example, the importance of fields of law as primary sources of lawyers' income in three states. Cited in ibid., 687.
27. For a description of this period, see Seligman, *The High Citadel*, 6–7. Grade reform, for instance, was not as extensive as it had been at Yale. Ibid., 13–15.
28. Quantitative studies of these times have now confirmed that many of these manifestations were primarily among elite groups, that is, they were more likely to happen at Yale or Stanford—with basically wealthier students—than they were at the University of Iowa or the University of Connecticut. Stevens, "Law Schools and Law Students," 551, 583–88, 602–6, 665–68, 681–84.
29. Herbold, "Law Is Where the Action Is," 27.
30. First, "Competition in the Legal Education Industry," 311.
31. Princeton University, "Princeton and Legal Education: A Preliminary Survey," 13 October 1975, mimeographed. The chairman of the committee was Donald E. Stokes.
In recording the repeated toes "dipped in" by Princeton, one wonders whether that university was mesmerized by the view of its most illustrious president. It was Woodrow Wilson who protested, in the 1880s, about the "narrowing influence" of the law, especially "its power to make a man . . . like a needle, a thing of one eye and one point." In 1900, he was to accuse John Austin of "having created the belief among lawyers who do not think, but swallow formulas, that law is somehow made independently of the bulk of the community, and that it is their business to accept it and apply it as it is

without troubling themselves to look beyond the statutes or decisions in which it is embodied." Wilson, *The Papers of Woodrow Wilson*, 2:357, 8:650.

32. First reported that seven schools made detailed feasibility studies, but they ultimately decided not to enter the law school market. The schools were the University of Nevada, Las Vegas; the University of Delaware; Claremont College; the University of New Orleans; Michigan State University; Pennsylvania State University; Queen's College (CUNY). First, "Competition in the Legal Education Industry II," 1074–75. Queen's College Law School was, however, scheduled to open in 1982.

33. The increasing control over entry became clear with the appointment of a full-time executive director of the AALS together with a permanent staff in 1962. In 1965, the association published the *Guideline Statement on the Establishment of New Schools*, "an exercise in cautious discouragement, firmly based on the elite-model law school." First, "Competition in Legal Education II," 1053–54. In addition to the heavy financial outlay, the AALS required "demonstrated need" for the new school. The *Guideline*'s standards and requirements were higher than those of the AALS and exceeded those of many members. Ibid., 1055–57. As a result of this approach, although the number of law students increased by 50 percent between 1967 and 1972, 94 percent went to previously established ABA-approved schools who, by 1972, held 98 percent of the market. Ibid., 1057.

   Moreover, inspections by the AALS began to examine not only AALS criteria but nonarticulated standards reflected in the question of whether the school was doing "as well as it could." Ibid., 1061. Both the ABA and the AALS subtly increased standards in the 1970s. Pace University, for instance, was denied provisional accreditation for its new law school in 1976 despite an "excellent" inspection report. It eventually achieved provisional accreditation in 1978. Ibid., 1070–73. The AALS also apparently had an unpublished standard rejecting all applicants for membership on the first attempt.

34. Dorsen and Gillers, "We Need More Lawyers," 7. Dorsen argued that "law, as a product, is no less essential than any other goods and services distributed by an organized society—and in our legal system, lawyers play the dominant distributive role." Ibid.

35. The deputy dean of the Yale Law School, Burke Marshall, reported that the classes of 1973 and 1974 were very different from the class of 1972 at Yale: "The students who entered more recently are more professionally oriented, less outwardly concerned about social injustice and more attentive to the technical intricacies of the law itself." Herbold, "Law Is Where the Action Is," 28. See also Papke, "The Browning of the Yale Law School," 17.

   In 1960, 61 percent of Harvard law students had gone directly into private practice; the percentage fell to 44 in 1967 and 1968. By 1973, the figure was up to 67 percent. Seligman, *The High Citadel*, 16.

36. The ABA predicted in 1972 that the number of law jobs available in 1974 would be 14,500, yet 30,000 law students were enrolled in the Class of 1974. For an extended analysis, see York and Hale, "Too Many Lawyers?," 1.

37. In 1960, roughly one out of two applicants had been accepted by the Harvard Law School; in 1974, roughly one out of nine. The median LSAT rose from 630 in 1960 (92d percentile) to 725 in 1974 (98th percentile). Seligman, *The High Citadel*, 8. See also chap. 6.

   The selectivity of the more elite schools also increased during the 1970s. The Chicago student body had a median LSAT in 1973 of 715 and a median grade point average of 3.70. By 1980, that had reached 736 and 3.75. During the same period at the University of Pennsylvania these figures went from 685 and 3.55 to 699 and 3.72. At

Pennsylvania the numbers applying rose from 3,000 to 3,500. *AALS Pre-Law Handbook, 1973–74;* and *AALS Pre-Law Handbook, 1980–82,* passim.
38. See "Law Students Facing a Job Shortage," *New York Times,* 6 February 1972, 33, col. 1; "Graduates and Jobs: A Grave New World," *Time,* 24 May 1971, 44.
39. American Bar Association, *Review of Legal Education, 1977.* For instance, the University of Santa Clara Law School, which had fewer than 300 students in 1969 had more than 800 in 1973. McKevitt, *The University of Santa Clara,* 302.
40. See Brickman, "Experience of the Lawyering Process through a New Delivery System," 1153; Statsky, "Paraprofessionals," 397. For more recent information on the progress of these members of the legal profession, see "Paralegals: Backup Team for Lawyers," *New York Times,* 22 March 1978, 13, col. 3; "Paramedic, Paralegal Training," *New York Times,* 20 December 1978, 13, col. 3.

By 1979, paralegals—predominantly women—were achieving the indicia of respectability. The New York State bar, for instance, allowed them to be listed on law firm letterheads. *National Paralegal Reporter,* July 1979, 2. There were also efforts to regulate the certification (although not to require licensing) of paraprofessionals. These efforts were defeated by the lobbying efforts of the National Federation of Paralegal Associations in Illinois and California, but appeared to be making progress in Kansas where the paraprofessionals were divided about the desirability of certification. Ibid., January 1979, 1.
41. Law had always been taught as part of business and similar undergraduate majors, normally at less prestigious institutions. It had not obtained any noticeable academic respectability. The new programs such as that at Hampshire College attempted serious academic respectability by suggesting that law should be an integral part of a liberal education. During the decade, similar programs were considered by MIT, Chicago, Yale, Buffalo, Berkeley, Columbia, Harvard, Pennsylvania, Wisconsin, SUNY-Binghamton. The Legal Studies Association was formed to represent these new undergraduate programs. Papke, "Legal Studies," 21.
42. See "Few New Law Schools Are Being Opened," *New York Times,* 25 February 1976, 20, col. 1.
43. See "Job Picture Bleak for Law Graduates," *New Haven Register,* 10 February 1975, 1; "Job Prospects for Young Lawyers Dim as Field Grows Overcrowded," *New York Times,* 17 May 1977, 1, col. 5; "Many Lawyers Find Practice Is Limited to Looking for Work," *New York Times,* 4 November 1980, B1, col. 1.
44. White, "Law School Enrollment Up Slightly But Leveling," 577. The ABA figures, which included accredited schools and those unaccredited schools that chose to report were 126,085 in 1977, 126,937 in 1978, and 126,915 in 1979. Of the 122,860 law students in accredited schools in 1979, 38,627 were women. (In 1963, 1,883 of 49,552 had been women and, in 1970, 7,031 of 82,499.) Perhaps the most telling statistic was the number of LSATs administered. The number rose from 39,406 in 1965 to 74,092 in 1970 and to 133,546 in 1975. By 1979, it had dropped to 111,235. American Bar Association, *Review of Legal Education, 1979,* 63–64. Increasing selectivity, however, was evident.
45. See Bloom, *The Trouble with Lawyers* (billed as "[t]he book that shows how the American middle class is victimized by inept, lazy and corrupt lawyers"); Siegel, *How to Avoid Lawyers.* In 1971, an organization called Lawyer Reform of the United States was founded in California. Its journal, *Lawyer Reform News,* announced its purpose: "To improve the honesty, openness, efficiency and relevancy to social welfare with which law is practiced."
46. This list, if anything, is longer. See Auerbach, *Unequal Justice:* "T[he] bar must be

judged by two standards (but not by a double standard): its sensitivity to the values and mores of society; and its implementation of the obligation to provide equal justice under the law." Ibid., 12. Green, *The Other Government*: "Though far less prominent than public officials, Washington lawyers have burrowed themselves into the federal establishment. They influence a whole range of policy matters that deal with the way we live—the drugs and food we consume, the cars we drive, the taxes we pay, the air we breathe, the things we view and read." Ibid., 3. Black, ed., *Radical Lawyers*; Nader and Green, eds., *Verdicts on Lawyers*, a collection of articles criticizing the ABA, business lawyers, government lawyers, judges, and the legal profession in general; Weinerstein and Green, eds., *With Justice for Some*.

Even the press got into the act. See, for example, "Those #*XIII#* Lawyers," *Time*, 10 April 1978, 56. "What works against lawyers is that they are at once indispensable and intimidating—a combination guaranteed to breed bitter resentment." Ibid., 58. "Too Much Law?" *Newsweek*, 10 January 1977, 42.

47. See Green, *The Other Government*, 163–85. The firm of Wilmer, Cutler and Pickering was picketed by law students from Georgetown and George Washington universities for defending General Motors on the issue of air quality. "It has been said that when the 1970 Clean Air Act was passed, Japan hired engineers, and Detroit hired lawyers." Ibid., 164.

48. "The Young Lawyers: Good-Bye to Pro Bono," *New York Magazine*, February 1972, 29. "Today's law students may talk like Danny the Red, but they wind up in Wall Street. What happened to sixties activism?" Ibid.

49. See Baird, "A Survey of the Relevance of Legal Training to Law School Graduates," 264; Erlanger and Klegon, "Socialization Effects of Professional Schools," 11; Koziol and Joslyn, "Have There Been Significant Changes in the Career Aspirations and Occupational Choices of Law School Graduates in the 1960's?," 95. For a discussion of this phenomenon in the context of general trends in legal education, see Gee and Jackson, "Bridging the Gap," 695, 951–61. The American Bar Foundation Studies suggested that by the late 1970s interest in public service careers had declined in law school. American Bar Association, *Law Schools and Professional Education*, 70 (1980).

50. Arnold, "And Finally 342 Days Later . . . ," 32.

51. "Legal Arts: Pay Now, Litigate Later . . . ," *New York Times*, 14 August 1970, 1.

52. See Partigan, *The Market for Lawyers*. See also York and Hale, "Too Many Lawyers," passim.

53. See Baker, "Bar Restrictions on Dissemination of Information about Legal Services," 483; Agate, "Legal Advertising and the Public Interest," 209; "Ethics Committee Draft Proposal Would Eliminate Code Ad Ban," *American Bar News*, November 1975, 1; "Should Lawyers Be Able to Advertise?," *The Reformer* [Brattleboro, Vermont], 19 December 1975, 5.

54. *Bigelow v. Virginia*, 421 U.S. 809 (1975). The Supreme Court declared that state restraints on advertising were violations of the First Amendment if they had no reasonable basis. For the ABA's reaction, see "Advertising Lawsuits and FTC Investigation Are Pending," 62 *ABA Journal* 1567 (1976); "Code Amendments Broaden Information Lawyers May Provide in Law Lists, Directories, and Yellow Pages," 62 *ABA Journal* 309 (1976); Hobbs, "Lawyer Advertising—Good Beginning But Not Enough," 735 (which pointed out the need for the public to have more information available for the selection of a lawyer); "Legal Profession Is Considering Code Amendments to Permit Restricted Advertising by Lawyers," 62 *ABA Journal* 53 (1976); "Supreme Court Will Hear Lawyer's Advertising Case from Arizona," 62 *ABA Journal* 1422 (1976); Walsh, "The Annual Report of the President of the American Bar Association," 1119.

Questioning the use of a lawyer's right to advertise continues today. Since the U.S. Supreme Court's declaration in *Bates* v. *State Bar of Arizona*, 433 U.S. 350 (1977), that lawyers have the right to advertise, ABA polls have shown that although the profession supports institutional advertising ("Lawpoll—Strong Support for Institutional Advertising," 65 *ABA Journal* 872 [1979]), individual lawyers remain reluctant to advertise. "Advertising Still Laying an Egg," 65 *ABA Journal* 1014 (1979).

55. In *Goldfarb* v. *Virginia State Bar*, 421 U.S. 773 (1975), the U.S. Supreme Court declared that the legal profession was subject to antitrust laws and that the bar's minimum fee schedule would violate such legislation. For a pre-Goldfarb review of the issues, see Allen, "Do Fee Schedules Violate Antitrust Law?," 565. For a post-Goldfarb discussion, with special emphasis on the decision's application to restrictions on advertising and solicitation, see Rigler, "Professional Codes of Conduct after Goldfarb," 185.

56. See Auerbach, "The Walls Came Tumblin' Down," 33.

For examples of support for the Legal Services Corporation, see Fellers, "President's Page," 261; Cramton, "The Task Ahead in Legal Services," 1339; Ehrlich, "Giving Low-Income America Minimum Access to Legal Services," 696.

For concern with ethics, see Manning, "If Lawyers Were Angels," 821; Martin, "Are Ethics In or Out?," 385.

For a discussion of new areas and means of research, see Harrington, "What's Happening in Computer Assisted Legal Research," 924; Rosenberg, "Anything Legislatures Can Do, Courts Can Do Better," 587.

For more recent concerns in all these areas, see ABA Section of Legal Education and Admissions to the Bar, *Report and Recommendations of the Task Force on Lawyer Competency: The Role of the Law Schools* (1979) (hereafter cited as *ABA Report on Lawyer Competency*).

57. See, for example, Johnstone and Hopson, *Lawyers and Their Work*, 459–531. "English solicitors are subject to a vast body of restrictions on their professional behavior, and our impression is that the general level of compliance is very high, certainly compared to that of American Lawyers." Ibid., 405. See also Gee and Jackson, "Bridging the Gap," 776; Leach, "The New Disciplinary Enforcement in England," 212.

58. Brown, *Loyalty and Security*, 109–14.

59. Schwartz, "Law Schools and Ethics."

60. Hazard, *Ethics in the Practice of Law*; Michael Kelly, "Teaching Ethics in Law School," mimeographed (1979).

61. For example, by 1975 Ohio asked for a dean's affidavit that the student had taken ten hours of instruction in the Code of Professional Responsibility. Indiana required successful completion of two semester hours of credit in legal ethics "regardless of the course name in the law curriculum." Yale Law School Files, Yale University, New Haven, Conn.

62. See Gee and Jackson, "Bridging the Gap," 714–16. See also Auerbach, "What Has Teaching of Law to Do with Justice?" 457; Hellman, "Considering the Future of Legal Education," 170.

63. Harris, "Minnesota C.L.E.," 23; *New York Times*, 8 April 1975, 18, col. 2.

64. Gee and Jackson, "Bridging the Gap," 263, 913–18; *New York Times*, 10 April 1975, 33, col. 3. A survey found that continuing education for lawyers was required in Colorado, Idaho, Iowa, Minnesota, Washington, Wisconsin, and Wyoming, and, in certain circumstances, in Arizona, California, Florida, New Mexico, and Texas. But see "Move to Require Continuing Education for Professionals Appears to Be Stalling," *Chronicle of Higher Education*, 17 November 1980, 1; *New York Times*, 9 September 1979, sec. G, p. 3.

The Profession and the Law Schools / 255

65. See Christensen, *Specialization*; Zehale, *Specialization in the Legal Profession*.
66. "Final Report, Committee on Specialization," 44 *California State Bar Journal* 493 (1969).
67. See, for example, Connecticut Bar Association, "Connecticut Pilot Plan on Legal Designation," Draft no. 4, 1975.
68. Mindes, "Lawyer Specialty Certification," 42.
69. Von Hoffman, "Legal Specialty: Newest Ripoff?," sec. 2, p. 4, col. 3.
70. The process was rejected by the New York Bar Association in 1979. Carlson, "Measuring the Quality of Legal Services," 287; Gee and Jackson, "Bridging the Gap," 711–14, 913–18; McKay, "Legal Education," 561–75. The then president-elect of the ABA, David Brink, however, predicted at an ABA Specialization Conference in New Orleans in May 1980 a resurgence in the specialization movement during the 1980s as part of the effort to insure competence in the bar. "In Brief—More Specialization," 66 *ABA Journal* 712 (1980). Cf. "A.B.A., Section Reps Blast Specialization Proposals," ibid., vol. 67, p. 692 (1981).
71. As late as 1951, thirty-five states allowed law office practice in lieu of law school. By 1980, only California, Vermont, Virginia, and Washington had such provisions. Some other states, including Alaska, Maine, New York, Texas, and Wyoming allowed a mixture of law school and law office work. American Bar Association, *Annual Review of Legal Education, 1979*, 71.
72. For example, "Burger Urges Curb on Trial Lawyers Not Fully Trained," *New York Times*, 27 November 1973, 1, col. 3; Cohen, "Certification of Trial Lawyers—a Judicial Effort to Restructure the American Legal Profession," 27.
73. Allen, "The Prospect of University Law Training," 127; "Law Schools Warned of Acrimonious Tension," *Chronicle of Higher Education*, 12 January 1976, 7; Vernon, "The Expanding Law School Curriculum Committee," 7.
74. At a 1979 ABA-sponsored conference on lawyer competence, the one hundred schools represented did not include Yale, Harvard, Chicago, Stanford, Berkeley, or Pennsylvania. "Absence of Leading Law Schools at Meet Noted," 65 *ABA Journal* 1035 (1979).
75. For all the egalitarianism of the 1970s, it was a decade obsessed with "ranking" law schools. For example, *The Reputation of American Professional Schools* (1974), ranked the following as the top nine law schools in descending order: Harvard, Yale, Michigan, Columbia, Chicago, Stanford, Berkeley, New York University, and Pennsylvania. In another survey, looking at the matter from various perspectives, Harvard and Yale came in first, but in the top eleven and in different order Virginia, Texas, and Georgetown appeared in addition to most of those schools previously listed. Flanigan, "Sizing Up the Graduate Schools," 64.
76. *New York Times*, 16 September 1975, 82, col. 1. See also Sovern, "A Better Prepared Bar—the Wrong Approach," 473. "Like the doctors who prescribe antibiotics for the common cold, the committee nevertheless proceeded to prescribe trial practice to cure an ailment not caused by lack of trial practice." Ibid., 475.
77. "Second Circuit Judicial Council Issues Statement on Proposed Admission Rules," 62 *ABA Journal* 516 (1976).
78. Gee and Jackson, "Bridging the Gap," 898–904; "What You Need to Know about the Proposed Federal Practice Rule," 65 *ABA Journal* 60, 61 (1976).
79. Gee and Jackson, "Bridging the Gap," 905–9.
80. The reaction of the state law schools also reflected the intellectual outlook of the academic hierarchy. The dean of the Indiana University Law School (Indianapolis), William Harvey, claimed, in 1981, that rule 9 was "splendid. It's been beneficial to the development of competency [in] attorneys." The associate dean at Indiana University

Law School (Bloomington), John Baker, said, "I don't like the rule at all. It's a very bad piece of policy." Slonim, "State Court Tells Law School What to Teach," 26, 27.
81. Givan, "Indiana's Rule 13," 16. In a similar vein, another writer suggested:

> The present agitation for a so-called competency training is merely a reflection of the fact that the skills learned in apprenticeship training have been forced out of the law school curriculum and must be obtained, if at all, in unsupervised practice. . . .
>   If law schools want to be schools of legal philosophy and their students do not wish to engage in the public practice of law, then they can do what they will with their students and structure any curriculum they see fit. However, when by their own long-term efforts the law schools have secured exclusive control of legal education so that no person can become a lawyer except by passing through their portals, then they cannot escape public scrutiny of their product. [Seidman, "Personal Viewpoint—the Responsibility of Law Schools," 638–39]

Cf. Boshkoff, "Indiana's Rule 13," 18. "Rule 13 confuses important information with essential knowledge." Ibid., 20.
82. Slonim, "State Court Tells Law School What to Teach," 26. The dean of the University of South Carolina Law School (Harry Lightsey, Jr.) was philosophical, possibly reflecting the fact that the original proposals had been even tougher: "This rule is about 60 of the 90 hours (that students must generally pass to graduate). . . . The rule is fairly broadly drawn. I don't see it as an intrusion on academic freedom. It's not about how (a subject) should be taught." Ibid., 27.
83. In Georgia, the dean of the University of Georgia Law School (J. Ralph Beaird) pledged to oppose the move. "I don't think the supreme court should determine the curriculum of the law school." Ibid. For details of the courses and examinations implementing Devitt, see Winter, "Federal Courts Implement Devitt Proposals," 550.
84. Slonim, "State Court Tells Law School What to Teach," 27.
85. Gee and Jackson, "Bridging the Gap," 909–10; Otorowski, "Some Fundamental Problems with the Devitt Committee Report," 713. On Rule 13, see Cutright and Boshkoff, "Course Selection, Student Characteristics and Bar Examination Performances," 127 (a study refuting the value of Rule 13 as a way to improve success rate on bar exam).
86. "Bar Unit Urges Law Schools to Shift Emphasis," *Chronicle of Higher Education*, 18 June 1979, 6; "Legal Education—Say More Dollars Crucial to Law School Improvement," 65 *ABA Journal* 1034 (1979); "Bar Panel Bids Law Schools Stress Practical Training," *New York Times*, 16 August 1979, sec. A, p. 10, col. 1.
  The *ABA Report on Lawyer Competency* urged law schools to take into account skills other than those reflected in the LSAT and not to lower standards as applications fell. It also urged the teaching of lawyer skills in small law school classes and on a cooperative basis, continuous evaluation rather than single examinations, a more structured curriculum even at the risk of "the loss of some teacher autonomy," the use of more part-time practitioners as teachers, and an improvement in faculty-student ratios. Although ability to teach was still to be the chief reason for appointment to the faculty, the report recommended that knowledge of skills and the law in action should be given greater emphasis.
  The ABA was urged to expand accreditation to include self-studies of lawyer-skill teaching and to increase both its financial support of and research into such development. The ABA was also urged to be flexible about course and term structures. The bar as a whole was urged to consider in its hiring the performance in skills evaluation as well as the results in traditional analytical examinations. In at least three different ways

the bar was reminded of its duty to support legal education financially. This same reminder was addressed to the federal government, in terms of financial aid programs, Title XI of the Higher Education Act, and the Legal Services Corporation. The state governments were also told to be generous.

87. The report suggested that "Bar-Admissions authorities, meanwhile, should not restrict law schools' opportunities to experiment with the curriculum." *ABA Report on Lawyer Competency*, 8. The dean of New York University Law School was quoted as saying: "Law schools should not have to choose between teaching law as an intellectual discipline and teaching skills. We can do both and each can enrich the other." Cited in Civiletti, "Clinical Education in Law School and Beyond," 576.

88. Late in 1980, the ABA began the process of attempting to add an accreditation requirement that would force law schools to "offer to all students at least one rigorous writing experience" and to "offer training in professional skills, including trial and appellate advocacy, counseling, negotiation and drafting." The draft rule was based on the *ABA Task Force on Lawyer Competency*. Reactions to the new regulation broke down along class lines. The dean of the University of the Pacific Law School (Gordon Scaber) welcomed the proposal: "Young lawyers feel they didn't get [such training], and law students feel they need it." Albert Sacks, dean of Harvard and then president of the AALS, noted: "One is tempted to treat the new proposal as a flyspeck to be ignored. I think . . . that this new, rather weak, proposal must be taken seriously. I hope it will be strongly resisted." Slonim, "New Accreditation Proposal Criticized," 1505.

89. The original proposal had included the requirement of trial and appellate advocacy, counseling, and negotiation. The 1980 compromise was limited to an interpretive paragraph calling for skills teaching, but it noted that "such instructions need not be limited to any specific skill or list of skills." Dean Albert Sacks, president of the AALS, announced that academic freedom was "substantially protected and preserved." "Lawyers' Group Softens Proposed Requirement That Law Schools Teach Specific Skills," *Chronicle of Higher Education*, 1 June 1981, 4.

90. Stevens, "Law Schools and Law Students," 559–60. The schools surveyed were Boston College, Connecticut, Iowa, Michigan, Pennsylvania, Southern California, and Yale. Ibid., 558. See also Baird, "A Survey of the Relevance of Legal Training to Law School Graduates," 264–94.

91. Marden, "CLEPR Origins and Program," 3; Stevens, "Legal Education," 43; Gee and Jackson, "Bridging the Gap," 881.

92. Pincus, "Clinical Training in the Law School," 479, 492.

93. Probably the most articulate spokesperson for intellectualized clinical legal education was Gary Bellow of the Harvard Law School. Seligman, *The High Citadel*, 164–73.

94. For instance, in 1977 CLEPR announced a program of grants to bring clinical legal salaries up to "regular" faculty salaries. Ibid., 164. See also Oliphant, "When Will Clinicians Be Allowed to Join the Club?," 34.

95. For a zealous statement from the trenches, see Barnhizer, "Clinical Education at the Crossroads," 1025. For an articulate statement, see Schrag, "Report from a CLEPR Colony," 581.

96. In 1978, the first funded year for Title XI, $1,000,000 was made available to thirty programs. The hope had been to expand this to $2,000,000 and forty programs in 1979. No line item was, however, included in President Carter's budget for fiscal year 1979, and the Reagan administration remained unsympathetic.

97. Gee and Jackson, "Bridging the Gap," 857–58. The *AALS Pre-Law Handbook, 1979–80*, reported:

A student begins his or her first year in September and follows a full-time academic program for three quarters until the end of May. He or she takes the traditional first-year curriculum as well as courses in legal practice and social theory, and constitutional law. In the beginning of June, the student starts the second year. He or she goes to work as a paid law clerk for the summer quarter or remains at the law school and takes upper-level classes full-time. At the end of three months the section that worked and the section that took classes exchange places and start a series of quarters that alternate work and study periods through the remainder of the second and third years. [P. 242]

98. The AALS Pre-Law Handbook, 1979–80 added:

> The [institute] represents an attempt to utilize the present system to solve many of the problems of the unrepresented of the inner city, through effective representation once reserved for the economically secure of the United States. The relationship of the law firm to the School of Law is analogous to that existing between a teaching hospital and the respective medical schools. The School of Law is structured around this legal aid clinic and must operate 12 months a year to serve the disadvantaged who qualify as clients of the firm. [P. 56]

See also Cahn, "Antioch's Fight against Neutrality in Legal Education," 41.

99. See "A Plan to Learn While You Defend," New York Times, 16 May 1971, 19, col. 3; Antioch School of Law, Newsletter, January 1973, 3.

100. See "Strife Impedes Antioch Law School's Reach for Goal: Clinical Education Test at Stake," Washington Post, 25 May 1977, 15, col. 3. Early in 1980, the founding deans were fired by the university. See "A Law School Comes to Judgment," Newsweek, 11 February 1980, 97. Later that year the acting dean's office was occupied by students demanding a 70 percent black presence, reflecting the racial composition of the District of Columbia. National Law Journal, 28 April 1980, 4.

101. See, for instance, the Law School of New College of California founded in 1972. Hyman, "A School for Advocates," 23.

102. AALS Curriculum Study Project Committee, Training for the Public Profession of Law (1971). However attractive the ideas in this report, the reasoning supporting them was not always impressive.

103. Manning, "Law Schools and Lawyer Schools—Two Tier Legal Education," 379. Manning was content to institutionalize a hierarchy of law schools: "To the law schools, which do not, after all, hold themselves out as 'lawyer schools,' should go those functions of teaching law that are essentially analytic, intellectual, and suited to classroom learning techniques. To the bar's training schools should go the functions of training lawyers in the operating skills of lawyering." Ibid., 382. In addition, however, he elegantly articulated the position that it is not the law schools' responsibility to solve all the bar's defects. Ibid., 380.

104. There was certainly evidence that the curricula of law schools was becoming more alike. Gee and Jackson, Following the Leader?.

105. Parker and Ehrlich, New Directions in Legal Education. The idea of a two-year law school also received support from President Bok of Harvard. See Bok, "A Different Way of Looking at the World," 41.

106. Stolz, "The Two-Year Law School," 37.

107. Sovern, "Training Tomorrow's Lawyers," 72.

108. "Columbia Plans Six-Year Course for Completion of Law Degree," New York Times, 19 March 1972, 64, col. 5. Such an approach was not unique; CCNY and New York Law School began a six-year integrated B.A.-J.D. program. "Law Course Start in

Freshman Year," *New York Times*, 10 January 1975, p. 1, col. 1.

109. Gee and Jackson, *Follow the Leader?*, 852; Stanley, "Comments on Current Problems Facing the Legal Profession," 109, 159–65; Stanley, "Two Years +," 18.

110. "Law Schools Are Cool to Chief Justice's Ideas on Reforming Curriculum," *Chronicle of Higher Education*, 15 January 1979, 10.

111. Dean Cramton of Cornell contended: "The proponents haven't carried the burden of proof." Samuel D. Thurman, chairman of the Section of Legal Education and Admissions to the Bar, said the two-year law school was "dead," explaining that the study of law was far too complicated to achieve in two years, since "most deans are tearing their hair out to do it in three." Dean Auerbach of Minnesota saw a two-year law school as "a confession of abject failure on our part." Ibid.

112. Stevens, "Law Schools and Law Students," 589–90. In another crumbling of the old order, in 1980 the council of the ABA Section of Legal Education voted to allow full-time law students to work twenty rather than fifteen hours a week while in law school.

113. See Oulahan, "The Legal Implications of Evaluation and Accreditation," 193, 195–97.

114. First, "Competition in the Legal Education Industry II," 1078–82.

115. Among the schools that gave up evening division programs in the 1960s were St. Louis, Emory, Southern California, Southern Methodist, New York University, and St. Mary's.

116. In 1972, fifty-six law schools had night divisions; thirty-three of those had both ABA and AALS accreditation; seventeen had only ABA accreditation; and six had neither ABA nor AALS accreditation. Sleeper, "The Renaissance of Night Law Schools," 6. Of the thirty-nine night-only programs, one was in a school with both ABA and AALS accreditation, four were in schools with only ABA accreditation, and thirty-four were in schools with no accreditation. Ibid.

117. American Bar Association, *Annual Review of Legal Education, 1978*, 65.

118. Three existed in Alabama, one in Arizona, one in Connecticut, four in the District of Columbia, four in Georgia, one in Illinois, two in Minnesota, one in Mississippi, two in Missouri, one in North Carolina, one in Tennessee, one in Texas, and one in Vermont. Ibid., 57–58.

119. It was in fact founded in 1911. By the mid-1970s its boom in enrollment caused it to limit the size of its freshman classes.

120. The People's College of Law had no dean and the governing body consisted of all faculty members and students. Ridenour, "Law and the People," 15. The first semester's enrollment was 40 percent Hispanic, 25 percent black, 5 percent Asian, and 30 percent white. Ibid.

121. Papke, "The Last Gasp of the Unaccredited Law Schools"; Stewart, "My Week in an Unaccredited Law School," 19.

At least some of the unaccredited law schools appeared to provide an important opportunity for minority students. For instance, 268 of the 1747 at Western State's Fullerton branch were minorities and 92 of the 961 at Atlanta Law School. American Bar Association, *Annual Review of Legal Education, 1979*, 55.

122. Resolution of the Coordinating Council of Higher Education, 3 April 1973. The resolution was based on O'Toole, "Legal Manpower Supply and Demand in California." "Policing Non-Accredited Law Schools," *Chronicle of Higher Education*, 18 February 1975, 4.

123. "Unaccredited Law Schools Face Scrutiny on Coast," *New York Times*, 16 April 1979, sec. A, p. 11, col. 1.

260 I Law School

Such developments were not unknown elsewhere in the country. In 1973, Anthony Doria was able to start a law school in the rustic Vermont village of South Royalton (the Vermont Law School), although he apparently had no law degree, a shell college with no students, a conviction for fraud in Pennsylvania (later overturned), as well as being defendant in thirty civil suits. As a member of the community reported, "The school came along at the right time. The chicken factory had closed and people were out of work." Haslow, "The Preposterous and Altogether Unlikely Case of Vermont Law School." After Doria was replaced as dean in 1974 (in 1980 Doria ran in the Republican primary for U.S. Senate) by a former Vermont attorney-general (Thomas Debevoise), the school flourished. In 1975, the school was given provisional approval by the ABA and in 1978 full approval. In 1982, it was approved by the AALS.

124. See Stevens, "Democracy and the Legal Profession," 12.

125. Western State University College of Law (WSU) was a thorn in the flesh of both the ABA and AALS. Although accredited by the state bar, its students could not participate in federal student-aid programs because it was not accredited by a "recognized accrediting agency." WSU then sought accreditation from the Western Association of Schools and Colleges (WASC). Both the ABA and AALS sought to organize a boycott of the WASC accrediting team. Despite this, a team was formed and WSU was given accreditation. WSU then filed a complaint against the ABA with the Office of Education. First, "Competition in the Legal Education Industry II," 1082–86.

126. This was a constant concern of law school deans and an increasing one as the universities found themselves in ever-straitening financial circumstances during the 1970s. See "Law Schools Warned of Acrimonious Tension," *Chronicle of Higher Education*, 12 January 1976, 7. Judith Younger resigned as dean of the Syracuse Law School in 1975, alleging that the law school had been "milked" by the university. Ibid. Alphonse Squillante, who resigned as dean of Ohio Northern Law School in 1975, noted: "I was supposed to be fund-raising, but every fund I raised seemed to end up in the university coffers." Ibid. Frederick Hart, dean of the University of New Mexico Law School, explained: "Law schools are historically underfunded and the law school is a small unit, so it is hard to win political battles in the university." Ibid. In contrast, President John Silber of Boston University said: "Every part of the university is related to every other part. If you can provide sound legal education and have an excess of income that the university can take back to fund other programs, there's nothing wrong with that." Ibid. At the AALS annual meeting, the president, Soia Mentschikoff, dean of the University of Miami Law School, warned that, as the higher education industry hurt for students, the "temptation to use the funds generated by law school enrollment to pay for the college becomes almost irresistible." *AALS Proceedings, 1974*, pt. 2, 70.

For a detailed analysis by one of the participants of the clash between the law school and the university administration at Hofstra, a clash that included both budget and tenure decisions, see Freedman, "Holding Law Schools Hostage," 16. For a detailed analysis of the broader issues, see Swords and Walwer, *The Costs and Resources of Legal Education*, chap. 5.

127. See "Bar Association May Lose Accrediting Status," 65 *ABA Journal* 683 (1979).

128. "Policing Non-Accredited Law Schools," *Chronicle of Higher Education*, 18 February 1975, 4.

129. "Two Groups to Continue Accrediting Law Schools," *Chronicle of Higher Education*, 14 October 1980, 4. The AALS was not the only body keeping an eye on the ABA. In 1981, under the threat of a restraining order from a federal judge, the ABA House of

Delegates changed the accreditation rules to delete the provision that had refused accreditation to those schools that discriminated against students on the grounds of religion. The suit had been brought on behalf of the Law School of Oral Roberts University in Tulsa, Oklahoma, which required students to sign an oath of religious faith and the faculty to be among the faithful. Whitney North Seymour, Sr., a former ABA president, argued: "It may be necessary to take a deep gulp and accept things we might not wish to accept in order to preserve the role of the A.B.A. in approving law schools." *New York Times*, 13 August 1981, 421.

130. "Unaccredited Law Schools Face Scrutiny on Coast," *New York Times*, 16 April 1979, sec. A, p. 11, col. 1.

131. Association of American Law Schools, *Opportunity for Negroes in Law* (1967); Carnegie Corporation, *A Step towards Equal Justice* (1973).

For more recent studies by blacks, see Ware, *From the Black Bar*; Leonard, *Black Lawyers*.

132. The big jump came in 1974, with an increase to 8,333. After that there was only a slow increase. In 1979, of the 10,008 minority students, 5,257 were black.

133. In 1980, the ABA House of Delegates called for "full opportunities" for minorities to study law as a requirement for accreditation. Dennis W. Areber, a black lawyer from Detroit, demanded the additional standard since minority groups had been "largely excluded from a profession of tremendous power and importance in this society." The change was supported by Erwin Griswold, former dean of Harvard and former solicitor-general, since "the only way to make progress in this area is to have a requirement." It was opposed by Gerhart Casper, dean of Chicago, as "a great danger to academic freedom." "Bar Units Spurs Minority Enrollment in Law Schools." *New York Times*, 7 August 1980, sec. B., p. 18, col. 1.

134. *DeFunis v. Odegaard*, 28 Wash. 2d. 11, 507 P. 2d 1169 (1973), *vacated as moot*, 416 U.S. 312 (1974). In *DeFunis*, a white law school applicant unsuccessfully challenged preferential minority admissions. See Zimmer, "Beyond Defunis," 317.

135. *Regents of the University of California v. Bakke*, 438 U.S. 265 (1978). Alan Bakke, a white applicant, challenged a decision that denied him admission to the University of California at Davis Medical School in 1973 and 1974. Bakke alleged that less well-qualified minority applicants had been accepted. The California supreme court upheld Bakke's contention that the special admissions policy was a violation of the Fourteenth Amendment. *Bakke v. California Board of Regents*, 19 Cal. 3d, 553 P. 2d 1152, 132 Cal. Rptr. 680 (1976). The U.S. Supreme Court affirmed the decision in part and reversed it in part. 438 U.S. 265, 320 (1978). Murray, "Special Admission Programs—the Bakke Case," 358.

136. *United Steelworkers of America v. Weber*, 99 S. Ct. 2721 (1980). In *Weber*, the union made an affirmative-action agreement with Kaiser Aluminum to reserve 50 percent of openings in in-plant craft-training programs for blacks until the percentage of black craft workers was proportionate to that in the labor force. A white applicant, Brian Weber, challenged this agreement as a violation of Title VII. The U.S. Supreme Court held that Title VII did not prohibit such race-conscious affirmative-action plans. Then, in 1981, the California Supreme Court held that law schools were entitled to treat minority racial status as a preferential factor. "Affirmative Action . . . Law School Admissions," 67 *ABA Journal* 642 (1981).

137. Between 1971 and 1974 none of the sixty black and Hispanic students who graduated from UC-Davis passed the bar, and the rate from UCLA was 38 percent as opposed to 80 percent for whites. *The Times Higher Education Supplement* [London], 22

November 1974.
138. California Bar Association, *Commission to Study the Bar Examination Process* (1974).
139. Green, "Taking the Bar Exam to Court," 2.
140. Anderson, "Black Lawyers in the 20 Largest Firms," 6.
141. See Auerbach, *Unequal Justice*, 184–88. "For no group of second-generation Americans did the New Deal serve as a more efficacious vehicle for social mobility and political power than for Jewish lawyers, who in many instances possessed every necessary credential for professional elite status except for the requisite social origins." Ibid., 185.
142. "The Jewish Law Student and New York Jobs—Discriminatory Effects in Law Firm Hiring Practices," 73 *Yale Law Journal* 625 (1964). The effects of discrimination against Jews was, however, still visible in Chicago. Heinz and Laumann, *Chicago Lawyers*, chap. 6. On the other hand, the percentage of Jewish students at the University of Chicago Law School dropped between the 1930s and the 1970s. Heinz and Laumann, *Chicago Lawyers*, passim.
143. Stevens, "Law Schools and Law Students," 573–74, 690.
144. American Bar Association, *Annual Review of Legal Education, 1978*, 86.
145. Spangler, Gordon, and Pipkin, "Token Women," 1.
146. Spangler and Pipkin, "Portia Faces Life: Sex Differences in the Professional Orientations and Career Aspirations of the Law Student," mimeographed (1978). See also, for instance, Leisberg, "Women in Law School Teaching," 226. In 1980, in the fifty largest law firms, 85 of the 3,987 partners (2.13 percent) were women and 1,297 of 6,034 (21.5 percent) of the associates were women. *National Law Journal*, 4 August 1980, 59.
    In 1970, 1 percent of lawyers in major Wall Street firms were women; in 1980, 9 percent were women. Of partners, 2 percent were women; of associates, 22 percent were women. In 1970, women had 2 percent of tenure track appointments in law schools; in 1979–80, they had 11 percent. "Despite the progress women lawyers still have far to go." Fossum, "Women in the Legal Profession," 67.
147. Turow recounts: "It is Monday morning, and when I walk into the central building I can feel my stomach clench. . . . By Friday, my nerves will be so brittle from sleeplessness and pressure and intellectual fatigue that I will not be certain I can make it through the day. . . . I am a law student in my first year at law, and there are many moments when I am simply a mess." Turow, *One-L*, 7.
148. Osborn, *The Paper Chase*. See also popular pieces such as Eliot M. Brown, "Dear Dr. Smith: About Law School—," 16.
149. For an annotated bibliography of statistical empirical studies over the last twenty years, see Barry and Connelly, "Research on Law Students," 751. The bibliography is not exhaustive. See, for example, Benthall-Neitzel, "An Empirical Investigation of the Relationship between Lawyering Skills and Legal Education," 373.
150. The parameters of this project appear in Boyer and Cramton, "American Legal Education," 221. The results of the studies are described in American Bar Association, *Law Schools and Professional Education* (Chicago, 1980).
151. Stevens, "Law Schools and Law Students," 653–63. See, especially: "For example, in the first semester, virtually no one spent fewer than ten hours per week studying. By the fifth semester, approximately one-fourth of the students devoted only that amount of time to their studies. Similarly, in the first semester virtually no one reported merely reading the material as his most frequent method of class preparation. In the fifth semester, the figure was about six out of seven. Finally, during the first semester, only a

third of the students reported 'seldom if ever' participating in informal discussions. By the fifth semester, the percentage had risen to about two-thirds of the interviewees." Ibid., 653. "In short, the popular conception of law student life as a mixture of long hours poring over casebooks and endless discussions of the contents of those books is more myth than reality. By the fifth semester many students have the equivalent of a two-day work week and discuss their studies rarely, if at all. At least intellectually law schools appear to be a part-time operation." Ibid. In later studies, particularly those by the American Bar Foundation, the "fall off" was pronounced, but it was not as dramatic as that of ten years earlier. American Bar Association, *Law Schools and Professional Education*, 38–41.

152. See, however, the successful strike by University of San Francisco law students in 1973, calling for better faculty-student ratios and more student aid. *San Francisco Chronicle*, 8 November 1973, 3. See also Carrington and Conley, "The Alienation of Law Students," 887.

153. That is the thesis of Seligman's *High Citadel*. Writing of Harvard in the mid-1970s, he claimed: "After a decade, the periphery of Dean Griswold's Harvard Law School had altered, but the center had not. Harvard Law School, as the dean once put it, continued to teach law in the grand manner." Ibid., 19.

THERE was an unhealthy dichotomy between the professional and scholarly approaches with which legal educators had been struggling since Langdell and Eliot first brought the professional school of law into the mainstream of the American liberal arts university. By the post-World War II era, this inherent conflict had developed into a massive case of intellectual schizophrenia. Thomas Bergin argued that "by compelling true academics, or those who have the potential for serious scholarship, to play out a Hessian-trainer role, and by compelling highly skilled Hessian-trainers to make believe they are legal scholars, the disease dilutes both scholarship and Hessian-training to the advantage of neither."[1] It was still unclear whether scholarship in the traditional sense was entirely appropriate in a law school.

The inherently conflicting academic purposes of the law school were also reflected in the increasingly purposive approach of the American lawyer. He had ceased to be a manipulator of principles and became more a searcher for precedents. The American lawyer had been accused of such things before; by seeking cases "on all fours" the lawyer seemed to have resorted to a somewhat mechanical search not for principles but for the magic case. Now the profession had gone one step further: the idea of a principle itself was for many no longer even seen as deciding or decisive. In this sense, the idea of law as a "brooding omnipresence" in the sky or even *in gremio magistratuum* had largely evaporated; American law had been secularized. Instead of searching for the law, the American lawyer had assumed a role as a facilitator—the person who used the system to enable the client or interest group to achieve its goal. The logic of Tocqueville had at last borne its full fruit.[2] This fact was increasingly accepted by leading scholars,[3] and thus it is not surprising that the articulated intellectual theories of American law were shallow.

It was perhaps not unnatural that out of the chaos of the Realist revolution and the war with Hitler—which latter event had given Realism, at least in some circles, the reputation of being "the jurisprudence of a sick society"[4]—an attempt would be made to piece together the old and the new. That attempt finally appeared in 1943. In the mid-1940s there were still grand designs at the intellectual level. In a mammoth article entitled "Legal Education and Public Policy," two post-Realist

Yale Professors, Harold Lasswell (a polymath political scientist) and Myres McDougal (an iconoclastic property lawyer) attempted to weld together the various intellectual themes of the 1920s and 1930s.[5] The result was a remarkable, albeit ultimately unsuccessful, synthesis. Although the importance of the article must not be overestimated, it provides a useful vehicle for examining the American approach to legal theory.

In what became known as the "Law, Science, and Policy" approach, the behavioralist aspects of the social sciences had pride of place. The authors argued that attempts during the previous two decades to integrate these aspects with law might have failed but that the failure was due neither to a lack of sophistication on the part of the social sciences nor to any absence of a need for such a merger. Rather, it was due to the lack of skill on the part of those making the earlier efforts. Lasswell and McDougal assumed that the social sciences were adequate to the task and that the need to integrate them with law was obvious.[6] More unexpected, the respectability of black-letter law (what Langdell had called principles and what the practitioner by then called precedents) was revived as one of the intellectually laudable factors going into the legal decision-making process. Most important of all, however, the authors were also able to support the increasing emphasis on legal skills by attempting to analyze which skills decision makers might need in light of the values that Lasswell and McDougal thought to be both relevant and quantifiable.

These are only some of the features of the elaborate "policy-science" schema that Lasswell and McDougal presented in their article. Their main purpose was to develop a plan for fundamental curricular reform that could be applied to law schools in the post-1945 period. The postulate that the role of the law schools was "training for policymaking"[7] led them to reject the type of functional reevaluation, which Columbia had attempted in the 1920s, as having been developed at too low a level of abstraction; in their view, policymaking required, in addition to functional skills, an understanding of values. Thus, after an inventory of legal skills and an analysis of the possible value system of the lawyer, the existing legal curriculum was weighed and found wanting.[8] In its place, the authors offered a curriculum built around the value principle and the skill principle.

The Lasswell-McDougal article was a tour de force. It was a historical landmark, both sifting and synthesizing the ideas and trends in legal education from the previous three-quarters of a century but, most especially, from the previous twenty-five years. It marked the clear beginning of the post-Realist period. Yet when all was said and done, the article itself, in terms of producing radical change in legal education, was almost completely unsuccessful.[9] Some scholars have been influenced by the "policy-science" approach,[10] but, for all practical purposes, law schools have not. Some critics have attributed this to the "policy-science" jargon,[11] others to the rigid formalism of the approach, and still others to the increasingly dated social science foundations of the system.[12] Another feature that may have limited its credibility was that the approach assumed, in its analysis of values, in a way that now seems embarrassingly dated, that the United States was the archetypal system of freedom and democracy.[13] Most important of all, the schema assumed the omnipotence and omnicompetence, as well as the homogeneity, of the lawyer in America.[14]

Ultimately, however, it may well be that all these objections were largely irrelevant factors in the lack of impact of the Lasswell-McDougal program. With respect to procedural reform in England, Maitland argued that although the forms of action were dead, they "still rule us from their graves." An analogous situation prevailed in American legal education. The historical roots of the system prevented the American law school from becoming a center for the study of policymaking. Lasswell and McDougal could, at most, influence rather than restructure; their approach was too elitist, too expensive, and too academic for most schools in the country. Despite all the rhetoric, the American law school was founded and developed as a professional school stressing the knowledge needed to pass the bar examination and to succeed in practice. Although some elite schools had gone beyond these objectives, most law schools retained this fundamental, practical orientation. Legal education's heritage was one of an inherent conflict between the professional and the scholarly.

Perhaps the Lasswell-McDougal plan was originally intended only to be applicable to a few schools, but it was elitist even by that standard. The bar in the years after 1945 was no more uniform than it had been when Reed first delivered his reports in the 1920s, or indeed when Langdell had instituted his reforms in 1870. If, as many still assumed,[15] Wall Street represented the pinnacle of the legal establishment, it was most heavily influenced by a narrow band of legal education. In the twenty largest firms more than 70 percent of the partners came from Harvard, Yale, and Columbia.[16] The work of the large firms differed remarkably from other forms of legal practice.[17] The work of the individual practitioner in Chicago bore only the most superficial resemblance to the work of the corporate lawyer. The latter might emphasize, from his comfortable position, the unitary nature of the bar, and he might be deeply concerned about the "ethics" of the less qualified who, in turn, might be deeply concerned about "unauthorized practice."[18]

Heinz and Laumann, in their recent studies of the Chicago bar, found such a continuing degree of differentiation among practitioners that they argued that "one could posit a great many legal professions, perhaps dozens."[19] Chicago was the home of Baker and McKenzie with almost 600 lawyers (many not American) in its thirty offices around the world. In 1979, although New York still had only one firm with more than 200 lawyers (Shearman and Sterling),[20] Houston boasted three, Chicago two, in addition to Baker and McKenzie, and Los Angeles, San Francisco, Cleveland, and Philadelphia all had one such firm. Nationwide, no less than fifty firms had 130 or more lawyers.[21] Branch lawyering had become so common that in 1980 it was reported that, between 1974 and 1980, twenty-nine New York law firms had opened offices in Florida.[22] Yet, as parts of the practicing profession moved into new areas, faced new concerns, and expanded their interests nationally and internationally,[23] as bar examiners fumbled with a multistate bar exam,[24] and as leading practitioners looked to the computer—especially LEXIS—to solve its research and office-management problems, the bulk of the profession operated either singly or in small firms doing the kind of practice that differed little from that which had faced practitioners in the 1880s. If Reed had been alive in 1980, he would have found the bar perhaps even more fragmented than he had found it fifty years earlier. Not only were almost half of all lawyers still individual practitioners pursuing a variety of local interests, but also new steps were being taken to insure the existence of other breeds of lawyer. The Legal Services Corporation, for instance, opened up the possibility of demands for legal services undreamed of even by Reginald Heber Smith.

For all this, the Carlin studies of the single practitioner in Chicago and the core practitioner in New York made it clear that the bulk of lawyers were still serving essentially as social workers, or at least business managers, to the middle-class and established communities in general, even if they did show an increasing sense of responsibility toward poorer groups. This scarcely fitted into the Lasswell-McDougal vision of the lawyer as the all-purpose decisionmaker, and even the portrait painted in the Smigel study of the Wall Street lawyer failed fully to reflect this image. It may be that at a few elite schools a number of students might have expected a career that would take them in and out of influential positions in the private sector and government, but such situations were highly atypical.[25] The bar might be strongly differentiated, but the different levels were still following their traditional roles within their groups. Even in California, where specialization of the bar had gone furthest and policymaking might be thought to be at its most potent, the highest degree of specialization came in negligence cases (11.1 percent) and probate and trusts (8.8 percent).[26] The various studies of other local bars during the 1960s confirmed these trends. For instance, in 1968 the primary interest of one-third of the Baltimore bar was negligence actions, and for Maryland lawyers, as a whole, 25 percent specialized in real property.[27] There may, of course, be "policy" issues in "personal injury" cases and land law, but to think of education for the Maryland bar as "training for public policy" was to misunderstand the role of lawyers.[28] Far from being policymakers, the majority of the members of the legal profession were performing their traditional and surprisingly differing roles.

Thus, although the Lasswell-McDougal assault failed to recognize this lack of policy orientation in the careers of American lawyers, it also assumed, incorrectly, that adequate funding would be available to develop legal education along the scholarly lines suggested. In fact, during the previous century, the inherent conflicts in the purposes of legal education had been seriously aggravated by its remarkable underfunding. Even the leading law schools had always had faculty-student ratios that would have been unheard of in any marginally acceptable college and unthinkable in any other graduate or other professional school.[29] This underfunding of legal education was almost certainly attributable to the Langdellian model, for the case method seemed to work as well with two hundred students as it did with twenty;[30] and, in fairness, no system had yet been devised that began to compete with the case method as a means of teaching the basic analytic skill of "thinking like a lawyer." It is possible that Langdell's greatest contribution to legal education was the highly dubious one of convincing all and sundry that legal education was inexpensive. Nothing that Lasswell and McDougal had to offer competed financially.

This Langdellian bequest was slowly appreciated in the post-1945 period. Esther Brown's 1948 study found that "society has long assumed that the needs of a law school are a building, a few instructors of professorial rank, and a small, specialized library."[31] A 1949 survey of the California law schools described the situation as "financial starvation."[32] Albert Harno in his semiofficial history did not hesitate to blame the case method for such parsimony.[33] At the moment the success of the case method resulted in the educational method becoming less attractive to many students and faculty members, its financial aspects led the university to expect the law school, almost alone among university departments or schools, not only to be self-supporting but also in some cases to subsidize other parts of the university. In the post-1945 period, law schools shared only marginally in the largesse of the foundations[34] and almost not at all in the vast infusion of federal funds into higher education.[35] Thus attempts at research programs, specialization, and clinical studies often foundered on the lack of faculty or for other financially motivated reasons. An ability to survive with limited funds by continuing large-class case-method instruction was one of several historical realities that faced Lasswell and McDougal, as it had faced those who came before and those who followed them.

The two authors also appeared to have misjudged the case method and its influence on legal education in ways other than the financial. One serious error was to underrate the advantages of the method. Although the case method had been subjected to various attacks over the years, especially in the post-1945 era, most legal educators and practitioners regarded it as an unparalleled method for training students to be lawyers. For all its failings, it was an impressive teaching device. It gave students a sense of "imaginative activity" that no other teaching techniques provided. Leon Green, as a Realist, continued to argue that it should be used through all three years of law school.[36] Edmund Morgan of Harvard said most emphatically that "it *is* the best method yet discovered or devised to lay the foundation for profitable, effective further study of the law by any method."[37] The ability of the case method to develop analytical skills and legal craftsmanship was widely accepted, even if not readily susceptible of proof. Moreover, it was no doubt suited to the teaching methods and research goals of the bulk of faculty members as well as to the professional goals of most students. In this respect, Lasswell and McDougal were almost certainly wrong to assume that the average student wanted a more scholarly or academic approach. Indeed, even when the case method came under virulent attack by radical faculty members[38] and students[39] in the late 1960s, it was as much for its alleged psychological impact[40] as for its pedagogical failings.

The Lasswell-McDougal approach, then, failed for many reasons, because it incorrectly assessed the nature and goals both of the American bar and of American law schools. In particular, it was overly academic for the context of American legal education. The bulk of the profession not unnaturally saw law schools as training grounds for lawyers; whether one liked it or not, the law school was seen as essentially a trade school.[41] Law students were still more interested in becoming lawyers—even if their career patterns were changing—than in becoming law professors.[42] No matter what the leaders of the academic profession liked to tell themselves, there were law schools—and they probably formed a majority—that did care how their graduates performed in bar examinations.

Far more than Lasswell and McDougal were prepared to admit, the law schools were tied into the bar requirements. It was the organized bar that determined the length of every law school program—even the most prestigious—just as it determined the length of terms and the length of the examination period. Through the bar examination process with its compulsory subjects and recommended courses,[43] the bar controlled and influenced, directly and indirectly, much of the content of legal education. The inability or unwillingness of Lasswell and McDougal to recognize that law schools were too tied to the profession to undertake major changes in the curriculum was not unique. The failure to recognize this basic feature of legal education had underlain all the grand failures in legal education and affected most aspects of legal education in addition to curricular reform.

Legal scholarship was yet another area whose purpose had been confused by the demands placed on the law schools as they both assumed their role as the sole point of entry for practice in the profession and also claimed legitimacy in the scholarly confines of the university. For a hundred years, commentators had been expressing surprise that despite the number of distinguished lawyers teaching in law schools, the output of scholarly literature was small. The collection and regurgitation of doctrine might have seemed scholarly to Langdell; it did not impress those in other disciplines in the twentieth century. As Columbia discovered in the 1920s and Yale found in the 1930s,[44] however, it was difficult to fit a scholarly orientation into an institution designed primarily for teaching purposes. In the law schools, teaching still took place of pride over scholarship,[45] and specialization was still the exception rather than the rule. The academic lawyer was primarily a generalist teacher committed to producing generalist lawyers. The professionalization of scholarship, begun by Charles Eliot, had had relatively little impact on the law schools.[46]

As a result of all this, what legal literature was produced was more likely to be of interest to the practitioner than to the scholar. In addition, even this type of literature became increasingly difficult to write. In contrast to the 1890s—when a limited and comprehensible area of substantive law was taught through case instruction—the law had accumulated such an extensive body of doctrine that a single individual found it difficult to comprehend even a significant fraction of the black-letter law.[47] Since the case method had long since become far more a vehicle for teaching methodology or process than for imparting knowledge of the substantive law,[48] it would be surprising if this mutation had not had a powerful effect on legal scholarship. By the 1950s, most leading members of the academic branch of the profession looked at research problems through the process approach. The high priests of the process school were at Harvard. The leading work was Henry Hart and Albert Sacks' *The Legal Process: Basic Problems in the Making and Application of Law* (1958), which profoundly influenced leading scholars during the 1950s and the 1960s and was especially significant in the way it opened up a semistructural and comprehensible approach to virtually all areas of the law. Like the case method at its best, the process approach merged the professional with the scholarly, or at least, left no clear divergence between them. At its best, the process approach was positively Burkean. Moreover, the approach, although reflecting a resurgence of interest in neutral principles, also led to an extended analysis of the law in action.

The emphasis of law professors on article writing flourished in the 1950s as the number of law reviews grew. Unlike the situation in more scholarly disciplines, at this time books about law (rather than law books) were virtually nonexistent, and publication proved difficult. On the other hand, legal articles in a discipline that did not know the constraints of the refereed journal were in great demand because of the law reviews' need to fill up the front part of their issues with faculty articles; students went through their own form of self-imposed academic legal apprenticeship with their edited comments and notes in the back part of the review. In general, the law review articles of the period—or at least those that were seen as trend setting—took a relatively narrow problem and addressed it doctrinally and in terms of goal-oriented solutions. There was little in the way of underlying theory and less doctrinal conceptualism than might be expected.[49]

This is not to suggest that there was not important literature in the reviews; the 1950s, after all, saw the flowering of the process school and the "forwards" to the *Harvard Law Review* achieved remarkable prestige and impact.[50] Such work was, however, geared primarily to problem solving. The institutional aspect of the process school was especially important to constitutional law,[51] labor law,[52] and criminal law.[53] Coupled with the renewed interest in the social sciences there were significant casebooks in family law as well as criminal law.[54] The research was often first-rate, and the level of debate on specific issues was considerably heightened; but on the spectrum of scholarly approach the work must be classified as eclectic, although the process approach challenged the profession in such a way that the best in the academic seemed relevant to the leaders of the bar.

While the process approach was to remain alive,[55] changes were beginning to appear during the 1960s. While politically that was to be a period during which anarchy increasingly appeared to be the preferred goal of the student population, the decade saw a renewed interest in a conceptualistic approach on the part of scholarly professors. There was some evidence of an increased concern with substantive doctrine, beyond the highly focused area.[56] The most important changes, however, came in grafts from other disciplines. The Realist-influenced casebooks had brought to a fine art the inclusion of the "snippet" from philosophy, sociology, or economics. The change that came over legal scholarship in the 1960s was that the underlying conceptualistic approaches of other disciplines were imported into, and frequently made the basis of, legal analysis, leading to a flurry of neoconceptualism. This sophisticated change was nowhere better illustrated than in Guido Calabresi's work.[57] Using underlying concepts of welfare economics, Calabresi and those who took their inspiration from him began examining torts (and later other substantive areas of the law) with the assumption that although legal doctrines might have become atomistic, unitary economic concepts, at least assumptions or instincts, underlay the reasoning of courts and, to some extent, legislatures.

In crude terms, Calabresi's organizing principle was risk avoidance, but by the 1970s the chic organizing principle, derived from classical economics, was the broader concept of efficiency, which was treated by its adherents as synonymous with the efficient allocation of resources through the operation of the free market. Based on the Law School of the University of Chicago (where Milton Friedman in the economics department of the School of Business was the high priest of market economics), the approach spawned its own journals,[58] and, inspired by Ronald Coase and led by Richard Posner, soon expanded from torts to other fields.[59] For those trained in the rhetoric of Realism and the process school, attacks on the "Chicago School" were easy,[60] but the overall impact of the importing of economic concepts to law was to make respectable once again the unified or monistic approach to law. Classical economics not only rested on the kind of basic assumptions that lawyers had jettisoned with the Realists, but it had about it the monocausal vision of the legal system that had underlain Langdell's work. Neoconceptualism had returned.[61] A new age of faith appeared to be dawning.

To say that the parentage of modern American legal thought is uncertain might be considered a charitable understatement. In the period after 1945, the field of legal theory was open to virtually anyone with the energy to attempt to fill it. The number of disciples of the "Law, Science, and Policy" approach, especially in the less prestigious law schools, was evidence of the need for a faith—and the apparent absence of one. In the more prestigious schools talk about the integration of law and the social sciences was frequently a substitute for rigorous intellectual analysis, at least with respect to legal theory.[62] Not all saw the need for faith or theory. Elegant among this group was Grant Gilmore, one of the most engaging legal thinkers to emerge during the 1960s and 1970s.

Gilmore, building on Llewellyn's view that Realism was not a theory but "merely a methodology,"[63] took the negative aspect of Realism to its nihilistic conclusion.[64] His *Death of Contract* (1974), chronicling the rise and fall of classical contract doctrines, was upsetting both to defenders of a doctrinal or conceptual approach and to the new wave of legal historians.[65] Gilmore's *Ages of American Law* (1977) in some respects shocked these observers even more, for Gilmore cast doubt on the vision, sanctified by generations on right and left, of the wisdom in having the biggest, and inevitably therefore the best, legal system in the world:

> As lawyers we will do well to be on our guard against any suggestion that, through law, our society can be reformed, purified, or saved. The function of law, in a society like our own, is altogether more modest and less apocalyptic. It is to provide a mechanism for the settlement of disputes in the light of broadly conceived principles on whose soundness, it must be assumed, there is general consensus among us. If the assumption is wrong, if there is no consensus, then we are headed for war, civil strife and revolution. . . .
>
> Law reflects but in no sense determines the moral worth of a society. The values of a reasonably just society will reflect themselves in a reasonably just law. The better the society, the less law there will be. In Heaven there will be no law, and the lion will lie down with the lamb. The values of an unjust society will reflect themselves in an unjust law. The worse the society, the worse law there will be. In Hell there will be nothing but law, and due process will be meticulously observed.[66]

If Gilmore's was the nihilistic position, it can certainly be claimed to be a legitimate lineal descendant of the Realist movement. The mainstream of the Realist movement, however, meandered on in a less pessimistic vein. The Realists underlined the procedural ethos of American law and its fragmentary nature. Not only did this position emphasize still more the atomistic nature of such theory as there was underlying the casebook mystique, it increasingly threw serious doubt on the value of the treatise. Although Corbin's massive and influential multivolume study of *Contracts* appeared after World War II, intellectually it belonged to the 1930s. Systematic expositions of substantive law, where they existed, became primarily the province of practitioners or teachers in less distinguished schools,[67] if not the province of faceless lawyers working for the commercial publishers. By the 1950s, it seemed as if the West Publishing Company, Sheppard's Citations, and the Commerce Clearing House Loose Leaf Service had taken over responsibility for recording and systematizing doctrine, while the intellectual elite either concentrated on practice in the law firms or, in the law schools, addressed themselves to articles or casebooks that eschewed underlying conceptual principles. Yet change was to come.

In some ways the most dramatic development, at least in terms of a recommitment to the conceptual and to a more mechanistic view of doctrine, was the increasing fascination during the 1960s with English linguistic philosophy as it applied to law. After an extended period of mediocrity, English jurisprudence was reunited once more with the appreciably more vibrant tradition of English philosophy with the appointment of Herbert Hart to the chair of jurisprudence at Oxford in 1951.[68] At that time, English philosophy was still heavily under the sway of Wittgenstein, who had dominated the field from his base in Cambridge during the 1930s. Hart adapted a modified Wittgensteinian linguistic philosophy to the still powerful Austinian approach of English law, turning the merged approach into a powerful analytic tool for approaching substantive doctrines, while admitting that doctrine was the primary focus, although not the exclusive base, for judicial decisions.[69]

In the early 1970s, Hart was succeeded in the chair of jurisprudence by Ronald Dworkin, an American who had been on the faculty at Yale. In elegant prose Dworkin surprisingly staked out what many regarded as a far narrower position. Although Dworkin's positions were in a constant state of flux, his general approach was to appear to argue that doctrine was all. If rules were not available to decide cases, then some underlying principle was available.[70] Because this approach might well be thought to be even narrower than the formalistic English tradition (or, conversely, savoring of some concept of fundamental or natural law), its arguments might have been expected to be greeted with skepticism by a generation bred on Realist suppositions and prejudices. Nothing could give greater evidence of the change that had come over American law in the 1970s and particularly its search for a new form of faith, than the fact that Dworkin became an important cult-figure.[71] His rule-principle dichotomy influenced leading scholars,[72] and *Taking Rights Seriously* took over as the most widely discussed book in the typical jurisprudence course. Although it is arguable that Dworkin attracted few "disciples," his obvious importance and his willingness to link legal philosophy more clearly with a revived political philosophy underlined the rebirth of neoconceptualism and further underlined the coming of the new age of faith.

As with all other intellectual movements in the law, the immediate impact of most of the approaches described was limited to relatively few schools. Moreover, even at these schools, there was an important counter-weight, a group that took a much more jaundiced view of the legal system. Yet even with these groups the need for a basic faith appeared vital. Led by Roberto Unger and Morton Horwitz at Harvard, the adher-ents of their approach shared a renewed interest in theory, a concern with the social sciences, and a political philosophy that was generally radical or sometimes Marxist. Intellectually, the leader of this group was Unger, whose two major books, *Knowledge and Politics* (1975) and *Law in Modern Society* (1976), set the stage for the general approach. Coming out of a strong continental philosophical tradition, Unger attributed the decline of community to the moment when law became separated from the state and thus began its demise. Reflecting in some respects Charles Reich's 1960s cult work, *The Greening of America*, Unger saw the need for law as itself evidence of the collapse of some mythical period of community.[73]

This "critical" approach underlay Morton Horwitz's *Transformation of American Law, 1780–1820* (1977). As an approach to American law, his theme was that "class bias" and "gross disparities of bargaining power" had come to be hidden behind a facade of "neutral and formal rules"[74] at least by the middle of the nineteenth century.[75] The Unger-Horwitz approach was increasingly attractive to a talented group of rising scholars[76] who formed an organization known as the Conference on Critical Legal Studies.[77] Somewhat like Realism forty years earlier, the conference probably reflected a general sense of intellectual dissatis-faction rather than clearly agreed-on goals or agendas or philosophies. Certainly the conference was more pluralistic than its European counter-parts who were unashamedly Marxist, and the American group was less paralyzed by the Soviet theorists such as Pashukanis than were their English equivalents. The leading members of the conference looked to Weber as their guide,[78] although their work increasingly took on the monocausal tone that characterized their contemporaries in Europe.

Sociologically, it was intriguing that scholars on both left and right sensed the need for some binding faith, conceptual or otherwise. It was not clear, however, how far the exponents of these new types of faith were able to influence curricula. As the bar was increasingly noticing, frustration and confusion had led legal educators to attempt innovation in curricula without changing the basic structure of bar examination-related courses.[79] Electives had sprung up everywhere; by 1970, at all "good" schools there was a veritable smorgasbord of seminars—from linguistic philosophy and African law to theories of decision making and empirical methodology. There were attempts to make offerings more programmatic, as at Yale with its divisional program, but such attempts at innovation seemed doomed to failure. Even if money, lack of interest in scholarship on the part of both the profession and of students preparing for the profession, and the "intellectual schizophrenia" of the legal educators themselves were not enough to deter any would-be reformer, there were other reasons that made fundamental changes in the law school impossible.[80] Perhaps as important as all of these were egalitarianism and entrenchment within law school faculties; like an Oxbridge college, American law schools largely ignored academic ranks (most faculty members were full professors), a process that undoubtedly enhanced independence of thought. Particularly when coupled with tenure at an early age, this security was no doubt one of the reasons why so many able persons were attracted to academic law. Yet such an arrangement did not make for easy change and restructuring, particularly at a time when deans appeared to have declining authority and influence. Walter Gellhorn put it crisply when he said: "We might as well be legal realists about the fact that you as a professor can't tinker very much with what another professor is doing."[81] It was noticeable that law school reform in the 1960s was most obvious at those schools, like the University of Southern California,[82] which had relatively small faculties with only a few tenured members.

There was, in fact, still considerable mystery surrounding the law teaching profession.[83] By the 1980s, law schools were said to be losing their brightest potential professors to the practicing profession because they could not offer attractive salaries to the young professors; yet at the same time there was concern that faculties were stable because the static state of higher education had finally invaded the law school.[84] Law professors began to unionize,[85] although the National Labor Relations Board held that law schools were to be treated as separate bargaining units because of their traditional remoteness from the university at large.[86] At the same moment, it was being dimly perceived that, with the decline in the number of law students, some law schools could expect a rough passage through the 1980s. For some of the less prestigious private schools, even accredited ones, it could be the end of the road.

Such potential changes, however, had led to no high degree of self-examination. Even the core case method had been subject to few empirical studies. In the late 1960s, the Socratic version of the case method had fascinated not only novelists but psychiatrists working in law schools.[87] It was a major cause of hostility among law students[88] and was perhaps most effectively assailed by Duncan Kennedy, then a law student at Yale.[89] Ten years later, by then a law professor at Harvard, Kennedy was reportedly a sympathetic teacher,[90] and in most schools the case method was said to be less rigorous than it once was. Since few have ever admitted to using the case method with all the ferocity that Kingsfield used it in *The Paper Chase*, the meaning of this observation is less than clear, although current research undertaken by the American Bar Foundation as part of its study of legal education may provide more accurate pointers to changes in teaching style.

With the exception of clinical legal education, there was some organic growth in the curriculum—in the areas of the environment and income security, for instance—and there was some "catching up" as middle-level schools added their versions of what were previously the preserve of the elite. The controversies in the conventional area of the curriculum, however, seemed much as before.[91] As Dean Soia Mentschikoff of the University of Miami Law School put it, "as a general position, we really haven't made much progress in 30 years."[92] Faculty members, being scholars, or having pretensions in that direction, had an urge to specialize through depth research; students, the vast majority seeking to be practitioners, sought breadth and practicality. Thus when, with considerable fanfare, Yale announced the Cluster Program, designed to implement Dean Goldstein's commitment to depth research and a sequential curriculum, only one student opted for it. Dean Sacks at Harvard, although credited with opening up the curriculum,[93] was not apparently successful in making the second and third years more intellectually meaningful. The underlying purpose of courses still often remained obscure and the sequential order of courses a mystery.

Indeed, at many of the leading schools during these years, there were forms of internecine warfare between the "practitioners" and the scholars, often cutting in a different way from the battles between the political liberals and conservatives in the faculty. Such a division, for instance, existed during the 1970s at Harvard, Pennsylvania, and Wisconsin. Appointments of deans at some schools revolved around disputes between the "schoolmen" and the Hessian-trainers. At schools such as Berkeley, although there was a reaching out to related disciplines, it seemed clear and understandable that such reaching out was from the center toward the periphery.[94] The basic professional purpose of the law school remained untouched, at the very moment the potential for conflict with the profession seemed greatest. It was an ironic situation.

Just as the law faculties were not enthusiastic about the prospect of returning respectability to clinical studies, so too the proposals for fragmentation of the curriculum and particularly the shortening of the basic law course had met with little enthusiasm. The proposals were probably even less attractive to members of the bar. Although some might sneer at law schools as high-grade schools of rhetoric, teaching by methods other than the casebook was probably not congenial to most law professors whose chief and sometimes only skill was the analytical one associated with the parsing of cases. There was understandable skepticism about venturing into other fields—"depth research" had frequently been an excuse for inexact analysis and sloppy scholarship. After all, law professors, like other mortals, had sometimes mistaken innovation for reform.

Even assuming that there were a greater willingness in the future for changes in legal education, would they be possible? Are students interested in changes other than those that take them into practice sooner? Are law professors interested in any change that might impinge upon their well-known independence? Is there any chance of developing forms of legal scholarship that are meaningful both to the profession and to the university community?[95] Would the profession, having achieved its goal of insuring that all lawyers passed through a graduate law program, be prepared to allow law schools to engage in serious scholarship? Would the new age of faith find broadly accepted philosophies or methodologies? Is there the remotest chance of finding the funds that would allow basic reform of legal education to proceed?

The historian, if he cannot afford to be an optimist, can at least sense the form the battle may take. Students will continue to reiterate the complaints about law schools that have been mouthed with remarkable regularity since the Harvard student survey of the 1930s. Faculty solutions will involve reforms requiring more student research in a period when students are apparently increasingly less interested in things academic, as well as require a faculty-student ratio that would be unthinkable even if universities were not in a financial crisis. To insure historical continuity, there will be demands for a final merging of law and the social sciences, and grand schemes based on the importation of theories and concepts from the other social sciences. In practice, that remarkable and resilient vehicle, the case method, will continue to dominate legal education.

Even more certain is that the debates about the unitary nature of the legal profession, the law schools, and the law—in which no side will concede that that is what the debate is about[96]—will take place between those who have probably never heard of the Reed Report and know little of the recent history of legal education. The fights over curriculum and the balance between the scholarly and professional (or the academic and the practical) will take place between those who know nothing of the battles at Columbia in the 1920s and 1930s and misperceive what the Realists wrought and what the alleged innovations of the 1950s were. The future requirements for admission to practice, oscillating between tougher and nationalized bar exams and a long period at an accredited law school, will be discussed on the assumption that the structure of American legal education dates from time immemorial rather than having been forged by the economic and social conditions of the Great Depression. In this context cyclical "reforms" are inevitable and law may well continue to be the only discipline that does not seem to claim a general theory. Finally, we may be sure that Langdell will continue to be blamed for things he never believed or at least never understood.

NOTES

1. Bergin, "The Law Teacher," 645–46. He continued:

> That this compulsion (I am using the word in as many senses as I lawfully may) exists in today's law schools seems to me plain upon inspection; for there is no fact more visible in our law schools than that teachers with extraordinary scholarly skills are being made to 'pay for their keep' by rule preaching and case parsing. The time they must give over to preparation for the Hessian-trainer roles makes it literally impossible to produce serious works of scholarship. The result is that we have so little authentic scholarship in our law schools that we are lucky not to be driven out of the academic herd.
>
> Almost as serious is the effect of this compulsion on the solid non-scholar Hessian-trainers. Since they are in a university environment (and not the Practicing Law Institute), and since the term 'scholarship' in a university environment is affectively connotative of 'the good,' it is not surprising that the non-scholars are as diluted by their painful attempts to produce works of scholarship as the scholars are by their attempts to teach their students how to be lawyers. As proof of the proposition that non-scholars are driven to produce vast tonnages of trivia each year in the name of scholarship, I refer the reader to that Forest Law of catalogues, The Index to Legal Periodicals.

See also Rutter, "Designing and Teaching the First Degree Law Curriculum," 7.

2. Woodard assimilated secularization to the three stages of legal education. "It has been transformed from a body of 'rules,' taught *ex cathedra* and learned by rote, to a system of 'principles,' searched for and inductively ferreted out of cases, and then to a bundle of skills which are brought to bear upon relevant data, legal or otherwise, in order to formulate public policy." Woodard, "The Limits of Legal Realism," 709.

3. Woodard cataloged various examples. Ibid., 705. For another type of example, see the words of Eugene V. Rostow in *Report of the Dean, Yale Law School, 1963–64* and *1964–65*: "[S]tudents and faculty . . . see law as part of the process of social change. They use law in the interest of improving society." Illogically, the acceptance of this approach to law by radical student groups in the late 1960s was to cause both concern and surprise to many political liberals.

4. Although the phrase is that of an Englishman, Sir Carleton Kemp Allen, professor of jurisprudence at Oxford, the view was more widespread in this country than is often appreciated. The early attacks had been judicial in temper. See Beutel, "Some Implications of Experimental Jurisprudence," 178. Philip Meacham of Iowa accused Realism of being a "jurisprudence of despair" ("The Jurisprudence of Despair," 672); and Morris Cohen warned that the approach "naturally leads to the assumption that what is, is

right" (review of Edward Robinson's *Law and Lawyers,* 22 *Cornell Law Review* 177 [1936]). Increasingly, the critics argued that Realism was an invitation to totalitarianism. See Hall, "Nulla Poena Sine Lege," 189; Bodenheimer, *Jurisprudence,* 316. The most devastating criticism, in terms of the threat of Nazism, was Fuller, *The Law in Quest of Itself,* 4. For an excellent survey of this period and literature, see Purcell, *The Crisis of Democratic Theory,* chap. 9.

5. Lasswell and McDougal, "Legal Education and Public Policy," 203.

6. "Heroic, but random, efforts to integrate 'law' and 'the other social sciences' fail through lack of clarity about *what* is being integrated, and *how* and *for what purpose.*" Ibid., 204.

7. "We submit this basic proposition: if legal education in the contemporary world is adequately to serve the needs of a free and productive commonwealth, it must be conscious, efficient, and systematic *training for policy making.* The proper function of our law schools is, in short, to contribute to the training of policy-makers for the ever more complete achievement of the democratic values that constitute the professed ends of American policy." Ibid., 206.

8. See section entitled: "Existing Curriculum Not Oriented toward Achievement of Democratic Values." Ibid., 232 ff.

9. Professor Macaulay of Wisconsin has noted that "it did not succeed in overturning the establishment." Macaulay, "Law Schools and the World Outside Their Doors," 619. See also Speidel, "A Matter of Mission," 606. Professor McDougal has been cited as expressing his disappointment with the results and impact and suggesting that things have gotten worse rather than better. Mayer, *The Lawyers,* 80–90.

10. For a sympathetic and perceptive treatment, see Moore, "Prolegomenon to the Jurisprudence of Myres McDougal and Harold Lasswell," 662.

11. What Dean Griswold of Harvard described as "a certain tendency towards grandiloquence." Griswold, "Intellect and Spirit," 292.

12. On this, see "Legal Theory and Legal Education," 79 *Yale Law Journal* 1153 (1970). See, especially, ibid., 1175–76.

13. "In our view the democratic values of our society can only be effectively fulfilled if all who have an opportunity to participate significantly in the forming of policy share certain ways of thinking, observing, and managing." Lasswell and McDougal, "Legal Education and Public Policy," 291.

14. "It should need no emphasis that the lawyer is today, even when not himself a 'maker' of policy, the one indispensable adviser of every responsible policy-maker of our society—whether we speak of the head of a government department or agency, of the executive of a corporation or labor union, of the secretary of a trade or other private association, or even of the humble independent enterpriser or professional man. As such an adviser the lawyer, when informing his policy-maker of what he can or cannot *legally* do, is, as policy-makers often complain, in an unassailably strategic position to influence, if not create, policy." Ibid., 208–9.

15. Many, but by no means all. "When all 500 law school graduates in the Class of 1975 from Harvard go into these public interest law firms, when Dewey, Ballantine has to go to Cumberland Law School, when the brain drain becomes so great . . . that finally we can say that we have arrived at a relatively sane deployment of legal manpower where the best legal minds are put on the greatest and most challenging problems of society, . . . then it would be very interesting to see the withering away of these corporate law firms and the assumption of their residual duties by house counsel." Nader, "Law Schools and Law Firms," 1. By 1975, the Harvard Law School class was once again choosing Dewey, Ballantine over public interest law.

16. In 1957, the 468 partners of the twenty largest firms in Wall Street (more than 50 lawyers) were 71 percent from Harvard, Yale, and Columbia law schools. By 1962, there were 543 partners in such firms, but the percentage from those schools was almost the same—71.8 percent. Smigel, *The Wall Street Lawyer*, 39. In Chicago, in firms with more than 25 partners, Carlin calculated that 21 percent had graduated from Harvard, 3 percent from Yale, and 1 percent from Columbia. A further 60 percent went to some other full-time university and 15 percent went to night school. Carlin, *Lawyers on Their Own*, 32–33. At least in the New York study, however, no less than 99 percent of the core lawyers had attended law school and 56 percent had had four years of college. Carlin, *Lawyers' Ethics*, 19. In Carlin's study of individual practitioners in Chicago, 11 percent had never attended college at all, and 54 percent had not graduated from college. Only 1 percent of them had attended an Ivy League law school, 32 percent had graduated from some other full-time schools, and 67 percent had attended a night school. Carlin, *Lawyers on Their Own*, 26, 35. A recent study of 548 Chicago attorneys by Zeman and Rosenblum found that 73 percent of members of large law firms had been to national law schools, as against 22 percent of solo practitioners. American Bar Association, *Law Schools and Professional Education*, 87.
17. Smigel, *Wall Street Lawyers*, 141.
18. See Johnstone and Hopson, *Lawyers and Their Work*, 179–84.
19. Heinz and Laumann, "The Legal Profession," 1111, 1117. In fairness it should be noted that Heinz and Laumann plump more clearly for a single fundamental split in the profession

> between lawyers who represent large organizations (corporations, labor unions or governments) and those who represent individuals or the small businesses controlled by these individuals. These two sorts of law practice are the two hemispheres of the profession. Most lawyers reside exclusively in one hemisphere or the other and seldom, if ever, cross the equator.
>
> The two sectors of the legal profession thus include different lawyers, with different social origins, who were trained at different law schools, serve different sorts of clients, practice in different office environments, are differentially likely to engage in litigation, litigate (if and when they litigate) in different forums, have somewhat different values, associate with different circles of acquaintance, and rest their claims to professionalism on different sorts of social power. . . . Only in the most formal of senses, then, do the two sorts of lawyers constitute one profession. [Heinz and Laumann, *Chicago Lawyers*, chap. 10]

20. In 1970, Shearman and Sterling had been the largest law firm in the nation with 164 lawyers.
21. *National Law Journal*, August 1979.
22. "New York Lawyers Branching Out to Florida," *New York Times*, 23 November 1980, 1, col. 1.
23. "Law Branches Grow Overseas," *New York Times*, 14 September 1979, sec. D., p. 4, col. 1.
24. Eckler, "The Multistate Bar Examination—August, 1974," 125.
25. A study undertaken in 1970 of the career patterns of the 1960 graduating classes of Boston College, Connecticut, Iowa, Pennsylvania, Southern California, and Yale concluded: "In the discussion of educational reforms, it is sometimes forgotten that the bulk of American lawyers are engaged in conveyancing, personal injury, and probate work. Our respondents [elite and 'semi-elite' schools] were less involved in these fields than lawyers generally. They were, however, still strongly engaged in conventional legal

jobs rather than 'policy' oriented roles." Statistics for "present occupation" showed that although 76 percent of the graduates of Boston College were in private practice, only a total of 14 percent were involved in some sort of government (legal or nonlegal) work. The comparable figures for other schools, respectively, were: Connecticut—63 percent, 8 percent; Iowa—57 percent, 9 percent; Pennsylvania—62 percent, 12 percent; U.S.C.—70 percent, 15 percent; and Yale—55 percent, 9 percent. Stevens, "Law Schools and Law Students," 560–62.
26. Stolz, "Training for the Law," 262.
27. Maryland Bar Association, Committee on Economics of Law Practice, *1968 Economic Survey of Maryland Law Practice* 26 (1969). See also a study showing that in Florida, Pennsylvania, and New Jersey, almost 70 percent of lawyers' incomes in the 1960s came from probate, conveyancing, and personal injury work. Florida Bar, *1966 Survey of the Economics of Florida Law Practice.*
28. For an analysis of what Lasswell and McDougal meant by policymaking, see Twining, "Pericles and the Plumber," 413–14.
29. For instance, a faculty-student ratio of one to six was standard for Ph.D. candidates in a good social science department. The best law schools aimed for a ratio of about one to twenty-five, whereas the ABA demanded only one to seventy-five. But even a one to twenty-five ratio, assuming a teaching load for the faculty of five hours a week, and students taking fifteen hours credit a term, presupposed a normal classroom relationship of one to seventy-five students.
30. See Mayer, *The Lawyers*, 83–84. "One striking advantage of the case method, noted by educational administrators, is its adaptability to large classes; indeed, there is an argument to be made for the proposition that the impersonality of the large class is helpful to the student called upon to perform under attack for the first time in his life. 'I prefer a hundred,' says Myres McDougal of Yale. 'I will work for a hundred and put on a good show; I'll go to sleep with ten or twelve. After you've taught a subject to a class of a hundred for two or three years, you can anticipate the questions and their timing. When I started, I was told, pick four or five points and keep coming back to them; find the bright students and play them like a piano. It works.' "
31. Brown, *Lawyers, Law Schools, and the Public Service,* 246.
32. *Legal Education and Admissions to the Bar in California, 1949,* 74.
33. Harno wrote:

> Apprenticeship training was cheap. The transition, from the apprentice system to lecture schools conducted by practitioners, was a natural one, but here again little expense was involved. All that these schools required was a lecturer, a few students, a room for the class, and, perhaps, a few books. . . . [L]egal education has never been able to dispel the widespread impression that it provides a relatively inexpensive type of instruction. . . .
> With the triumph of the case method, legal education accepted the tenet that law was self-contained. And so long as legal education is confined to the study and the teaching of cases, it will be an inexpensive affair. Further, so long as legal research is restricted to the study and analysis of cases, it, too, . . . will be relatively inexpensive. [Harno, *History of Legal Education,* 133–36]

For a study of the economics of law schools in the 1960s, see Nicholson, *The Law Schools of the United States*; and Association of American Law Schools, *Anatomy of Legal Education* (1961), passim.
34. And such as there was went to a very few. Between 1955 and 1966, 60 percent of the $41,000,000 given by foundations to legal education went to five law schools. Ten

schools absorbed 78 percent; 22 percent was distributed among the remaining 150 schools. *AALS Proceedings, 1968*, pt. 1, sec. 2, 51–52. In 1967, just over 1 percent of all foundation-giving went for legal research. Ibid., 53.

35. Ibid., 51–54. For the fiscal year 1966–67, the Yale Law School, with some 600 students, received some $2,709 from all federal government sources and nothing from the state in a total budget of $2,205,122. In the same year, the Yale Medical School, with some 400 students, received $14,336,145 from the federal government and $1,169,971 from the state government out of a total budget of $22,963,488. Part of the federal largesse directed toward medical schools resulted from their close connection with service activities—something the law schools still generally avoided—but much of the support also went for basic research, as it did in the physical sciences generally.

36. "Perhaps the failure to integrate the subject matter of a curriculum as a unit and prepare materials in support accounts for much of the difficulty encountered in maintaining the interest of students in later years of their law school careers. They continued to be treated like first year students. It can be ventured that in this respect the possibilities of the use of case materials have by no means been exhausted." Green, "Advocacy and Case Study," 21.

37. "It gives him [the student] training in the analysis of states of fact and in distinguishing the legally material from the immaterial. It enables him to recognize and state accurately the legal problem involved. . . . It gives him a perception of the kind of argument which appeals to the judicial mind, of the extent to which logical reasoning is checked by practical considerations and judicial experience. . . . It requires him to do some independent thinking and to form his own judgments upon legal questions." Morgan, "The Case Method," 84.

38. See Savoy, "Towards a New Politics of Legal Education," 444. See also Watson, "The Quest for Professional Competence," 93.

39. See Kennedy, "How the Law School Fails," 71.

40. See the Ralph Nader view: "Harvard Law's most enduring contribution to legal education was the mixing of the case method of study with the Socratic method of teaching. . . . These techniques were tailor-made to transform intellectual arrogance into pedagogical systems that tumbled the student into accepting its premises, levels of abstraction and choice of subjects. Law professors take delight in crushing egos in order to acculturate the students to what they call 'legal reasoning' or 'thinking like a lawyer.' The process is a highly sophisticated form of mind control that trades off breadth of vision and factual inquiry for freedom to roam in an intellectual cage." Nader, "Crumbling of the Old Order," 20. William Pincus, president of CLEPR, in arguing the advantages of clinical education, described the psychological impact of law school education (as well as education in general) from a slightly different point of view, noting the fact that "our present prolonged system of higher education, coming on top of lengthy primary and secondary school experience, retards the emotional development of the individual." Cited in Seligman, *The High Citadel*, 161.

41. For the classic statement of this position, see Cantrall, "Law Schools and the Layman," 909.

42. This tone comes through in a useful comment, "Modern Trends in Legal Education," 64 *Columbia Law Review* 710 (1964). The 1970 study of the class of 1960 of various law schools was revealing in this matter. From this class, ten years later, none of the respondents from Boston College had gone into legal education, nor had any at Connecticut or the University of Southern California. At Iowa, only one respondent (or 2 percent) had entered legal education; at Pennsylvania, 3 (or 4 percent) had; and at Yale, 10 (or 8 percent) had. Stevens, "Law Schools and Law Students," 562.

43. For details of these, see National Conference of Bar Examiners. *The Bar Examiners' Handbook*, 132–33.

44. The pressure of practical demands, arrogance about other disciplines, and obsession with practical short-term interests all contributed to make the interaction of law and the social sciences erratic and relatively unfruitful. Harry Kalven, Jr., "The Quest for the Middle Range," in Hazard, ed., *Law in a Changing America*, 56. Lawyers were sometimes hazy about distinguishing between the social sciences and social service. See, for example, Griswold, "Intellect and Spirit," 292. Partly as a result of this, the basic discussions about curricular reform, which Yale and Columbia, among others, encountered fifty or sixty years ago, have been reargued in each succeeding decade, because the discussants have been unaware that the issues have even been discussed before. In terms of research, the wheel has been reinvented with depressing frequency. See Reich, "Towards the Humanistic Study of Law," 1402; Wallace, "Philosophy and the Future of the Law School Curriculum," 24; Haber and Cohen, eds., *The Law School of Tomorrow*.

45. "In the received tradition, law schools are viewed as teaching institutions, whose research activities are essentially incidental." Cavers, "Legal Education in Forward-Looking Perspective," in Hazard, ed., *Law in a Changing America*, 145. A similar view was expressed by Professor Geoffrey Hazard, who served as executive director of the American Bar Foundation in the 1960s:

> Aside from the fact of inadequacy of outside resources, research in legal processes is impeded by the intractability of inside professional conceits in the law school. We are so good at doctrinal analysis that we are resistant to the idea that brilliance of intuition ought in any way to be qualified by going out and finding out what really happens. It is kind of cheating to find facts. And the whole pressure in the law school world is to preserve the integrity of that Socratic process that shows we are all so smart *a priori*. The evidence for this is the low social status that researchers have in law school. In the law schools, such as Columbia, Harvard, Yale, Michigan, Chicago . . . Berkeley—and these are pretty good schools—the research people are all second-class citizens. [U.S. Senate, *Hearings before the Subcommittee on Government Research of the Committee on Government Operations, National Foundation for Social Sciences*, 90th Cong., 1st sess. (1967), 307]

The divergences between at least some of the strands of legal theory were highlighted by Harry Kalven's "slogan for the future"—"let us 'empiricize' jurisprudence and intellectualize fact-finding." Harry Kalven, Jr., "Quest for the Middle Range," in Hazard, ed., *Law in a Changing America*, 56. See also, generally, "Legal Theory and Legal Education," 79 *Yale Law Journal* 1153 (1970).

46. Indeed at elite schools not only did few professors have the research degree of Ph.D., the legal research degree of S.J.D. was looked down upon.

47. Despite this situation the law schools did not show themselves as particularly innovative toward the use of programmed learning for teaching substantive law. Freeman, "Legal Education," 272; O'Donovan, Twining, and Mitchell, "Legal Eagles or Battery Hens: An Examination of Kelso's 'Programmed Introduction to the Study of Law,' " 6; Kelso, "Programming Shows Promise for Training Lawyers," 243.

48. It is arguable that, in recent years, this has been less true. The classical casebook had several cases on a single subject, an ideal basis for teaching methodology or process. The more recent trend toward a single case on one topic may represent more of a return to conceptualism; it certainly makes the teaching of legal method more difficult.

49. White argued that it was more conventional: "Scholarship from the period was narrow

in its focus, modest in its goals, and saturated with the conventional patterns of approved professional reasoning of the time, which stressed careful distinctions between fact situations, explicit attention to logical analysis, and a thorough marshalling of relevant arguments. Case analysis was the nub of an article: the scholar appeared as the balanced voice of reason." White, *Tort Law in America*, 212. White added that "the object of scholarship in the 1950s was less to develop new or original theoretical perspectives in law than to reinforce the versatility of a common professional methodology." Ibid., 213.

50. It was these articles that emphasized the reasoned elaboration approach. See, especially, Louis Jaffé, "Forward to the Supreme Court, 1950 Term," 107; Sacks, "Forward to the Supreme Court, 1953 Term," 96; Henry Hart, "The Supreme Court—1958 Term—Forward," 84. Also significant during this period were Bickel and Wellington, "Legislative Purpose and the Judicial Process," 1; Wechster, "Toward Neutral Principles in Constitutional Law," 1 (the 1959 Holmes Lecture). By the 1960s, the battle had moved on to the dispute over judicial activism and judicial restraint. White, *Patterns of American Legal Thought*, 144–53.

51. See Bickel, *The Least Dangerous Branch*; Bickel, *The Supreme Court and the Idea of Progress*; Black, *The People and the Court*.

52. See Wellington, *Labor and the Legal Process*.

53. See Goldstein, *The Insanity Defense*.

54. Goldstein and Katz, *The Family and the Law*; Goldstein, Dershowitz, and Schwartz, *Criminal Law*.

55. See, for instance, Brest, *Processes of Constitutional Decision-making*; Ely, *Democracy and Distrust*. Although he would see himself in a more philosophical tradition, it is arguable that the process school is most elegantly reflected in the work of Bruce Ackerman, which, although more theoretical than that of the previous generation, steered away from the extreme conceptualism of the late 1970s while retaining a strong problem-solving approach. See Ackerman, *Social Justice in the Liberal State*. The process approach probably explains the attractiveness to lawyers of the post-utilitarian reasoning in Rawls, *A Theory of Justice*.

56. See, for instance, Gilmore and Black, *The Law of Admiralty*; Davis, *Administrative Law*; Gilmore, *Security Interest in Personal Property*; Bittker, *Federal Taxation of Income Estate and Gifts*.

57. See, especially, Calabresi, *The Costs of Accidents*.

58. Both *Law and Economics* and the *Journal of Legal Studies* have been important forces in advancing this general approach. Equally important has been the willingness of proponents of this viewpoint to conduct extensive evangelism. See, for instance, the work of Henry Manne at the University of Rochester, the University of Miami Law School, and, more recently, Emory University Law School. Tibeau, *The University of Miami*, 384.

59. See, especially, Posner, *Economic Analysis of Law*.

60. For criticism of Posner, see, especially, Leff, "Economic Analysis of Law," 451; Dworkin, "Is Wealth a Value?", 191.

61. G. Edward White has traced the impact of the new conceptualism on the leading tort casebook, Keeton and Keeton (which is, incidentally, the lineal descendant of the first torts casebook published by James Barr Ames in 1874):

The 1957 and 1964 editions of the Keeton casebook were striking in their strong emphasis on numerous discrete cases, heavily edited, and in their relative absence of conceptual order or theoretical perspective. The message of those editions was essentially that conveyed by Thurston and Seavey's 1942 edition, which, as noted, abandoned previous subject matter organizations for an unstructured presentation of discrete, but artfully grouped, appellate cases. While the editors of the 1957 and 1964 editions had become more conscious of the "study of the legal process in tort cases" and accordingly presented some cases where courts contrasted their role as lawmakers with that of legislatures, their intent was clearly to teach methodology as much as substantive doctrine and to avoid any explicit theoretical overview of the subject of torts itself. In 1971 a new edition appeared, and the editors announced that they had "substantially reduce[d] the emphasis heretofore given to negligence law and increase[d] the attention focused on alternatives." They referred specifically to "the strong impact of economic considerations on tort doctrines" and the rising interest among legal scholars in "the influence of . . . economic factors" and "the potential usefulness to judges . . . of theories and methods of analysis current among economists." By 1977 their relatively narrow consideration of economic theory as it related to no-fault automobile insurance programs had broadened to a discussion of the "moral, economic and social premises" of compensation systems generally. The discussion referred to choices. . . . Excerpts from works on moral philosophy and economic theory were presented "to identify contrasting perspectives that may help explain influences in tort law beyond those that are explicitly examined in judicial opinions." [White, *Tort Law in America*, 216]

62. There was, however, greater funding for law and the social sciences provided by the Russell Sage Foundation, the Walter E. Meyer Institute, the National Science Foundation, and the American Bar Foundation.
63. Gilmore, *The Ages of American Law*, 138.
64. On Gilmore, see Teachout, "Gilmore's New Book," 229.
65. See, for example, Robert Gordon, Review of *The Death of Contract*, by Grant Gilmore, *Wisconsin Law Review* 1216 (1974); Morton Horwitz, Review of *Death of Contract*, by Grant Gilmore, 42 *University of Chicago Law Review* 787 (1975); Mooney, "The Rise and Fall of Classical Contract Law," 155; Speidel, "An Essay on the Reported Death and Continued Vitality of Contract," 1161.
66. Gilmore, *Ages of American Law*, 109–11. Teachout argues that in the original lectures (the book is based on the Storrs Lectures given at Yale) Gilmore painted an even more nihilistic picture. Teachout, "Gilmore's New Book," 263n.
67. Of course there were exceptions to this. The Harvard faculty continued to contain some outstanding professors who commanded great respect from leading practitioners, while figures like James William Moore at Yale worked away at producing revised editions on his multivolume treatises on *Bankruptcy* and *Federal Practice* as if there had been no Realist "revolution."
68. Twining, "Academic Law and Legal Philosophy," 557.
69. See Hart, *The Concept of Law*. For example, p. 12, "In most important cases there is always a choice."
70. Dworkin, *Taking Rights Seriously*. See, especially, chaps. 2, 3, and 4.
71. Efforts were made by Harvard, Yale, and Princeton to hire Dworkin; he held tenured visiting appointments at NYU and Cornell; at least one distinguished reviewer—Marshall Cohen—called for his appointment to the Supreme Court. Cohen, "He'd Rather Have Rights," 37, and news magazines frequently sought his wisdom about Supreme Court cases. See "Treating People as Equals," *Newsweek*, 5 September 1977, 54.
    Other scholars were skeptical of his work. "Excuse Me," *Legal Times of Washington*,

8 December 1980. For some of the conflicting interpretations of Dworkin's work, cf. Richards, "Taking *Taking Rights Seriously* Seriously," 1265; Griffiths, "Legal Reasoning from the External and the Internal Perspectives," 1124.

72. See Wellington, "Common Law Rules and Constitutional Double Standards," 221.

73. See, especially, Unger, *Law in Modern Society*, chap. 2.

74. See, especially, Horwitz, *Transformation of American Law*, 99, 188, 201.

75. Horwitz's scholarship has been severely attacked. See Simpson, "The Horwitz Thesis and the History of Contract," especially 600: "Through an unsatisfactory and loose use of evidence, he has made a complex, confused story fall into a preordained pattern."

76. See Abel, "Law Books and Books about Law," 175; Kennedy, "Form and Substance in Private Law Adjudication," 1685. For an overview of the approach, see Tushnet, "Post Realist Legal Scholarship," 20. For a political manifesto from one of the group, see Duncan Kennedy, "Utopian Proposal or Law School as a Counter Regemanic Enclave," Harvard Law School, mimeographed (1980).

77. Luxenberg, "Moving toward the Legal Left," 18.

78. Trubek, "Max Weber on Law and the Rise of Capitalism," 720.

79. In 1961, the Curriculum Committee of the AALS undertook the task of projecting what the basic syllabus would be in 1981. It was generally agreed that the first year would consist of contracts, torts, property, procedure, and a course along the lines of legal method. York, "The Law School Curriculum Twenty Years Hence," 160. This conservative projection proved surprisingly accurate.

In 1925, the first year of the Yale Law School called for the teaching of legal method, procedure, contracts, criminal law, equity, property, torts; in 1975, the first semester called for torts (4 units), contracts (4 units), constitutional law (4 units), and procedure (3 units), with criminal law (4 units) and property (4 units) compulsory (normally) in the second semester.

80. This is in addition to Cornford's contribution: "The principle of Unripe Time is that people should not do at the present moment what they think right at that moment, because the moment at which they think it right has not yet arrived." Cornford, *Microcosomographia Academia*, 16.

81. Gellhorn, "Commentary," 538. In 1948, a reviewer said of Esther Brown's proposals: "[N]either law-school deans nor curriculum committees seem to possess that totalitarian authority over the prima donnas who make up the law school faculties, especially those buttressed by permanent tenure, which would be necessary to effectuate such far-reaching changes in the immediate future." See Thomas I. Emerson, Review of *Lawyers, Law Schools, and The Public Service*, by Esther Brown.

82. Mayer, *The Lawyers*, 91–92; Riesman, "Some Observations on Legal Education," 63.

83. There were still allegations of inbreeding among law teachers. Sixty percent of the nation's law teachers at the 160 accredited schools had been produced by 20 schools (Harvard, Yale, Columbia, Michigan, Chicago, NYU, Georgetown, Texas, Virginia, Berkeley, Pennsylvania, Wisconsin, Northwestern, Stanford, Iowa, Illinois, Minnesota, Cornell, Duke, and George Washington). At the 20 most prestigious schools, 90 percent of the faculty were from these 20 schools. Fossum, "Law Professors," 501, 508.

84. An Association of American Law Schools' committee, chaired by Dean Michael Kelly of the University of Maryland, is currently studying this problem.

85. See, for instance, the fight between the University of San Francisco and its law school faculty which sought unionization when all university salaries were frozen during a financial crisis. *San Francisco Chronicle*, 17 August 1973, 18.

86. See, for example, "Fordham University," 193 *National Labor Relations Board* 134 (1971); "Syracuse University," 204 *National Labor Relations Board* 641 (1973). Law

professors had in fact a vested interest in being regarded as a separate bargaining unit. It helped avoid the leveling effect of collective bargaining contracts.

87. See, for example, Stone, "Legal Education on the Couch," 392. According to Stone: "The goal should be to relieve the oppressive atmosphere of the Socratic method by altering the power relationships without compromising the intensity of the intellectual inquiry which, after all is said and done, is the legitimate justification of Socratic teaching." Ibid., 418. For a typical recent study, see Beck and Burns, "Anxiety and Depression in Law Students," 270.

88. See Stevens, "Law Schools and Law Students," 591, 637–45.

89. Kennedy, "How the Law School Fails."

90. See Seligman, *The High Citadel*, 157. For a more general and recent study, see Smith, *Cognitive Styles in Law Schools*.

91. See, for example, Gee and Jackson, *Following the Leader?*, 315; Jackson and Gee, *Bread and Butter?*.

92. AALS Proceedings, 1974, pt. 2, 69.

93. See Seligman, *The High Citadel*, 212.

94. But note the establishment of such important journals as the *Law and Society Review* and the *American Bar Foundation Research Journal*.

95. The former Master of Balliol, in attempting to explain the seriousness with which lawyers treat Sir Edward Coke, may inadvertently have given the answer to the question raised above: "Coke can hardly be left out of an inquiry into the intellectual origins of the English Revolution, yet he presents difficulties. He was a lawyer, not an intellectual. The confusion and self-contradiction in his writings are so great that one is apt to dismiss them, as of no significance for our purposes. Yet the legal historians have no doubt of his importance." Hill, *Intellectual Origins of the Revolution*, 227.

96. A sharp reminder of the ultimate control of law schools by the profession came in the spring of 1970 when the New York Court of Appeals made it clear to New York University Law School that if it curtailed its spring term to protest the invasion of Cambodia and the killings at Kent State, the students at that school would not be qualified to take the New York bar exams. *New York Times*, 13 May 1970, 18, col. 1.

Bibliography

Books and Dissertations

Abbott, Nathan. *The Undergraduate Study of Law*. Denver, 1901.

Abel-Smith, Brian, and Stevens, Robert. *In Search of Justice: Society and the Legal System*. London, 1968.

————. *Lawyers and the Courts: A Sociological Study of the English Legal System, 1750–1965*. London, 1967.

Ackerman, Bruce A. *Social Justice in the Liberal State*. New Haven, 1980.

Ahern, Patrick Henry. *The Catholic University of America, 1887–1896*. Washington, D.C., 1948.

Ames, James Barr. *Lectures on Legal History and Miscellaneous Essays*. Cambridge, Mass., 1913.

Archer, Gleason L. *Building a School*. Boston, 1919.

————. *The Educational Octopus: A Fearless Portrayal of New and Old Events in the Old Bay State, 1906–1915*. Boston, 1915.

————. *The Impossible Task*. Boston, 1926.

————. *Suffolk Law School Systems and the Case Method of Teaching Law*. Boston, 1924.

Arnold, Thurman. *Fair Fights and Foul: A Dissenting Lawyer's Life*. New York, 1965.

————. *The Folklore of Capitalism*. New York, 1937.

Association of American Law Schools. *Select Essays in Anglo-American Legal History*. Edited by Ernst Freund et al. Boston, 1907.

Auerbach, Jerold L. *Unequal Justice: Lawyers and Social Change in Modern America*. New York, 1976.

Baldwin, Joseph G. *The Flush Times of Alabama and Mississippi*. San Francisco, 1899.

Barber, John T. *Missouri Lawyer*. St. Louis, 1949.

Barnes, Thomas G. *Hastings College of Law: The First Century*. San Francisco, 1978.

Benson, Lee. *The Concept of Jacksonian Democracy*. Princeton, 1961.

Beveridge, Albert J. *The Life of John Marshall*. 4 vols. Boston, 1919.

Bickel, Alexander. *The Least Dangerous Branch: The Supreme Court at the Bar of Politics*. Indianapolis, 1962.

————. *The Supreme Court and the Idea of Progress*. New York, 1970.

Bittker, Boris. *Federal Taxation of Income, Estate and Gifts*. Boston, 1981.

Black, Charles L. *The People and the Court: Judicial Review in a Democracy*. New York, 1960.

Black, J., ed. *Radical Lawyers: Their Role in the Movement and the Courts*. New York, 1971.

Blaustein, Albert P., and Porter, Charles O. *The American Lawyer: A Summary of the Survey of the Legal Profession*. Chicago, 1954.

Bledstein, Burton J. *The Culture of Professionalism: The Middle Class and the Development of Higher Education in America*. New York, 1976.

Bloom, Murray T. *The Trouble with Lawyers*. New York, 1968.

Bloomfield, Maxwell. *American Lawyers in a Changing Society, 1776–1876*. Cambridge, Mass., 1976.

Bodenheimer, Edgar. *Jurisprudence*. Cambridge, Mass., 1962.

Bok, Derek, ed. "Issues in Legal Education." Mimeographed. Cambridge, Mass., 1970.

Boorstin, Daniel. *The Americans*. Vol. 3, *The National Experience*. New York, 1965.

Bouseman, J. "The Pulled Away College: A Study of the Separation of Colleges from the Young Men's Christian Association." Ph.D. dissertation, University of Chicago, 1970.

Bowen, Claude G. *Beveridge and the Progressive Era*. New York, 1932.

Bowen, William G. *Economics of Major Private Universities*. New York, 1968.

Brackenridge, H. M. *Recollections of Persons and Places in the West*. Philadelphia, 1834.

Brenner, James E. *Bar Examinations and Requirements for Admission to the Bar*. Chicago, 1952.

Brest, Paul. *Processes of Constitutional Decision-making*. Boston, 1975.

Brown, Elizabeth G., with Blume, William W. *Legal Education at Michigan, 1859–1959*. Ann Arbor, 1959.

Brown, Esther L. *Lawyers, Law Schools, and the Public Service*. New York, 1948.

_____. *Lawyers and the Promotion of Justice*. New York, 1938.

Brown, Ralph S. *Loyalty and Security*. New Haven, 1958.

Bruce, P. A. *History of the University of Virginia*. Vol. 2. Charlottesville, 1922.

Bryce, James. *The American Commonwealth*. 3d ed. London, 1895.

Buck, Paul. *Social Sciences at Harvard, 1860–1920: From Inculcation to the Open Mind*. Cambridge, Mass., 1965.

Butler, Benjamin F. *Plan for the Organization of a Law Faculty in the University of the City of New York*. New York, 1835.

Calabresi, Guido. *The Costs of Accidents: A Legal and Economic Analysis*. New Haven, 1970.

Calhoun, Daniel H. *Professional Lives in America: Structure and Aspiration*. Cambridge, Mass., 1965.

Cardozo, Benjamin. *The Growth of the Law*. New Haven, 1927.

_____. *The Nature of the Judicial Process*. New Haven, 1922.

Carlin, Jerome. *Lawyers' Ethics: A Survey of the New York City Bar*. New York, 1966.

_____. *Lawyers on Their Own: A Study of Individual Practitioners in Chicago*. New Brunswick, N.J., 1962.

Chan, F. H. *Lemuel Shaw*. Boston, 1918.

Christensen, Barlow F. *Specialization*. Chicago, 1967.

Chroust, Anton Herman. *The Rise of the Legal Profession in America*. Vol. 2. Norman, 1965.

Clark, Charles E. *Real Convenants and Other Interests Which "Run with Land."* Chicago, 1929.

_____, and Shulman, Harry. *A Study of Law Administration in Connecticut: A Report of an Investigation of the Activities of Certain Trial Courts of the State*. New Haven, 1937.

Clary, William W. *History of the Law Firm of O'Melveny & Myers*. Vol. 1. Los Angeles, 1966.

Cochrane, Rexmond C. *Measures for Progress: A History of the National Bureau of Standards*. Washington, D.C., 1966.

Cohen, Morris R. *American Thought: A Critical Sketch*. Glencoe, 1954.

Cornford, Francis M. *Microcosomographia Academia: Being a Guide for the Young Academic Politician*. Cambridge, England, 1908.

Cover, Robert M. *Justice Accused: Anti-Slavery and the Judicial Process.* New Haven, 1975.
Cramer, C. H. *The Law School at Case Western Reserve University: A History, 1892–1977.* Cleveland, 1977.
Crick, Bernard. *The American Science of Politics: Its Origins and Conditions.* Berkeley, 1960.
Cross, Alfred Rupert. *Precedent in English Law.* Oxford, 1961.
Curtis, Merle, and Carstensen, Vernon. *The University of Wisconsin: A History, 1848–1925.* Vol. 1. Madison, 1949.
Dabney, Lillian G. "History of Schools for Negroes in the District of Columbia, 1807–1947." Ph.D. dissertation, Catholic University, 1949.
Davis, Kenneth. *Administrative Law.* 1951. 2d ed. St. Paul, 1958.
Davis, William E. *Glory Colorado!: A History of the University of Colorado, 1858–1963.* Boulder, 1965.
Dawson, John P. *The Oracles of the Law.* Ann Arbor, 1968.
Dean, Arthur H. *William Nelson Cromwell.* New York, 1957.
Douglas, William O. *Go East, Young Man.* New York, 1974.
Durkin, Joseph T., S.J. *Georgetown University: The Middle Years, 1840–1900.* Washington, D.C., 1963.
Dwight, Timothy. *Travels in New England and New York.* Vol. 4. New Haven, 1821.
Dworkin, Ronald. *Taking Rights Seriously.* Cambridge, Mass., 1977.
Earle, Walter K. *Mr. Shearman and Mr. Sterling and How They Grew.* New Haven, 1963.
Eliot, Charles W. *A Late Harvest.* Boston, 1924.
Ellsworth, Frank. *Law on the Midway: The Founding of the University of Chicago Law School.* Chicago, 1977.
Ely, John. *Democracy and Distrust: A Theory of Judicial Review.* Cambridge, Mass., 1980.
English, William F. *The Pioneer Lawyer and Jurist in Missouri.* Columbia, 1947.
Epstein, Sandra. "Law at Berkeley: The History of Boalt Hall." Ph.D. dissertation, University of California, Berkeley, 1979.
Ferrier, William W. *Origin and Development of the University of California.* Berkeley, 1930.
Fisher, Samuel H. *Litchfield Law School, 1774–1833: Biographical Catalogue of Students.* New Haven, 1946.
Fiske, John. *Outline of Cosmic Philosophy: Based on the Doctrine of Evolution with Criticism of the Positive Philosophy.* Vol. 1. Boston, 1874.
Flexner, Abraham. *Medical Education in the United States and Canada.* New York, 1910.
Frank, Jerome. *Courts on Trial.* Princeton, 1949.
French, John. *A History of the University Founded by Johns Hopkins.* Baltimore, 1960.
Friedman, Lawrence M. *A History of American Law.* New York, 1973.
Friedman, Milton. *Capitalism and Freedom.* Chicago, 1962.
Fuller, Lon L. *The Law in Quest of Itself.* Chicago, 1940.
Furniss, Edgar S. *The Graduate School of Yale: A Brief History.* New Haven, 1965.
Galpin, W. Freeman. *Syracuse University.* Syracuse, 1960.
Gawalt, Gerard W. *The Promise of Power: The Emergence of the Legal Profession in Massachusetts, 1760–1820.* Westport, 1979.
Gee, E. Gordon, and Jackson, Donald W. *Following the Leader?: The Unexamined Consensus in Law School Curricula.* New York, 1975.
Gellhorn, Walter. *Individual Freedom and Governmental Restraints.* Baton Rouge, 1956.
Gest, John Marshall. *Legal Education in Philadelphia Fifty Years Ago.* Philadelphia, 1929.

Gilb, Corinne L. *Hidden Hierarchies*. New York, 1966.
_____. "Self-Regulating Professions and the Public Welfare: A Case Study of the California State Bar." Ph.D. dissertation, Radcliffe College, 1956.
Gilmore, Grant. *The Ages of American Law*. New Haven, 1977.
_____. *Security Interests in Personal Property*. Boston, 1965.
_____, and Black, Charles. *The Law of Admiralty*. 1957. 2d ed. Brooklyn, 1977.
Gittinger, Roy. *The University of Oklahoma, 1892–1942*. Norman, 1942.
Goebel, Julius, ed. *A History of the School of Law, Columbia University*. New York, 1955.
Goetsch, Charles. *Essays on Simeon E. Baldwin*. West Hartford, 1981.
Goldman, Marion S. *A Portrait of the Black Attorney in Chicago*. Chicago, 1972.
Goldstein, Abraham S. *The Insanity Defense*. New Haven, 1967.
Goldstein, Joseph; Dershowitz, Alan M.; and Schwartz, Richard D. *Criminal Law: Theory and Process*. New York, 1974.
Goldstein, Joseph, and Katz, Jay. *The Family and the Law: Problems for Decision in the Family Process*. New York, 1965.
Goodhart, Arthur L. *Essays in Jurisprudence and the Common Law*. Cambridge, England, 1931.
Green, Leon. *The Judicial Process in Tort Cases*. St. Paul, 1931.
Green, Mark J. *The Other Government: The Unseen Power of Washington Lawyers*. New York, 1975.
_____, ed. *With Justice for Some: An Indictment of the Law by Young Advocates*. Boston, 1970.
Haber, David, and Cohen, Julius, eds. *The Law School of Tomorrow*. New Brunswick, N.J., 1968.
Hadley, Morris. *Arthur Twining Hadley*. New Haven, 1948.
Haldeman, Harold W., Jr., and Goetsch, Charles. *A History of the First One Hundred Years of the Connecticut Bar Association, 1875–1975*. Hartford, 1974.
Hamlin, Paul M. *Legal Education in Colonial New York*. New York, 1939.
Handlin, Oscar. *Boston's Immigrants, 1790–1880*. Cambridge, Mass., 1959.
Harbaugh, William H. *Lawyer's Lawyer: The Life of John W. Davis*. New York, 1973.
Harno, Albert J. *Legal Education in the United States*. San Francisco, 1953.
Harris, Barbara. *Beyond Her Sphere: Women and the Professions in American History*. Westport, 1978.
Hart, Herbert L. A. *The Concept of Law*. Oxford, 1961.
Harvard Law School Association. *Centennial History of the Harvard Law School, 1817–1917*. Boston, 1918.
Haskell, T. *The Emergence of Professional Social Science*. Urbana, 1977.
Hastings College of Law. *Golden Jubilee Book, 1878–1928*. San Francisco, 1928.
Hathaway, Grace. *Fate Rides a Tortoise: A Biography of Ellen Spencer Mussey*. Philadelphia, 1937.
Hazard, Geoffrey C., Jr. *Ethics in the Practice of Law*. New Haven, 1978.
_____, ed. *Law in a Changing America*. Englewood Cliffs, N.J., 1968.
Heinz, John P., and Laumann, Edward O. *Chicago Lawyers: The Professions of the Bar*. Chicago, 1982.
Herman, Beaumont A. *Western New England College: A Calling to Fulfill*. Springfield, Mass., 1980.
Heuston, Robert F. V. *Lives of the Lord Chancellors, 1885–1940*. Oxford, 1964.
Hicks, Frederick C. *Yale Law School: The Founders and the Founders Collection*. New Haven, 1935.

————. *Yale Law School: From the Founders to Dutton, 1845–1869.* New Haven, 1936.
————. *Yale Law School: 1869–1894.* New Haven, 1937.
————. *Yale Law School: 1895–1915, Twenty Years of Hendrie Hall.* New Haven, 1938.
Higham, John, with Kreger, Leonard, and Gilbert, Felix. *History.* New York, 1965.
Hill, Christopher. *Intellectual Origins of the English Revolution.* Oxford, 1965.
Hoffman, David. *A Course of Legal Study.* Baltimore, 1836.
Hofstadter, Richard, and Smith, Wilson, eds. *American Higher Education: A Documentary History.* 2 vols. New York, 1961.
Hogan, Peter E. *The Catholic University of America, 1896–1903.* Washington, D.C., 1949.
Hohfeld, Wesley N. *Fundamental Legal Conceptions as Applied in Judicial Reasoning.* Edited by Walter Wheeler Cook. New Haven, 1923.
Holmes, Oliver Wendell. *The Common Law.* Boston, 1881.
Honnold, John. *The Life of the Law.* New York, 1964.
Hopkins, C. *The History of the Y.M.C.A. in North America.* New York, 1951.
Horton, John T. *James Kent: A Study in Conservatism.* New York, 1939.
Horwitz, Morton J. *The Transformation of American Law, 1780–1860.* Cambridge, Mass., 1977.
Howe, Mark DeWolfe. *Justice Oliver Wendell Holmes.* Cambridge, Mass. Vol. 1, 1957. Vol. 2, 1963.
————, ed. *The Correspondence of Mr. Justice Holmes and Harold J. Laski.* 2 vols. London, 1953.
————. *The Correspondence of Mr. Justice Holmes and Sir Frederick Pollock, 1874–1932.* London, 1961.
Hurst, James Willard. *The Growth of American Law: The Law Makers.* Boston, 1950.
————. *Law and Conditions of Freedom in the Nineteenth-Century United States.* Madison, 1956.
————. *Law and Economic Growth: The Legal History of the Lumber Industry in Wisconsin, 1836–1915.* Cambridge, Mass., 1964.
Hutchins, R. "Birth and Development of the Salmon P. Chase College School of Law within the Structural Organization of the Y.M.C.A." Ph.D. dissertation, University of Ottawa, 1960.
Jackson, Donald W., and Gee, E. Gordon. *Bread and Butter?: Electives in American Legal Education.* New York, 1975.
Jackson, Frederick H. *Simeon Eben Baldwin: Lawyer, Social Scientist, Statesman.* New York, 1955.
James, Henry. *Charles W. Eliot.* Vol. 1. London, 1930.
Jefferson, Thomas. *Writings of Thomas Jefferson.* Edited by Thomas A. Lipscombe. Vol. 1. New York, 1903.
Jessup, Philip C. *Elihu Root.* Vol. 1. Hamden, 1938.
Johnson, William R. *Schooled Lawyers: A Study in the Clash of Professional Cultures.* New York, 1978.
Johnstone, Quintin, and Hopson, Dan. *Lawyers and Their Work.* Indianapolis, 1967.
Kamenka, Eugene, et al., eds. *Law and Society: The Crisis in Legal Ideals.* London, 1978.
Kayser, Elmer Louis. *Bricks Without Straw: The Evolution of George Washington University.* New York, 1970.
Keener, William A. *A Selection of Cases on the Law of Quasi Contracts.* Cambridge, Mass., 1888–89.
Kelso, Charles, ed. *Study of Part-Time Legal Education.* Washington, D.C., 1972.
Kirkwood, Marion, and Owens, William. "A Brief History of the Stanford Law School."

Mimeographed. Stanford University, 1961.
Kitch, Edmund W., ed. *Clinical Education and the Law School of the Future*. Chicago, 1969.
Kucklich, Bruce. *The Rise of American Philosophy*. Cambridge, Mass., 1977.
Langdell, Christopher Columbus. *A Selection of Cases on the Law of Contracts*. 1871. 2d ed. Boston, 1879.
Larson, Magali. *The Rise of Professionalism*. Berkeley, 1977.
Laski, Harold J. *The American Democracy: A Commentary and Interpretation*. New York, 1948.
Lee, Edward T. *The Study of Law and Proper Preparation*. Chicago, 1935.
Leonard, Walter J. *Black Lawyers: Training and Results, Then and Now*. New York, 1977.
Levy, Leonard W. *The Law of the Commonwealth and Chief Justice Shaw*. Cambridge, Mass., 1957.
Llewellyn, Karl N. *The Bramble Bush*. New York, 1930.
————. *The Common Law Tradition: Deciding Appeals*. Boston, 1960.
————, and Hoebel, E. Adamson. *The Cheyenne Way: Conflict and Case Law in Primitive Jurisprudence*. Norman, 1941.
McDougal, Myres S., and Haber, David. *Property, Wealth, Land: Allocation, Planning, and Development*. Charlottesville, 1948.
McGloin, John B., S.J. *Jesuits by the Golden Gate*. San Francisco, 1972.
McGrave, Reginald C. *The University of Cincinnati: A Success Story in Urban Higher Education*. Cincinnati, 1963.
McKevitt, Gerald, S.J. *The University of Santa Clara: A History, 1851–1977*. Santa Clara, 1979.
McKown, Dave R. *The Dean: The Life of Julien C. Monnet*. Norman, 1972.
Marshall, Leon C. *Business Administration*. Chicago, 1921.
Martin, George. *Causes and Conflicts; The Centennial History of the Association of the Bar of the City of New York, 1870–1970*. Boston, 1970.
Mason, Alpheus T. *Brandeis: A Free Man's Life*. New York, 1946.
————. *The Brandeis Way*. Princeton, 1938.
Massey, Robert V., Jr. *Dechert, Price and Rhoads: A Law Firm Centennial, 1975*. Lancaster, 1975.
Mayer, Martin. *The Lawyers*. New York, 1967.
Mays, David J. *The Pursuit of Excellence: A History of the University of Richmond Law School*. Richmond, 1970.
Meyers, Marvin. *The Jacksonian Persuasion: Politics and Beliefs*. Stanford, 1957.
Miller, Perry. *The Legal Mind in America: From Independence to the Civil War*. Garden City, 1962.
————. *The Life of the Mind in America: From the Revolution to the Civil War*. New York, 1965.
Mills, C. Wright. *Sociology and Pragmatism: The Higher Learning in America*. New York, 1966.
Mitchell, J. Pearce. *Stanford University, 1916–1941*. Stanford, 1958.
Montana State University. *Dedication and History: School of Law*. Missoula, 1961.
Moore, Philip S. *A Century of Law at Notre Dame*. South Bend, 1969.
Morais, Herbert M. *The History of the Negro in Medicine*. New York, 1967.
Morison, Samuel Eliot. *Three Centuries of Harvard, 1636–1936*. Cambridge, Mass., 1936.
Nader, Ralph, and Green, Mark, eds. *Verdicts on Lawyers*. New York, 1976.
Nelson, William E. *Americanization of the Common Law: The Impact of Legal Change on Massachusetts Society, 1760–1830*. Cambridge, Mass., 1975.

Nicholson, Lowell S. *The Law Schools of the United States*. Chicago, 1958.
O'Connor, Michael J. L. *Origins of Academic Economics in the United States*. New York, 1944.
Odum, Howard W. *American Sociology: The Story of Sociology in the United States through 1950*. New York, 1951.
Oliphant, Herman. *Summary of the Studies on Legal Education by the Faculty of Law of Columbia University*. New York, 1928.
Osborn, John J., Jr. *The Paper Chase*. Boston, 1971.
O'Toole, J., Jr. "Legal Manpower Supply and Demand in California." Xeroxed report. Sacramento, 1972.
Packer, Herbert, and Ehrlich, Thomas. *New Directions in Legal Education*. New York, 1972.
Parsons, Theophilus. *Law of Contracts*. 3d ed. Boston, 1857.
———. *Memoir of Theophilus Parsons*. Boston, 1859.
Partigan, B. Peter. *The Market for Lawyers: The Determinants of the Demand and Supply of Lawyers*. Washington, D.C., 1976.
Patterson, Edwin W. *Jurisprudence: Men and Ideas of the Law*. Brooklyn, 1953.
Pedersen, Gilbert J. *The Buffalo Law School: A History, 1887–1962*. Buffalo, 1962.
Pepper, George Wharton. *Philadelphia Lawyer*. Philadelphia, 1944.
Pierson, George Wilson. *Yale: College and University, 1871–1937*. 2 vols. Vol. 1, *Yale College, 1871–1921*. New Haven, 1952; Vol. 2, *Yale: The University College, 1921–1937*. New Haven, 1955.
Pink, Louis, and Delmage, Rutherford. *Candle in the Wilderness: A Centennial History of the St. Lawrence University, 1856–1956*. New York, 1957.
Porter, Earl W. *Trinity and Duke, 1892–1924: The Foundations of Duke University*. Durham, N.C., 1964.
Posner, Richard A. *Economic Analysis of Law*. Boston, 1972.
Purcell, Edward A., Jr. *The Crisis of Democratic Theory*. Lexington, 1973.
Rahl, James, and Schwerin, Kurt. *Northwestern University School of Law: A Short History*. Chicago, 1960.
Rawls, John. *A Theory of Justice*. Cambridge, Mass., 1971.
Redlich, Josef. *The Common Law and the Case Method in American University Law Schools*. New York, 1914.
Reed, Alfred Z. *Present-Day Law Schools in the United States and Canada*. New York, 1928.
———. *Training for the Public Profession of the Law: Historical Development and Principal Contemporary Problems of Legal Education in the United States with Some Account of Conditions in England and Canada*. New York, 1921.
Reed, G. I., ed. *Bench and Bar of Ohio*. Chicago, 1897.
Reed, John P. *Chief Justice: The Judicial World of Charles Doe*. Cambridge, Mass., 1967.
Reppy, Alison, ed. *David Dudley Field: Centennial Essays*. New York, 1949.
Ritchie, John. *The First Hundred Years: A Short History of the School of Law of the University of Virginia for the Period 1826–1926*. Charlottesville, 1978.
Roalfe, William. *John Henry Wigmore*. Evanston, 1977.
Roback, A. A. *History of American Psychology*. New York, 1952.
Robinson, Edward. *Law and Lawyers*. New Haven, 1935.
Robinson, William. *A Study of Legal Education*. New York, 1895.
Rosenberg, J. Mitchell. *Jerome Frank: Jurist and Philosopher*. New York, 1970.
Rudolph, Frederick. *The American College and University*. New York, 1962.
Rumble, Wilfred E., Jr. *American Legal Realism*. Ithaca, 1968.

Sack, Saul. *History of Higher Education in Pennsylvania.* Harrisburg, 1963.

Savage, Howard J. *Fruit of an Impulse: Forty-five Years of the Carnegie Foundation, 1905–1950.* New York, 1953.

Sayre, Paul L. *The Life of Roscoe Pound.* Iowa City, 1948.

Schlesinger, Arthur M., Jr. *The Age of Jackson.* New York, 1946.

Seligman, Joel. *The High Citadel: The Influence of the Harvard Law School.* Boston, 1978.

Shaw, George Bernard. *The Doctor's Dilemma.* London, 1909.

Sherman, Charles P. *Academic Adventures: A Law School Professor's Recollections and Observations.* New Haven, 1944.

Siegel, Edward. *How to Avoid Lawyers.* New York, 1969.

Smigel, Erwin O. *The Wall Street Lawyer: Professional Organization Man?* New York, 1964.

Smith, Alan McKinley. "Virginia Lawyers, 1680–1776: The Birth of An American Profession." Ph.D. dissertation, Johns Hopkins University, 1976.

Smith, Alfred G. *Cognitive Styles in Law Schools.* Austin, 1979.

Smith, Reginald Heber. *Justice and the Poor.* New York, 1919.

Stephenson, Nathaniel W. *An Autobiography of Abraham Lincoln.* Indianapolis, 1926.

Stevens, Rosemary A. *American Medicine and the Public Interest.* New Haven, 1971.

Stevens, Robert. *Law and Politics: The House of Lords as a Judicial Body, 1800–1976.* Chapel Hill, 1978.

Stone, Harlan Fiske. *Law and Its Administration.* New York, 1915.

Storr, Richard J. *Harper's University.* Chicago, 1966.

Story, Joseph. *Miscellaneous Writings.* Edited by William W. Story. New York, 1852.

Strong, Theron G. *Joseph H. Choate.* New York, 1917.

Sullivan and Cromwell: A Century at Law, 1879–1979. New York, 1979.

Sutherland, Arthur E. *The Law at Harvard: A History of Ideas and Men, 1817–1967.* Cambridge, Mass., 1967.

Swaine, Robert T. *The Cravath Firm and Its Predecessors, 1819–1948.* New York, 1948.

Swords, Peter DeL., and Walwer, Frank K. *The Costs and Resources of Legal Education: A Study of the Management of Educational Resources.* New York, 1974.

Taft, Henry W. *A Century and a Half at the New York Bar: Being the Annals of a Law Firm and Sketches of Its Members with Brief References to Collateral Events of Historical Interest.* New York, 1938.

Tibeau, Charlton, W. *The University of Miami: A Golden Anniversary History, 1926–1976.* Coral Gables, 1976.

Tinnelly, Joseph T. *Part-time Legal Education: A Study of the Problems of Evening Law Schools.* Brooklyn, 1957.

Tocqueville, Alexis de. *Democracy in America.* Edited by Phillips Bradley. New York, 1956.

Trout, Charles H. *Boston, the Great Depression and the New Deal.* New York, 1977.

Tugwell, R. G. *The Brains Trust.* New York, 1968.

Turow, Scott. *One-L.* New York, 1977.

Twining, William. *Karl Llewellyn and the Realist Movement.* London, 1973.

Unger, Roberto. *Law in Modern Society: Toward a Criticism of Social Theory.* New York, 1976.

University of Southern California. *Dedication Ceremonies: School of Law Building.* Los Angeles, 1926.

Van Schaak, Henry C. *The Life of Peter Van Schaak.* New York, 1842.

Veblen, Thorstein. *Higher Learning in America.* New York, 1918.

Veysey, Lawrence. *Emergence of the American University.* Chicago, 1965.

Walsh, Mary Roth. *"Doctors Wanted: No Women Need Apply."* New Haven, 1977.
Wambaugh, Eugene. *The Study of Cases.* 2d ed. Boston, 1894.
Ware, Gilbert. *From the Black Bar: Voices for Equal Justice.* New York, 1976.
Warren, Charles. *A History of the American Bar.* Vol. 1. Boston, 1911.
————. *History of the Harvard Law School and of Early Legal Conditions in America.* New York, 1908.
Warren, Edward. *Spartan Education.* Boston, 1942.
Weber, Max. *Max Weber on Law in Economy and Society.* Translated and edited by Max Rheinstein and Edward Shils. Cambridge, Mass., 1954.
Weinerstein, Bruce, and Green, Mark, eds. *With Justice for Some: An Indictment of the Law by Young Advocates.* New York, 1970.
Wellington, Harry H. *Labor and the Legal Process.* New Haven, 1968.
Wertenbaker, Thomas Jefferson. *Princeton, 1746–1896.* Princeton, 1946.
White, G. Edward. *Patterns of American Legal Thought.* Indianapolis, 1978.
————. *Tort Law in America: An Intellectual History.* New York, 1980.
White, Morton. *Social Thought in America: The Revolt against Formalism.* Boston, 1957.
Wigdor, David. *Roscoe Pound: Philosopher of Law.* Westport, 1974.
Williams, T. Harry. *Huey Long.* New York, 1969.
Williston, Samuel. *Life and Law.* Boston, 1940.
Wilson, Woodrow. *The Papers of Woodrow Wilson.* Edited by Arthur Link et al. Vols. 2 and 3. Princeton, 1966, 1972.
Wylie, T. *Indiana University, 1820–1890.* Indianapolis, 1890.
Zehale, Richard H. *Specialization in the Legal Profession: An Analysis of Current Proposals.* Chicago, 1975.

Articles

Abel, Richard. "Law Books and Books about Law." 26 *Stanford Law Review* 175 (1973).
Agate, Carol. "Legal Advertising and the Public Interest." 50 *Los Angeles Bar Bulletin* 209 (1975).
Allen, Charles Claffin. "The St. Louis Law School." 1 *Green Bag* 283 (1889).
Allen, Francis A. "The Prospect of University Law Training." 29 *Journal of Legal Education* 127 (1978).
Allen, Richard B. "Do Fee Schedules Violate Antitrust Law?" 61 *American Bar Association Journal* 565 (1975).
Amstary, A. E. "The Term of Study of the Law Student." 10 *Chicago Legal News* 354 (1878).
Anderson, Charles. "Black Lawyers in the 20 Largest Firms: It's Better Than Before and Worse Than Ever." *Juris Doctor*, January 1973, 6.
Arant, Herschell. "Survey of Legal Education in the South." 15 *Tennessee Law Review* 179 (1938).
Arnold, Mark R. "And Finally 342 Days Later . . . " *Juris Doctor*, September 1975, 32.
Arnold, Thurman. "The Restatement of the Law of Trusts." 31 *Columbia Law Review* 800 (1931).
Askin, Frank. "The Case for Compensatory Treatment." 24 *Rutgers Law Review* 65 (1970).
Auerbach, Jerold S. "Born to an Era of Insecurity: Career Patterns of Law Review Editors, 1918–1941." 17 *American Journal of Legal History* 12 (1973).

_____. "The Walls Came Tumblin' Down." *Juris Doctor*, January 1976, 33.
_____. "What Has Teaching of Law to Do With Justice? 53 *New York University Law Review* 457 (1978).
Babb, James E. "Union College of Law, Chicago." 1 *Green Bag* 330 (1889).
Bachelder, George S. "Christopher C. Langdell." 18 *Green Bag* 440 (1906).
Baird, Leonard L. "A Survey of the Relevance of Legal Training to Law School Graduates." 29 *Journal of Legal Education* 264 (1978).
Baker, Valerie. "Bar Restrictions on Dissemination of Information about Legal Services." 22 *University of California Los Angeles Law Review* 483 (1974).
Baldwin, Simeon E. "Education for the Bar in the United States." 9 *American Political Science Review* 437 (1915).
_____. "The Readjustments of the Collegiate to the Professional Course." 8 *Yale Law Journal* 1 (1898).
_____. "The Recitation System." 2 *Columbia Jurist* 1 (1885).
_____. "The Study of Elementary Law: The Proper Beginning of a Legal Education." 13 *Yale Law Journal* 1 (1903).
Ballantine, Henry. "Adapting the Case Book to the Needs of Professional Training." 2 *American Law School Review* 135 (1908).
Barnes, Janette. "Women and Entrance to the Legal Profession." 23 *Journal of Legal Education* 276 (1971).
Barnhizer, David. "Clinical Education at the Crossroads: The Need for Direction." 1977 *Brigham Young Law Review* 1025.
Barry, Kenneth H., and Connelly, Patricia A. "Research on Law Students: An Annotated Bibliography." 1978 *American Bar Foundation Research Journal* 751.
Bartlett, Alfred L. "Report of the Committee of the Section on Legal Education on Co-operation between the Law Schools and the Bar." 9 *American Law School Review* 32 (1938).
Beale, Joseph H. "The Law School as Professor Redlich Saw It." 23 *Harvard Graduates' Magazine* 617 (1915).
_____. "Professor Langdell—His Later Teaching Days." 20 *Harvard Law Review* 9 (1906).
Beck, Phyllis W., and Burns, David. "Anxiety and Depression in Law Students: Cognitive Intervention." 30 *Journal of Legal Education* 270 (1980).
Bell, Derrick A., Jr. "In Defense of Minority Admission Programs: A Response to Professor Graglia." 119 *University of Pennsylvania Law Review* 364 (1970).
Benthall-Neitzel, Deedra. "An Empirical Investigation of the Relationship between Lawyering Skills and Legal Education." 63 *Kentucky Law Journal* 373 (1975).
Benton, J. H. "Annual Address." 3 *Proceedings of the Southern New Hampshire Bar Association* 227 (1894).
Bergin, Thomas F., Jr. "The Law Teacher: A Man Divided against Himself." 54 *Virginia Law Review* 646 (1968).
Beutel, Frederick K. "The New Curriculum at the University of Nebraska College of Law." 25 *Nebraska Law Review* 177 (1946).
_____. "Some Implications of Experimental Jurisprudence." 48 *Harvard Law Review* 178 (1934).
Bickel, Alexander, and Wellington, Harry. "Legislative Purpose and the Judicial Process: The Lincoln Mills Case." 71 *Harvard Law Review* 1 (1957).
Biener, A. G. C., Jr. "Address of the Chairman to the Ninth Annual Meeting of the National Conference of Bar Examiners." 9 *American Law School Review* 390 (1939).
_____. "Retrospect and Prospect." 9 *American Law School Review* 1 (1938).

Black, Hugo. "Reminiscences." 18 *Alabama Law Review* 1 (1965).

Bloomfield, Maxwell. "The Texas Bar in the Nineteenth Century." 32 *Vanderbilt Law Review* 261 (1976).

Bok, Derek. "A Different Way of Looking at the World." 20 *Harvard Law School Bulletin* 41 (1969).

Boshkoff, Douglas G. "Indiana's Rule 13: The Killy-Loo Bird of the Legal World." 3 *Learning and the Law* 18 (1976).

Boyer, B. F. "Smaller Law Schools: Factors Affecting Their Methods and Objectives." 20 *Oregon Law Review* 281 (1941).

Boyer, Barry, and Cramton, Roger C. "American Legal Education: An Agenda for Research and Reform." 59 *Cornell Law Review* 221 (1974).

Bradway, John. "The Beginning of the Legal Clinic of U.S.C." 3 *Southern California Law Review* 36 (1932).

————. "Case Presentation and the Legal Aid Clinic." 1 *Journal of Legal Education* 280 (1948).

————. "Classroom Aspects of Legal Aid Clinic Work." 8 *Brooklyn Law Review* 373 (1939).

————. "Clinical Preparation for Admission to the Bar." 8 *Temple Law Quarterly* 185 (1934).

————. "Education for Law Practice: Law Students Can Be Given Clinical Experience." 34 *American Bar Association Journal* (1948).

————. "Legal Aid Clinic." 7 *St. John's Law Review* 236 (1933).

————. "Legal Clinics and Law Students: Rocks and Cement for a Better Legal Education." 41 *American Bar Association Journal* 425 (1955).

————. "Objectives of Legal Aid Clinic Work." 24 *Washington University Law Quarterly* (1939).

————. "Practical Legal Training: No Cause for Alarm." 35 *Journal of the American Judicature Society* 52 (1951).

————. "Some Distinctive Features of a Legal Aid Clinic Course." 1 *University of Chicago Law Review* 469 (1934).

Bradwell, Myra. "Admission of Women to the Bar." 11 *Chicago Legal News* 179 (1887).

Brenner, James. "Bar Exam Research in California." 5 *Bar Examiner* 29 (1936).

————. "Post Exam Appraisal of California Bar Exam System." 16 *California State Bar Journal* 89 (1941).

————. "A Survey of Unemployment Conditions among Young Attorneys in California." 2 *Bar Examiner* 175 (1933).

Brickman, Lester. "Expansion of the Lawyering Process through a New Delivery System: The Emergence and State of Legal Paraprofessionalism." 71 *Columbia Law Review* 1153 (1971).

Bronson, H. A. "The Advisability of a Longer Law School Course and of a Higher Standard of Admission." 67 *Central Law Journal* 85 (1908).

Brooke, Edward W. "Disadvantaged Students and Legal Education—Programs for Affirmative Action." 1970 *University of Toledo Law Review* 277.

Brosman, Paul. "Modern Legal Education and the Local Law School." 9 *Tulane Law Review* 517 (1935).

Brown, Eliot M. "Dear Dr. Smith: About Law School—." *Juris Doctor*, December 1972, 16.

Brown, Elizabeth G. "The Bar on a Frontier: Wayne County, 1796–1836." 14 *American Journal of Legal History* 136 (1970).

Bryson, Gladys. "The Emergence of the Social Science from Moral Philosophy." 42 *Inter-*

national Journal of Ethnics 304 (1932).

Bryson, W. Hamilton. "The History of Legal Education in Virginia." 14 *University of Richmond Law Review* 155 (1979).

Cahn, Jean Camper. "Antioch's Fight against Neutrality in Legal Education." 1 *Learning and the Law* 41 (1974).

Cantrall, Arch. "Law Schools and the Layman: Is Legal Education Doing Its Job?" 38 *American Bar Association Journal* 909 (1952).

Carlson, Rick J. "Measuring the Quality of Legal Services: An Idea Whose Time Has Not Come." 11 *Law and Society Review* 287 (1976).

Carrington, Paul D., and Conley, James J. "The Alienation of Law Students." 75 *Michigan Law Review* 887 (1977).

Carusi, Charles. "Legal Education and the Bar." 2 *American Law School Review* 91 (1907).

Casner, James. "Faculty Decisions on the Report of the Committee on Legal Education." 3 *Harvard Law School Bulletin* 10 (1961).

Cavers, David F. "The First-Year Group Work at Harvard." 3 *Journal of Legal Education* 39 (1950).

_____. "In Advocacy of the Problem Method." 43 *Columbia Law Review* 453 (1943).

_____. "New Fields for the Legal Periodical." 23 *Virginia Law Review* 23 (1936).

_____. "Skills and Understanding." 1 *Journal of Legal Education* 396 (1949).

_____, et al. "Issues in Legal Education." 16 *Cleveland Marshall Law Review* 9 (1967).

Chase, Anthony. "The Birth of the Modern Law School." 23 *American Journal of Legal History* 329 (1979).

Chase, George. "Methods of Legal Study." 1 *Columbia Jurist* 69 (1885).

Chafee, Zechariah. "Colonial Courts and the Common Law." 68 *Massachusetts Historical Society Proceedings* 132 (1952).

Civiletti, Benjamin R. "Clinical Education in Law School and Beyond." 67 *American Bar Association Journal* 576 (1981).

Clark, Charles E. "Underhill Moore." 59 *Yale Law Journal* 192 (1950).

_____, and Shulman, Harry. "Jury Trial in Civil Cases—a Study of Judicial Administration." 43 *Yale Law Journal* 867 (1934).

Clark, Herbert. "Some Random Comments by a Former Member of the Committee of Bar Examiners." 18 *California State Bar Journal* 5 (1943).

Clark, John Kirkland. "A Contrast: The Full-Time Approved School Compared with Unapproved Evening School." 20 *American Bar Association Journal* 548 (1934).

_____. "Qualification for Bar Admission." 8 *American Law School Review* 3 (1934).

Clements, Andrew. "Law School Curricula—a Reply: Doctors and Lawyers." 25 *New York State Law Bulletin* 36 (1953).

Coates, Albert. "The Story of the Law School at the University of North Carolina." 47 *University of North Carolina Law Review* 1 (1968).

Cohen, Harry. "Certification of Trial Lawyers—a Judicial Effort to Restructure the American Legal Profession." 3 *Journal of the Legal Profession* 27 (1978).

Cohen, Marshall. "He'd Rather Have Rights." *New York Review of Books*, 26 May 1977, 37.

Colby, James F. "The Collegiate Study of Law." 19 *Reports of the American Bar Association* 521 (1896).

Corbin, Arthur L. "Democracy and Education for the Bar." 19 *Handbook of the Association of American Law Schools* 143 (1921).

_____. "Democracy and Education for the Bar." 4 *American Law School Review* (1922).

_____. "The Law and the Judges." 3 *Yale Review* 234 (1914).

Cormack, J., and Hutcheson, C. "Relations of Pre-legal Studies and Intelligence Tests to

Success in Law School." 14 *Southern California Law Review* 35 (1940).

Cramton, Roger C. "The Task Ahead in Legal Services." 61 *American Bar Association Journal* 1339 (1975).

Crawford, Albert. "Use of Legal Aptitude Test in Admitting Applicants to Law School." 1 *Bar Examiner* 151 (1931).

Cribbet, John E. "The Evolving Curriculum—a Decade of Curriculum Change at the University of Illinois." 11 *Journal of Legal Education* 230 (1958).

Crotty, Holmer D. "Who Shall be Called to the Bar?" 20 *Bar Examiner* 86 (1951).

Currie, Brainerd. "The Materials of Law Study, Parts I and II." 3 *Journal of Legal Education* 331 (1951).

———. "The Materials of Law Study, Part III." 8 *Journal of Legal Education* 1 (1955).

Curtis, Benjamin R. "The Boston University Law School." 1 *New England Magazine and Bay State Monthly* 218 (1886).

Cutright, Phillip S., and Boshkoff, Douglas G. "Course Selection Study Characteristics and Bar Examination Performance: The Indiana Law School Experience." 27 *Journal of Legal Education* 127 (1975).

Danaher, Franklin M. "Courses of Study for Law Clerks." 25 *Reports of the American Bar Association* 559 (1902).

Day, Alan F. "Lawyers in Colonial Maryland, 1660–1715." 17 *American Journal of Legal History* 145 (1973).

Delafield, Lewis L. "The Conditions of Admissions to the Bar." 7 *Pennsylvania Monthly* 960 (1876).

Del Duca, Louis F. "Continuing Evaluation of Law School Curricula—an Initial Survey." 20 *Journal of Legal Education* 309 (1967).

Dennis, William. "Object-Teaching in Law Schools." 21 *American Law Review* 228 (1887).

Dickman, Franklin J. "The Demand for a High Standard of Legal Culture and Education." 3 *Western Reserve Law Journal* 109 (1897).

Dieffenbach, C. Maxwell. "The Origin and Development of the Salmon P. Chase College of Law." 1 *Northern Kentucky State Law Forum* 10 (1973).

Dillon, John. "Methods and Purposes of Legal Education." 2 *Counsellor* 10 (1892).

Dobie, Otis P. "An Approach to 'Clinical' Legal Education: The University of Louisville Briefing Service." 3 *Journal of Legal Education* 121 (1950).

Dorris, George B. "Admission to the Bar." 6 *Oregon Bar Association Proceedings* 43 (1896).

Dorsen, Norman, and Gillers, Stephen. "We Need More Lawyers." *Juris Doctor*, February 1972, 7.

Duke, R. T. W. "Some Thoughts on the Study and Practice of Law." 3 *Virginia State Bar Association Reports* 133 (1890).

Dwight, Theodore. "Admission to the Bar." 13 *Albany Law Journal* 142 (1876).

———. "Columbia College Law School of New York." 1 *Green Bag* 146 (1889).

———. "Education in Law Schools as Compared with That in Offices." 2 *Columbia Jurist* 157 (1885).

———. "What Shall We Do When We Leave Law School?" 1 *Counsellor* 63 (1891).

Dworkin, Ronald. "Is Wealth a Value?" 9 *Journal of Legal Studies* 191 (1980).

———. "There Oughta Be a Law." *New York Review of Books*, 14 March 1968.

Eaton, Clement. "A Mirror of the Southern Colonial Lawyer: The Law Books of Patrick Henry, Thomas Jefferson and Waightstill Avery." 3d ser. 8 *William and Mary Quarterly* 520 (1951).

Eckler, John. "The Multistate Bar Examination—August, 1974." 43 *Bar Examiner* 125 (1974).

Ehrenzweig, Albert. "The American Casebook: 'Cases and Materials,'" 32 *Georgetown Law Journal* 235 (1944).

Ehrlich, Thomas. "Giving Low-Income America Minimum Access to Legal Services." 64 *American Bar Association Journal* 696 (1978).

————, and Headrick, Thomas. "The Changing Structure of Education at Stanford Law School." 22 *Journal of Legal Education* 452 (1970).

Erlanger, Howard, and Klegon, Douglas. "Socialization Effects of Professional Schools: The Law School Experience and Student Orientations to Public Interest Concerns." 13 *Law and Society Review* 11 (1978).

Ethridge, George H. "Unjust Standards for Law Practice." 2 *Mississippi Law Journal* 276 (1929).

Fellers, James D. "President's Page." 61 *American Bar Association Journal* 261 (1975).

Fessenden, Franklin C. "The Rebirth of the Harvard Law School." 33 *Harvard Law Review* 493 (1920).

Finn, James F. "The Law Graduate—an Adequate Practitioner?" 1 *University of Detroit Law Journal* 84 (1954).

First, Harry. "Competition in the Legal Education Industry." 53 *New York University Law Review* 311 (1978).

————. "Competition in the Legal Education Industry II: An Antitrust Analysis." 54 *New York University Law Review* 1074 (1979).

————. "Legal Education and the Law School of the Past: A Single Firm Study." 8 *University of Toledo Law Review* 135 (1976).

Flanigan, William. "Sizing Up the Graduate Schools." *New York Magazine*, 10 January 1977, 64.

Fossum, Donna. "Law Professors: A Profile of the Teaching Branch of the Legal Profession." 1980 *American Bar Foundation Research Journal* 501.

————. "Law School Accreditation Standards and the Structure of American Legal Education." 1978 *American Bar Foundation Research Journal* 515.

————. "Women in the Legal Profession: A Progress Report." 67 *American Bar Association Journal* 578 (1981).

Foster, Jonathan A. "Report of the Committee on Legal Education and Admission to the Bar." 6 *Reports of the Alabama State Bar Association* 124 (1884).

Frank, Jerome. "Both Ends against the Middle." 100 *University of Pennsylvania Law Review* 20 (1951).

————. "Why Not a Clinical Lawyer-School?" 81 *University of Pennsylvania Law Review* 908 (1932).

Freedman, Monroe C. "Holding Law Schools Hostage." 4 *Learning and the Law* 16 (Spring 1977).

Freeman, Harrop A. "Administrative Law in the First-Year Curriculum." 10 *Journal of Legal Education* 226 (1957).

————. "Legal Education: Some Further-Out Proposals." 17 *Journal of Legal Education* 272 (1965).

Freilich, Robert H. "The Divisional Program at Yale: An Experiment for Legal Education in Depth." 21 *Journal of Legal Education* 443 (1969).

Fuller, Lon L. "Legal Education and Admissions to the Bar in Pennsylvania." 25 *Temple Law Quarterly* 250 (1952).

Garrison, Lloyd K. "Address." 15 *University of Cincinnati Law Review* 165 (1941).

————. "Developments in Legal Education at Michigan, Illinois, Chicago, Northwestern, Minnesota and Wisconsin." *American Bar Association Annual Review of Legal*

Education 28 (1936).
_____. "Results of the Wisconsin Bar Survey." 32 *Association of American Law Schools Proceedings* 58 (1934).
Gavit, Bernard C. "Indiana's Constitution and the Problem of Admission to the Bar." 16 *American Bar Association Journal* 595 (1930).
_____. "Legal Education and Admission to the Bar." 6 *Indiana Law Journal* 67 (1930).
Gawalt, Gerald W. "Massachusetts Legal Education in Transition, 1766–1840." 17 *American Journal of Legal History* 27 (1973).
Gee, E. Gordon, and Jackson, Donald W. "Bridging the Gap: Legal Education and Lawyer Competency." 1977 *Brigham Young Law Review* 695.
_____. "What You Need to Know about the Proposed Federal Practice Rule." 65 *American Bar Association Journal* 60 (1976).
Gellhorn, Ernest. "The Law School and the Negro." 6 *Duke Law Journal* 1069 (1968).
Gellhorn, Walter. "Commentary." 21 *University of Miami Law Review* 538 (1967).
_____. "Second and Third Years of Law Study." 17 *Journal of Legal Education* 1 (1964).
Gilmore, Grant. "Legal Realism: Its Cause and Cure." 70 *Yale Law Journal* 1037 (1961).
Givan, Robert M. "Indiana's Rule 13: It Doesn't Invite Conformity, It Compels Competency." 3 *Learning and the Law* 16 (1976).
Goldstein, Abraham S. "Research into Administration of Criminal Law: A Report from the United States." *British Journal of Criminology* 27 (1966).
Goodhart, Arthur L. "Case Law in England and America." 15 *Cornell Law School Quarterly* 173 (1930).
Goodrich, Herbert. "Law School and Bar Examiners." 18 *American Bar Association Journal* 101 (1932).
Gorhan, T. H., and Crawford, A. E. "The Yale Legal Aptitude Test." 49 *Yale Law Journal* 1237 (1940).
Gray, John Chipman. "Cases and Treatises." 22 *American Law Review* 756 (1888).
Green, Leon. "Advocacy and Case Study." 4 *Journal of Legal Education* 21 (1952).
_____. "Legal Education and Bar Admission." 20 *American Bar Association Journal* 105 (1934).
_____. "A New Program in Legal Education." 17 *American Bar Association Journal* 299 (1931).
_____. "Who Shall Study Law?" 14 *Tennessee Law Review* 578 (1939).
Green, Mark J. "The Young Lawyers: Good-Bye to Pro Bono." *New York Magazine*, 21 February 1972, 29.
Green, Milton D. "Realism in Practice Court." 1 *Journal of Legal Education* 422 (1949).
Green, Wayne. "Taking the Bar Exam to Court." *Juris Doctor*, January 1974, 2.
Griffiths, John. "Legal Reasoning from the External and the Internal Perspectives." 55 *New York University Law Review* 1124 (1978).
Griswold, Erwin N. "Intellect and Spirit." 81 *Harvard Law Review* 292 (1967).
Hall, Jerome. "Nulla Poena Sine Lege." 47 *Yale Law Journal* 189 (1937).
_____. "An Open Letter Proposing a School of Cultural Legal Studies." 4 *Journal of Legal Education* 181 (1951).
Hammond, W. G. "Legal Education and the Present State of the Literature of the Law." 1 *Central Law Journal* 292 (1874).
_____. "Legal Education and the Study of Jurisprudence in the West and North West." 8 *Journal of Social Sciences* 165 (1870).
_____. "The Legal Profession—Its Past—Its Present—Its Duty." 9 *Western Jurist* 1 (1875).

Hand, Richard L. "Preparation for the Bar." 53 *Albany Law Journal* 119 (1896).

Handler, Milton. "What, If Anything, Should Be Done by the Law Schools to Acquaint Students with the So-Called New Deal Legislation and Its Workings." 8 *American Law School Review* 164 (1935).

Hansen, Millard. "The Early History of the College of Law: State University of Iowa, 1865–1884." 30 *Iowa Law Review* 31 (1944).

Harno, A. J. "Professional Ethics at the University of Illinois." 21 *Tennessee Law Review* 821 (1951).

Harrington, William G. "What's Happening in Computer Assisted Legal Research." 60 *American Bar Association Journal* 924 (1974).

Harris, Frank V. "Minnesota C.L.E.: The End of Licensing for Life?" *Trial*, July/August 1975, 23.

Harris, Michael H. "The Frontier Lawyer's Library: Southern Indiana, 1800–1850, as a Test Case." 16 *American Journal of Legal History* 239 (1972).

Harris, Whitney R. "The Inculcation of Professional Standards at Southern Methodist University School of Law." 21 *Tennessee Law Review* 823 (1951).

Harsch, Alfred. "The Four-Year Law Course in American Universities." 17 *North Carolina Law Review* 244 (1939).

Hart, Henry. "The Supreme Court—1958 Term—Forward: The Time Chart of Justice." 73 *Harvard Law Review* 84 (1959).

Haslow, Jonathan E. "The Preposterous and Altogether Unlikely Story of Vermont Law School." *Juris Doctor*, May 1974.

Heinz, John P., and Laumann, Edward O. "The Legal Profession: Client Interests, Professional Roles, and Social Hierarchies." 76 *Michigan Law Review* 1111 (1978).

Heinz, John P., et al. "Diversity, Representation, and Leadership in an Urban Bar: A First Report on a Survey of the Chicago Bar." 1976 *American Bar Foundation Research Journal* 717.

Hellman, Lawrence K. "Considering the Future of Legal Education, Law Schools and Social Justice." 29 *Journal of Legal Education* 170 (1978).

Henn, Harry G. "The Cornell Law School—Its History and Traditions." 37 *New York State Bar Journal* 146 (1965).

Herbold Scott, R. "Law Is Where the Action Is." *Yale Alumni Magazine*, January 1972, 27.

Hobbs, Charles. "Lawyer Advertising—Good Beginning But Not Enough." 62 *American Bar Association Journal* 735 (1976).

Holmes, Oliver Wendell, Jr. "The Uses and Meaning of Law Schools, and Their Method of Instruction." 20 *American Law Review* 923 (1886).

Horack, Claude. "Securing Proper Bar Exams." 33 *Illinois Law Review* 89 (1939).

Houck, Stanley. "The State Acts to Suppress Unauthorized Practice." 16 *Tennessee Law Review* 235 (1940).

Houts, Marshall W. "A Course in Proof." 7 *Journal of Legal Education* 418 (1955).

Hunter, Robert M. "Motion Pictures and Practice Court." 2 *Journal of Legal Education* 426 (1949).

Hutchins, Harry B. "The Cornell University School of Law." 1 *Green Bag* 473 (1889).

———. "Legal Education: Its Relation to the People and the State." 1 *Publications of the Michigan Political Science Association* 1 (1895).

Hutchins, Robert M. "The Autobiography of an Ex-Law Student." 1 *University of Chicago Law Review* 511 (1934).

———. "Modern Movements in Legal Education: A Symposium." 26 *Association of American Law Schools Proceedings* 32 (1928).

———, and Slesinger, Donald. "Some Observations on the Law of Evidence." 28 *Columbia Law Review* 432 (1928).

Hyman, Harvey. "A School for Advocates." *Juris Doctor*, January 1975, 23.

Jackson, Marilyn. "N.U. Law School: An Untraditional Tradition." *Northeastern Today*, May 1976, 10.

Jacobson, Robert C. "Bar Unit Urges Law Schools to Shift Emphasis." *Chronicle of Higher Education*, 18 June 1979, 6.

Jaffé, Louis. "Forward to the Supreme Court, 1950 Term." 65 *Harvard Law Review* 107 (1959).

Jenks, Edward. "Legal Training in America." 3d ser. 4 *Journal of Comparative Legislation and International Law* 152 (1922).

Johnstone, Quintin. "Law School Legal Aid Clinics." 3 *Journal of Legal Education* 535 (1951).

Jones, Harry W. "Local Law Schools vs. National Law Schools: A Comparison of Concepts, Functions and Opportunities." 10 *Journal of Legal Education* 287 (1958).

———. "Notes on the Teaching of Legal Method." 1 *Journal of Legal Education* 22 (1948).

Jones, Richard C. "Report of the Committee on Legal Education and Admission to the Bar." 21 *Alabama State Bar Association Proceedings* 97 (1898).

Jones, Shirley Penrose. "The George Washington University Law School." *Res Gestae* (1915).

Jones, Vonciel. "Texas Southern University School of Law—the Beginning." 4 *Texas Southern University Law Review* 197 (1976).

Jordan, David Starr. "Pettifogging Law Schools and an Untrained Bar." 19 *The Forum* 350 (1895).

Kales, Albert. "A Further Word on the Next Step in the Evolution of the Case Book." 4 *Illinois Law Review* 11 (1909).

Kalven, Harry, Jr. "Law School Training in Research and Exposition: The University of Chicago Program." 1 *Journal of Legal Education* 108 (1948).

Katz, Wilbur G. "A Four-Year Program of Legal Education." 4 *University of Chicago Law Review* 530 (1937).

Keener, William A. "The Inductive Method in Legal Education." 17 *Reports of the American Bar Association* 473 (1894).

Kelso, Charles. "Programming Shows Promise for Training Lawyers: A Report on an Experiment." 14 *Journal of Legal Education* 243 (1961).

———. "Symposium on Legal Education: Curricular Reform for Legal School Needs of the Future." 21 *University of Miami Law Review* 26 (1967).

Kennedy, Duncan. "Form and Substance in Private Law Adjudication." 89 *Harvard Law Review* 1685 (1976).

———. "How the Law School Falls: A Polemic." 1 *Yale Review of Law and Social Action* 71 (1970).

———. "The Structure of Blackstone's Commentaries." 28 *Buffalo Law Review* 205 (1979).

Kennerly, W. T. "299 a Year!" 13 *Tennessee Law Review* 224 (1936).

Keyserling, Leon H. "Social Objectives in Legal Education." 33 *Columbia Law Review* 455 (1933).

King, George. "The Law School 45 Years Ago." *Res Gestae* (1915).

King, Willard L. "A Pioneer Court of Last Resort." 20 *Illinois Law Review* 575 (1925).

———. "Riding the Circuit with Lincoln." 6 *American Heritage* 48 (1955).

Kingsley, Robert. "Teaching Professional Ethics and Responsibilities: What the Law Schools Are Doing." 7 *Journal of Legal Education* 84 (1954).

Kinnane, Charles. "Recent Tendencies in Legal Education." 25 *American Bar Association Journal* 563 (1939).

Kirkwood, Marion R. "Requirements for Admissions to Practice Law." 20 *Bar Examiner* 18 (1951).

Klein, M. Millen. "New York Lawyers and the Coming of the American Revolution." 55 *New York History* 383 (1974).

———. "The Rise of the New York Bar: The Legal Career of William Livingston." 3d ser. 15 *William and Mary Quarterly* 334 (1958).

Kocourek, Albert. "The Redlich Report and the Case Method." 10 *Illinois Law Review* 321 (1915).

Koziol, Frank, and Joslyn, Nancy. "Have There Been Significant Changes in the Career Aspirations and Occupational Choices of Law School Graduates in the 1960's?" 8 *Law and Society Review* 93 (1973).

Langdell, Christopher Columbus. "Harvard Celebration Speeches." 3 *Law Quarterly Review* 123 (1887).

Larson, Arthur. "An 'Inductive' Approach to Legal Education." 1 *Journal of Legal Education* 287 (1948).

Lasswell, Harold, and McDougal, Myres. "Jurisprudence in Policy-Oriented Perspective." 19 *University of Florida Law Review* 486 (1966).

———. "Legal Education and Public Policy: Professional Training in the Public Interest." 53 *Yale Law Journal* 203 (1943).

Leach, W. Barton. "Property Law Taught in Two Packages." 1 *Journal of Legal Education* 35 (1948).

Leach, P. A. "The New Disciplinary Enforcement in England." 61 *American Bar Association Journal* 212 (1975).

Lee, Edward. "Evening Law Schools." 1 *American Law School Review* 290 (1905).

Leff, Arthur A. "Economic Analysis of Law: Some Realism about Nominalism." 60 *Virginia Law Review* 451 (1974).

Leflar, Robert A. "Survey of Curricula in Small Law Schools." 9 *American Law School Review* 259 (1939).

Leisberg, D. Kelly. "Women in Law School Teaching: Problems and Progress." 30 *Journal of Legal Education* 226 (1979).

Lewis, William Draper. "Agreements and Differences between the Report of the Committee on Which the Action of the Association Was Taken and the Carnegie Foundation Report." 8 *American Bar Journal* 39 (1922).

Libby, Charles F. "Legal Education." 7 *Maine State Bar Association Proceedings* 2 (1894).

Lindsay, John M. "John Saeger Bradway—the Tireless Pioneer of Clinical Legal Education." 4 *Oklahoma City University Law Review* 6 (1979).

Llewellyn, Karl N. "The Current Crisis in Legal Education." 1 *Journal of Legal Education* 215 (1948).

———. "On What Is Wrong with So-Called Legal Education." 35 *Columbia Law Review* 653 (1935).

———. "Some Realism about Realism." 44 *Harvard Law Review* 1233 (1931).

Lockhart, William B. "The Minnesota Program of Legal Education—the Four-Year Plan." 3 *Journal of Legal Education* 234 (1950).

Lucas, Paul. "Blackstone and the Reform of the Legal Profession." 77 *English Historical Review* 456 (1962).

Luxenberg, Stan. "Moving toward the Legal Left." *Change*, February–March 1980, 18.

Macaulay, Stewart. "Law Schools and the World Outside Their Doors: Notes on the Margin of 'Professional Training in the Public Interest.'" 54 *Virginia Law Review* 619 (1968).

McClain, Emlin. "Law Department of the State University of Iowa." 1 *Green Bag* 374 (1889).

McCoy, Philbrock. "Unlawful Practice of the Law: Some Recent Prosecutions." 10 *California State Bar Journal* 294 (1935).

MacDonald, Edward. "Bar Admission and Legal Education." 16 *Michigan State Bar Journal* 69 (1937).

_____. "Limitations on New York Bar Admissions Recommended." 5 *Bar Examiner* 115 (1936).

McDougal, Myres. "The Law School of the Future: From Legal Realism to Policy Science in the World Community." 56 *Yale Law Journal* 1353 (1947).

McGuire, O. R. "The Growth and Development of American Law Schools." 8 *Rocky Mountain Law Review* 91 (1939).

McKay, Robert. "Legal Education." *1977 Annual Survey of American Law* 561 (1978).

McKelvery, John Jay. "The Law School Review, 1887–1937." 50 *Harvard Law Review* 873 (1937).

Mackenzie, Robert. "Farrah's Future: The First One Hundred Years of the University of Alabama Law School, 1872–1972." 25 *Alabama Law Review* 121 (1972).

McKirdy, Charles R. "A Bar Divided: The Lawyers of Massachusetts and the American Revolution." 16 *American Journal of Legal History* 205 (1972).

_____. "Before the Storm: The Working Lawyer in Pre-Revolutionary Massachusetts." 11 *Suffolk University Law Review* 46 (1976).

_____. "The Lawyer as Apprentice: Legal Education in Eighteenth-Century Massachusetts." 28 *Journal of Legal Education* 124 (1976).

Maggs, Douglas. "How the Common Objectives of Bar Examiners and Law Schools Can Be Achieved." 13 *Oregon Law Review* 147 (1934).

Mandelker, Daniel K. "Legal Writing—the Drake Program." 3 *Journal of Legal Education* 583 (1951).

Manning, Bayless. "If Lawyers Were Angels: A Sermon in One Canon." 60 *American Bar Association Journal* 821 (1974).

_____. "Law Schools and Lawyer Schools—Two Tier Legal Education." 26 *Journal of Legal Education* 379 (1974).

Marden, Orison S. "CLEPR Origins and Program." In Council on Legal Education for Professional Responsibility, *Clinical Education for the Law Student*, 3. New York, ⁻1973.

Martin, Ellen A. "Admissions of Women to the Bar." 1 *Chicago Law Times* 76 (1886).

Martin, Mark. "Are Ethics In or Out?" 38 *Texas Bar Journal* 835 (1975).

Maxwell, Lawrence. "The Importance of a Pre-Legal Education as a Preparation for the Practice of Law." 4 *American Law School Review* 29 (1915).

Meltsner, Michael, and Schrag, Philip G. "Report from a CLEPR Colony." 76 *Columbia Law Review* 581 (1976).

Mewett, Alan W. "Reviewing the Law Reviews." 8 *Journal of Legal Education* 188 (1955).

Miller, Charles H. "Clinical Training of Law Students." 2 *Journal of Legal Education* 298 (1950).

Miller, Samuel F. "The Ideals of the Legal Profession." *1874–1881 Iowa State Bar Association Proceedings* 194 (1879).

Mindes, Marvin W. "Lawyer Specialty Certification: The Monopoly Game." 61 *American Bar Association Journal* 42 (1975).

Mooney, Ralph James. "The Rise and Fall of Classical Contract Law: A Response to Professor Gilmore." 55 *Oregon Law Review* 155 (1976).

Moore, John N. "Prolegomenon to the Jurisprudence of Myres McDougal and Harold Lasswell." 54 *Virginia Law Review* 662 (1968).

Moore, Underhill, and Callahan, Charles C. "Law and Learning Theory: A Study in Legal Control." 53 *Yale Law Journal* 1 (1943).

Moore, Underhill, and Sussman, Gilbert. "Legal and Institutional Methods Applied to the Debiting of Direct Discounts." 40 *Yale Law Journal* 381 (1931).

Moreland, Roy. "Legal Writing and Research in the Smaller Law Schools." 7 *Journal of Legal Education* 49 (1954).

Morgan, Edmund M. "The Case Method." 4 *Journal of Legal Education* 84 (1952).

Morrison, William. "Frames of Reference for Legal Ideals." In *The Crisis In Legal Ideals*. Edited By Eugene Kamenka et al. London, 1978.

Morse, Oliver. "Let's Add Another Year." 7 *Journal of Legal Education* 252 (1954).

Mueller, Addison, and James, Fleming, Jr. "Case Presentation." 1 *Journal of Legal Education* 129 (1948).

Mueller, Gerhard P. W. "Pre-Requiem for the Law Faculty." 18 *Journal of Legal Education* 413 (1966).

Murray, John R., Jr. "Special Admission Programs—the Bakke Case." 28 *Journal of Legal Education* 358 (1977).

Nader, Ralph. "Crumbling of the Old Order: Law Schools and Law Firms." *New Republic*, 15 November 1969, 20.

————. "Law Schools and Law Firms: The Mordant Malaise or the Crumbling of the Old Order." 7 *Harvard Law Record* 47 (1968).

Nighswander, Arthur N. "Should Study in a Law Office Be Abolished as a Qualification for Admission to the Bar?" 30 *Bar Examiner* 31 (1961).

Nilsson, George W. "Legal Education and Admission to the Bar." 6 *Journal of the American Judicature Society* 104 (1922).

Nolan, Dennis R. "The Effect of the Revolution on the Bar: The Maryland Experience." 62 *Virginia Law Review* (1976).

————. "Sir William Blackstone and the New American Republic: A Study of Intellectual Impact." 51 *New York University Law Review* 731 (1976).

Norton, Charles P. "The Buffalo Law School." 1 *Green Bag* 421 (1889).

Nutting, Charles B. "An Experiment in Intraprofessional Education." 7 *Food, Drug, Cosmetic Law Journal* 44 (1952).

O'Donovan, Katherine; Twining, William L.; and Mitchell, Roy. "Legal Eagles or Battery Hens: An Examination of Kelso's 'Programmed Introduction to the Study of Law.'" 10 *Journal of the Society of Public Teachers in Law* 6 (1968).

Oleck, Howard L. "The 'Adversary Method' of Law Teaching." 5 *Journal of Legal Education* 104 (1952).

Oliphant, Herman. "A Return to Stare Decisis." 14 *American Bar Association Journal* 23 (1928).

Oliphant, Robert E. "When Will Clinicians Be Allowed to Join the Club?" *Learning and the Law*, Summer 1976, 34.

Osborn, John R. "Annual Address." 2 *Ohio State Bar Association Reports* 71 (1881).

Otorowski, Christopher L. "Some Fundamental Problems with the Devitt Committee Report." 65 *American Bar Association Journal* 713 (1979).

Oulahan, Courts. "The Legal Implications of Evaluation and Accreditation." 7 *Journal of Law and Education* 193 (1978).

Papke, David. "The Browning of the Yale Law School." *Change*, April 1973, 17.
———. "The Last Gasp of the Unaccredited Law Schools." *Juris Doctor*, August 1973.
———. "Legal Studies: Here Today, Boom Tomorrow?" *Change*, November 1977, 21.
Patterson, C. Stevart. "The Law School of the University of Pennsylvania." 1 *Green Bag* 99 (1889).
Peairs, C. A. "Legal Bibliography: A Dual Problem." 3 *Journal of Legal Education* 61 (1949).
Pemberton, John DeJ., Jr. "Report of the National Law Student Conference on Legal Education—Conference Report." Part I, 1 *Journal of Legal Education* 73–97 (1948); Part II, 1 *Journal of Legal Education* 221–50 (1948).
Petters, Isabella Mary. "The Legal Education of Women." 38 *Journal of Social Science* 234 (1900).
Pincus, William. "Clinical Training in the Law School: A Challenge and a Primer for the Bar and Bar Admissions Authorities." 50 *St. John's Law Review* 479 (1976).
Pipkin, Ronald M. "Legal Education: The Consumer's Perspective." *1976 American Bar Foundation Research Journal* 1161.
Pound, Roscoe. "The Call for a Realist Jurisprudence." 44 *Harvard Law Review* 697 (1931).
———. "The Scope and Purpose of Sociological Jurisprudence." 24 *Harvard Law Review* 591 (1911).
Powell, Thomas R. "Law as Cultural Study." 4 *American Law School Review* 336 (1917).
Pritchett, Henry S. "The Story of the Establishment of the NBS." 15 *Science* 281 (1902).
Prosser, William L. "Legal Education in California." 38 *California Law Review* 197 (1953).
———. "The Ten-Year Curriculum." 6 *Journal of Legal Education* 149 (1953).
Raysor, Thomas H. "Necessity of Preparation for the Bar." 7 *Southern California Bar Association Reports* 57 (1891).
Reed, Alfred Z. "Cooperation for the Improvement of Legal Education." In *Twenty-Sixth Annual Report of the Carnegie Foundation for the Advancement of Teaching, 1931*, 51.
———. "Criticism of Carnegie Foundation Bulletin." 7 *American Bar Association Journal* 8 (1922).
———. "The Lawyer as a Privileged Servant of Democracy." 6 *Journal of the American Judicature Society* 154 (1922).
———. "Legal Education during the War." In Carnegie Foundation for the Advancement of Teaching, *Review of Legal Education*. New York, 1918.
———. "Legal Education, 1925–28." 6 *American Law School Review* 771 (1930).
———. "Scholarship or Opinions." 35 *Harvard Law Review* (1922).
Reese, Willard. "The Standard Law School Admission Test." 1 *Journal of Legal Education* 124 (1948).
Reich, Charles A. "Towards the Humanist Study of Law." 74 *Yale Law Journal* 1402 (1965).
Richards, David A. J. "Taking *Taking Rights Seriously* Seriously: Reflections on Dworkin and the American Revival of Natural Law." 52 *New York University Law Review* 1265 (1977).
Richards, Harry S. "Progress in Legal Education." 15 *Handbook of the Association of American Law Schools* 15 (1915).
———. "Shall Law Schools Give Credit for Office Study?" 24 *Reports of the American Bar Association* 514 (1901).

Ridenour, Ron. "Law and the People." *Juris Doctor*, May 1975, 15.

Riesman, David. "Some Observations on Legal Education." 1 *Wisconsin Law Review* 63 (1968).

Rigler, Douglas V. "Professional Codes of Conduct after Goldfarb: A Proposed Method of Antitrust Analysis." 29 *Arkansas Law Review* 185 (1975).

Robinson, James J. "Admission to the Bar as Provided For in the Indiana Constitutional Convention of 1850–1851." 1 *Indiana Law Journal* 209 (1926).

Robinson, William C. "A Study of Legal Education." *Catholic University Bulletin, 1895.*

Rodell, Fred. "Goodbye to Law Reviews." 23 *University of Virginia Law Review* 38 (1936).

——. "Goodbye to Law Reviews—Revisited." 48 *University of Virginia Law Review* 279 (1962).

Rogers, Henry Wade. "The Law Department of Michigan University." 3 *Western Jurist* 129 (1869).

——. "Law School of the University of Michigan." 1 *Green Bag* 189 (1889).

——. "Legal Education." 21 *Illinois State Bar Association Proceedings*, pt. 2, 53 (1897).

Rogers, James G. "The American Bar Association in Retrospect." In New York University School of Law, *Law: A Century of Progress, 1835–1935.* Vol. 1. New York, 1937.

——. "Democracy versus High Standards: The American Lawyer's Dilemma." 7 *Rocky Mountain Law Review* 1 (1935).

Rosenberg, Maurice. "Anything Legislatures Can Do, Courts Can Do Better?" 62 *American Bar Association Journal* 587 (1976).

Rutter, Irvin C. "Designing and Teaching the First Degree Curriculum." 37 *University of Cincinnati Law Review* 7 (1968).

Sacks, Albert. "Forward to the Supreme Court, 1953 Term." 68 *Harvard Law Review* 96 (1954).

Savoy, Paul N. "Towards a New Politics of Legal Education." 79 *Yale Law Journal* 444 (1970).

Schlegel, John Henry. "American Legal Realism and Empirical Social Science: From the Yale Experience." 28 *Buffalo Law Review* 459 (1980).

——. "American Legal Realism and Empirical Social Science: The Singular Case of Underhill Moore." 29 *Buffalo Law Review* 195 (1981).

Schouler, James. "Cases Without Treatises." 23 *American Law Review* 1 (1889).

Scott, James B. "The Study of the Law." 2 *American Law School Review* 1 (1906).

Schwartz, Murray L. "Law Schools and Ethics." *Chronicle of Higher Education*, 9 December 1974, 20.

Seavey, Warren A. "The Association of American Law Schools in Retrospect." 3 *Journal of Legal Education* 158 (1950).

Seidman, Marshall J. "Personal Viewpoint—the Responsibility of Law Schools." 62 *American Bar Association Journal* 639 (1976).

Shafroth, Will. "Bar Examiner and Examinees." 17 *American Bar Association Journal* 375 (1931).

——. "Bar Examiners Take Steps toward Permanent Organization." 16 *American Bar Association Journal* 699 (1930).

——. "National Conference of Bar Examiners." 7 *Indiana Law Journal* 134 (1931).

——. "The Next Step in the Improvement of Bar Admissions Standard." *Annual Review of Legal Education* 13 (1935).

——. "The Part of the Bar Association in Fixing Standards of Admissions." 6 *Indiana Law Journal* 512 (1931).

——. "The Problem of the Lawyer's Qualification." 6 *Indiana Law Journal* 268 (1931).

————. "Recent Change in Bar Admission Requirements." 22 *American Bar Association Journal* 304 (1936).

Shepard, Charles. "The Education of the Lawyer in Relation to Public Service." 81 *Central Law Journal* 220 (1915).

Simpson, A. W. Brian. "The Horwitz Thesis and the History of Contract." 46 *University of Chicago Law Review* 533 (1979).

Simpson, Sidney P. "Developments in the Law School Curriculum and in Teaching Methods." 8 *American Law School Review* 1040 (1938).

Slack, Charles W. "Hastings College of Law." 1 *Green Bag* 518 (1889).

Sleeper, Peter. "The Renaissance of Night Law Schools." *Juris Doctor*, December 1972, 6.

Slonim, Scott. "New Accreditation Proposals Criticized." 65 *American Bar Association Journal* 1505 (1980).

————. "State Court Tells Law Schools What to Teach." 67 *American Bar Association Journal* 26 (1981).

Smith, Eugene L. "Is Education for Professional Responsibility Possible?" 40 *University of Colorado Law Review* 509 (1968).

Smith, G. H. "History of the Activity of the American Bar Association in Relation to Legal Education and Admission to the Bar." 7 *American Law Review* 1 (1930).

Smith, Young. "Training the Law Teachers through Graduate Work." 29 *Association of American Law Schools Proceedings* 93 (1931).

————, and Rogers, James G. "The Overcrowding at the Bar and What Can Be Done about It." 7 *American Law School Review* 565 (1932).

Snyder, Orvill C. "The Problem of the Night Law School." 20 *American Bar Association Journal* 109 (1934).

Sovern, Michael J. "A Better Prepared Bar—the Wrong Approach." 50 *St. John's Law Review* 473 (1976).

————. "Training Tomorrow's Lawyers: A Response to the Chief Justice's Challenge." 11 *Columbia Journal of Law and Social Problems* 72 (1974).

Spangler, Eve; Gordon, Mosha; and Pipkin, Ronald. "Token Women: An Empirical Test of Kanter's Hypothesis." 85 *American Journal of Sociology* 1 (1978).

Speca, John M. "Panel Discussions as a Device for Introduction to Law." 3 *Journal of Legal Education* 124 (1950).

Speidel, Richard. "An Essay on the Reported Death and Continued Vitality of Contract." 27 *Stanford Law Review* 1161 (1975).

Spencer, William, and Harno, Albert. "The Correlation of Law and College Subjects." 4 *American Law School Review* 85 (1922).

Stanley, Justin. "Comments on Current Problems Facing the Legal Profession." 57 *Chicago Bar Record* 109 (1975).

————. "Two Years +: The Third Year of Schooling Should Cater to the Special Demands of State Law." 3 *Learning and the Law* 18 (1976).

Starr, Merritt. "The Value to the Lawyer of Training in the Classics." 15 *School Review* 409 (1907).

Statsky, William P. "Paraprofessionals: Expanding the Legal Service Delivery Team." 24 *Journal of Legal Education* 397 (1972).

Steigler, Mayo H. "Reconstruction of NCLE." 1966 *Legal Aid Briefcase* 279 (1966).

Stein, Peter. "Attraction of the Civil Law in Post-Revolutionary America." 52 *Virginia Law Review* 403 (1966).

Stein, Robert A. "In Pursuit of Excellence: A History of the University of Minnesota Law School." Parts 1–3, 62 *Minnesota Law Review* 485, 857, 1161 (1978); Parts 4–6, 63 *Minnesota Law Review* 229, 809, 1101 (1979).

Stephenson, Edward L. "Academe to Agora: Bridging the Gap." 28 *Connecticut Bar Journal* 163 (1954).

Stevens, Robert. "Aging Mistress: The Law School in America." *Change in Higher Education*, January–February 1970, 32.

———. "American Legal Education: Reflections on the Light of Ormrod." 35 *Modern Law Review* 242 (1972).

———. "Democracy and the Legal Profession." 3 *Learning and the Law* 12 (1976).

———. "Law Schools and Law Students." 59 *Virginia Law Review* 551 (1973).

———. "Legal Education: Historical Perspective." In Council on Legal Education for Professional Responsibility, *Clinical Education for the Law Student*, 43. New York, 1973.

———. "Preface." *1976 Brigham Young University Law Review* 695.

———. "Unexplored Avenues in Comparative Anglo-American Legal History." 48 *Tulane Law Review* 1086 (1974).

Stewart, James B., Jr. "My Week in an Unaccredited Law School." *American Lawyer*, August 1980, 19.

Stolz, Preble. "Clinical Experience in American Legal Education: Why Has It Failed?" In Edmund W. Kitch, ed., *Clinical Education and the Law School of the Future*. Chicago, 1969.

———. "Training for the Public Profession of the Law (1921): A Contemporary Review." In Herbert Packer and Thomas Ehrlich, *New Directions in Legal Education*. Berkeley, 1972.

———. "The Two-Year Law School: The Day the Music Died." 25 *Journal of Legal Education* 37 (1973).

Stone, Alan A. "Legal Education on the Couch." 85 *Harvard Law Review* 392 (1971).

Stone, Harlan F. "Dean Stone's Rejoinder to Mr. Reed's Reply." 8 *American Bar Association Journal* 7 (1922).

———. "Dr. Redlich and the Case Method in American University Law Schools." 17 *Columbia University Quarterly* 262 (1915).

———. "Legal Education and Democratic Principle." 7 *American Bar Association Journal* 639 (1921).

Stone, Phil. "The Greatest Good for the Greatest Number." 2 *Mississippi Law Journal* 290 (1929).

Storke, Frederic P. "Devices for Teaching Fact-Finding." 23 *Rocky Mountain Law Review* 82 (1950).

Stricker, Joseph. "Unauthorized Practice and the Public Relations of the Bar." 23 *American Bar Association Journal* 278 (1931).

Strong, Frank R. "A New Curriculum for the College of Law of the Ohio State University." 11 *Ohio State Law Journal* 44 (1950).

———. "Pedagogical Implications of Inventorying Legal Capacities." 3 *Journal of Legal Education* 555 (1951).

Sullivan, Russell N. "The Professional Associations and Legal Education." 4 *Journal of Legal Education* 412 (1952).

Surrency, Edwin C. "The Lawyer and the Revolution." 8 *American Journal of Legal History* 125 (1964).

Sutherland, Arthur. "One Man in His Time." 78 *Harvard Law Review* 7 (1964).

Swaffield, Roland G. "Unlawful Practice of the Law: The Professional Responsibility in Relation Thereto." 5 *Southern California Law Review* 181 (1932).

Swan, Thomas W. "Reconstruction and the Legal Profession." 28 *Yale Law Journal* 794 (1919).

Swasey, George R. "Boston University Law School." 1 *Green Bag* 54 (1889).

Swindlehurst, Albert. "Legal Education and Law Practice." 34 *American Law Review* 214 (1900).

Teachout, Peter R. "Gilmore's New Book: Turning and Turning in the Widening Gyre." 2 *Vermont Law Review* 229 (1977).

Tiedeman, Christopher. "Methods of Legal Education." 1 *Yale Law Journal* 150 (1892).

Trubek, David. "Max Weber on Law and the Rise of Capitalism." 3 *Wisconsin Law Review* 720 (1972).

Tushnet, Mark. "Post Realist Legal Scholarship." N.S. 15 *Journal of the Society of the Public Teachers of Law* 20 (1980).

Twining, William. "Academic Law and Legal Philosophy: The Significance of Herbert Hart." 95 *Law Quarterly Review* 557 (1979).

──────. "Pericles and the Plumber." 83 *Law Quarterly Review* 396 (1967).

Vance, William R. "The Function of the State Supported Law School." 3 *American Law School Review* 410 (1914).

Van Dyke, Jon. "Bakke v. The Regents of the University of California." 3 *Hastings Constitutional Law Quarterly* 891 (1976).

Venny, Courtney. "The Case Method of Teaching Law." N.S. 16 *Journal of the Society of Comparative Legislation* 182 (1916).

Vernon, David H. "The Expanding Law School Curriculum Committee: The Move by Courts and the Organized Bar to Control Legal Education." 27 *Journal of Legal Education* 7 (1976).

Vold, L. "Improving North Dakota Bar Association Requirements." 13 *Quarterly Journal* 59 (1923).

Volz, Marlin. "The Legal Problems Courses at the University of Kansas City." 7 *Journal of Legal Education* 91 (1954).

Von Hoffman, Nicholas. "Legal Specialty: Newest Ripoff?" *Chicago Tribune*, 2 January 1975, sec. 2, p. 4, col. 3.

Wallace, J. E. "Philosophy and the Future of the Law School Curriculum." 44 *University of Denver Law Review* 24 (1967).

Walsh, Lawrence E. "The Annual Report of the President of the American Bar Association." 62 *American Bar Association Journal* 1119 (1976).

Walton, Joseph P. "Notes on the Early History of Legal Studies in England." 22 *Reports of the American Bar Association* 501 (1899).

Ward, Bernard J. "The Problem Method at Notre Dame." 11 *Journal of Legal Education* 100 (1958).

Washburn, Emory. "Legal Education: Why?" 7 *Western Jurist* 213 (1873).

Washington, Harold R. "History and Role of Black Law Schools." 18 *Howard Law Review* 385 (1974).

Watson, Andrew S. "The Quest for Professional Competence: Psychological Aspects of Legal Education." 37 *University of Cincinnati Law Review* 93 (1968).

Weaton, Carl. "Law Teaching and Pragmatism." 25 *Georgetown Law Journal* 338 (1937).

Wechster, Herbert. "Toward Neutral Principles in Constitutional Law." 73 *Harvard Law Review* 1 (1959).

Weisberg, D. Kelly. "Women in Law School Teaching: Problems and Progress." 30 *Journal of Legal Education* 226 (1976).

Wellington, Harry H. "Common Law Rules and Constitutional Double Standards: Some Notes on Adjudication." 83 *Yale Law Journal* 221 (1973).

Werner, Joseph. "Need for State Reviews." 23 *Virginia Law Review* 49 (1936).

Wicker, William H. "Legal Education Today and in the Post War Era." 18 *Tennessee Law*

Review 700 (1945).

Wickser, Philip J. "Law Schools, Bar Examiners and Bar Associations: Co-operation versus Insulation." 7 *American Law School Review* 734 (1933).

Weihofen, Henry. "Education for Law Teachers." 43 *Columbia Law Review* 427 (1943).

Wellman, Francis L. "Admission to the Bar." 15 *American Law Review* 295 (1881).

White, James J. "Women in the Law." 65 *Michigan Law Review* 1051 (1967).

White, James P. "Law School Enrollment Up Slightly But Levelling." 65 *American Bar Association Journal* 577 (1979).

Wigmore, John Henry. "Juristis Psychoyemetrology—Or How to Find Out Whether the Boy Has the Makings of a Lawyer." 24 *Illinois Law Review* 454 (1930).

Wilson, Lyman. "Preparation for the Bar Exam." 1 *Bar Examiner* 128 (1931).

Winter, Bill. "Federal Courts Implement Devitt Proposals." 67 *American Bar Association Journal* 550 (1981).

Woodard, Calvin. "The Limits of Legal Realism: An Historical Perspective." 54 *Virginia Law Review* 689 (1968).

Woodruff, Edwin H. "History of the Cornell Law School." 4 *Cornell Law Quarterly* 91 (1919).

York, John C., and Hale, Rosemary D. "Too Many Lawyers?: The Legal Service Industry: Its Structures and Outlook." 26 *Journal of Legal Education* 1 (1973).

York, Kenneth M. "The Law School Curriculum Twenty Years Hence." 15 *Journal of Legal Education* 160 (1965).

Zimmer, Michael J. "Beyond DeFunis: Disproportionate Impact Analysis and Mandate 'Preferences' in Law School Admissions." 54 *North Carolina Law Review* 317 (1976).

Zimmerman, Paul. "A History of the Youngstown Law School." Paper written in behalf of the committee to write the history of the Youngstown University, Youngstown, Ohio, 1976.

Index

107 (n. 37); and depression, 197–98, 203 (nn. 55, 56); funding of, 198, 216 (n. 3); admissions policy of, 221 (n. 38)

Hazard, Geoffrey, 284 (n. 45)

Hefley, Norman, 78–79

Henry, Peter James, 201 (n. 34)

Hoffman, David, 4, 12 (n. 17), 93

Hohfeld, Wesley, 116, 134, 144–45 (n. 29)

Holmes, Oliver Wendell, Jr., 36, 131, 155; on case method, 62–63, 122–23; and Langdell, 71 (n. 88), 134, 142 (n. 1)

Horack, Claude, 173, 175, 177, 185 (n. 49), 194, 196, 201 (n. 29)

Horwitz, Morton, 9, 275

Houston, law firms in, 267

Howard University Law School, 217 (n. 6), 247 (n. 2); establishment and fortunes of, 81, 89 (nn. 63, 67), 195–96, 202 (nn. 44, 45); women at, 83, 90 (n. 79), 91 (n. 88)

Howell, David, 12 (n. 15)

Humphrey's Law School, 220 (n. 32)

Hurst, Willard, 9

Hutchins, Robert, 141, 145–46 (n. 35), 150 (n. 73), 152 (n. 86), 166 (n. 17)

Hutchinson, J. A., 30 (n. 28)

Idaho, bar in, 254 (n. 64)

Illinois: bar in, 19 (n. 70), 43 (n. 8), 174, 182 (n. 26), 193; paralegal personnel in, 252 (n. 40); law schools in, 259 (n. 118)

Immigrants: desire of for legal education, 74, 75, 184 (n. 41); access of to legal education, 74, 79, 81, 88 (n. 46), 184 (n. 41), 198, 203 (n. 60); ABA-AALS efforts to exclude, 100–101, 126 (n. 18); and depression, 187 (n. 54)

Indiana, bar admission in, 9, 14 (n. 42), 18–19 (nn. 69, 70), 25, 174, 177, 185 (n. 46), 217–18 (nn. 9, 11), 239, 254 (n. 61)

Indiana University Law School, 43 (n. 7), 213, 226 (n. 66)

Industrialization, and legal profession, 9, 20, 22, 23, 92

Institute of Human Relations (Yale University), 140, 146 (n. 35), 151 (n. 78)

Institute of International Studies (Harvard), 222 (n. 42)

Institutionalization: and professionalism, 20–22, 24, 100; and legal education, 21,

24, 82

Integrated bar, 10 (n. 1), 182–83 (n. 29)

International law, 39, 40, 45 (n. 21), 48 (n. 41), 49 (nn. 43, 46), 211, 222 (n. 42)

Iowa, bar in, 15 (n. 44), 19 (n. 70), 82, 254 (n. 64)

Jacksonian Democracy: and legal profession, 5–10, 14 (n. 40), 235; and legal education, 8, 10, 15 (n. 46)

Jefferson, Thomas, 10–11 (n. 5), 71 (n. 86)

Jefferson College, 16 (n. 47)

Jewish lawyers and students, 100–101, 184 (n. 41), 246, 262 (nn. 141, 142)

John F. Kennedy University Law School, 220 (n. 32), 244

John Marshall Law School, 130 (n. 62), 164 (n. 12), 187 (n. 54), 193, 201 (n. 24), 207, 220 (n. 26)

John Randolph Neal College of Law, 194

Johns Hopkins Institute for the Study of Law, 139, 140, 151 (n. 76), 233

Johns Hopkins University, 28 (n. 4)

Johnson, Hugh, 168 (n. 44)

Jones University Law School, 199, 204 (n. 65)

Jordan, Alice Ruth, 83

Jordan, David Starr, 73

Journal of Legal Education, 213

Journal of Legal Studies, 285 (n. 58)

Kales, Albert, 41

Kalven, Harry, 284 (n. 45)

Kansas: bar in, 182 (n. 26), 217 (n. 9); paralegal personnel in, 252 (n. 40)

Kansas City Law School, 183 (n. 33)

Kasm, Caesar, 16 (n. 50)

Keane, John Joseph, 77

Keener, William, 41, 55, 56–57, 59, 60, 61, 68 (n. 40), 119

Kelly, Michael, 287 (n. 84)

Kennedy, Duncan, 276, 287 (n. 76)

Kent, James, 4, 10 (n. 5), 12 (n. 15), 17 (n. 52), 23; *Commentaries* of, 4, 30 (n. 28), 31 (n. 33), 48 (nn. 38, 39)

Kent College of Law, 201 (n. 31)

Kentucky, bar admission in, 174

Kepley, Ada, 82

Kidd, Alexander, 147 (n. 53)

tions, 252 (n. 40)
National Labor Relations Board, 276
National Law School, 183 (n. 33), 207
National Lawyers Guild, 244
National Origins Act, 92
National Reporting System, 132, 143 (n. 10)
National Science Foundation, 286 (n. 62)
National University Law School, 74, 85 (n. 15)
National Youth Administration, 187 (n. 53)
Nelles, Walter, 153 (n. 86)
Neoconceptualism, 272, 274
Nevada, bar admission in, 218 (n. 11)
New College of California Law School, 258 (n. 101)
New Deal: participation of lawyers and law professors in, 137, 141, 160, 168–69 (nn. 44, 45), 178; and Realism, 141, 155, 168–69 (n. 5); and public law in curriculum, 160, 168 (n. 40)
New Hampshire, bar admission in, 7, 9, 25, 94–95, 104 (n. 12)
New Jersey, bar in, 14 (n. 43), 32 (n. 41), 126 (n. 22), 282 (n. 27)
New Mexico, bar in, 183 (n. 29), 217 (n. 9), 254 (n. 64)
New Orleans, black lawyers in, 89 (n. 62)
New York: condition of bar in, 3, 267; bar admission in, 11 (n. 5), 25, 26–27, 33 (nn. 46, 48), 94, 174, 182 (n. 26), 255 (n. 71)
New York City: law schools in, 76, 187 (n. 54), 247 (n. 2); bar in, 89 (n. 68), 92, 187 (n. 56), 267
New York Law School, 75, 86 (n. 21), 183 (n. 33), 214, 247 (n. 2), 258 (n. 108)
New York Legal Aid Society, 85 (n. 17)
New York University Law School, 160, 255 (n. 75), 257 (n. 87), 288 (n. 96); establishment and revival of, 4, 8, 12 (n. 18), 21–22, 28 (n. 9); diploma privilege at, 26; case method at, 66 (n. 14), 123 (n. 5); funding of, 72 (n. 90); clinical program at, 230 (n. 96); night program at, 259 (n. 115); and academic inbreeding, 287 (n. 83)
Niagara University, 85 (n. 13)
Nicholas, George, 12 (n. 15)

Night schools. *See* Part-time schools
Niles, John B., 18 (n. 70)
Norfolk College Law School, 180 (n. 2), 190 (n. 76)
Northampton Law School, 5
North Carolina, bar and law schools in, 32 (n. 41), 78, 259 (n. 118)
North Carolina Central University Law School, 217 (n. 6)
North Dakota, bar in, 183 (n. 29)
Northeastern University Law School: origin of, 80; faculty of, 200 (n. 12); case method at, 192, 198; women at, 194; and AALS, 195, 198; role of, 198, 203 (n. 59); refounded, 233; clinical program at, 241
Northern Indiana Normal School and Business Institute. *See* Valparaiso University
North Texas School of Law, 199, 204 (n. 65)
Northwestern College of Law, 74
Northwestern University Law School, 70 (n. 81); curriculum content and change at, 41, 159–60, 162, 165 (n. 14), 171 (n. 70), 224 (n. 53), 226 (n. 68); admissions policy of, 45 (n. 18), 193, 200 (n. 18); case method at, 60–61, 69 (nn. 54, 73), 113, 123 (n. 5); funding of, 72 (n. 90); origin and growth of, 77–78, 87 (n. 36); women at, 82; four-year program at, 159, 167 (n. 27); clinical program at, 162; problem method at, 228 (n. 84); and academic inbreeding, 287 (n. 83)

Oakland College of Law, 199, 204 (n. 65)
Oberlin College, 81
Ocean College of Law, 244
Office of Economic Opportunity (OEO), legal services program, 237, 241
Ohio: apprenticeship in, 14 (n. 2), 15 (n. 45), 174; condition of bar in, 16 (n. 50), 19 (n. 70); bar admission in, 32 (n. 41), 174, 182 (n. 26), 217 (n. 9), 254 (n. 61)
Ohio Northern University Law School, 260 (n. 126)
Ohio State University Law School, 213, 214–15, 226 (n. 66), 227 (n. 78)
Oklahoma, bar admission in, 217 (n. 9)
Oleck, Howard, 214